Thomas Moore of Liverpool: One of our Oldest Colonists

Essays & Addresses to Celebrate 150 years of Moore College

Peter G. Bolt

Studies in Australian Colonial History No. 1

Thomas Moore of Liverpool: One of our Oldest Colonists

*Essays & Addresses
to Celebrate 150 years
of Moore College*

Peter G. Bolt

Thomas Moore of Liverpool
One of our Oldest Colonists
Studies in Australian Colonial History No. 1

© Peter G. Bolt 2007
Bolt Publishing Services Pty Ltd, Sydney
ACN 123024920

www.boltpublishing.com.au

Bolt, Peter, 1958 – .
Thomas Moore – one of our oldest colonists: essays & addresses to celebrate 150 years of Moore College.

1st ed.
Bibliography.
Includes index.
ISBN 9780980357912 (hbk).

ISBN 9780980357905 (pbk).

ISBN 9780980357929 (e-book).

1. Moore, Thomas, 1762–1840. 2. Moore Theological College – History. 3. Pioneers – New South Wales – Biography. I. Title. (Series: Studies in Australian colonial history; 1834–6936; no. 1).

994.02

Cover design and layout by Lankshear Design Pty Ltd
lanksheardesign.com

Printed by **Ingram Spark**

DEATH NOTICE:
At his residence, Liverpool, on Thursday the 24th instant,
in the 79th year of his age, Thomas Moore, Esq.
Mr Moore was one of our oldest colonists, and much esteemed
for his piety and charity.

Sydney Gazette, 29th December 1840
Sydney (Morning) Herald, 28th December 1840

To the lovely Alice, for patiently listening to things about Thomas on many different occasions.

Table of Contents

	Preface to the Series	xi
	Preface	xii
1.	Moore Circularity: A College Thanking God for a Man Thanking God with a College	1
2.	But, Who Was Thomas Moore? An Overview of his Life	7
3.	An Overdue Birth Announcement: In Quest of the Long-Lost Family of Thomas Moore	29
4.	Moore and the Merino	43
5.	Thomas Moore: S/Purveyor of Timber	61
6.	A Man, A Church, A College: Thomas Moore and St Luke's Liverpool	105
7.	Thomas Moore's Bookshelf	115
8.	Liverpool and the Lash: The Magistrate Thomas Moore	211
9.	Portrait of The Late Thomas Moore, Esq.	233
10.	Training Colonial Clergy After Moore's Will and before Moore's College	249
	Abbreviations	295
	Bibliography	297
	Index of Names	309
	Thomas Moore Index	327

Preface to the Series

THIS IS THE FIRST VOLUME in a new series entitled *Studies in Australian Colonial History*.

There are signs in our society that a new interest in Australian history is emerging. The aim of this series is to bring to light aspects of the earliest period of the history of Colonial Australia, as revealed by careful examination of the relevant primary sources.

Preface

Thomas Moore's most public legacy is a Theological College bearing his name, presently situated in Newtown, NSW. The celebration of the 150th year of the College in 2006, presented an opportunity to remember the life of its benefactor. Although known as a quiet, pious man of good character, Thomas Moore (1762–1840) exerted a profound influence on many of the institutions and activities of Colonial New South Wales. Arriving as an adventurer, he settled as the Colony's Master Boat Builder, before moving to his property 'Moore Bank' as one of the pioneers of the Liverpool district. Here he played an important role, firstly, in building the township, and then in the long-term as its first resident magistrate. Across his long life, his contributions to the civic and Christian life of the colony were many and varied. It has been a pleasure to uncover something more about this most interesting man.

These essays and addresses were written and/or delivered across the course of the celebratory year. Although my research kept advancing at the same time as the addresses were being given, their original form has mostly been kept, and, when necessary, notes have been added to point the reader to where latest updates can be found.

Thomas Moore is important as the benefactor of Moore College, but he also had a wider significance to the early life of Sydney. While honouring his memory occurred in a particular sub-section of Sydney contemporary life, these essays and addresses seek to place him in the wider context of earliest colonial Australia.

CHAPTER 1

MOORE CIRCULARITY

*A College Thanking God for
a Man Thanking God with a College*[1]

THIS YEAR MOORE COLLEGE celebrates its sesquicentenary. In 2006, as 315 students sit in crowded classrooms in Newtown, listening to 20 faculty, they are the latest group to join the College which began 150 years ago in Liverpool with just 3 students, under one teacher.[2] Like generations of students before them, this latest group stands indebted to the man who gave the college both its name and its existence. Moore College exists because of a godly man who gave thanks for everything God had given him.

The May 1937 issue of *Societas* included an article by the third Principal of the College, Arthur Lukyn Williams.[3] Since he began as Principal at the bright age of twenty-five in July 1878, then Williams would have been about eighty-four when he wrote this article—which may well be an age record for *Societas*, I don't know![4] This elderly former Principal offered *Societas* readers some reminiscences of the College in his day—which was then still at Liverpool. Lukyn Williams did not really enjoy the location, preferring his vacations, for 'we were not sorry to leave for a bit the rather dull little township of Liverpool'. He tells of how—perhaps to break up the dullness of his surrounds!— in the midst of his other activities, he sought out some of the old people of the town, to record their memories of our college's founder.[5] Having died in 1840 after a long life as one of Liverpool's chief citizens, Thomas Moore was still part of living memory. Indeed, this living memory survived into the twentieth century, for F.B. Boyce, writing in 1914, knew that 'one aged and highly respected resident of the town still lives who was a scholar [at Liverpool school], and has a kindly recollection of [Moore] often coming to the school and showing a warm concern in its doings'.[6]

Lukyn Williams discovered some interesting stories about Moore.

> The legend ran that he secreted a large sum of money somewhere in the house, which could not be found after his death. Yet a tenant came, with no money worth speaking of, who suddenly went to a distant part of Australia as a well-to-do man; and the story ran that he had found the lost treasure under the stairs of the house. Whether the tale is true or not, I do not know.

Principal Williams has probably labelled the 'legend' correctly. If there was such a fortunate tenant, however, there seems to be a limited window of opportunity for his fortunate fortune finding: between June 1843 and February 1847. Almost immediately after Moore's Will was read, Rev. John Duffus, the minister at Liverpool, was granted permission to live in Moore's old home, which he did from April 1841 until the end of June 1843.[7] In 1847, Mr J.J. Galloway was granted permission to occupy the premises, undertaking to make some improvements.[8] By the end of that year, Moore's old home again became the residence of the incumbent of St Luke's Liverpool, now Rev J. Walker,[9] who stayed in the house until he died in 1854,[10] providentially opening up the possibility of then using the house according to the intention of Moore's Will, as a college for the education of Protestant youth.[11]

Another story struck Williams as rather odd:

> [Moore] must have been a queer old fellow; while he was dying, he was asked if he would not leave something to his nephew, but he replied: "No, God gave it all to me, and I shall give it all back to Him."

Thomas Moore was no 'queer old fellow' when he began his time in Australia. He was about thirty years old when he first touched these shores in 1792, before deciding to settle here in 1796. At a much later time, Bishop Broughton would say that

> all people who come to a Colony come to push their fortune; that is, to make money and to raise themselves on the scale of society; and in the endeavour to do this, some (that is, a great many) will break through all sumptuary regulations: and some (that is, not a few) will lose their respect for moral obligations.[12]

Things may have been different when Moore arrived, for most of those in the colony were here at the invitation of the British government, either to serve time, or to look after those who were serving time! But those seeking their fortunes soon made their presence felt. In 1796, when Thomas Moore left his position as ship's carpenter on the ship *Britannia*, to shortly after become the Master Boat Builder of the Colony, the number of free settlers in the town was small enough to ensure that all were to some extent acquainted with each other. Moore took his place amongst them as a civil officer in the Government service, as well as engaging in his own commercial enterprises. Although his motives for originally settling in the colony are unknown,[13] over the next 40 years, it is certainly true that Moore became one of the largest landholders and one of the wealthiest people in the colony.

Far from 'losing their respect for moral obligations' (with Broughton), or even being regarded as 'a queer fellow' (with Williams), it seems from all reports that people held Mr Moore in the highest esteem throughout his days, and when he died, it was not just his wealth that received comment from the Sydney newspapers, but his evident piety.

> At his residence, Liverpool, on Thursday, the 24th instant, in the seventy-ninth year of his age [...] Mr Moore was one of our oldest colonists and much esteemed for his piety and charity.[14]

Others may have come to the colony in pursuit of the kind of material wealth that Moore gained. Whatever his own motivations at the beginning, his testimony at the end of his life was quite simple: 'God gave it all to me'.

These are not the words of a queer old fellow, but the words of a Christian man, struck by the generosity of his God. The story that Lukyn Williams had heard in the Liverpool old folks home (so to speak), can be echoed from Bishop Broughton's own experience of Moore. When the Bishop first saw Moore's Will in 1838, it reminded him 'of the pious and humble purposes which the men of former days used to manifest, of providing for the advancement of God's glory upon earth after their own departure from it'.[15] As an answer to the pressing needs for ministry in the growing colony, Broughton had found a man who wished to leave his money to further Christ's work. Broughton understood Moore's plans against the highest backdrop:

> I must regard it as a remarkable interposition of Divine Providence, looking upon our poverty, and by the most unexpected means supplying a share of daily bread for his Church in a quarter where, unless I am an utterly false and incompetent prophet, its services will thereafter be more called for, and its fidelity more put to the proof, than perhaps in any other spot upon the earth.[16]

But this was no sudden decision on Moore's part. For a long time, even during the period when Broughton was first in Australia as our second Archdeacon (1829–34), Moore's intentions were clear.

> [Moore] frequently, during my former residence in this country even, threw out hints of his wish to make some disposal of property for the benefit of the Church.[17]

There is also a hint in a codicil to the Will of his stepson, Andrew Douglas White, that Moore's plans may have even been in place as early as 1827,[18] thirteen years before he died, and well before the Bishop can be credited with any undue influence! For many, many years, this Christian man had been planning to bestow his considerable worldly goods to assist the Christian cause. And why did he do it? According to Broughton's report, Thomas Moore was moved 'in gratitude, as he very becomingly expressed himself, to God who had given him all'.[19]

For those who now stand in the tradition of the college

bearing his name, this generosity was not the act of some 'queer old man'. Perhaps the oddity for Williams was Moore's passing over of his surviving relatives —we know of a brother, a sister and a nephew in England.[20] However, this was not a sudden act of pique, it was a settled decision over many years. It was the act of a man who considered his accumulated fortune, and found the hand of God in it all. And he was thankful.

The College, in which the largest ever student body is now being served, is a legacy of Thomas Moore responding to his God. As we praise God for the last 150 years, the Moore which now gives thanks, arises from the Moore who once gave thanks.

Notes

1. A slightly shorter version of this essay was published in the Moore College student magazine, *Societas '06*, 6–7.
2. When the college opened at Liverpool, it was placed in the hands of the Acting Principal, William Macquarie Cowper, who brought with him from Stroud the first three students, Stanley Mitchell, Thomas Kemmis, and Marcus Blake Brownrigg. See Loane, *Centenary History*, 20–21.
3. See Loane, *Centenary History*, Ch. 4. Donald Robinson suggested to me (personal conversation, 1st December 2006) that the reminiscences in the *Societas* article may have come by way of T.C. Hammond, who, on the eve of his departure to become the eighth Principal, was farewelled by a meeting in Cambridge chaired by Williams (see Loane, *Centenary History*, 140).
4. He lived beyond the article for another six years, dying in Cambridge on 6th October 1943; Loane, *Centenary History*, 60.
5. Williams says that he deposited the reminiscences he collected in the Bishop's Registry. To date, I have been unable to locate them, and they do not appear to be in the Sydney Diocesan Archives.
6. Boyce, *Thomas Moore*, 9.
7. *Trustees Minute Book*, vol. 1, 10 February 1841: authority granted to Rev. J. Duffus to reside in the residence. J. Layton to move him in from 1st April for 12 months. (Cf. *Trustees Record Book*, p.6). J. Duffus to Trustees, 1 April 1842 (SDA 851 CH, item 7, doc. 11), requests permission to stay until 1/4/1843. *Trustees Minute Book*, vol. 1, 20 April 1843, permission granted. J. Duffus to Trustees, 1 May 1843 (SDA 852 CH, item 8, doc 30, he then requests a further period until 30th June 'as the Parsonage will not be fit for me to go into sooner'. *Trustees Minute Book*, vol. 1, pp. 41–42, permission granted until 30th June 1843, and J. Duffus is then to find a tenant.
8. *Trustees Minute Book* 1, p.82: 20 Feb 1847: 'That Mr J.J. Galloway's application for the temporary occupation of "Moore College" at Liverpool was referred back for a more

specific statement of what improvements Mr Galloway would undertake to make'; p.83, 1 Mar 1847, accepted Mr Munroe's tender for repairs totalling £18, and 'Mr Galloway was also authorized to enter into possession of the premises upon the terms stated in his note [of 27 Feb]'.
9. Walker, 'Early Churches', 441–42; Loane, *Centenary History*, 9.
10. *Trustees Minute Book 1*, p.155: 23 Nov 1854, 'The Agent having reported that the Reverend J. Walker, who with consent of the Trustees temporarily occupied the Late Mr Moore's residence at Liverpool had died, the Trustees directed that the Churchwardens of Saint Luke's Church be informed that the future Incumbent would not be allowed the use of that building; but that for the present the widow of the Reverend Mr Walker might continue in charge of the premises'. The Minute Book contains no earlier reference to the consent mentioned here, so perhaps it was at the permission of the Agent.
11. Loane, *Centenary History*, 9, 16.
12. Broughton to Coleridge, 8th May 1850.
13. What can we learn from the snide comment made by his dismissed predecessor as Master Boat Builder, Daniel Paine, that Governor John Hunter's 'good Intentions have too often been frustrated by giving his Confidence to those Persons who considering their private Interests and Views alone in their Councils proved themselves unworthy of it. Something of this kind appears in the Person appointed to my Situation a Mr Moore who was the Second Mate and Carpenter of the *Britannia*, Captn Raven in preference to the Carpenters of His Maj's Ships *Reliance* and *Supply* who indisputably had a Priority of Right to the Situation', 22 August 1796, Paine, *Journal*, 31.
14. *Sydney (Morning) Herald*, 28 December 1840; *Sydney Gazette*, 29 December 1840.
15. Broughton to Watson, 29 November 1838.
16. Broughton to Watson, 29 November 1838.
17. Broughton to Coleridge, 25 February 1839.
18. See Robinson, 'Thomas Moore & Early Life', 186 (24).
19. Broughton to Coleridge, 25 February 1839.
20. See Broughton to Watson, 29 November 1838; Broughton to Coleridge, 27 December 1841. At the time of the Societas publication, the identity of these relatives had not come to light. See now, the essays to follow in this volume.

CHAPTER 2

BUT, WHO WAS THOMAS MOORE?

An Overview of his Life[1]

As Moore College celebrates its sesquicentenary this year, it seems right to honour the memory of the benefactor who gave our college its name and the seed-funding to bring it into existence. But, who was Thomas Moore? What can we know about him?

Donald Robinson's article, 'Thomas Moore and the Early Life of Sydney',[2] and Eric Russell's work—produced during the days of the Gosford tourist attraction *Old Sydney Town*—under the title *Thomas Moore & The King's Dock Yard 1796–1816*,[3] have substantially illuminated Moore's life from his arrival in the colony through to his retirement as Master Boat Builder at the King's Dock Yard. This was the period when Moore lived and worked in Sydney Town (1792–1809). The details of Moore's life both before and after that period, however, have been hitherto clothed in some mystery.[4] The issue with the latter years is simply that of uncovering the sources (of which there are many) and documenting what can be known from them. The issue with Moore's earlier years is not that simple.

Who was the Early Thomas Moore?

On Christmas Eve, 1840, when Thomas Moore died in his home

at Liverpool he was in his 79th year.⁵ Working backwards, this means that he was born in 1762, and when he first arrived in Australia in 1792 he was already 30 years old. The Thomas Moore of these first thirty years has, until this sesquicentenary year, remained elusive.

For at least the last decade of his life, Moore had been speaking with William Grant Broughton, the first and only Bishop of Australia, about leaving the bequest that would eventually bring Moore College into existence and assist the Church of England in Sydney in other ways.⁶ Initially Broughton did not encourage these plans, for Rachel Moore and her son Andrew Douglas White were still alive, and so he regarded them as having a prior claim on Thomas' property.⁷ It was only after, first, his step-son (November 1837) and then, one year later, his dear wife passed away (November 1838),⁸ that Mr Moore received the Bishop's encouragement to change his Will in favour of the Church. According to Broughton's report, it was only at this late stage that he discovered that Thomas also had a brother and a nephew still alive and well in England.

> For it is somewhat remarkable that on the very day of my conversation with Mr Moore ~~on the day of~~ after his wife's funeral, in which conversation it was assumed by me that, having now no remaining ties, he was at liberty to dispose of his property as he thought fit, I learned that he had still a brother and a nephew living in England. This he confirmed yesterday when I put the question to him, before he declared what disposal he had now determined to make of his property. I urged him, as strongly as I could, to leave to these relatives a suitable proportion: but he seems, on what account I know not, to have little feeling of affection for them: saying they are not badly off, and he shall send them a few hundred pounds during his life time, which will be quite enough.⁹

At the end of 1841, Broughton reveals that he had been in correspondence with Moore's surviving relatives, but at this stage, the nephew has been replaced by a sister. 'I am sorry to learn that the old gentleman has left a brother and sister in very narrow circumstances, for whom we trusted he had made provision'.[10] These relatives were keen to have a copy of Moore's Will, and Broughton was a little fearful that the Church in Australia may end up being deprived of its first major native benefaction.

Although this information about his relatives only emerges in sources either just before or just after Moore died, they may provide some clues about his mysterious early years.

In 1838, when Broughton mentioned Moore's brother and nephew to Joshua Watson, he stated that, 'they live I believe in the North of England near to Archdeacon Scott, through whom some communication has been once or oftener made to them'.[11]

By the end of 1841, because of Broughton's fears about Moore's Will being challenged, he was keenly soliciting legal advice from his English connections, and had sent a copy of Moore's Will to England for this purpose. Because Thomas's brother and sister had requested a copy, Broughton asked Coleridge to forward the copy in his possession, informing him that:

> Moore's family are in communication with Revd Archdeacon Scott, Whitfield Rectory, Hayden Bridge, Northumberland; and with the Revd George Fielding, Bishop-Auckland, through either of whom the papers might be conveyed to them: most readily I believe by the latter.[12]

If we can assume that his relatives had a more settled life than the adventurous Thomas, these comments may provide us with some clues to Thomas Moore's origins. Although it has been claimed that he was born in Ireland,[13] in view of the location of these surviving relatives it is more likely that he was born in England. Since these surviving relatives are in touch with Scott in Northumberland, and Fielding in the Durham area, then it is also likely that Thomas Moore hailed from the Northeast of England.

Whitfield is a rural area, in the hills of Northumberland, where lead had been mined for over a century. Thomas Hobbes Scott first visited Australia as the secretary to Commissioner Bigge, sent to inquire into the state of the colony in 1819. On his return to England in 1821, he received Holy Orders and, probably because of a family connection, assumed the living of Whitfield, which was under the patronage of the Ord family of Whitfield Hall, into which his sister had married. As a result of a paper he had written about an education system for the colony, in 1825 he arrived as the first Archdeacon of Australia, and spent three rather turbulent years in the colony, before resigning and returning to the peaceful surrounds of Whitfield to live out his days.[14] Assuming a more settled nature in rural regions, it was my early guess that this was the area that Moore may have spent his early days, and that Scott was still in connection with some of his family. There were (and are still!) several families of Moor(e)s in the district, and there were Moor(e)s who were in the long-term employ of the Ords at Whitfield Hall, including during Scott's time,[15] as well as others with possible family connections.[16] Was Thomas a far-flung relative of the Moor(e)s of Whitfield Hall?

Rev George Fielding was the grandson of the famous politician and author Henry Fielding, of *Tom Jones* fame, whose father Allen and brother Charles were both in the ministry. George began his ministry at Bishop Auckland, near Durham (1827–1845), and concluded it at N. Ockendon, Essex (1845–1869).[17] According to Broughton, he is the one through whom contact with the surviving relatives could most easily be made. The Census returns show several Moores in Bishop Auckland, and, in particular, in 1851 the 76 year old widow Isabella Moor_ was living with her 44 year old daughter Jane (Johnson) on the Market Place, where the Fielding's abode was also situated.[18] This neighbourly connection is intriguing, and, once again at an earlier stage of my research, I wondered if these were Thomas's relatives.

Family connections are, of course, not proved by mere speculations, and so, before I had made my later discoveries, I had to be content to operate on the basis of these 'educated guesses'.[19] Even if the details remained obscure, I assumed that Thomas Moore came from the Northeast, in order to seek further information to fill out the picture of his (potential) origins.

Chapter 2 ~ But, Who Was Thomas Moore?

When Thomas Moore first arrived in Australia, he was the ship's carpenter on the ship, *Britannia*, whose master and part owner was Captain William Raven—the other part owner being John St Barbe of London. The *Britannia* sailed from Falmouth on 15th February 1792,[20] as the first of three ships commissioned to carry stores for the settlement at Port Jackson, 'twelve months' clothing for the convicts, four months' flour, and eight months' beef and pork for every description of person in the settlements, at full allowance, calculating their numbers at four thousand six hundred and thirty-nine'.[21]

Being owned by John St Barbe, the *Britannia* was part of the Southern Fisheries, and so it is no surprise that Raven was set on fishing in the waters off Australia. At this stage, however, the East India Company had the monopoly, and so the *Britannia* had come equipped with a three year fishing licence granted by the Company.[22] During his visit to Dusky Bay, on the remote South West tip of New Zealand, Captain Cook had noticed many seals, and Raven was keen to make some profit from their loss. Given the practices of the day, his crew—including Moore—would share in the profits. But on the eve of their departure, the *Britannia* was commissioned by the officers of the New South Wales Corps for a voyage to the Cape of Good Hope, which became the first of several such trading voyages for Captain Raven and his crew. Not to be daunted from his first object, after leaving Sydney on 22nd October 1792, Raven firstly dropped off his second mate William Leith, with eleven men under him, to acquire some sealskins from the herds at Dusky Bay, while he continued to the Cape via Cape Horn.

The ship's carpenter, Thomas Moore, was with them.[23] After felling timber for the needs of the *Britannia*, once she left he then oversaw the men in the building of a house for them to live in. When this first dwelling made by Europeans in New Zealand was completed, Moore then turned to the next project: to build New Zealand's first European vessel—in case Raven's *Britannia* failed to return. Return she did, however, on 27th September 1793, but not before Moore had built a vessel of 60 or 70 tons, to within a month or two of being able to sail away. The ship was left on the stocks at Dusky Bay, but after reaching Norfolk Island, Captain Raven spoke of it to Lieut. Gov. King in words of high praise:

> What excited my admiration was the progress they had made in constructing a vessel of the following dimensions:—40 ft. 6 in. keel, 53 ft. length upon deck, 16ft. 10 in. extreme breadth, and 12 ft. hold. She is skinned, ceiled and decked, and with the work of three or four men for one day would be ready for caulking. Her frame knees and crooked pieces are cut from timber growing to the mould. She is planked, decked, and ceiled with the spruce fir, which in the opinion of the carpenter is very little inferior to English oak.
>
> Her construction is such that she will carry more by one-half than she measures, and I am confident will sail well. The carpenter has great merit, and has built her with that strength and neatness which few shipwrights belonging to the merchant service are capable of performing.[24]

The ship was actually completed, fitted and sailed, two years later, by Captain William Bampton, who christened it the *Providence*.[25] He did not consider that it sailed very well at all, but it was better than his *Endeavour* which was in very bad shape indeed and was left at Dusky Bay. But the positive report from Raven to King almost certainly contributed to the enhancement of Moore's reputation as a shipbuilder, such that in a relatively short time he had been appointed Master Boat Builder to the colony of New South Wales.[26]

Given Raven's glowing report of Moore's shipbuilding prowess, Robinson finds it 'regrettable that we know nothing of where Moore may have received his earlier training'.[27] But, if it is a fair guess that he originated in the Northeast of England, it is also a fair guess that this was where he learned his trade as a ship's carpenter. If his work was as good as his reputation suggests, it is almost certain that he served an apprenticeship. An apprenticeship usually lasted for seven years, and since a boy may have begun as early as twelve years old, Moore would have been serving his apprenticeship from approximately 1774 to 1781, give or take a couple of years.

In the last quarter of the eighteenth century, rapid advances were occurring in the Northeastern shipbuilding industry around Sunderland.[28] By 1819, a contemporary source claimed that Sunderland's shipbuilding industry stood 'the highest of any in the United Kingdom, and gives employment to a great number of carpenters'.[29] In 1801, there were nine shipbuilding establishments in Sunderland. Even though there may have been slightly less to choose from twenty five years earlier, this gives us some idea of the kind of options available to Moore as he served his apprenticeship.[30] Although Sunderland's output would not peak until 1840, when 251 vessels were built, it was still something of a record that 19 were completed in 1790.[31]

Although some derogatory comments were cast from time to time, in general Sunderland ships were of a high standard and the Sunderland carpenters had a good reputation. There were numerous small firms, and small to medium vessels were the norm, and Sunderland carpenters were especially used to working with mixed woods, as a variety of timber was readily available in the port.[32]

Another piece in the puzzle presents itself in the fact that the vessel which brought Moore to Australia, the *Britannia*, was actually built in Sunderland in 1783, and she also had some damage repaired there in September two years later.[33] In other words, she was being finished as Moore was freshly emerging from his apprenticeship. It is possible that he was even engaged in her building, before he joined her as her carpenter and she became his first vessel. If he was already part of her crew by 1790, he would have sailed under W. Warng and/or D. Young to the Straits, and then, just prior to his journey to Australia he would have sailed to Antigua under Wm. Raven (1791–1792),[34] the same master who then brought him to Australia.

Who was the Later Thomas Moore?

Once Thomas Moore was in Australia, there is more information about him, especially for the latter years of his life when he lived at Liverpool. Even though there are still mysteries about Mr Moore in this period, this is the period when our sources are much more abundant, and the problem is simply one of gathering and explaining them.[35]

By the time Thomas Moore resigned his position at the Dock Yard, and permission was granted for him to do so, he had already built a house on the George's River, which he called Moore Bank.[36] By this stage he was already one of the Colony's larger landowners, having a property that stretched from Petersham to the Cook's River, as well as the grant at George's River—which is originally referred to as being in Banks Town, the extent of civilization at that stage in that direction. Rachel and Thomas were therefore amongst the earliest settlers in the Georges River district.[37]

Lachlan Macquarie was Governor of NSW from 1809 to 1821.[38] Almost as soon as he arrived in the Colony, he began the development and building for which he became famous—or infamous, depending on one's perspective! His was a great time of building in and around Sydney. After he had settled numbers of people on land grants at some distance from Sydney, he then sought to build townships to act as centres of government administration under the supervision of magistrates and constables, as well as being depots for receiving grain, and other farm produce.[39] With this goal in mind, in 1810, he laid out five new townships: Windsor, Richmond, Pitt Town, Wilberforce, and Castlereigh, as well as proclaiming a site for a township on the banks of the Georges River which would act as a centre and a depot for the storage of grain for the district of Holsworthy and Airds. This town he named Liverpool.[40]

Governor Macquarie selected the site for the township of Liverpool on Wednesday, 7th November, 1810. Having stayed the night before at Parramatta, he and his official party arrived early the next morning at Thomas and Rachel Moore's river-bank home.

> At 6am I set out [...] for George's River, and arrived at Mr. Moore's house at 8 o'clock, having crossed the River in a boat [...]. Between 10 and 12 o'clock we all set out [and crossed the

river ...] to view and survey the Ground intended for the new Township [...] having surveyed the ground and found it in every respect eligible and fit for the purpose, I determined to erect a Township on it, and named it *Liverpool* in honour of the Earl of that Title—now the Secretary of State for the Colonies.[41]

The next day, the Governor and his party, including Thomas Moore, toured the Minto district. Still using Thomas Moore's home as a base, just after daybreak on the Friday, they went to some farms in the Banks Town district. They got lost, but eventually returned 'home'—presumably the Moore's—at about 10:30 am, then inspected more farms at Minto.[42]

Once the site was chosen, building could begin. Thomas Moore had a major role in the laying out[43] and the building of the town, acting as the supervisor of public works until 1823,[44] and he would be one of its leading citizens until his death in 1840.

In 1810, Macquarie also proclaimed Thomas Moore a Magistrate. Across almost thirty years he would faithfully fulfil the many and varied duties that came to him in that capacity. Like other early colonial magistrates, this required him not only to dispense justice, but also to act as the government representative in Liverpool. In this capacity he was responsible for publicising Government policy and its changes, for assigning convicts as they arrived in the colony, for conducting Government 'musters' (censuses) from time to time, and a whole host of other duties.[45]

Macquarie was also a great builder of churches. New South Wales' oldest surviving Anglican[46] church buildings were constructed under his governorship:[47] St Matthew's Windsor,[48] Christ Church Newcastle,[49] St Peter's Campbelltown,[50] St Thomas' Port Macquarie,[51] St James Sydney, as well as the two towers at St John's Parramatta and the original foundation stone for St Andrew's Cathedral, and, of course, as the second of the Macquarie churches, St Luke's Liverpool.[52]

Rev. and Mrs Youl were present when Governor Macquarie laid the foundation stone of St Luke's on the 7th April 1818.[53] Thomas and Rachel Moore were also present, as well as Governor

Macquarie's four-year-old son, Lachlan who, as the Governor noted in his diary, 'assisted me in a very active, manly manner'. The friendship and respect between the Governor and the Moores is exemplified by the fact that they were appointed to be Lachlan junior's guardians, should anything happen to his parents while in the colony. The other person who attended that day was the future architect of the building, Francis Greenway.[54]

Thomas Moore was given the job of superintending the building of St Luke's,[55] but the contracted builder was Nathaniel Lucas, whose gravestone now rests outside the Northwestern wall of the Church. Lucas had already built the parsonage, which he completed at the end of 1816.[56]

Lucas and Moore would have known each other from when they both lived in Sydney, after Lucas arrived with his large family when Norfolk Island was reduced in 1805.[57] The two men shared the same profession, for Lucas had formerly been the boat builder at Norfolk Island, and set himself up in Sydney as a builder. Perhaps this gave the two men some affinity. On the other hand, Francis Greenway and Nathaniel Lucas did not see eye to eye. When Lucas took his own life after a bout of drunkenness following a disagreement with the architect, some blame was imputed to Greenway, provoking his strong assertion that their differences were merely professional. It would be interesting to know how Greenway got on with Thomas Moore, during the building of St Luke's.[58]

Thomas and Rachel were keenly involved with the congregation from before St Luke's even existed, right through until they were each buried from the Church. Thomas and Rachel were evidently quite hospitable people. It seems that throughout the 1810s and into the 20s, they often entertained Governor Macquarie, with or without his entourage.[59] In 1833, we find them entertaining the surveyor Felton Mathew, and his wife Sarah, who also greatly enjoyed the fellowship of St Luke's. On June the 11th, 1833, *en route* to Campbelltown, their party pitched camp 'in our old spot near the water course in Mr. Cartwright's paddock'.[60] The next day, Mrs Felton Mathew informs us, the camp was sent on to Campbell Town:

> while we called on the Cartwright's who seemed delighted to see us, and on the Moore's who also welcomed us kindly. The Cartwrights had removed to their new house close to the church, an ill contrived, tasteless building but roomy and convenient, though I should greatly prefer their pretty secluded cottage "Mary Vale".[61]

On their return, they again camped near Mr Cartwright's place at Liverpool, and on 23rd June 1833, being a Sunday, they were able to join the St Luke's service.

> Walked into Liverpool to church: it is almost a treat to spend a Sunday near this place for it is the only church in the colony where the service is reverently, and decently performed, at least the only one I have been in, and I have visited almost all—We afterwards dined with the Moores, and walked out to our tents by moonlight: the nights are very lovely, the stars shine with the brilliancy of an English frosty night: and the constellations of the Southern Hemisphere are certainly more splendid than those of the Northern: the most striking is that, which is called the "Southern cross" presenting the exact figure, by four stars of superior size and lustre, a fifth, included in the constellation, is too small to interrupt the exact resemblance of the figure.[62]

In 1838, Bishop Broughton wrote of the frequent hospitality he enjoyed in the Moore's home.[63] They were obviously keen members of St Luke's, who used their home to extend the fellowship that was enjoyed during the times of the service.

Their home was known for its devotion to Christ. Loane's comment that '[Moore's] home, with its habits of household prayers each day and of worship in St Luke's Church every Sunday, was a model of ordered piety and simple contentments',[64] can be supported from several sources. An incidental reference in the Journal of the Quaker, Mr George Washington Walker, for example, which he writes on the 13th September 1836, notes:

> We breakfasted with Thomas Moore and his wife, the oldest

inhabitants in Liverpool, having been the first to locate themselves in what was a wilderness. Thomas Moore is a magistrate, and an active promoter, by his influence and example, of the welfare of the community. After reading the Scriptures my companion had some appropriate counsel to offer, under the renewed feeling of gospel love, which was well received.[65]

The plaque erected to Rachel's memory in St Luke's Liverpool, also points in this direction, for one of the things she is remembered for is her 'devotion to family prayers'.[66]

Thomas Moore was also involved in the missionary cause. There was quite a large missionary presence in those early days at Liverpool.[67] Before St Luke's was built, services at Liverpool were presided over by Samuel Marsden, whose interest in the New Zealand mission is, of course, well known. Rowland Hassall, the ex-missionary to Tahiti was also involved, taking lay services. John Youl, the first Chaplain at Liverpool, who had twice been a missionary in Tahiti,[68] and his successor, Robert Cartwright (1819–1836) had been recruited by Marsden and both proved to be great evangelists. Richard Taylor left for the New Zealand mission after being incumbent at Liverpool 1836–1838.

But Moore did not simply rub shoulders with the missionary-minded, he also took an active interest in the missionary cause. In 1817, he was a founding member of the Bible Society, whose committee in those days were active in doorknocking homes in order to offer the Scriptures to those who did not have a copy.[69] His interests did not stop with the mission at home. In a letter from 1818, Samuel Hassall told his brother James that: 'Mr Moor [sic] of Liverpool for some time past has been using all his influence to prevail on me to go to New Zealand—but under present existing circumstances I cannot consent'.[70] Evidently Moore wished Samuel to follow in his grandfather's footsteps by joining the mission in New Zealand.[71]

According to Boyce, he was also involved in some capacity in the founding of an Auxiliary of the Church Missionary Society in New South Wales in 1824 or 1825,[72] although I have not yet been able to substantiate this claim. Apparently he also presided over an earlier meeting in Sydney, 'held to forward missions abroad'.[73] Loane (and Dickey) is correct in reporting that he was involved in 'the Liverpool committee Wesleyan Auxiliary Missionary Society,'[74] for he was appointed to the (Wesleyan) Missionary Committee in Parramatta in, for example, 1829[75] and again in 1836.[76] The first Wesleyan services were held in the Government buildings at Liverpool by Rev Samuel Leigh,[77] who became a fellow member with Moore on the first committee of the Bible Society. Later Moore donated land to build the first Methodist church in Liverpool.[78] Both Thomas and Rachel were subscribers to the construction of Wesleyan chapels.[79]

Although I have not yet verified all of the claims made for Moore's missionary concerns, there certainly seems to be sufficient evidence to justify Boyce's statement that:

> The sending of the good news of the Great Redeemer's work to the heathen world was evidently very near [Thomas Moore's] heart. To the end of his life the interest was maintained. He would have known all leading particulars of Marsden's seven missionary voyages to New Zealand, most probably have heard them from his own lips, and the importance of all were doubtless written in his mind.[80]

ON FRIDAY NOVEMBER 2ND, 1838, the faithful of the colony were called together for a concerted time of prayer. For three years, the colony had been in the grip of one of the severest droughts in memory, and it had become dependent upon supplies coming from overseas, which were themselves insufficient. Bishop Broughton asked the Governor to proclaim a day of humiliation and prayer, which he did for this day.[81]

> On this morning, as the people throughout the Colony began to gather in the churches to offer their supplications, with their confessions of sin before the Throne of Grace, soft and gentle rain began to fall, increasing in strength as we prayed,

developing into a steady downpour, and continuing until the longed for saturation of the ground was effected.[82]

Although we cannot be sure, it is probable that Thomas was adding his prayers to those of St Luke's that morning. However, shortly after this great cause for thanksgiving, he suffered his own loss when his beloved Rachel finally left his side, dying on 13th November at the age of 76 years.[83] Perhaps providing some return for the Moore's care and hospitality for him on his many visits to and through Liverpool, Bishop Broughton conducted Rachel's funeral service on 16th November 1838.[84]

Just over two years later, on Christmas Eve, 1840, Thomas Moore himself died quietly in his home, aged 78. His death was announced in the Sydney papers a few days later,[85] and his funeral took place at St Luke's at 11 am, on Tuesday, 29th December, conducted by Rev. John Duffus.[86] When his Will was proved the following February, Moore's lasting legacy became publicly known.

Moore the Wealthy Benefactor

Thomas Moore died a very wealthy man. With perhaps only a little exaggeration, we could say that Moore was acquiring land almost from the beginning of his time in Australia through to the end of his life, first at Bulanaming (between Petersham and Cook's River), then along the George's River (from Liverpool southwards, his 'Moore Bank' property), then around the township of Liverpool, in Argyle, Sutton Forrest, and elsewhere. His property interests enabled him to accumulate a great deal of his wealth.

In 1797, he bought some of the first merinos in Australia, although he doesn't seem to have maintained a long-term interest in sheep,[87] preferring cattle and horses. As his farming interests expanded at Liverpool, his cattle made him one of the major suppliers of meat to the Government stores.

Over time, he also gained a reputation for breeding horses of good quality. In an age before the motor car and, indeed, even before the railway, the horse was an important and valuable commodity. The list of the names of the various horse-owners in the early Colony, reads like a 'who's who' of the colony, evoking from one writer the comment that 'already we see the pattern that was to remain for the next century—the leaders in our political, commercial (and later our agricultural) life were those same people most prominent as breeders and owners'.[88] In this august company, we find Thomas Moore.

His interest in horses began while he was still living in Sydney. Buying his first horse in 1798,[89] by 1800, Moore owned four horses,[90] and by 1802 (if not before) he was set up for breeding, owning 1 horse and 5 mares.[91] By 1804 he owned 10 of the colony's 404 horses (3 stallions and 7 mares), which presumably he kept on his Petersham/Bulanaming property.[92] He continued to breed good horses on Moore Bank, and beyond the 'ordinary' services they no doubt rendered in the Colony, it seems that some of Moore's fine horses may have even brought their owners a little money at the race-track![93]

During his time at Liverpool, Thomas Moore acted in a range of capacities, providing civic leadership to his town and to the colony. His duties as the principal magistrate at Liverpool[94] gradually expanded to require two, then three or four days work per week.[95] As noted above, the colonial magistrates had a much broader function than those of today.

Moore led an active political life, and was involved in many causes that placed him amongst the 'liberals' of his day. The year before he left Sydney, his signature was amongst those who requested the arrest of Governor Bligh in the colony's famous 'Rum rebellion'. Influenced, no doubt, by the fact that he was married to an ex-convict, he was clearly amongst those with 'emancipist' sympathies, and was a close friend of Governor Macquarie, and a close associate of his three emancipist magistrates Thompson, Lord, and Redfern. He was involved in the long-term struggle for the right of trial by jury and for representative government. His political activity seemed to continue almost to the day of his death, for even on 26th December 1840, that is, two days after he had died, *The Australian* and the *Gazette* ran a notice that the central committee of the 'Australian Immigration Association' intended to invite various citizens to form District Committees of the Association, and Mr T. Moore was at the top of the list of the eight men for the Liverpool committee.[96]

Moore was certainly interested in education. He had shown an active interest in the Liverpool School from its inception, and he visited the children well into his old age.[97] But when it came to education, however, it is difficult to know whether his weight was thrown in with the 'radicals' or the 'conservatives'. He was a supporter of Richard Bourke in other areas, did he support him in his educational reforms? The issue is clouded somewhat by a little bit of politics that was regarded as manipulative at the time, even though it may have been a simple mistake. In 1836, Bishop Broughton chaired a meeting which drew up a petition against the proposal to introduce the Irish system of General Education. This meeting, held on the 14th July, respectfully invited other Protestants to form local committees for the purpose of obtaining signatures. Thomas Moore was amongst those invited to form the Protestant Committee at Liverpool.[98] These 'Protestant Associations' set up to collect signatures for the petition, sought to protect the right of the Protestant churches to teach their Faith as part of a child's education. Certainly Thomas Moore strongly supported the Protestant cause, and was an associate of Broughton in some regards, so he could have been part of this committeee, heart and soul. However, as the days went on it was revealed that the people listed in the newspapers as forming local committees had not actually been asked, and, in fact, some of them were opposed to the aims of the Protestant Association in regard to education. Until further evidence is uncovered, it is difficult to know whether Moore was a 'genuine' member, and so a 'conservative', or there by mistake, and so possibly a 'radical'.

We do know, however, that he would certainly have supported Christian, and Protestant, education in its proper place (whatever he may have regarded that to be). For, whatever other personal and public motivations may have been behind his many and varied interests, Thomas Moore was, above all a Christian gentleman. In what can perhaps be described as his last act in this world, after decades of thinking about it, he left his considerable wealth to benefit the work of Christ in the land that he now called home. In his Will, his Christian faith coalesced with his long-term interest in education, as he provided a considerable benefaction towards a college that would educate young men of the Protestant persuasion according to the principles of the united Church of England and Ireland.

In 2006, the college that resulted from his bequest has been opened for 150 years.

Notes

1. A shorter version of this essay was delivered as the address at the Supporters' Lunch at Moore College 27th April 2006.
2. Robinson, 'Thomas Moore & Early Life'.
3. Russell, *Thomas Moore and the King's Dockyard 1796–1816*.
4. Robinson, 'Thomas Moore & Early Life', 192 (30) n.127, himself laid down the challenge for the latter years of Moore's life: 'There is room for a further study of Moore's years at Liverpool, 1810–1840, his place in the life of the colony during those years, and of the history of his benefactions to the present day'. The sesquicentenary celebrations have been the impetus for my own research in response to this challenge.
5. His death notice: 'At his residence, Liverpool, on Thursday the 24th instant, in the 79th year of his age, Thomas Moore, Esq. Mr. Moore was one of our oldest colonists, and much esteemed for his piety and charity'; *Sydney (Morning) Herald* 28 December 1840 and *Sydney Gazette* 29 December 1840. His funeral announcement appeared in the two papers on the same day as the event, Tuesday 29th December 1840.
6. Broughton to Coleridge, 25 February 1839: '[Moore] frequently, during my former residence in this country even, threw out hints of his wish to make some disposal of property for the benefit of the Church'. Broughton's 'former residence' was between 1829 and 1834. A codicil to Andrew Douglas White's Will suggests that Moore may have made up his mind about the benefaction as early as 1827; see Robinson, 'Thomas Moore & Early Life', 186 (24).
7. Broughton to Coleridge, 25 February 1839.
8. Both are buried with Thomas in Pioneer Park at Liverpool. Their inscriptions read 'sacred to the memory of', respectively, 'Captain A.D. White, of the Royal Engineers, who died 24th Nov. 1837 aged 44 years'; 'Rachel Moore, the beloved wife of Thomas Moore Esq. J.P., who died 13th Nov. 1838, aged 76 years'; 'Thomas Moore, Esq. J.P., founder of Moore College and Donor of other church benefactions, who died 24th

Dec. 1840, aged 78 years'. Rachel also has a high-relief marble memorial inside St Luke's Liverpool.
9. Broughton to Watson, 29 November 1838.
10. Broughton to Coleridge, 27 December 1841. Robinson, 'Thomas Moore & Early Life', 192 (30) n.123, mistakenly reports the date of this letter as the 22nd.
11. Broughton to Watson, 29th November 1838.
12. Broughton to Coleridge, 27th December 1841.
13. Australian Encyclopedia[2], 'Moore, Thomas (1762–1840)', 145.
14. See Cunningham-Browne, 'Scott, Thomas Hobbes (1773–1860)' and Border, 'Scott, Thomas Hobbes (1773–1860)'; Wyatt, 'Wine Merchant'.
15. 1851 Census, Whitfield HO 107/2416 (AIGS), item 47, shows 34 year old Thomas Moor_, Agricultural labourer, with wife and four children living in the Whitfield Office. The Ord family erected inscriptions in the Whitfield church to John Moor_ (M.I. Nbl 7 [AIGS], items 17 & 49) who died 23/8/1858 after working as the agent for William Ord, Esq. and Revd. J.A.B. Ord for 41 years, and for his niece Mrs Blackett Ord; and to George Moor_ (items 18 & 48), land agent to William Ord, Esq. for 44 years (d. 3/6/1832), and a younger George, son of John, who died 8/1/1851 at the age of 20.
16. 1841 Census, Whitfield HO 107/843/12 (AIGS) shows a Mr Robson lived with Scott in the rectory. There were family ties between some Robson and Moore families in the district.
17. Cambridge Alumni List; Crockfords.
18. 1851 Census HO 107/2385/folio 208, fiche 5 (AIGS): Bishop Auckland, item 70.
19. For the further evidence which came to light in the course of my research, see the later essays in the present volume.
20. Nicholson, *Log of Logs*, p.73. Raven's *Britannia* has often been confused with the *Britannia* which came out in the third fleet under Captain Melville in July 1791. This mistake is behind Boyce's comment that the ship had 'a long and wearisome voyage of about eight months' (*Thomas Moore*, 2), whereas it was actually 'a comparatively fast journey of five and a half months', Robinson, 'Thomas Moore & Early Life', 167 (3). Loane, 'Moore, Thomas', 254, and Dickey, "Moore, Thomas', 266, also confuse the vessels.
21. Collins, *Account*, 174.
22. Several years later, Thomas Moore received his own commission from the Company, as a second Lieutenant under the authority of Fort William, Bengal, with the right to seize French ships as lawful prizes. East India Company, Commission to Thomas Moore, 18th December 1795.
23. For the next several paragraphs, see Robinson, 'Thomas Moore & Early Life', 167–172 (3–8).
24. King to Dundas, 19 Nov 1793, Enclosure: Raven to king, 2 Nov 1793, *HRNSW* II. 95.
25. Nicholson, *Log of Logs*, p.425.
26. 'Mr Thos. Moore is appointed to the place of master boat-bulder, in the room of Mr Daniel Paine, commencing on the 2nd instant'. John Hunter, General Order, 13th September 1796. *HRNSW* III. 115.
27. Robinson, 'Thomas Moore & Early Life', 170 (6).
28. Smith & Holden, *Where Ships are Born*, 10. I have also entertained the possibility that Thomas was apprenticed in South Shields, another up and coming shipbuilding area. See Flagg, *Notes on the History of Shipbuilding*.
29. Cited in Smith & Holden, *Where Ships are Born*, 1.

30. Smith & Holden, *Where Ships are Born*, 2, 22. If I have discerned these establishments correctly, they would be those associated with the following families/persons: Goodchilds (pp.7–8), Burns (p. 8), Collins (p. 8), Henry Rudd (p. 9), Reay (p. 9), Thomas Havelock (p. 9), Tiffin (p. 9), Nicholsons (p. 96), Pile (p. 18).
31. Smith & Holden, *Where Ships are Born*, 10, citing the House of Commons Report of 1806. http://www.thisisthenortheast.co.uk/the_north_east/history/shipbuilding generalises this number by saying 'by 1790 Sunderland was building around nineteen ships per year'. Smith & Holden give the actual figures from the House of Commons Report in 1806 as: 1790: 19; 1791: 6; 1804: 51. Average tonnage built 144, 202, 163 respectively; and largest tonnage: 312, 356, 349.
32. For further history of shipbuilding in Sunderland, especially in the nineteenth century, see the following exchange: Ville, 'Rise to Pre-Eminence'; Clarke, 'Comments on Simon Ville'; Ville, 'Sunderland Shipbuilding: Pre-Eminence Restated'; Craig, 'A Note on Shipbuilding'; Ville, 'Craig on Sunderland Shipbuilding'.
33. *Lloyds Register of British and Foreign Vessels*, volumes for 1790, 1791, 1792. These records also tell us that *Britannia* was 296 tons, sheathed in copper over boards, surveyed in London, owned by St Barbe & Co (therefore a Southern Fisheries vessel), and registered as a Ship (not a Brig). She was classified A1, the highest rating—see Blake, *Lloyds Register of Shipping 1760–1960*, 6.
34. *Lloyds Register of British and Foreign Vessels*, volumes for 1790, 1791, 1792.
35. As this volume goes to press, I am still in the process of gathering these sources, with a view to completing a substantial biography of Moore by about 2010. See end papers.
36. The site is now commemorated with 'Thomas Moore Park', in Whelan Avenue, Chipping Norton, which looks down the river towards Liverpool and Lake Moore.
37. According to the G.W. Walker the Moores were '[...] the first to locate themselves in what was a wilderness'; Backhouse, *Life of Walker*, 253; cf. Boyce, *Thomas Moore*, 10.
38. McLachlan, 'Macquarie, Lachlan'; Freame, 'Early Days', 2.
39. Freame, 'Early Days', 3–4.
40. For this paragraph, Freame, 'Early Days', 4.
41. Macquarie's Journal Entry for 7th November 1810, cited from Havard, 'Note on the Naming of Liverpool, N.S.W.', 370.
42. 'The official tour of the district commenced on the following morning [i.e. Nov 8th, 1810], Governor Macquare [sic], being accompanied by Dr. Redfern, Captain Antill, Mr. Meehan (surveyor), and Mr. Moore (settler). They set out to view the farms in the Minto district, and Governor Macquarie declared that Mr. Thompson's farm, called St. Andrew's, and Dr. Townson's farm, "to be by far the finest soil and best pasturage I have yet seen in the colony"', Freame, 'Early Days', 5.
43. Broughton to Watson, 29 Nov 1838: '[...] the old gentleman was always forward in contributing to the support of the Church; the building of which he, it seems, had superintended, as well as the laying out of the township (Liverpool) in which he resides'.
44. See his request to resign from this position and Goulburn's acquiescence to his request; Moore to Goulburn [19] May 1823; Goulburn to Moore 18 October 1823, SDA 0853CH, Item 9, docs. 1 and 2.
45. I further explored this role later in the year, at Moore College's celebratory Thomas Moore dinner (28th October 2006), under the heading, 'Liverpool and the Lash: the Magistrate Thomas Moore'. See now, Chapter 8 of the present volume.
46. The oldest surviving building is the chapel at Ebenezer, which has long been in Presbyterian hands. For a brief account of its earliest period, see White, *The Challenge of the Years*, Chapter 1.

47. These are listed by Cowper, *Autobiography*, 24–25, but not in historical order.
48. Foundation stone laid 11th and then again on 13th October, 1817; Walker, 'Early Churches', 439. For a more detailed account of the troubled building programme, see Ellis, *Greenway*, 113–119.
49. Building commenced 1817, although a temporary building was on the same site since 1812; Walker, 'Early Churches', 439–440.
50. Erected 'about 1824'; Walker, 'Early Churches', 442
51. This building is very similar in appearance to St Luke's. Its foundation stone was laid in 1824, and it was opened in 1828; Walker, 'Early Churches', 442.
52. See Walker, 'Early Churches', 441–42.
53. Loane, *Hewn From The Rock*, 29, mistakenly attributes the energy for St Luke's foundation to Robert Cartwright and Moore: 'Thomas Moore was a staunch churchman and must have seen Cartwright as a truly kindred spirit. Through their combined efforts the foundation stone for the Church of St. Luke was laid in 1819, and the church was built on the plan of St. Matthew's Windsor'. Cartwright's appointment to Liverpool was announced in the *Sydney Gazette* on 18th December 1819, whereas the foundation stone was laid in April of the year before, when Youl was still presiding.
54. Ellis, *Greenway*, 95. Ellis provides a list of Greenway's first buildings on pp.112–113. Greenway and the surveyor of St Luke's, William Stone, each received 3/– per day. In 1818 Stone also received £1 travelling expenses while he was surveying St Matthew's Windsor, and St. Luke's Liverpool; Freame, *St Luke's*, 21.
55. Macquarie's diary has records of payment to Mr James Smith for alterations to St. John's Church, Parramatta, and to Nathaniel Lucas for the building of Liverpool parsonage, which was in progress; Ellis, *Greenway*, 64. SG 2/11/1816: Police Fund Accounts for quarter ending 30th September 1816: 'Nathaniel Lucas, in part payment of his Contract for erecting the Parsonage House and Offices at Liverpool, 27-0-0 sterling'. SG 8/2/1817: Police Fund account for quarter ending 31st December 1816: 'Mr. Nathaniel Lucas, in full payment of the Balance due him on account of his Contract, for erecting the Parsonage House and Offices at Liverpool, 123-0-0'.
56. 'He had thirteen children, eleven at Norfolk Island between 1789 and 1803, of whom two (twins) died in infancy, and two more in Sydney in 1805 and 1807', Herman, 'Lucas, Nathaniel (1764–1818)', 139. The twin girls were killed on 2nd February 1792, when they were just 18 months old, when Nathaniel set fire to two trees when clearing, and one fell on the house. See 'Children of Nathaniel and Olivia', http://www.jdark.linkt.com.au/childrenhtml.html (5/8/2005), which alludes to a grief-filled letter in Nathaniel's name, but now believed to be written by Olivia herself, dated four years later in 1796. How much did this tragedy play upon the mind of the troubled Nathaniel even at a later period?
57. His sons would also be known for the boats they would later build at Port Dalrymple, where they moved after his death.
58. Broughton to Watson, 29 Nov 1838: '[…] the old gentleman was always forward in contributing to the support of the Church; the building of which he, it seems, had superintended, as well as the laying out of the township (Liverpool) in which he resides'.
59. For example, on 28th June, 1814, Thomas and Rachel entertained Gov. Macquarie and Col. and Mrs Molle at his house, Moore Bank, Liverpool, and on 26th July, 1814, Gov. and Mrs Macquarie. *Macquarie Memoranda*, pp. 80, 82 (ML: A772). In addition, they entertained the Governor and Mrs Macquarie and their suite at Moore Bank, Nov 30–Dec 5th 1820. *Governor Macquarie's Diary*, pp.174–179 (ML: A774).

CHAPTER 2 ~ But, Who Was Thomas Moore? [27]

60. Havard, 'Mrs Felton Mathew's Journal', 117, where the note identifies this as 'Brickmakers Creek, which joins Cabramatta Creek before the latter's junction with George's River'.
61. Havard, 'Mrs Felton Mathew's Journal', 117–118.
62. Havard, 'Mrs Felton Mathew's Journal', 123. On Tuesday 15th October, 1833, they were again at Liverpool and called on the Cartwrights and Moores (p.174).
63. Broughton to Watson, 29 Nov 1838: 'They were always very civil and hospitable to me in my visits to their house travelling through the country'.
64. Loane, 'Moore, Thomas', 255.
65. Backhouse, *Life of Walker*, 253. Cf. Boyce, *Thomas Moore*, 10.
66. As an indirect testimony to the pious practices of their home, we can refer to a recently discovered list of Moore's books, which shows that he owned a large selection of devotional material, including several volumes particularly focusing upon family prayers. See 'Thomas Moore's Bookshelf', chapter 7 in this present volume.
67. Freame, *St Luke's*, 6–7.
68. Stancombe, 'Youl, John'.
69. Thompson, *Australia*, 34–35.
70. S.O. Hassall to Rev. J. Hassall, Sept 19, 1818; Hassall Correspondence, vol. 4, p. 656 (ML A1677-4).
71. Boyce, *Thomas Moore*, 9. The claim is repeated in *Australian Encyclopedia*[2], 'Moore, Thomas', 145. He does not appear in the early records of CMS Australia, but he could have been associated with the Corresponding Committee in NSW, formed and dissolved in 1821; see Yarwood, Marsden—Survivor, 206, 223.
72. At this stage, it could have been the CMS mission or the Wesleyan.
73. Boyce, *Thomas Moore*, 9.
74. Loane, 'Moore, Thomas', 255; Dickey, 'Moore, Thomas', 266.
75. *The Australian* 9 October 1829, presuming that 'T. Moore' refers to him.
76. SG 9th October 1836, again, presuming that 'T. Moore' refers to him. The editor of the *Australian* took the opportunity to compare the reports of 'so many extraordinary conversions' amongst the islands of the pacific, with the continuance of the natives of New Holland 'engulphed in spiritual darkness'.
77. Freame, *Early Days*, 23.
78. Freame, *Early Days*, 36.
79. E.g. SG 23/11/1827, 3f: Mrs Moore, Liverpool, subscribes to Richmond Wesleyan Chapel—although to be certain we need to establish that this was not the wife of Joshua John Moore, who also gave to charitable causes.
80. Boyce, *Thomas Moore*, 9.
81. Cowper, *Autobiography*, 115.
82. Cowper, *Autobiography*, 116. Presumably his vivid description is of the events as they occurred in Stroud.
83. Death of Rachel Moore, at Liverpool, aged 76 years. Announced in SG 20/11/1838, p.3. Freame, *St Luke's*, 8, mistakenly has 1832, but the date is correct on p.17.
84. *St Luke's Burial Register*, 16 November 1838.
85. *Sydney (Morning) Herald* 28 December 1840, p.3; SG 29 December 1840, p.3.
86. For funeral notice, see *Sydney Herald* 29/12/1840; for Duffus, see *St Luke's Register*.
87. I further explored this later in the year in a library lecture at Moore College, under the title: 'Moore and the Merino', see ch. 4 in this present volume. According to the muster, in 1800 he had a flock of 40 sheep, but by the following year, they were all gone;

Baxter, *Musters & Lists. 1801–1802*, List 2 (1800), items AB010–012, compared with List 7 (1802), item AG478. Moore still has no sheep on the return 14/8/1804 (*HRNSW* V, 432–433), but has 3 mares, 7 stallions, 1 bull, 13 cows, 4 oxen, 6 male hogs and 7 sows. He has 700 acres pasture, 470 acres fallow (total 1170); He is victualled from the stores, but his wife is not; one of his convicts is on the stores and two are not.
88. Barrie, *The Australian Bloodhorse*, 12.
89. *Thomas Moore's Business Notebook*, SDA 0884CH, Item 1, lists the age of his mares from 1798–1812.
90. In Baxter, *Musters & Lists. 1801–1802*, List 2 (1800), items AB 010–012, he is listed as having 4 horses (not differentiated with regard to sex), along with 40 sheep, 6 pigs, and 8 cattle on his Bulanaming property, 470 acres of which came from his own grant, 30 from John Jeffries, and 30 from Robert Abell, 20 acres of wheat sown on his own property and 5 on Jeffries'. He has five convicts in his employ (List 9, items AJ 088–92). In the 1801 muster (List 5, item BE 021) on his original grant (470 acres) he has only 5 cleared, 1 horse, 5 hogs, 1 assigned convicts. Incidentally, when they were still convicts, Jeffries and Abel were both engaged to unload *The Lady Juliana*, upon which Rachel arrived, and by the end of the week were each flogged with 200 lashes for somehow purloining sugar between the ship and the shore inventory-taking; see Rees, *The Floating Brothel*, 200–201, 209.
91. Baxter, *Musters & Lists. 1801–1802*, List 7 (1802), item AG 478. This list also gives him a grant of 530 acres, 100 under cultivation, 5 acres of maize; 1 m. cattle, 10 cows, 2 m. hogs and 2 sows, as well as his horses; 20 [bushels?] of wheat in hand and 50 maize; and 2 servants on the stores, 1 off.
92. *HRNSW* 5.433–444. For some comparison, at the same time Major Johnstone owned 15 horses (4, 11), John Palmer 21 (10, 11), Richard Fitzgerald 12 (2, 10), William Kent 19 (5, 14), and John Macarthur 26 (12, 14). In April of the same year, Robert Campbell imported the Colony's second pure Arab stallion and sold it to Governor King who then bartered it to the Government.
93. See, for example, the notice in *Sydney Gazette* 2 February 1811: 'Strayed, a Dark Grey Gelding, 15 hands high, white star in the forehead, white fetlocks, has a small wen or wart under the left ear, was bred at George's River by Mr Moore; ran at the last Races, and is well known by the Name of *Bryan Boroo*, being the property of Captain Glenholme, of the 73rd Regiment; any Person restoring him to whom, will receive Five Guineas Reward'.
94. *Bigge Report 1*, 80: Moore was 'assisted occasionally by Mr. Brookes and Mr. Broughton, and at one period by Mr. Redfern'. Redfern was the third and last emancipist (after Andrew Thompson and Simeon Lord) appointed to the magistracy by Macquarie, a policy criticised by Bigge (and others), see pp. 84–90.
95. *Bigge Report 1*, 80: 'The duties of these magistrates have latterly so much increased, that their attendance at Parramatta, Windsor and Liverpool, which was in the year 1818 only twice in the week, is now required on three or four days, and that of the police magistrate of Sydney is on every day, and sometimes protracted to a late hour'.
96. *The Australian* 26th December 1840.
97. Boyce, *Thomas Moore*, 9, writing in 1914, knew that 'one aged and highly respected resident of the town still lives who was a scholar [at Liverpool school], and has a kindly recollection of [Moore] often coming to the school and showing a warm concern in its doings'.
98. *The Australian* 19th July 1836.

CHAPTER 3

AN OVERDUE BIRTH ANNOUNCEMENT

In Quest of the Long-Lost Family of Thomas Moore[1]

ON CHRISTMAS EVE, 1840, Thomas Moore Esq., the first appointed magistrate of Liverpool, NSW, departed this life at his home, after a short period of illness.[2] He was 78 years old, and had spent the last 48 years of his life in the colony of NSW.

Once his funeral service at St Luke's Liverpool was over (29th December),[3] and his Will proved (2 February 1841),[4] what the Bishop of Australia, William Grant Broughton, had already known for a couple of years became public. Thomas Moore's rather substantial fortune had been left, in one way or another, to the Anglican Church. In particular, special provisions were made for the founding of a College for the training of young men of 'the Protestant persuasion in the principles of Christian Knowledge [...] according to the principles of the United Protestant Church of England and Ireland'.[5]

Moore's old house in Liverpool very quickly became known as Moore College,[6] even though it was simply tenanted for a number of years and it was only when Bishop Barker arrived that a proper college began there, exactly 150 years ago, in March 1856.[7]

Thomas Moore probably thought of leaving his estate to these purposes as early as 1827—perhaps earlier[8]—well before Broughton arrived on the scene as Australia's second Archdeacon, to replace the controversial Thomas Hobbes Scott.[9] But after Broughton arrived,

Moore had spoken to him of his plans, even during the time that Broughton was Archdeacon (i.e. 1829–34).[10] After Broughton returned to Australia for his second tour of duty (1835), now as the first and only Bishop of Australia, Moore once again pressed this idea upon him. By this time, Thomas Moore had amassed wealth in the colony through his property, his trading, his farming, and his banking. He felt that God had blessed him greatly, and now, at the end of his long life, he wanted to give his fortune to God's work, in gratitude for what the Lord had done for him.[11]

Bishop Broughton listened, but he did not encourage these plans.[12] After all, Thomas Moore had a family and surely they had to be given the first claim on Moore's estate. Bishop Broughton was referring to Thomas's wife Rachel and her son Andrew, or Douglass, as he was known to the Moores.

Rachel had originally come to Australia when she was Rachel Turner.[13] She had arrived as a convict on the *Lady Juliana* in 1790, serving a 7 year sentence for theft of goods from the London household in which she had worked as a servant.[14] Once she arrived in Sydney, she was assigned to Surgeon John White. She subsequently became his mistress and on 23 September 1793, bore him a son, Andrew Douglass White.[15] When John White returned home at the end of the following year, he left Rachel and the infant behind.[16]

Thomas Moore had arrived in the colony in 1792, as ship's carpenter aboard William Raven's ship, *Britannia*.[17] It is almost certain that Thomas became acquainted with Rachel on one of the occasions when the *Britannia* was in Sydney Cove between voyages, whether 1792, 1794, or 1795.[18] Perhaps she was one of the reasons he eventually decided to leave the adventuring life on the *Britannia* and to settle in Sydney.[19] Be that as it may, in September 1796, he was appointed Master Boat Builder for the colony,[20] a post he held for the next 13 years. In January 1797, Thomas married Rachel, with Richard Johnson officiating.[21] For almost half a century from that day, he would be devoted to Rachel,[22] and to her son Andrew (or Douglass).[23]

CHAPTER 3 ~ *An Overdue Birth Announcement* [31]

When Bishop Broughton didn't encourage Moore's plans to give his fortunes away, on the grounds that he should care for Rachel and her son, Moore would have taken this very seriously indeed. He therefore did nothing further, at this stage, about changing his Will.

But Providence then took a different turn. Thomas Moore had doted on the young Andrew (or Douglass), who spent several years in Moore's home as his stepson.[24] I have recently discovered some accounts in Sydney Diocesan Archives that show that Thomas Moore also paid for Andrew's schooling in England at Charterhouse, which he attended between 1806 and 1808.[25] And it is likely that he paid for Andrew's Military Commission after that.[26] By 1812 the young man was an officer in the Royal Engineers, just in time to be at Waterloo in 1815. He returned to Australia for six months in 1823,[27] and eventually returned for good, probably to assist his aging step-father and to be reunited with his beloved mother. In due course (1835), Andrew married Mary Ann Mackenzie,[28] but just two years later, after a short illness, he died,[29] predeceasing both mother and stepfather.

Sadly for Thomas, within a further twelve months, Rachel also died (13 November, 1838).[30] Bishop Broughton took the funeral service from St Luke's Liverpool (16 November).[31] Almost immediately after Rachel was buried,[32] Thomas took the opportunity to speak with Bishop Broughton about his old plan. He could now leave his fortune to the Church, because both wife and stepson were gone, and so their prior claim on his estate no longer prevailed. Broughton agreed and Thomas went off to the good judge Burton to change his Will accordingly.[33]

However, it was also at this time that Bishop Broughton encountered another potential snag. Make no mistake, despite Broughton's previous reluctance to encourage Moore's plans, he certainly wanted to benefit from Moore's money. He was in almost constant anxiety about the need for clergy and churches to bring the ministry of the Church of England to this vast new land.[34] It is a tribute to him that he sought to have Moore deal honourably with his family, even if this may have meant that the Church, so full of need, would receive no legacy from Thomas Moore. As he buried Rachel, Bishop Broughton would have known that the last legitimate alternative claim on Moore's money was now placed in her grave.

But then came the snag. After Rachel's funeral, Broughton learned that Thomas Moore had several other surviving relatives. From some of his letters to his friends in England, we learn of his discovery of a sister, a brother, and a nephew, but, unfortunately for future researchers, he did not use their names, nor did he say precisely where they actually lived. What he did say, however, was that contact could be made with them via two clergymen, Thomas Hobbes Scott, former Archdeacon of NSW, now at the parish of Whitfield, Northumberland, and the Rev. George Fielding, Rector of Bishop-Auckland, Co. Durham.[35]

These surviving relatives were of great concern to Broughton. But he sends rather mixed messages. On the one hand, he urged Thomas Moore to make some provision for them in the Will, which Thomas refused to do, saying he would instead send some ready cash, while he was still alive.[36] I have recently discovered some letters in our Diocesan Archives, which prove that Moore heeded the Bishop's advice and sent some much-welcomed funds to his family and that they were also cared for by the Trustees after Thomas died.[37]

But, on the other hand, Broughton desperately needed money and he had welcomed Moore's generosity as a signal provision of Providence, and relished the thought of the property and funds that would come his way on Moore's demise. He was already dreaming dreams. Now that there were surviving relatives at home, there was the potential for Thomas's Will to be legally challenged, and then there would be no providential gift to the Anglican Church, and so there would be no future Moore College. Once Thomas had died, Broughton was in correspondence with these relatives, but at the same time he sent copies of the Will to his friends in England[38] so that they could seek legal advice, as to how the issue could be solved in such a way that the Anglican Church would still retain the benefits at Moore's hands.

To put the matter bluntly, Moore College only exists because

CHAPTER 3 ~ *An Overdue Birth Announcement* [33]

Thomas Moore had no surviving heirs and because the English relatives that *did* survive him did not, or could not, mount a legal challenge in a bid to grab his cash. In a sense, therefore, it is best not to know who these people were, in case we felt sorry for them and wanted perhaps to hand back the College to any of *their* surviving relatives!

But there are also good reasons to want to know who these relatives were. Thomas Moore arrived in Australia in 1792, already 30 years old. As to his early life, he has always been like Melchizedek, 'without father or mother or genealogy' (Hebrews 7:3). Even as long ago as 1914, just two generations after Moore's death, when Archdeacon F.B. Boyce wrote the first biographical essay on Thomas Moore, he could say that very little was known about the man.[39] Those who contributed other short dictionary articles[40] continued to bewail this deficiency, as did Donald Robinson, who wrote the only major and scholarly inquiry into Thomas Moore thus far.[41] Each writer on Moore has contributed a little further to our knowledge of this important early Colonial free settler and Anglican layman.[42] But none of them were able to illuminate Thomas Moore's origins or the first 30 years of his life. In fact, there was even dispute about which country he came from. One dictionary article[43] claimed his roots were in Ireland, although all others (rightly as it turns out) opted for England. Because of Broughton's reference to Archdeacon Scott at Whitfield and Rev. George Fielding at Bishop Auckland, Donald Robinson implied that Moore's origins lay in the North East of England.[44] Thus, to track these relatives down and so to locate Thomas Moore's beginnings seemed to be an important step towards filling the blanks and so adding to our understanding of the man.

Donald Robinson's 1970 article focused upon the period from Moore's arrival in NSW in 1792 to the end of his time as Master Boat Builder at the Dockyard in 1809. At the conclusion of his article, Bishop Robinson laid down the challenge for others to take up the inquiry into the Liverpool years (1810–1840) and also into the earliest years of Moore's life.[45]

In 2005, since I had a period of study leave and since Moore College was about to have its sesquicentenary in 2006, I thought I would take up both challenges, and this has now led to a major project, which will, in due course, issue in a serious biography of the man.[46] But as I began my study leave, I did so with the early period in mind: Perhaps I could, at last, find the early Thomas Moore.

Where do you start such a quest? I soon became familiar with the Mormon's massive project to collect genealogical material together on a website, www.FamilySearch.org, known as the International Genealogical Index. But what do you search for?

I knew Thomas Moore's name, and could deduce from his age at death that he was born in 1762, so there may be a christening record from that year. But he was married in Australia and he died in Australia and he had left England (in fact, the planet!) well before the 1841 census, so the sources of relevance to my search were rather limited.

At his death, we knew that he had at least three surviving relatives, a sister, a brother and a nephew—but we did not know their names. So how do you search for them? We knew that these surviving relatives were in touch with two clergymen in the North East of England, so did the Moores come from the Durham/Northumberland area?

From these barest of hints, I worked out a number of criteria that enabled me to search for potential candidates who may have been *our* Thomas Moore. My search gave me about half a dozen potential candidates for the whole of England who were christened about the right time. At the top of my list was a Thomas Moore, christened on 18th June 1762 in the Northumberland parish of Lesbury. On the positive side, he was born in the right year and from the right area. Although in Northumberland in England's North East, the coastal village of Lesbury was, however, a long way from Whitfield or Durham.

Anyway, I then set to examining all kinds of other records to find the sister, brother and nephew of my top candidates and built up many, many partial family trees of various Moores in the North East.

CHAPTER 3 ~ *An Overdue Birth Announcement* [35]

Towards the end of my 2005 study leave, I stumbled across an interesting connection between the past and the present. I was in pursuit of Thomas Moore's apprenticeship certificate, since, if it could be located, it would yield a lot of information about his origins. Since Moore was a ship's carpenter, I got in touch with the Most Worshipful Company of Shipwrights to see if they had any of these old records. Their Honorary Historian informed me that they did not. But he then added an 'oh, by the way'. His name happened to be David Moor (no 'e') and he happened to have a family tree stretching right back, which he had checked, and he happened to have noticed that he had a Thomas Moor, christened in 1762 at the parish church in Lesbury. I made a few half-baked and unsuccessful attempts to get in touch with David Moor further, but I had already gone cold on the Lesbury Thomas in favour of some other options, and my study leave was at an end, so, as it happened, I did not pursue David Moor's family tree any further.

When I started back at College, I had plenty of other things to do apart from my pursuit of Thomas Moore. When I did turn to my Thomas Moore research again, I took a different direction, turning from his early origins (with some disappointment at having been unsuccessful), to take up the second of Donald Robinson's challenges, the Liverpool period (1809–1840). In the last twelve months I have spent many a spare hour in front of the microfiche viewers in the Mitchell library with Government Records and early Newspapers becoming engrossed in these years when Thomas was Liverpool's resident magistrate.

But then, fairly recently, I decided to start into the collection at the Sydney Diocesan Archives. I had several things to pursue there relating to Moore's later period, but the quest for his origins still burned, even if at the back of my mind. By the kindness of Donald Robinson I had previously come across a transcript of some letters from Governor Macquarie to Thomas Moore—they had become good friends during Macquarie's time in NSW. A letter from 1824 mentioned that a nephew of Thomas Moore's had visited Macquarie in London, because he was interested in emigrating to NSW.[47] Was this the same nephew Broughton would later mention? Or was it a *fourth* mysterious relative? The difference on this occasion was that Governor Macquarie mentioned the nephew's name: he was a 'Mr N. Clarke'. Here was another person to search for.

I wanted to verify Donald Robinson's transcript of the Macquarie Correspondence against the originals and this is one of the things that sent me to the Sydney Diocesan Archives, for the transcript indicated that this was where the original letters were housed. When I arrived, I found a number of boxes of material collected by the Trustees of Moore's Estate, and, with the permission of the present-day Trustees, I began to sift through it all.[48] And here, amongst this material, most of which has not been touched perhaps for over a century, I have been fortunate enough to make some wonderful discoveries.

Amongst the various receipts and documents relating to the administration of Moore's Estate, I came across several bundles of personal papers from Mr Moore himself. On the 25th July 2006, I came across three letters that make it possible, at last, for us to know something of Thomas Moore's origins.

I have discovered a letter from Thomas's father,[49] written in March 1806 informing his children that their mother had died and been buried. In the course of doing so, he mentions a number of the children by name and provides the names of other people who are connected with the family.

I have also discovered two letters from Thomas Moore's brother, written in 1839.[50] The letters obviously respond to Thomas's correspondence and speak of the financial needs of the brother, his son, and their sister and her son. About this time, Bishop Broughton had urged Thomas to care for any surviving relatives and these two letters prove that Thomas had done so, sending cash and inquiring about further help that might be required.[51] They also speak of several other family connections and events. They also show a warm Christian fellowship existed between the two brothers, and so provide further witness to Thomas Moore's faith and piety.

CHAPTER 3 ~ *An Overdue Birth Announcement* [37]

And, of course, as you have no doubt already noticed, the discovery of these letters meant that, after 18 months of searching, I had at last discovered the elusive brother, sister, and nephew—along with a 'bonus' nephew to boot! And above and beyond the satisfaction and excitement that brought me, I also gained much more bonus information about the Moor(e)s. Thomas Moore's 'shady' origins were now coming into the light!

When I saw where these letters originated, further connections were made. Thomas's father wrote in 1806 from the Northumberland village of Lesbury—where my original top candidate had been born. I have subsequently got in touch with David Moor again, and have now gained access to his family tree. We have now worked out that David is our Thomas Moore's 5th Cousin, 5 times removed.[52]

The 1839 letters from Thomas's brother originated in a little village in County Durham, by the name of South Church, which is near Bishop-Auckland. They also mention how Thomas's correspondence has come by way of a friend in that town, and that Archdeacon Scott had also been in touch—thus confirming the hints we had already gained from Bishop Broughton's letters.

Since these discoveries, I have been engaged in a delightful email conversation between myself, David Moor, and another very helpful local historian from the Lesbury area—Mrs Lorna Gilroy,[53] whose enthusiasm for someone else's project has been astounding, and who has been looking up records on my behalf. Together we have been able to map out some family relationships—and I have also been able to locate the extra Moore Nephew who visited Macquarie, Mr Nathaniel Clarke who, in fact, did make it to Sydney in 1825, but died within the year.[54] We now have a fairly good sketch of the wider connections and family friendships of the Moore clan.

The information we have uncovered, when coupled with a bit of guesswork, might also enable some of the movements of the family during Thomas's growing up years to be pieced together. His family roots go back to Holy Island, that is, Lindesfarne—

famous for the beautifully illuminated Lindesfarne Gospels.[55] At one stage, I speculated that in about 1772, when Thomas was just about old enough to begin an apprenticeship, the family may have moved to the town of South Shields.[56] I have now reverted to an earlier theory that he may have been apprenticed to someone in Sunderland. Both towns were in what was fast becoming one of England's leading ship-building regions:[57] the perfect place for Thomas to learn his trade.

In 1783 one of the ships built in Sunderland was the *Britannia*, and in 1785 she returned there for repairs.[58] This was the very same vessel that arrived in Sydney Cove in 1792, with a 30 year old ship's carpenter by the name of Thomas Moore.[59]

And so, in the year that Moore College is celebrating its sesquicentenary, I am most privileged to be able to make a birth announcement that has hitherto been impossible to make.

In 1762, Thomas Moor(e), future benefactor of Moore College and of the Diocese of Sydney, was born to Joseph and Mary Moor, of the village of Lesbury, Northumberland. He was christened on 18th June 1762 in the Parish Church,[60] St Marys. His parents already had a daughter (Elizabeth) before Thomas was born, and they went on to have several other sons and daughters (Joseph, William, Henry, Sarah ['Sally'] and Mary).

The origins of this important Anglican layman, who was so prominent in the early colony of NSW, are no longer obscure.

As we celebrate 150 years of the College that bears his name, it is lovely to be able to announce to the Anglican Historical Society, that now, at last, Thomas Moore himself has a history.

Notes

1. Originally delivered as an address to the Anglican Historical Society, Sydney Diocese, on 2 September 2006, and subsequently published in the Society's journal (Vol. 51, No. 2, December 2006). Some discrepancies will be found between references to the Sydney Diocesan Archive material cited here and those of the earlier version, for I have since made some improvements in the classification of Moore's papers.

CHAPTER 3 ~ *An Overdue Birth Announcement* [39]

2. *Sydney Gazette* 29 December 1840, Death Notice: 'At his residence, Liverpool, on Thursday the 24th instant, in the 79th year of his age, Thomas Moore, Esq. Mr. Moore was one of our oldest colonists, and much esteemed for his piety and charity'. See also the headstone on his grave, Pioneer Cemetery, Liverpool NSW. Amongst his papers in the Sydney Diocesan Archives there are several indications that Moore was subject to some illness in his last months.
3. The notice of his funeral was published on the same day as the event; *Sydney Gazette* and *Sydney Herald* 29/12/1840.
4. *Trustees Minute Book* 1, 2/2/1841 (SDA): 'The Executors of the late Mr Moore attended this day at the Supreme Court, Sydney, and proved the Will and Codicil'.
5. *Trustees Record Book*, 3–4 (SDA). For excerpt, see Loane, *Centenary History*, 8–9.
6. The Trustees kept records of the income and distributions according to the various divisions named in the Will, including under the heading 'Moore College'; see the accounts in *Trustees Minute Book* (SDA).
7. See Loane, *Centenary History*, Ch. 2, esp. p.20.
8. See Robinson, 'Thomas Moore & Early Life', 186–189 (24–25). Moore had a clear interest in education, providing funds for several educational ventures during his lifetime. Now that his family of origin has come to light (see below), we know that his uncle James was the schoolmaster in Lesbury. Perhaps this was another influence that can now be added to those listed by Robinson.
9. T.H. Scott first came to the colony as assistant to Commissioner Bigge (1819–1821). After taking holy orders, he returned for a short but turbulent period as Australia's first Archdeacon (1825–1829). See further, Wyatt, 'Wine Merchant'.
10. Broughton's letters are held in the Moore College Library. Broughton to Coleridge, 25 February 1839: '[Moore] frequently, during my former residence in this country even, threw out hints of his wish to make some disposal of property for the benefit of the Church'. On 28 November 1838, Moore made an entry in his account book, *T. Moore's Account book, 1828–1840*; SDA 885CH, Item 6, indicating that he adjusted his Will several days after Rachel's funeral (see below, note 33).
11. Broughton to Coleridge, 25 February 1839; Williams, 'Moore College 1878–1884'.
12. Broughton to Watson, 29 November 1838.
13. For this paragraph, see Robinson, 'Thomas Moore & Early Life', 174–175 (10–11). The *Lady Juliana* arrived at Port Jackson on 3 June 1790. For an account of the journey of this vessel to Australia, and of those upon her, see Rees, *Floating Brothel*.
14. Her trial at the Old Bailey can be found at http://www.oldbaileyonline.org/html_units/1780s/t17871212-13.html.
15. He was christened by Richard Johnson on 30th; St Philip's Register (SAG 90), 30 September 1793. The Register also records his birth date.
16. Robinson, 'Thomas Moore & Early Life', 174 (10), initially followed Rienits, 'Biographical Introduction', 28, in thinking Andrew had returned to England in 1794 with his father, but later appended a 'Postscript' (now held in Moore College library) reassessing this opinion in the light of further evidence found in the Waterhouse papers. Robinson argues that Andrew probably stayed in the colony until he returned to England with Henry Waterhouse in 1800.
17. For the story, see Robinson, 'Thomas Moore & Early Life', 167–168 (3–4). His predecessor, Daniel Paine, informs us that he was the second mate at the time of Moore's appointment as master boat builder, Paine, *Journal*, 22nd August 1796, p.31. Earlier, when *Britannia* went to Dusky Bay, William Leith occupied this position.
18. The *Britannia* was in Sydney five times: between 26th July and 24th October, 1792;

? June and 8th September, 1793 (although Moore was not with her); 1st June and 1st September, 1794; 2nd March and 18th June, 1795; and 11th May to 29th September, 1796. See Robinson, 'Thomas Moore & Early Life', 167–168, 169, 171–172 (3–4, 5, 7–8).
19. So Boyce, *Thomas Moore*, 3; cf. Loane, 'Moore, Thomas', 254.
20. 'Mr Thos. Moore is appointed to the place of master boat-builder, in the room of Mr Daniel Paine, commencing on the 2nd instant', Government and General Order, 13 September 1796 (ML Col.Sec. 6037, ML Safe 1/18b); *HRA* I.I, 698.
21. See St Philip's Register (SAG 90), 11th January 1797. NSW Registry of BDM: 380 Vol. 3A and 240 Vol. 4.
22. The memorial to Rachel in St Luke's Liverpool, several comments from Moore's own pen when she died, and several letters of consolation from friends, all point to Thomas's great affection for his dear wife.
23. As some of the evidence for this affection, we could list the following: Moore named his Bulanaming farm, Douglas's Farm, in honour of his step son; he paid for his schooling, and possibly his military commissioning (see Robinson, 'Postscript'); he speaks fondly of Andrew when he visits Sydney for six months in 1823; some of Andrew's early handwriting books are still amongst Thomas's papers in the Sydney Diocesan Archives (SDA 0884CH, Items 2 and 3 [1805]).
24. On the assumption he stayed in the colony until 1800, see above, note 16.
25. Isaac Clementson to Thomas Moore, 21/2/07, SDA 0853CH, Item 11, doc. 2; *Charterhouse Register* 1769–1872, p.401.
26. Robinson, 'Postscript'.
27. Rienits, 'Biographical Introduction', 31, implies that he stayed in Australia—followed by Robinson, 'Thomas Moore & Early Life', 186 (24). That this was simply a six month visit, is shown by a note on the day of his arrival (7 February) and departure (17 August) in Moore's *Memorandums and Occurrences*, SDA 884 CH, Item 5, as well as by arrival (13/2/1823) and departure notices (7/8/1823) in *Sydney Gazette* (21/8/1823). This is confirmed by a postscript to a letter to Moore from ex-Gov. Macquarie, written in 1824, which adds that he had recently seen Andrew in London, Gov. L. Macquarie to T. Moore, 1 June 1824, SDA 853 CH, Item 4, doc. 12.
28. *Australian* 19/6/1835.
29. He died on 24th November, 1837; *Australian* 28/11/1837; Headstone, Pioneer Cemetery, Liverpool NSW.
30. Entry for 13 November, *T. Moore's Account book, 1828–1840*; SDA 885CH, Item 6; Sydney *Morning Herald*, 21 November 1838; Headstone, Pioneer Cemetery, Liverpool NSW; Memorial, St Luke's Liverpool.
31. Entry for 16 November 1838, *T. Moore's Account book, 1828–1840*; SDA 885CH, Item 6; St Luke's Register, 16/11/1838.
32. Broughton to Watson, 29 Nov 1838: 'The week before last however the old lady died: and after the funeral Mr Moore again spoke to me about his Will, which he said must now be altered again. It was therefore arranged that he should meet Mr Justice Burton and myself yesterday that we might receive his testamentary dispositions, and enable him to carry them into effect'.
33. Broughton to Watson, 29/11/1838; *T. Moore's Account book, 1828–1840*; SDA 885CH, Item 6, entry for 28 November: 'Went to Sydney to alter my Will [...] Deeds to Sydney to be made out to the Deed of Gift to the Church'.
34. This is a constant theme of his letters to his English friends. See ch. 10 in this volume, 'Training Colonial Clergy'.

35. Broughton to Watson, 29 Nov 1838: 'I learned that he had still a brother and a nephew living in England. They live I believe in the North of England near to Archdeacon Scott, through whom some communication has been once or oftener made to them'. Broughton to Coleridge, 27 Dec 1841: 'the old gentleman has left a brother and sister. [...] Moore's family are in communication with the Reverend Archdeacon Scott, Whitfield Rectory, Haydon Bridge, Northumberland, and with the Reverend George Fielding, Bishop-Auckland'. The memory of this nephew survived in the memories of those around Liverpool, see the reminiscences of Arthur Lukyn Williams, 'Moore College 1878–1884'. There was also another nephew who had emigrated to NSW in 1825, but died shortly after his arrival; see below.
36. Broughton to Watson, 29 Nov 1838. See also the anecdotal evidence provided by Arthur Lukyn Williams to the same effect, 'Moore College 1878–1884'.
37. William Moor to Thomas Moore, 24 Dec 1839, SDA 851 CH, Item 6, doc. 35; William Moor to Broughton, 5 Nov 1842 and 7 July 1842 (copy), SDA 851 CH, Item 7, doc. 65; George Fielding to Trustees, 12 July 1847, SDA 852 CH, Item 10, doc. 45.
38. Broughton to Coleridge, 15 Feb 1841 no. 1 and 2; 4 Dec 1841; 14 Feb 1842; 14 April 1842.
39. Boyce, *Thomas Moore*, 1.
40. [Australian Encyclopedia²], 'Moore, Thomas', 145; Loane, 'Moore, Thomas', 254–255; Bernard, 'Moore, 12' and 'Moore Theological College'; Dickey, 'Moore, Thomas', 265–266.
41. Robinson, 'Thomas Moore & Early Life'.
42. Moore provides one case study towards the project called for by Fletcher, 'Christianity and free society', 94: 'the religious beliefs and pursuits of free persons considered as a group have not received the attention they deserve. While the response of convicts to efforts to arouse their faith has been the subject of a major study, [i.e. Grocott, *Convicts*], no attempt has been made systematically to examine the relationship between free persons and the churches'.
43. Australian Encyclopedia², 'Moore, Thomas', 145.
44. Robinson, 'Thomas Moore & Early Life', 167 (3) n.11.
45. Robinson, 'Thomas Moore & Early Life', 187 (25) n.127.
46. For information, see end papers of this volume.
47. Gov. L. Macquarie to T. Moore, 1 June 1824, SDA 853 CH, Item 4, doc. 12.
48. I am glad to acknowledge the assistance of Dr Louise Trott, the Diocesan Archivist, over several months of my bothering her, whilst sitting at her left hand!
49. Joseph Moor to children, 20 March 1806 (SDA 853 CH, Item 11, doc. 1b).
50. William Moor to Thomas Moore, 2 July 1839, SDA 853 CH, Item 8, doc. 9; William Moor to Thomas Moore, 24 Dec 1839, SDA 851 CH, Item 6, doc. 35; cf. the copy resent on 28/1/1840: 853 CH, Item 8, doc. 10.
51. See also William Moor to Broughton, 7 July 1842 and 5 Nov 1842, SDA 851 CH, Item 7, docs. 28 and 65.
52. David Moor to Peter Bolt, 9 August 2006, per email.
53. I originally came across Lorna through a query about Alnwick Grammar School, in pursuit of possible places in which Thomas may have been educated. Although this quest is still incomplete, Lorna expressed her interest in local history and volunteered her assistance in whatever way might help. I have been very glad to have the information she has dug out.
54. Subsequently I have learned that Nathaniel was the son of Thomas's sister Sarah ('Sally') and William Clarke, who lived in London (St Mary's, Lesbury, Burial Register,

16 January, 1787). He was a twin to Joseph and both boys were christened in Lesbury on 4 June 1786 (St Mary's, Lesbury, Baptismal Register). Joseph died on 16th January the following year, and was buried in Lesbury (St Mary's, Lesbury, Burial Register). After visiting Macquarie in June 1824, Nathaniel did in fact proceed to NSW, arriving in 1825 and taking up residence in the city. However, by the end of the year he was dead, after a painful illness, which resulted in a 'burst artery' in his oesophagus and him choking to death; *SG* 7/11/1825. He died on 3rd November, aged 40, and was buried on the 4th; see St Philip's Register (SAG 90), 1825 No. 1145. His death is registered with NSW Registry of BDM: V18256640 2C/1825 and V18251145 8/1825. The journal of his journey to Australia found its way into Moore's possession—he used the unused portion to keep his accounts!—and now resides in the Sydney Diocesan Archives (SDA 885 CH, Item 5 (a)).
55. David Moor's family tree.
56. This was the state of my thought at the time of my address to the Anglican Historical society. It was based upon the following argument: David Moor's family tree had the possibility of two Elizabeths amongst Thomas's siblings. In searching for records for Elizabeth the younger and her sister Mary, I noticed that when Thomas's brother Joseph 'junior' was married in 1790, it was in South Shields, Co. Durham, where he was a resident at the time. Pursuing things a little further, I discovered that a Joseph and Mary Moore christened two daughters at St Hilda's South Shields: Mary on 19th July 1772, and Elizabeth on 23rd April 1775 (See IGI records: 442757/ 0119/ 059508 and 459177). The names and dates seemed to fit well with what I had already discovered, and so I guessed that this was the same family. This led to the proposal that the family began at Lesbury, but, after Henry died (1772), they moved to South Shields for a time, in time for Thomas's apprenticeship years. Joseph and Mary then eventually returned to Lesbury, where they subsequently finished the course of their days. Evidence from the letters in the Sydney Diocesan Archives has confirmed that Elizabeth was Thomas's older sister, who actually lived longer than he did. She had married rather late (age 35—the IGI usually guesses 25 if the birthdate is unknown), and the wedding record was therefore hers, thus removing the need for a second Elizabeth. The pair of girls christened in St Hilda's are therefore most probably another family.
57. Smith & Holden, *Where Ships are Born*, 10; for South Shields, see Flagg, *Notes*.
58. *Lloyds Register of British and Foreign Vessels*, 1791 to 1796 editions.
59. It is possible that Thomas Moore joined the vessel for earlier voyages. The one immediately prior to the trip to NSW was to Antigua and before that, the Straits [of Malacca or of Magellan—either way indicating the territory of the East India Company].
60. Baptismal Register, St Mary's, Lesbury, 18 June 1762: 'Thomas, Son of Joseph & Mary Moore of Lesbury, Baptized'.

CHAPTER 4

MOORE AND THE MERINO[1]

*I*N 2006 MOORE COLLEGE HAS been training men and women for the work of Christian ministry for 150 years. This celebratory year provides the opportunity to remember with thankfulness our founder, Mr Thomas Moore of Liverpool. As a small contribution to that task, my topic this afternoon will be 'Moore and the Merino'. Now, it has been said that Australia was built on the sheep's back, but what has the founder of our theological college got to do with wool?

Although Australia began as a penal colony, it was only a matter of time before questions began to be asked about its future as a nation. If it were to grow towards maturity, it would need to break free from its reliance upon the government stores and develop its own economy and industry. It was in this context that a small number of people began to look for Australian products that could be exported in order to return a profit. And wool was one of the products, which, at least in the eyes of some, held great potential.

When the First Fleet arrived in Australia in January 1788, it brought a small handful of sheep from England.[2] Exactly one hundred years later, Australia was proclaimed to be 'the first among the nations in the production of wool'.[3] One of the key factors in Australia gaining this position of prominence was the development of our distinctive fine wool through the introduction and selective breeding of the merino.

One of the long-running debates of Australian history concerns the question: who really deserves the credit for introducing the merino into Australia? Is it the colourful ex-Captain of the NSW Corps, John McArthur? Or is it the famous Chaplain, Samuel Marsden,[4] whom Governor King called 'the best practical farmer in the colony'[5]?

But this year we celebrate another man with a surname beginning with 'M'. On hearing my topic today, you could imagine that I am going to propose something rather radical. Am I going to say that it was really Thomas Moore who introduced the merino? This may even sound reasonable when we recall that Thomas Moore was one of the major landholders in the early days of the colony, and much of the wealth that he eventually bequeathed to the Anglican Church was gained from his pastoral industry.

But my object this afternoon is not so grand. Despite wishing to honour our founder, to propose that he had a major role in the development of the Australian wool industry would be running roughshod over the evidence—to say the least. As we shall see, he did not. That honour rightly belongs to the other two 'M's', McArthur and Marsden, along with a couple of others, such as Alexander Riley and his family.[6]

My interest this afternoon is in a packet of material that is housed in our library that was originally in the possession of our benefactor, Thomas Moore. Although I won't be solving any large-scale puzzles in Australian history, this packet of material does enable us to solve a small-scale puzzle, and, of course, even such small-scale solutions are valuable in setting the record straight.

One of the most interesting items in our library's packet is a copy of the lease to the property known as 'The Vineyard' at Parramatta. This was one of the first four land grants in NSW. These grants were each issued on the same day by Arthur Phillip to four men, of whom the most famous would probably be James Ruse. The lease to 'The Vineyard' was issued to the German,

Phillip Schäffer, who was brought to the colony for his expertise in farming. However, he did not really perform as well as expected and eventually sold his farm to Captain Henry Waterhouse. We have a copy of the document transferring the lease from Schäffer to Waterhouse.

Thomas Moore first arrived in New South Wales in 1792: 30 years old and the ship's carpenter on board William Raven's *Britannia*. After several years of further adventuring, he left the *Britannia* in 1796 to become the Master Boat Builder at Sydney Cove. He held this post until 1809, after which he retired to his property on the George's River, known as Moore Bank. He then went on to become one of the leading citizens of Liverpool, where he played an active civic role, and where he continued to pursue his farming interests, until he died on Christmas Eve, 1840, at the age of 78.

During the dockyard years (1796–1809), Moore lived in the Rocks and for some of that time Henry Waterhouse was his neighbour.[7] They were involved together in several official capacities,[8] but they also became good friends. They continued to have contact after Henry Waterhouse returned to England, not only because of their friendship, but because there was a family connection. It is probable that Thomas Moore had sent his stepson Andrew Douglas White to England when Henry returned, and that Andrew then lived with Waterhouse's family[9]—which included Henry's sister Elizabeth, who married the famous explorer George Bass. Our library's packet of material contains several letters from members of the Waterhouse family to Thomas Moore, which bring him news of Andrew's welfare.[10]

When Henry Waterhouse departed from the colony in March 1800,[11] he left his property in the hands of others. However, this did not work out happily, and on 24 April 1812 he wrote to Thomas Moore for assistance. Impressed by Thomas Moore's character, Henry gave him power of attorney over his affairs in conjunction with Colonel Davey,[12] and requested that they both 'justly dispose' of his property in New South Wales.

In a matter of months, however, Thomas received news from William Waterhouse,[13] Henry's father, that Henry had passed away. William was also impressed with Thomas Moore's character, and so he handed the power of attorney solely into Moore's hands. He requested that Thomas Moore sell Henry's stock and property as soon as he was able. The sale went through in March and May of the following year, and many of the documents in our packet are documents relating to this sale.[14]

But what about the merino?

The potential value of wool to Australia only began to be widely understood in 1812 when, for various reasons, some of Marsden's fleeces fetched enormous prices in the English market, as did fleeces from Marsden, McArthur and Riley in the following year.[15] This continued to happen, until this first boom peaked about 1825, before the harder times of the second quarter of the century.[16] Without a doubt, in these early days the two significant names were those of Marsden and McArthur.[17]

As 'Australia's first major entrepreneur',[18] McArthur's motives were undoubtedly connected to his 'ruthless pursuit of wealth',[19] whereas Marsden's agricultural pursuits in large part arose from his view of Christian mission as a civilizing force in the world.[20] But, despite their different motivations, both these men had a far-sighted vision of the place of wool as a future export for the colony. While other farmers were largely killing their sheep for mutton,[21] these men were carefully breeding theirs to produce better wool. And the key to this programme in these early days was the introduction of the merino to the colony.

But who deserves the praise for this introduction of 'the Spanish sheep', as they were called? According to the long-standing debate, was it McArthur, or was it Marsden?

It seems reasonably clear that the person behind the claim that John McArthur was responsible for introducing the merino, was John McArthur himself.[22] But once he had started the rumour, it seemed to stick, probably because of his subsequent importance for the wool industry. So, for example, in 1828, the London papers the *Morning Herald* and the *Quarterly Review* spoke of Macarthur having introduced the merino.[23]

On the other side of this debate, Samuel Marsden had his supporters—once again, probably because of his obvious significance in the early days of Australian wool and because when he sailed from England in late 1809 he brought five Merino sheep from the flocks of George III.[24] Even as late as 1902 the *Yorkshire Daily Observer*, and *Dalgety's Review*, claimed that Marsden held the honour of introducing the merino to Australia.[25]

This question has been debated for a long time, from the early nineteenth century through to at least the 1960s![26]

Along the way, some have felt that the whole debate is pointless. This was the view of the *Sydney Gazette* in 1826:

> Whether Mr. Macarthur was or was not the first *bona fide* importer of merino sheep is a matter of little moment. To cavil on that point is as absurd as it would be to attribute the merit if there is any to the ship that conveyed them. It is not in the importation of one or two sheep where the merit lies, it lies in the improvement of them—in the facilities afforded for their propagation—in bringing their wool to such perfection as to render it one of the greatest and most important exports of an infant colony [...] It is in all this that the honour lies, and it is in the exercise of all this that we recognise the transcendent merits of Mr. John Macarthur as regards woolgrowing.[27]

Despite this fine piece of early Australian pragmatism, which attempts to shift the focus towards outcomes and successful achievement, others were not satisfied with the dismissal of the historical question of fact.

Two years later, the *Sydney Gazette* published a letter that had been addressed to the editor of London's *Morning Herald*, which attempted to set the record straight.[28]

> (To the Editor of the Morning Herald)
> Sir:— in your paper of Saturday (Jan. 20.) the introduction of Merino sheep into New South Wales is attributed to Mr. McArthur. The last number of the "Quarterly Review," in

noticing "Mr. Cunningham's Letter upon the actual State of Society in that Colony," also ascribes their introduction by the same gentleman. Upon what foundation Mr. McArthur's claim to be so considered rests the accompanying letters will show. The individuals who really conferred that benefit upon the Colony being deceased, it is to them of no consequence to whom the palm is awarded; but, as a matter of fact, it may as well be correctly transmitted to posterity—I am, Sir, yours, &c, A CONSTANT READER[29]

Following his letter, the *Gazette* then published a brief exchange of letters between Sir Joseph Banks and Captain Henry Waterhouse, dating to 1806.[30] Prior to that time, McArthur had been in London, seeking to arouse interest in his scheme for a greater production of Australian wool. His predictions were rather unrealistic, and, at that stage, Sir Joseph Banks was not in favour of supporting his scheme.[31] Banks, however, continued to seek further information from various people, and in this connection he wrote to Waterhouse stating:

> I much wish to procure accurate information respecting the introduction of the Spanish breed of sheep at Port Jackson, from which so much is expected, and some good will, I have no doubt, be in time realised.[32]

Waterhouse is happy to furnish the facts.

> In *1797* I arriv'd in the *Reliance* at the Cape of Good Hope, together with the *Supply Capn Kent*, and *Brittania* Transport, on board the *Reliance* was the Commissary for the purpose of purchasing Cattle for the Settlement on board the *Brittania*[33] Govr King and Colonel Paterson on their way to England. Both which Gentlemen had been acquainted with Colonel Gordon who lost his life there—*Col^n Gordon* had imported a few Spanish sheep to the Cape which had increas'd to *thirty two*. *Mrs Gordon* was then going to Europe and for some reason did not chuse to leave any thing that had belong'd to her late Husband at the Cape, she gave *three* Spanish sheep to *Govr King* and *three* to *Col^n Paterson*, the remainder I understood

were offerd [sic] to the *Commissary*, but he *declin'd to purchase them* on the part of Government. They were then offer'd to *me*, as I could not afford to purchase the whole, Captn Kent (that they might not be lost to the Colony) offer'd to *take half, a[nd he] receiv'd thirteen*, and I took Govr Kings on [board] the Reliance, *Col^n Paterson* took his to *England* to present to Sir *I Sinclair*, we paid Mrs Gordon *four pounds*[32] apiece for them, the expences on delivery, was about *one pound ahead* more, the expence for food for the passage was very considerable, unfortunately Govr Kings sheep had been brought to the Cape Town some time before ours, and put with some others, by which they became *diseas'd* and communicated it to ours, his *three died* soon after they came onboard, I do not recollect the numbers I had alive when I arrived at Port Jackson,[35] but think more *than half*, Cap^n Kent who I understood shared his with Lieut *Braithwait*, I believe lost all, from the circumstance of his applying to me for one immediately on my arrival, I do not recollect if Lieut Braithwaite had one or two alive.

By republishing this correspondence, this 'CONSTANT READER' of the *Gazette* sought to set the record straight. Despite Macarthur's subsequent success in breeding the merino, he was not the one to introduce them to the colony. This honour actually belongs to a man who admitted he was no farmer: the naval Captain, Henry Waterhouse.

Having purchased the sheep, Waterhouse then had to acquire some land on which he could keep them, and so he quickly purchased 'The Vineyard' from Phillip Schäffer.[36] This is the lease already mentioned held in our library. About the same time, he also received a grant of a further 4.5 acres of land abutting 'The Vineyard', and a copy of this grant is also amongst the material in our library.

But if this letter from Waterhouse to Banks helps to solve the big issue of who holds the honour of introducing the merino to NSW that I am not really addressing, it also raises the small-scale puzzle that our library packet helps to solve.

In his letter to Banks, Waterhouse also tells what happened to the Spanish sheep when they arrived in the colony. He did not keep them all, but he expressly desired to distribute them amongst the other colonists.

> I offer'd all mine to the *Governor* but I suppose he was satisfy'd as they were in the *Colony*, as he declin'd purchasing them.
>
> Cap^n McArthur then offerd fif*teen Guineas* a head provided I would let him have *the whole* this I *declined* wishing to distribute them
>
> I supply'd Cap^n Kent, Cap^n McArthur, Cap^n Rowley, and Mr Marsden. As the Spanish Ewes had Lambs (none but Spanish Rams running with them) I supplyd Mr Williamson, Mr Moore, Government and in fact any person who wish'd to have them.[37]

As I am sure everyone has already noticed, amongst those listed by Waterhouse as purchasing some of the first merinos there is a 'Mr Moore'. This introduces our minor historical puzzle: who was this 'Mr Moore' who became the proud owner of a couple of Spanish sheep?

The identity of this Mr Moore is left open by both the Mitchell Library Card Index and the Index to the *Sydney Gazette*.[38] Unsure of who he was, these indexes are content to leave him as a mystery Moore.

However, not content with the mystery, two different identifications have been made. When publishing Waterhouse's letter amongst the Banks Papers, the State Library website identifies this Moore as the colony's first solicitor William Henry Moore.[39] However, this cannot be correct. Solicitor Moore did not arrive in the colony until 1814, so he could not have purchased merinos in 1797.[40]

A better candidate would be another William Moore, who enlisted in the NSW Corps on the 7th March 1795,[41] arriving in the colony as an Ensign[42] and later being promoted to the rank of Lieutenant. This Moore was in the colony when Thomas Moore was Master Builder at the Dock Yard. Both Moores appear on various lists of officers of the colony, William being a military

CHAPTER 4 ~ *Moore and the Merino* [51]

officer, and Thomas being a civil officer of the crown. Occasionally they were confused in the government records, such as when William was listed as the Master Builder,[43] most probably simply by a slip of the pen.

But it does not seem likely that William was the Moore who purchased the merino. Whenever he is referred to in the records, his military title is usually used.[44] Whereas Captain Waterhouse in his letter says that sheep went to *Cap*ⁿ Kent, *Cap*ⁿ McArthur, and *Cap*ⁿ Rowley, he then says that some went to *Mr* Moore.

In addition, Ensign Moore seems to have been absent from Sydney when the sheep arrived. He was serving in Norfolk Island from 1796 to 1801, which would make it rather difficult for him to purchase Waterhouse's merino. After his arrival on board the *Marquis Cornwallis* on 11 February 1796,[45] the next month (on 21/3/1796) he was called to give evidence at the inquiry into the mutiny that took place on that ship.[46] Almost immediately after the inquiry, he was posted to Norfolk Island, where he stayed for several years. In October and November 1796 he began supplying pork to the Government at Norfolk Island, and he was still supplying pork as well as maize in December 1798.[47] He is on the NSW Corps pay lists for Norfolk Island during this period—although there are gaps in the record.[48] In addition, William Moore is not listed as holding any land grants in NSW before 1801,[49] after he had returned to serve at Parramatta.[50]

Although serving in NSW in 1801, and again, after a tour of duty at Risdon Cove in 1803–04,[51] it seems to be pretty clear that Ensign William Moore was not in NSW when the first Spanish sheep arrived, and so he could not have been the Moore who gave some of them a home.

Which leaves only one serious candidate for who this purchaser actually was:[52] Thomas Moore, later benefactor of Moore College. He was certainly in the colony when the sheep arrived, having settled here in 1796. He is always referred to as 'Mr. Moore' in the sources, especially as time went on, to distinguish him from both Ensign (or Lieutenant) Moore, and much later, from Solicitor

W.H. Moore. And, as already mentioned, he was a good friend of Henry Waterhouse, the one selling the sheep.

One potential snag to this identification arises from the fact that the first record of land granted to Thomas Moore was a parcel of 470 acres, granted by Governor Hunter in October 1799,[53] that is, two years after the sheep arrived. If this was the first time he received land, since he probably only purchased a couple of sheep at the most, presumably he could have housed them on someone else's property.[54] But, it seems more likely that, in fact, he already owned—or occupied— some land. He may have received a grant of land even prior to him settling in the colony, during the period when Major Grose was in charge, when records were not well kept.[55] Or, alternatively, he may have purchased someone else's land grant prior to 1799. Such a purchase would not appear in the records, just like Waterhouse's purchase of Phillip Schäffer's property 'The Vineyard' does not appear in the official records, yet the deed in our library proves that it actually occurred. It is also interesting to notice that the records of Thomas Moore's first land grant in 1799 are annotated in such a way as to allow for the possibility that he may have already held the land for some time. So, when Hunter submitted his return of 6th February 1800, which reported on lands granted since 1st August 1796, it is clear that Moore received this land earlier than Hunter's period, for his 470 acre grant is listed as being given 'by different Governors, but renewed in one grant by Governor Hunter'.[56]

So it seems likely that Thomas Moore is a good candidate for the Mr Moore who purchased some merino sheep in 1797.

And at this point we can return to the packet of material housed in Moore College Library.

Amongst this packet, there are a number of letters between Henry Waterhouse and Thomas Moore. On the 20th October 1804, Waterhouse wrote to Moore, obviously in response to Moore sending him a report of the bad state of his farm. After asking Thomas to assist Captain Rowley in doing anything that may improve the situation, Waterhouse then ventures an opinion on the future of Australian wool. He says,

> The spanish wool, and some of the woods of N.S. Wales, I believe will shortly be an object of attention to Government, from which I think you may profit, by keeping your wool & & c.[57]

Although we could wish that he had spelled out what he meant by '& & c', this tantalisingly brief comment is most illuminating for the purposes of our puzzle.

Amongst his other duties, Thomas Moore was at this stage the official 'S/Purveyor of Timber' for the colony.[58] In view of England's urgent need of timber for shipbuilding, the Australian timber was being touted as another potential export for the colony. Indeed, the letter from Moore to which Waterhouse was responding, had been conveyed by the *Calcutta*, which had returned to England laden with samples of Australian timber for this purpose—loaded by Moore's endeavours.[59] Waterhouse now encourages Moore by informing him that 'some of the woods of N.S. Wales, I believe will shortly be an object of attention to Government'.

But, for our purposes today, his mention of the other potential Australian export is noteworthy. In Waterhouse's opinion, the Government will soon turn its attention to Australia's 'spanish wool'. This being so, if the market is about to begin its boom, then those holding Spanish sheep will, of course, begin to make a profit. Waterhouse therefore counsels his old friend that he also may soon begin to make some money, 'by keeping your wool & &c'.[60]

Here is the confirmation we are after: Waterhouse knew that Thomas Moore had some Spanish sheep. How did he know this? Well, isn't this because Waterhouse himself had sold the sheep to Moore in 1797?

What Waterhouse did not realise, however, is that by the time of this letter, Thomas Moore had already gotten rid of his sheep. In the muster of 1800, Moore had a flock of 40 sheep, but he appears to have dispensed with these by the muster of the following year.[61] By the time Waterhouse wrote to him in 1804, he had a total of 1170 acres, stocked with 3 mares, 7 stallions, 1 bull,

13 cows, 4 oxen, 6 male hogs and 7 sows—but no sheep.[62] Already at this stage, even before Thomas Moore left the dockyard and moved his pastoral interests to the George's River, his future leanings can be seen. His 3 mares and 7 stallions hint towards his future reputation as a breeder of fine horses, and his 1 bull, 13 cows and 4 oxen, hint towards his future role as one of the largest suppliers of meat to the government stores. But Thomas Moore had gotten rid of his sheep. Well before the early boom in interest in the fine wool of the Australian-bred Spanish merino, Thomas Moore had got out. He would accumulate a great deal of wealth from his farming, but it would not be through wool.

The record should be set right: Thomas Moore, benefactor of Moore College, was the Mr Moore who purchased some of the first merinos brought to Australia. However, Moore's farming interests subsequently moved on, and after a brief flirtation, Moore left the merino to others.

Notes

1. The original form of this essay was delivered as a library lecture at the Moore College Library Open Day, 1st July 2006.
2. When Governor Phillip reported home in July, there were 26 sheep still alive. Phillip to Sydney, 9 July 1788, Enclosure 1: An Account of Livestock, 1st May 1788 (*HRA* 1.1, 52) shows: 1 stallion, 3 mares, 3 colts, 2 bulls, 5 cows, 29 sheep, 19 goats, 49 hogs, 25 pigs, 5 rabbits, 18 turkeys, 29 geese, 35 ducks, 122 fowls, 87 chickens. A note is appended saying that since that return 3 of the sheep have died, and the cows and bulls lost. To put this in proportion, 1030 people were landed and Phillip reports that 966 of these were victualled (*HRA* 1.1, 51 and 727).
3. Morrison, *Aldine Centennial History*, 1.268: 'Australia attaches more importance to her pastoral, agricultural, mineral, and commercial interests than to any other. She is one of the leading pastoral countries of the world. [...] She is the first among the nations in the production of wool, and America comes second.' At this time, the comparative value of wool per annum was: Aust: £20,000,000; USA: £14,500,000.
4. Samuel Marsden arrived in NSW as a Chaplain in December 1794, receiving a grant of 100 acres in the district known as Hunter's Hill, that is, the area north of the Parramatta River through to the Hawkesbury. By 1802 he had received 201 acres in grants and another 239 by purchase and had cleared 200 acres, and by 1805 his holdings totalled 1730 acres. In 1802 he owned 480 sheep, and by 1805 this figure had grown to over 1000, and he was recognised by Governor King as 'the best practical

farmer in the country'. Loane, *Hewn From The Rock*, 11; who draws upon Smith, *Quench Not the Spirit*, 29–30. After 1815 Marsden took up land around Bathurst. In 1827 he had received 3631 acres by grant, 1600 by purchase. He kept accumulating more land, and by his death his total holdings were over 10000 acres.
5. Gov. King to Sir Joseph Banks, 14 August 1804; *HRNSW* V, 450; Gov. King to Lord Hobart, 14 August 1804; *HRNSW* V, 427. A similar thing had been said about Chaplain Richard Johnson, see Tench, *Sydney's First Four Years*, ?
6. See Ker, 'The Wool Industry', Parts 1 and 2.
7. For these years, see Robinson, 'Thomas Moore & Early Life'.
8. For example, Henry Waterhouse, Thomas Moore, and Matthew Flinders, were on the Vice-Admiralty Court held 20 Aug 1798 in regard to the mutiny on the *Barwell* (*HRNSW* III.453ff.). They were also both involved in the trial of Isaac Nichols.
9. This suggestion was made by Donald Robinson in an unpublished 'Postscript' to his article, 'Thomas Moore & Early Life', held in Moore College library. The suggestion arises from evidence contained in the packet under review in this article.
10. William also passes on news of Andrew in W. Waterhouse to T. Moore, 9/6/1813, 18/12/1813, 28/7/1814 (SDA 0852CH, Item 7, docs. 4, 5, 6, and 7); 16/8/1816 (SDA 0202 LT 0851 CH, Item 4, doc. 8) and 9/12/1819 (SDA 0852CH, Item 7, doc. 7). Other correspondents also kept Thomas informed of his step-son: Isaac Clementson to Thomas Moore 21 Jan 1807 (0853CH, Item 11, doc.2); J. Harris to T. Moore, 31 May 1811 (SDA 0854CH, Item 1, doc. 17); Gov. L. Macquarie to T. Moore, 20 Dec 1819 and 1 June 1824 (SDA 0853CH, Item 4, docs. 4 and 12).
11. [*Australian Encyclopaedia*[2]], 'Waterhouse, Henry', IX, 213–214.
12. Henry Waterhouse to Thomas Moore, 24 April 1812. This letter, and that granting power of attorney, is held in Moore College library.
13. William Waterhouse to Thomas Moore, 21 Sept 1812. Henry died on 27 July 1812.
14. The property was valued by Samuel Marsden and Rowland Hassall on 17 March 1813, and subsequently sold to Hannibal McArthur; the stock was auctioned by D. Bevan on 6 May 1813.
15. Ker, 'Wool Industry', Part 1, 28, 36, 37–38.
16. Ker, 'Wool Industry', Part 2, 31–34.
17. 'Marsden must be linked with John Macarthur as the founder of sheep breeding and wool growing in this country', Loane, *Hewn From The Rock*, 12.
18. Ker, 'Wool Industry', Part 1, 18.
19. According to Ker, 'Wool Industry', Part 2, 50, this was part of the criticism made of Macarthur amongst his contemporaries, even though they were prepared to discount such things in the light of his positive contribution to the colony.
20. British agriculture went alongside expansion into other lands. Although out of step with other thinkers about mission, Marsden believed civilization preceeded evangelization. See Yarwood, *Marsden-Survivor*, 'I may be too fond of the Garden, the Field, and the Fleece. These would be the first objects of my attention were I placed amongst a savage nation'. He introduced Duaterra, the maori chieftan who lived with him and embraced Christianity (Yarwood, ch. 5), to agriculture because, thought Marsen, this 'will add greatly to their civilization and comfort, and prepare the way for greater blessings to be communicated to them, even the blessings of Christianity'. In keeping with these principles, Marsden built a house for his New Zealanders at his 'Newlands' property at Parramatta, and alongside general and religious education, he taught them how to farm, Hassall, *In Old Australia*, 161, 168.

21. According to Ker, 'Wool Industry', Part 1, 31, a symptom of seeking to replicate English small farming practices in New South Wales.
22. Evidence of John Macarthur to J.T. Bigge, cited from Clark, *Select Documents*, 1.267: 'In the year 1796 (I believe) [he was wrong, it was 1797] the two sloops of war on this station were sent to the Cape of Good Hope, and as their Commanders were friends of mine, I requested them to enquire if there were any wool-bearing sheep at the Cape. At the period of their arrival at the Settlement there was a flock of Merino sheep for sale, from which about twenty were purchased'. Enclosure in letter addressed to Elizabeth 19/8/1816: Copy of letter to Lord Bathurst (undated), 'Your Lordship is without doubt informed of the extent and nature of my establishment in N.S. Wales: [...] I allude, My Lord to the introduction into that distant Colony of a breed of Merino Sheep, specimens of the Wool of which I once had the honour to submit to your Lordship's notice. The approbation your Lordship was pleased to express upon that occasion excite hopes that any additional evidence may not be unacceptable of the progressive advancement ...'; Macarthur Onslow, *The Macarthurs*, 268–269. For Macarthur's selfmade legend see Yarwood, *Marsden-Survivor*, 90.

   It is clear, however, that McArthur knew who was really responsible, for he wrote to Henry Waterhouse on 4 March 1804, of 'the improvement of the Wool, produced by the Spanish Breed of Sheep that you introduced into that Colony, [...]'. Macarthur-Onslow, *The Macarthurs*, 83–84.
23. See the letter by A Constant Reader, in the *Sydney Gazette*, 25 July 1828.
24. See Marsden, *Marsden*, 50–51.
25. The Appendix to Hassall, *In Old Australia*: The Origin of the Australian Wool Trade, a reprint from *Dalgety's Review* March 1902, cites the Yorkshire *Daily Observer*: 'There are various claimants for the honour of being the first to introduce the merino sheep into Australia, but that honour appears to belong to a countryman of our own in the person of the Rev. Samuel Marsden'; Hassall, *In Old Australia*, 199.
26. Ker, 'Wool Industry', Part 1, 29: 'The fact that these sheep arrived is of great importance, it is relatively valueless to quibble over who was responsible for bringing them'. Cf. Part 2, 50–51, where she speaks of 'the much-debated first imports' and cites the *Sydney Gazette* of 26 August 1826 saying the issue is 'a matter of little moment', and 'to cavil on that point is [...] absurd'—a view similar to her own.
27. *Sydney Gazette* 26 August 1826. Also cited by Ker, 'Wool Industry', Part 2, 50–51.
28. *Sydney Gazette* 25 July 1828.
29. On the basis of the evidence discussed below, his friendship with Henry Waterhouse, and of his close interest in the *Gazette* over many years, it is tempting to think that this Constant Reader may have been Thomas Moore himself.
30. The letter is published online by the State Library of NSW, amongst the Banks papers. (See note 39 below).
31. Sir Joseph Banks to Mr Fawkener, Sept. 1803, *HRNSW* V.225: 'I confess, therefore, I have my fears that the Captain [i.e. McArthur] has been too sanguine in his wishes', 'what as yet is a mere theoretical speculation'. Cf. Sir Joseph Banks to [Capt. McArthur—see note], 31 March 1804, *HRNSW* V.365; Sir Joseph Banks to Gov. King, 29 Aug 1804, *HRNSW* V.459: 'I do not think you need to trouble yourself about getting possession of the fine-woolled sheep for Government. If the project for breeding them succeeds, [...].
32. Banks to H. Waterhouse, 8 July 1806, portion cited from *SG* 25/7/1828.
33. This was William Raven's vessel, upon which Thomas Moore originally came to Australia, on its way home.

CHAPTER 4 ~ *Moore and the Merino* [57]

34. 1828 *Gazette* version has 'or 4 guineas'.
35. 1828 *Gazette* version has 'on my arrival'.
36. Henry Waterhouse to William Waterhouse, 20 Aug 1797, *HRNSW* 3.287–288: 'In consequence of having so much stock, I thought it necessary to get a farm, and found the cheapest way was to purchase one. I have therefore given one hundred and forty pounds for one, with a good house, &c, on it. I am at present so pleased with it that I do not mean ever to part with it'.
37. *Gazette* version: 'I supplied Capt. Kent, Capt. McArthur, Mr Marsden, Mr Laycock, Mr Williamson, Capt. Rowley, Mr Moore, Mr Grimes, and in fact any person who wished to have them'.
38. SG Index: *Sydney Gazette* 25/7/1828, 3c: A Mr Moore purchased Merino sheep from Capt. Waterhouse in 1797 when he brought them from the Cape.
39. http://www.sl.nsw.gov.au/banks/series_23/23_43.htm.
40. W.H. Moore was 'one of the solicitors sent out by the British government on a salary of three hundred pounds per annum to practise under the charter of justice', arriving on the *Broxbornebury* with Jeffrey Hart Bent and the assistant chaplain Rev. Benjamin Vale (Clark, *History* I.306)—three characters who would each become rather infamous in the colony. See also McKay, 'Moore, William Henry'.
41. This is the date according to which his rank in the regiment is calculated in the Return of Officers of the New South Wales Corps, 31/12/1801 *HRNSW* IV, 650.
42. Ker mistakes the 'Moore' as Moore, William Ensign NSW Corps; Ker, 'Wool Industry', Part 1, 29 n.11.
43. This appears to have been the case in two Statements of Return of Officers on the Civil Establishment, King to Portland 21 Aug 1801, Enclosure, and 21 May 1802, Enclosure 4 (*HRA* 1.3, 153 and 494 respectively).
44. Whether Ensign, or, after promotion, Lieutenant, then Captain.
45. Hunter to Portland, 3/3/1796 (*HRA* I.1, 555); Hunter to Portland, 28/4/1796 (*HRA* I.1, 556).
46. *HRNSW* 3, 102ff.; *HRA* I.1 657.
47. 13/10/1796 he supplied Norfolk Island Government with 988 lbs Pork (King papers, C.189, p.75); 24/11/1796 he supplied Norfolk Island Government with 1066 lbs Pork (King papers, C.189, p.72); 31/12/1798 Receives £51.7.0 for pork supplied to the Government (King Papers C189, p.157); 31/12/1798 Ensign in NSW Corps Norfolk Is, receives £25 for maize from the government (King Papers C189, p.163).
48. In 1796, and from 25/7/1798–31/12/1799 Ensign, NSW Corps Pay Lists. Macarthur Papers vol. 102A, pp.3 et sqq; A2998.
49. In the 1801 muster, Ensign Moore is listed as not having received any land grant, although he owns one horse (*HRNSW* IV, 649). According to Baxter, *Musters & Lists. 1801–1802*, List 5 (1801), Item BE 036, he has no land, and no stock. In December of that year, however, he purchased a farm of 48 ac known as Moore's Folley [sic]. The 10/12/1801 deed is stated to be enclosed with the letter from T. Hassall to Capt. Clark 8/7/1822; (Hassall Correspondence vol. 4, p.212; A1677-4).
50. In August 1801 he is listed as on duty at Parramatta: General Return of His Majesty's New South Wales Corps, 21/8/1801 (*HRNSW* IV, 495). In September of that same year, after John McArthur was arrested fighting a duel with his superior officer, Lieut.-Col. Paterson, Moore was one of four Ensigns who examined the pistols McArthur had used, signing that they were defective; *HRNSW* IV, 561. In October 1801, he and Lieut. Hobby prevented soldiers from seizing some spirits which the

constables had detained, which were said to be a gift from John McArthur to the detachment; Lieutenant Hobby to Governor King, 5/10/1801, and, Ensign Moore to Lieutenant-Colonel Paterson, 30/10/1801 (*HRNSW* IV, 581, 582).

51. 1803 August, left in charge at Risdon Cove; the *SG* 26/8/1804 announces he arrives from Risdon Cove; Aug 15 grant 60 ac at Eastern Farm [ML cards], known as Moor's farm [sic], adjoins Kent's. Cf. Ryan, *Land Grants*, p.129, #899: Thomas Taleby's grant, originally given Nov 12 1799, of 30 acres in the district of the Eastern farms, consolidated into a new grant given to Lieutenant Moore 1803. Ryan, *Land Grants*, p.138, Thomas McKenny, Mar 12 1800, Granted 30 acres in the district of the Eastern Farms, consolidated into a new grant given to Lieut. Moore by order of Gov. King, 1803.

52. William Moore is the only other Moore listed in *HRNSW* IV and V. In February 1800, Hunter's return of lands granted since 1st August 1796 shows no other Moores receiving land in that period; Hunter to Portland, 6/2/1800, *HRNSW* IV, 37–48. The only other potential candidates for being the purchaser, would come from the Moore's who were amongst the settlers of the Hawkesbury, but 1) it is unclear whether they were there in 1797; 2) they do not appear to be significant enough in the life of the colony to be simply listed as 'Mr. Moore'; 3) they may have been ex-convicts, and so Waterhouse would have probably preferred Thomas Moore over them as purchaser.

53. In the 1801 muster, Thomas Moore, Master Boatbuilder is listed as having received one land grant, given by Hunter in October 1799, of 470 acres, with only 5 acres cleared, and none sown with wheat and maize. At this time he had one horse and five hogs. One convict had been assigned him. *HRNSW* IV, 648.

54. The same return lists the following persons having sheep: Governor King (8) [NB: with no land of his own]; Judge-Advocate Atkins (134); Commissary John Palmer (650); Chaplain Samuel Marsden (340); Storekeeper Rowland Hassall (5); Magistrate Thomas Arndell (50); Chief Constable George Barrington (25); Superintendents Richard Fitzgerald (95) and Nicholas Divine (5).

55. Grose largely ignored his instructions regarding the granting of land, *HRA* I.1, 469 n.251, cf. p.441 n.237. His summary of land grants does not agree with the tabular statement he transmitted: 3 x 110 ac, instead of 2; 5 x 100 ac instead of 6; 35 x 30 ac, instead of 34. Donald Robinson, 'Thomas Moore & Early Life', 180 (16), speculates that Thomas Moore could have received an allotment as early as 1794. Robinson argues that the note about Hunter consolidating previous grants 'presumably means that Moore had acquired some sort of title to land even before the arrival of Hunter in 1795, that is while he, Moore, was still on *Britannia*. He was, as we remember, on shore for a time during 1794 when Grose was acting governor and again from March to June 1795 in Paterson's administration. His name does not appear among the Bulanaming allotments on Grimes' 'Plan of the Settlements in New South Wales' of 1796 (*HRNSW* III, frontespiece), and neither does Smyth's, but he may have had some sort of holding nevertheless'. The practice of occupying land well before receiving it as a grant goes back as far as the very first land grants (e.g. Phillip Schäffer and James Ruse), and a version of this practice may have continued in later periods.

56. Hunter to Portland, 6/2/1800 (*HRNSW* IV, 45).

57. Henry Waterhouse to Thomas Moore, 20th Oct 1804 (Moore College, Waterhouse Papers).

58. Government and General Order, 7 May 1803: 'His Excellency having appointed Mr. Thomas Moore, master boat-builder, to be surveyor of timber throughout the colony for naval purposes, neither him, nor any person employed under his direction, are to

be hindered or molested in marking, cutting down, and removing such trees and timber as he may fix on'. *HRNSW* V.107. For more on this subject, see chapter 5 in the present volume, 'S/Purveyor of Timber'.
59. Gov. King to Sir Joseph Banks, Sept 1803, *HRNSW* V.229: 'A great quantity of timber is now collected, ready for the *Calcutta*, which we are in hourly expectation of seeing. I hope to have a compleat [sic] load ready for her on her arrival; and I hope the captain will be better disposed towards us than Captain Colnett [of the *Glatton*] was'.
60. This suggestion was made by Donald Robinson in an unpublished 'Postscript' to his article, 'Thomas Moore & Early Life', held in Moore College library; '[Waterhouse] introduced the first merino sheep into N.S.W. from the Cape of Good Hope in 1797, and supplied lambs to Macarthur and Marsden, with well-known consequences. Did he also sell lambs to Moore? In October 1804 he wrote to Moore: "The Spanish wool ... I believe will shortly be an object of attention to the Government, from which I think you may profit, by keeping your wool etc.".'
61. Baxter, *Musters & Lists. 1801–1802*, List 2 (1800), Items AB010–012 he is listed with 40 sheep, 6 pigs, 4 horses, 8 cattle on his Bulanaming property, 470 acres of which came from his own grant, 30 from John Jeffries, and 30 from Robert Abell, 20 acres of wheat sown on his own property and 5 on Jeffries'. He has five convicts in his employ (List 9, Items AJ 088–92). In the 1801 muster (List 5, Item BE 021) on his original grant (470 acres) he has only 5 cleared, 1 horse, 5 hogs, 1 assigned convicts.

Baxter, *Musters & Lists. 1801–1802*, List 7 (1802), Item AG478. This list also gives him a grant of 530 acres, 100 under cultivation, 5 acres of maize; 1 m. cattle, 10 cows, 2 m. hogs and 2 sows, as well as his horses; 20 [bushels?] of wheat in hand and 50 maize; and 2 servants on the stores, 1 off.
62. King to Hobart, 14/8/1804 (*HRNSW* V.432–433). He has 700 acres pasture, 470 acres fallow (total 1170); He is victualled from the stores, but his wife is not; one of his convicts is on the stores and two are not.

CHAPTER 5

THOMAS MOORE
S/Purveyor of Timber

A SHIP'S CARPENTER BY TRADE, Thomas Moore officially left the sea on 13th September 1796, having been appointed Master Boat Builder of the Colony of New South Wales.[1] In May 1803, when he was more than half-way through his time in this position and had established an excellent reputation for his work, Sydney received notification that his position also included the duties of 'Surveyor of Timber throughout the colony for naval purposes'.[2]

> His Excellency having appointed Mr. Thomas Moore, master boat-builder, to be surveyor of timber throughout the colony for naval purposes, neither him, nor any person employed under his direction, are to be hindered or molested in marking, cutting down, and removing such trees and timber as he may fix on.[3]

Timber 'for naval purposes' had been on the agenda for a long time before 1803, but this official announcement came at a crucial moment in history. Thomas Moore's job at the dockyard in the little colony in Port Jackson was about to be strongly shaped by international affairs. From 1801 to 1804, 'the adequate supply of Naval timber was the [British Government's] paramount consideration' and in 1803–04, Britain's long-standing shortage of this necessity reached its greatest crisis ever, at precisely the moment Napoleon was poised on the brink of her invasion.[4]

1. The Urgent Need for Naval Materials

When the First Fleet arrived in January 1788, it came with specific orders preventing the building in the colony of boats with a keel of more than twenty feet, in order to protect the trade monopoly of the East India Company.[5] However, the need for a dockyard in the island settlement at the other side of the world became obvious very quickly, not only for vessels to bring supplies to the colony and for traffic to and from the sister settlement at Norfolk Island, but also for the ongoing repairs needed by vessels already present in the colony as well as those visiting. Gradually plans were made that eventually issued in the King's Dockyard.[6]

But there was also a much larger agenda behind these plans. Although the establishment of the dockyard would certainly serve local needs, the Naval Administration had a more international concern for this fledgling establishment, or at least for its Master. As preparations were made for John Hunter to come to NSW, 'the Administration renewed its efforts to make the colony a supplier of naval materials, having Hunter seek out a person "to fill the office of boatbuilder &c at Port Jackson".'[7]

Since the seventeenth century, England's need of 'naval materials', especially timber, had been a growing concern. In the mid-eighteenth century, home-grown English oak and crooked and compass (or great) timber especially was in short supply, and, despite repeated warnings, the situation steadily grew worse.[8]

It took a lot of timber to keep a wooden navy afloat, both for building new ships and repairing the existing fleet. Each ship consumed an enormous amount. To build a seventy-four gun ship of the line at the beginning of the 19th century, for example, required approximately 3000 loads of timber, and more was required for re-equipping and repair every two and one half years. A load was fifty cubic feet (1.5 cubic metres), and an average oak tree contained one load.[9] This demand for timber grew with the size of the ships, and by the 1840s the size of ships was reaching the safe limit for timber vessels.[10] In the earlier period of our interest, however, the timber shortage was not due to ships being too large, but because of a whole 'raft' of other problems.

The Navy had a strong prejudice in favour of English oak for their ships, but since the oak tree took about 100–120 years to reach the maturity needed to supply shipbuilding timber,[11] and the English had been engaged in a long period of sea-going warfare, supplies were dwindling. 'Crooked Timber' and 'compass timber'—the timber which grew in the right shapes and sizes for specialist pieces in the wooden vessels—was in drastic short supply.[12] By the end of the Seven Years War (1763), Britain had already become the master of the seas,[13] but if this mastery was to be retained, supplies of ship-building timber were absolutely essential. The American War of Independence (1775–1783), and then the outbreak of war with France (1793–) put timber supplies under further strain. The prejudice for English oak meant a corresponding prejudice against other kinds of timber and timber from elsewhere. Even when the Navy reluctantly moved towards utilising this other timber to a limited degree, there was a constant problem in securing supply—especially when the nation was at war. England may have been master of the seas, but the one who had control of the land was often the effective master of the trees![14] For these and other reasons, as the new colony was struggling to get on its feet at Port Jackson, the 'timber crisis' for the English Navy was becoming acute.

Although the war with France would not end until after the battles of Trafalgar (1805) and Waterloo (1815),[15] there was a brief, 14 month peace when the Treaty of Amiens was signed on 25th March 1802. Just before Moore was announced to have the duties of 'Surveyor', many were thinking that, at last, peace was here to stay.

John Jervis, *aka* Lord St Vincent, was apparently one of those people. After years of others crying for reform, St Vincent was the man who took action. As soon as he was appointed First Lord of the Admiralty (March 1801), he set about reforming the dockyards and the timber contracting systems.[16] His reforms ultimately failed, because 'well-intentioned but untimely',[17] and, in fact, Britain never succeeded in reforming the dockyards, and the problems remained until the end of the era of wooden ships.

St Vincent's predecessor, Lord Middleton, had managed to sustain the timber supplies, despite the long war with France (1793–1802), by requiring stockpiles containing three years supply.[18] When war resumed with France in 1803, St Vincent's 'reforms' had run the supply of ship timber down to dangerously low levels.[19]

The crisis hit with a vengeance in 1803–04. This was provoked by three problems: the problem of dry rot; the long-standing prejudice about where ship-building timber came from, and the politics associated with corruption and St Vincent's attempted reforms. Over many years, supply of naval timber had become the domain of the Timber Trust.[20] This monopoly situation was associated with a whole range of corrupt practices. By increasing prices, the Timber Trust precipitated 'one of the gravest crises in the history of the timber problem'.[21] To counter St Vincent's reforms, they cut off supply as Napoleon threatened England with invasion.

These reforms were one of the many disputes between the Navy Board and the Lords of the Admiralty. The Navy Board wished to retain supply through the Timber Trust, which would entail the acceptance of corrupt practices. St Vincent wished to break their monopoly and clean up the dockyards. In 1801 he structured the inspection of timber in the dockyards by appointing 'timber masters'.[22] This provoked bitter opposition from the Timber Trust, which attacked this new office throughout 1803–04. In 1802, probably believing the Peace of Amiens would last, St Vincent cancelled the Timber Trust contracts, in favour of individual contractors. This resulted in a direct decrease in timber supplies and the alienation of the suppliers who controlled its replenishment.[23] When hostilities resumed in May 1803, the dockyards were almost completely empty, with less than one year's supplies in reserve.[24]

By February 1803, the contractors were seriously in arrears, just months before the resumption of war. Early in 1804, the shortage was at its worst, especially of English oak and the crooked timber so crucial to wooden ship-building. When Lord

Melville replaced St Vincent in 1805, this shortage began to encourage the development of new designs, such as the 'wall-sided' vessels and the use of iron-knees to diminish the need for crooked timber, and also to the commencement of ship-building in India, close to the supply of teak.[25] Thomas Moore was himself an early innovator,[26] but it was another solution that probably had the biggest impact upon his role at the dockyard.

The timber shortage meant that the navy was at the centre of English politics from 1801 to 1806.[27] When St Vincent was appointed First Lord of the Admirality, he discovered the naval yards did not have the required three years' reserves of timber. At this stage the Navy Board expressed its intention to 'import such Timber from abroad as may be judged proper for Naval Purposes which although perhaps, not of so good a quality as Oak Timber of the growth of this Country will be found useful in many instances'.[28] Consequently, large sums of public money were spent in the pursuit of timber supplies from the eastern Mediterranean and the Black Sea, and yet 'the Navy Board ultimately failed to tap this considerable source'.[29] Given that French and Spanish agents were also searching for supplies, this pursuit had to be done in some secrecy, and the changing politics of war-torn Europe meant that timber-supplying areas became blocked to the British, and that stockpiles of timber paid for with British money never saw service in a British ship.[30] Despite these set-backs, however, Britain's mastery of the waves enabled her quest for timber to encompass the globe, and with some success.[31] Napoleon could stop timber from Europe, but he could do nothing to stop the supply from the Americas, Asia, Africa, and the South Seas. During the Napoleonic decade (1805–1815), 'the Navy was supported by Britain's overseas possessions'.[32] The 1803 announcement of Moore's position as 'Surveyor' has to be seen as an antipodean response to this critical situation at home.

But Moore was not the first person to have some responsibility for naval timber in New South Wales. There was one other who held the position of Master Builder before him—even if only briefly.

2. Daniel Paine

Even though Arthur Phillip had drawn attention to Sydney's need of 'one or two good shipwrights' to keep the local marine craft in good repair as early as 1792,[33] it was the timber situation that apparently led to John Hunter being instructed to find someone 'to fill the office of boatbuilder &c at Port Jackson'. Out of curiosity and a desire to see foreign climes, one Daniel Paine from the Deptford Naval Dockyard applied and was accepted. Paine had served his apprenticeship there, under William Hunt (1784–1791),[34] and he presented to Hunter as 'a Clever young man from Deptford Yard [...] well recommended to me both for his Theoretical and practical knowledge'.[35] Travelling with John Hunter on Captain Henry Waterhouse's *Reliance*, in company with George Bass, Matthew Flinders, and the Australian Aboriginal, Benelong, on his homeward journey,[36] Daniel Paine arrived in Sydney on 7th September 1795,[37] to begin his duty as Master Boat Builder.

Although Paine left a journal, it does not reveal much about his role.

> Paine is curiously and disappointingly silent where we might have almost wished him to be eloquent. Apart from describing the qualities of some fifteen varieties of New South Wales timber, he offers few details of his work, which must have constituted the substantial beginning of Australian boat-building.[38]

In fact, it is rather unclear whether Paine made any real 'beginning' to Australian boat-building at all.[39] Presumably his duties centred upon the boat-shed constructed on the east of Sydney Cove by Mr Reid, carpenter of the *Supply*, in December 1788, but construction of the dockyard proper only commenced in Moore's time, June 1797.[40] He may have 'clearly performed his official duties diligently',[41] but there is little evidence to prove that he did.

His own relative silence about his activities is matched by a similar silence in the official record. He is listed on the Return of Civil Officers in October 1795, and he is still on the Return of 20th September 1796—despite him having been replaced by Thomas Moore on the 2nd.[42] The only duty in which Paine is named is during Hunter's attempt at registration of the boats of the colony, which are ordered to be presented to him, so that he could mark them. However, this order was given on the 18th July 1796,[43] which means that the series of events which led to Paine's dismissal had already begun, and we can wonder how much he would have personally been involved in marking boats at this time.

In December 1795, Hunter was concerned about the urgent need to rebuild or repair the boats of the colony, being convinced that 'no time must therefore be lost in putting them in such a state as to render them safe and useful'.[44] From Paine's journal,[45] however, it seems that the new Master Builder was otherwise occupied at this time. As his only entry for December 1795, he states that he 'was busily employed in getting a House fitted up in the Town'. He had been staying out of town on Nicholas Divine's farm, but this had proved too inconvenient. To be fair, his move was apparently motivated by his work, for he comments that his workmen require close supervision. But nevertheless, his own lodgings seemed to take his entire attention in December. This continued into January, when he was 'fully employed in fitting up my Premises with Stock Yard and other conveniences and preparing the Garden for the production of Roots and Vegetables &c'. There is not much evidence that Hunter's Master Boat-Builder shared the Governor's urgency for boat repairs.

The record does, however, contain several items of work which would naturally fall under the purview of his position.

In January, the American vessel, *Otter*, called in for repairs, departing 18th February.[46] Since Hunter reported that his locals assisted in these repairs, no doubt Paine was also involved.[47] When the *Otter* left Sydney, it was discovered that Thomas Muir, one of the famous 'Scottish Martyrs' had escaped upon her.[48] From a 'radical' family himself,[49] Paine had been associating with this group since his arrival. When he fell foul of the authorities at the end of his time, this association proved detrimental to his reputation. Although unsubstantiated, rumours circulated that George Washington had sent the *Otter* to extract Muir and any of the other Martyrs who wished to leave.[50] If Paine had access to the *Otter* during her repairs, we can wonder whether he helped prepare for Muir's escape.[51]

On 24th March 1796, his fellow-passengers on the *Reliance*, Bass and Flinders, departed on their second voyage of discovery. Paine may have supervised the building of the second *Tom Thumb*, which served them on this journey.[52]

If there is only a little information about Paine's boat building and repairs, there is even less for his timber-gathering, but this is probably not the kind of 'event' that would often make it into the record. It is likely, however, that this was one of his major interests. The need for naval supplies lay behind his original appointment. His *Journal* shows that he had become familiar with the native timbers, describing about fifteen varieties in the midst of his remarks on New South Wales.[53] When it abruptly ends, he is in the Philippines with clear plans to set up a sawmill to harvest the country's native timber.[54] Being a child of Deptford, the need for naval timber would have been deeply ingrained in him, and this may well have been where he spent his energies in New South Wales.

Paine was eventually dismissed as Master Boat Builder as a result of a series of events arising from the robbery of his house on 5 July 1796.[55] One of his servants, David Lloyd, used Paine's gun to kill the intruder, and was then found guilty of manslaughter and sentenced to 600 lashes. Paine forcibly expressed his disagreement, and was found guilty of contempt of court. When he would not agree to make an appropriate concession to the court, he was dismissed from his position and, on 2nd September 1796, Thomas Moore was appointed 'in his room'.

During David Lloyd's trial (8/7/1796), a deponent mentioned in passing 'a black man that had been up with Mr Paine's people cutting timber'.[56] The editors of his *Journal* comment that 'this remark suggests that Paine drew on Aboriginal knowledge to identify suitable timbers and locate stands of them'.[57] Soon after Hunter arrived, he had issued orders to prevent indiscriminate cutting of timber on crown land (8/12/1795):

in order to preserve as much as possible such timber as my be of use either for building or for naval purposes, the King's mark will be forthwith put on all such timber, after which any person or persons offending against this Order will be prosecuted. This Order extends only to grounds not granted to individuals, there being a clause in all grants from the Crown expressly reserving for the use thereof such timber as may be growing, or to grow hereafter, upon the said land which may be deemed fit for naval purposes.[58]

Presumably it would have been Paine's responsibility to seek out these trees and to mark them with the King's mark—probably the broad arrow traditionally used for this purpose.[59] This, in itself, would have been a time-consuming exercise. The comment at the deposition, however, also indicates that some cutting of the timber had probably also begun. Normally timber was stored and seasoned for a matter of years before it was used in ship-building, but with only Reid's boat shed to work from, and a proper dockyard still in the future, it is difficult to imagine Paine having the advantage of a seasoning shed for cut timber. When combined with the small amount of evidence of actual ship-work, this may indicate that in the short couple of months Paine was Master Boat-builder, he spent much of his time marking naval timber, without necessarily cutting much of it down.

Given his experience with Paine, we are left wondering if Hunter's thoughts included his master boat builder when he complained that 'in many of those people recommended to Govern't at home to fill little offices here much imposition has been practis'd'. Given the rumours he had already heard about Paine's successor, we can also wonder if he numbered Thomas Moore amongst 'some of the ingenious people who are sometimes to be found here', whose appointment would not only cheaper, but better.[60] Whatever Hunter's thoughts, a few years after taking over from Mr Paine, Thomas Moore would find himself timber-gathering at a rather frantic pace.

3. Timber for naval purposes in the antipodes

The need for naval timber had been on the Australian agenda since the First Fleet. Indeed, consistent with the fact that the need for timber was advanced as one of the reasons for the settlement of New England and Canada,[61] some Australian historians have suggested that this need was also a primary reason for forming the new colony at Port Jackson.[62] Even if the penal nature of the early colony of New South Wales is sufficient evidence for why Pitt sent the First Fleet, it is probably also true—at least in some circles—that 'the region was valued for its capacity to provide flax and timber required by the Royal Navy for the rigging, sails and masts of its warships'.[63]

In 1798, Lord Hawkesbury had suggested drawing on reserves in Canada and other parts of the world in case the Baltic states started using the supply of timber to England as a political weapon, as subsequently happened in 1801–1806.[64] The experience of the Navy Board in Croatia and Southern Russia—and in more distant regions—had shown how difficult it was for the Navy Board 'to secure the supply of vital war materials in areas outside its control'.[65] On the other hand, the Cape of Good Hope, India, Canada, New Zealand and Australia were more accessible to sea transport, and to the protection of British seapower.[66] By 1802, timber from more remote lands was being discussed, and by 1804 it had started to roll in.

Until 1804 only four kinds of timber were used, but the crisis of 1803–04 meant that these old prejudices had to be broken down and soon dozens of kinds of timber were arriving from every continent, and some were even noted as the peer of English oak.[67] For some time, reports had been coming home with South Seas Captains about glorious forests of timber right down to the water's edge, of sufficient quantity to solve Britain's timber problem forever. In the midst of this crisis, 'Admirals and Captains on every station, diplomats and consuls at every post were urged to co-operate in relieving the situation. Samples by the dozens were submitted'.[68]

New colonies also presented the opportunity of overcoming previous barriers to the timber supply. The Royal Navy had been frustrated by the supply of timber by contractors, especially as their power had grown.[69] Reform had also been somewhat hampered by the presence in Parliament of the Lords, since it was their forests which largely supplied oak to the contractors! New territories allowed for new contracting arrangements and for new practices, designed to yield the Government greater control.

One controversial practice was the reservation of trees by the crown, even on private land, such as in the system of *martelage* practiced in France.[70] In Tudor and early Stuart Britain, a system of 'purveyance of timber' theoretically enabled trees to be seized for the king, even if this did not often occur. In the decade before the civil war, Parliament opposed this system and the king modified the policy. Under Cromwell's Protectorate it was abolished altogether, having become associated with tyranny. At a later date, therefore, the English despised the French *martelage* as a sign of a despotic system and as being against the spirit of English freedoms. Given this history, it was a bold move when St Vincent attempted to reintroduce the system as part of his reforms. When Parliament refused him, it was probably not for any worthy political reasons, but more likely because it was the owners of the English timber who were the ones voting!

Despite the high-sounding philosophical principles forged across years of English history, however, the Parliament was not so strict on the trees of Ireland or the colonies.[71] As British colonies sprang up, the practices resisted by the Lords to protect their own trees at home were permitted in lands far away. Those in the new world weren't too happy about this inconsistency, however, and the use of the broad arrow to reserve trees to the crown was one of the major grievances that led to the American Revolution.[72] This, in turn, led to the Navy turning to areas which were likely to remain under British control long-term, such as Canada.[73]

On this criterion, a penal colony like New South Wales must have been considered extremely controllable. For despite the trouble caused in the American experience, Australian naval timber was reserved to the crown from the very first leases. When James Ruse, Phillip Schäffer and their companions read the fine print, they found that their leases explicitly reserved 'such timber as may be growing, or to grow hereafter, upon the said land which may be fit for naval purposes'.

When Governor Hunter was sent to Australia, he was instructed to continue this reservation.[74] He soon extended this to crown lands, forbidding indiscriminate felling, and informing the colony that 'in order to preserve as much as possible such timber as may be of use either for building or for naval purposes, the King's mark will be forthwith put on all such timber'.[75]

Of course, this reservation was not simply theoretical. Some months before Moore first arrived in Australia, Governor Phillip had sent a shipment of timber specimens home to be assessed for their suitability for naval purposes.[76]

> Specimens of the timber of this country are put on board the *Gorgon* [sailed 18 Dec 1791].[77] The natives so very frequently setting the country on fire, is I apprehend the reason we find so little timber that is sound. It must injure the very young trees which it does not destroy, and so very scarce is the sound timber, which is proper for masts, that there has been some trouble to get the *Supply* masted.[78]

By 1803, the potential of the NSW timber would once again come before the Navy Board.

4. Thomas Moore as Purveyor of Timber

By the 1803 announcement, Thomas Moore had already earned a reputation for his assessment of timber. His abilities were first noticed soon after he arrived in 1792, on William Raven's *Britannia*. Once Raven had discharged his cargo of supplies for the hungry settlement, he set out for Dusky Bay, New Zealand, to look for the seals Captain Cook had noticed some years before. Having also picked up a commission from the military officers of the colony to acquire more supplies, the *Britannia* left the seals to a party of eleven men offloaded at Dusky Bay, before speeding on to the Cape of Good Hope.

Thomas Moore, the *Britannia's* carpenter was left with them.[79] After felling timber for the *Britannia's* own refitting before she left, Moore then supervised the building of a house to shelter the sealers. He then turned to building a ship in case Raven's *Britannia* failed to return. When Raven arrived to pick them up, on 27th September 1793, Moore had built a vessel of 60 or 70 tons, to within a month or two of being able to sail away. The ship was left on the stocks at Dusky Bay, only to be completed, fitted and sailed, two years later, by Captain William Bampton. Taking it as a replacement for his *Endeavour*, which was practically falling apart, Bampton christened the vessel the *Providence*.[80]

When Captain Raven reached Norfolk Island, he was so impressed with Moore's little schooner that he spoke of it to Lieut.-Governor King in words of high praise:

> What excited my admiration was the progress they had made in constructing a vessel of the following dimensions:— 40 ft. 6 in. keel, 53 ft. length upon deck, 16ft. 10 in. extreme breadth, and 12 ft. hold. She is skinned, ceiled and decked, and with the work of three or four men for one day would be ready for caulking. Her frame knees and crooked pieces are cut from timber growing to the mould. She is planked, decked, and ceiled with the spruce fir, which in the opinion of the carpenter is very little inferior to English oak.
>
> Her construction is such that she will carry more by one-half than she measures, and I am confident will sail well. The carpenter has great merit, and has built her with that strength and neatness which few shipwrights belonging to the merchant service are capable of performing.[81]

Given the long-standing prejudice at home, Moore's comment that the New Zealand spruce fir being little inferior to English oak is a very strong endorsement of the native timbers. Moore's ability with New Zealand timber was well-recognised. While commenting on the New Zealand timbers, Robert Murry, Fourth Officer[82] on the *Britannia* cites Moore as his authority:

> the timber which grows here would answer very well for plank, for the Ship Builder, Joiner, or Cabinet Maker. This is the opinion of our Carpenter in the *Britannia*, he being as well acquainted with its properties as any man of his profession.[83]

Presumably Raven also drew upon Moore's opinion when he said:

> There are various kinds of timber in Dusky Bay, but that which is principally fit for shipbuilding is the spruce fir, which may be cut along the shore in any quantity or size for the construction of vessels from a first-rate to a small wherry.[84]

When the party was picked up, the *Francis* accompanied the *Britannia* from Sydney. On her return, the *Francis* reported Raven as naming 'the spruce fir of that country to be the finest wood that he had observed for ship-building'. In telling the story, David Collins enhanced Moore's reknown, by commenting that, 'the carpenter of the *Britannia*, an ingenious man, and master of his profession, compared it to English oak for durability and strength'.[85] Once again, when set against the centuries-long debates about the superiority of English oak, especially its 'durability and strength', Moore's comments on this timber are high commendation.

It was traditional for shipwrights themselves to be involved in the fetching of timber. Although the development of the Timber Trust contracting system had led to the decline of this practice in England, resulting in increased wastage, in foreign supply areas the Navy usually employed an expert to work with the timber agents, 'an inspector who understood the quality of timber necessary to the Navy'.[86] This shipwright assisted with the conversion of felled trees into the timber desired for shipbuilding.[87] When Raven mentioned cutting timber 'growing to the mould', this refers to the various moulds traditionally used by shipwrights to select timber where it grew, before the trees were felled and converted on the spot.[88] South Seas conditions necessitated a return to traditional practices.

Raven's positive report to King on Norfolk Island, probably

contributed to the enhancement of Moore's reputation in Government circles, not only as a shipbuilder, but also as someone who knew how to select and convert ship-building timber. This latter quality may have been an especially important influence on Hunter appointing Moore, given that the timber problem originally lay behind the appointment of a Boat Builder for Sydney. Hunter certainly had no doubts about Moore's understanding of timber, for in mid 1802 he confidently informed the Navy Board that 'a person properly qualified for the Selection of [timber] may be found at Port Jackson'.[89]

In 1803, it was announced that this 'ingenious man' was New South Wales' Surveyor of Timber. Since he had been engaged in the duties already, the announcement must signal that he was now officially appointed Surveyor on behalf of the Navy Board, as part answer to their present crisis.

If Hunter's December 1795 order was in response to indiscriminate timber cutting on Crown land, newspaper advertisements suggest that the theft of timber from other people's grants was also quite common in the early days of the colony. Even Thomas Moore's Bulanaming property suffered, necessitating a warning in the *Sydney Gazette*.[90]

As we have seen, from the first land grants in NSW 'timber for naval purposes' was specifically reserved for the crown. The lease from one of Moore's own holdings can be cited as an example: 'such timber as may be now growing or that may grow hereafter upon the said lands which may be deemed fit for Naval Purposes to be had reserved for the use of the Crown ...'.[91]

In 1803, timber theft would be viewed even more seriously, given the new dimension added by the worsening international situation. Another warning published in the *Gazette* reflects Moore's new position and awareness:

> NOTICE IS HEREBY GIVEN, There being great quantities of TIMBER cut down and destroyed on my and Captain BUNKER's FARM adjoining to it, near Sydney, which would have been useful for Naval Purposes, It is therefore particularly

> requested, that no Person will cut down, unbark, or otherwisel [sic] damage any of the Trees, Posts, Paling, Shingles, &c on the said Premises, unless for the above Use, else they will be prosecuted to the utmost rigour of the Law provided against such Offenders. T. Moore[92]

Thomas Moore was involved in timber long before the crisis. Not only is there a record of a gang sent out to cut 'crooked timber for the boat-builder' from 1798,[93] it stands to reason that from the time he took over from Paine, he would have continued to criss-cross the colony placing the 'broad arrow' upon trees reserved to the crown, according to Hunter's order. In June 1797, in the first year of Moore's reign, boat building activity moved from Reid's small boat-shed on the east side of the cove, when construction of what would become the King's Dockyard began on the western side.[94] The various returns show that, with a properly established dockyard, there was a consequent increase in activity. The timber-gathering side of things must have also increased, for 1797 a steamer for seasoning plank was built, indicating that timbers were being brought to the yard for the preparation thought essential for shipbuilding.[95]

In 1802, John Hunter, now back in England,[96] continued to give advice, having heard of plans to send convict ships to Australia in both spring and autumn.[97] To minimise the expense of such voyages, he recommends a return cargo of timber.

> With respect to such articles as that settlement in its present state can best furnish as a return by those ships to this country, I would recommend the sending back such timber as may be thought fit for naval purposes, of which I think there are several kinds, viz., that called by us stringybark. It is something similar to the teak of India, and is, in general, sound.[98]

He then provides a long inventory of the timbers of NSW. In the midst of listing the box-tree, the cedar and the she-oak, he draws upon Thomas Moore's work, when he comments that

> the crooked limbs of most of the gum-trees, when sound, are very fit for ship timbers or ribs, and are uncommonly durable.

> The fact I proved by the raising the frame of a vessel of 160 tons, which, for want of strength, I could not finish before I left the country, but she stood in frame, exposed to the weather, upwards of two years without the smallest appearance of any decay.[99]

Hunter also has a 'Plan B':

> If the timber to be sent from New South Wales should not be approved in our dockyards, it would be found a convenient and valuable article for fuel or other purposes at the Cape, which lays so conveniently in the route homeward.[100]

Hunter is clearly applying gentle pressure to move towards a freer situation to trade, in the same letter mentioning the possibility of trading with the Cape and with India. As potential exports he mentions coal, bark (for tanning), flax, sheep, tobacco and indigo, in order 'to show that in due time much may be done to lessen the expences of that settlement [i.e. Sydney]; but at the same time I conceive the timber and coals may be found the only articles by which a part of its expences may be immediately relieved'.[101]

When Henry Waterhouse offers his advice, his experience probably also draws upon Thomas Moore as the source of his information and the artificer behind the achievements:[102]

> In speaking of the timber of New South Wales, and of its ability for naval purposes, I confine myself to what experience I had of it in His Majesty's ship *Reliance* whilst under my command.

Waterhouse tells of repairs made in 1797 (i.e. under Moore's supervision) to the *Reliance* from Australian timber, which performed very well and when he left the ship in 1801, none of these timbers had shrunk, rent, or decayed. He points out that the ship was at the time of writing lying at Sheerness, where the various articles made from the NSW timber could be inspected. The timber was not painted 'nor seasoned as ship timber generally is'. Because of its gum, NSW timber resists decay, and Waterhouse has been persuaded that it is 'more durable than oak or the teak'. Masts have been made of it, with approval from the ships commanders who used them.

> The carpenters, when in getting the timber for the repairs of the *Reliance*, stated that the timber necessary was in great abundance, but they were sometimes obliged to go for the crooked timbers that exactly suited their purpose some distance, but the ship was then lying alongside the rocks in the town of Sydney. Any quantity of strait or crooked timber was to be got close to the water's edge (I mean fit for naval purposes) through the whole harbour of Port Jackson, which is nearly seventeen miles in length, with almost numberless coves on each side, the parts cleared for cultivation being in general some distance inland. Rough timber may be fashioned where the tree is fallen, and in the heaviest gale of wind a small boat can go to any part of the harbour, it being in general considerably less than a quarter of a mile wide; consequently, water carriage is always certain.[103]

As well as being convinced that timber for masts could be shaped where it was felled, and there are any number of places large ships could be moored in the harbour to receive such timbers aboard, Waterhouse enthusiastically lists the various parts of the ship that could be built from NSW timber, feeling that it is especially suited for the gun carriages, and other places where a great deal of friction takes place. He felt that a convict ship, returning with a cargo of timber, could make the round trip in 12 months. And convicts could be assigned in preparation of the various articles. In short, Waterhouse has thought through this plan down to the finest detail.

Since Moore was the one in charge of these timber-gathering enterprises, this memorandum from Waterhouse also hints that he was 'old-school'—probably because of the circumstances of the colony, if nothing else—in that the timbers were fashioned in the bush.

> [...] the pit could be made under the tree where fallen, and the plank when cut shaded till seasoned. It is customary to do so in that country [...;] made masts could be finished in the woods, and be brought down in separate pieces to the water side.[104]

Waterhouse's comments also reveal the high claims being made for Australian timber at this stage—by Moore, no doubt:

I am therefore induced to think the wood of New South Wales more durable than oak or the teak.

When Hunter passes on Waterhouse's report, it is also clear that a return supply of timber for a convict transport will be of great cost-saving enterprise.[105] In times of war, they could also bring many men for service in the navy from amongst the emancipated convicts.[106] His arguments no doubt contributed to a decision being made. His (and Waterhouse's) report seems to be reflected in Lord Hobart's comments in the same year, when he listed timber amongst the 'produce of our Settlement at New South Wales which Ships carrying out Convicts may return with':

> Stringy Bark Tree similar to the Teak Wood in India. The Box Tree. Cedar Species of Mahogany. Most of the Gum Trees. The above are fit for Ship Timber and the Gum Trees in particular not only for Ship Timber, but also for Blocks, Gun Carriages and other Articles subject to great Friction.[107]

It was in May of the following year that King appointed Hunter's Master Builder to be the Colony's 'Surveyor of Timber'. By this time, Moore had already been engaged in loading the *Glatton*, the first of the ships under the new plan to arrive with convicts and leave with timber.

In April of the year before, the Board of Admiralty had informed the Home Secretary of their decision to require *HMS Glatton* to fetch a backload of timber.[108] By May,[109] Hunter has informed the board that 'a person properly qualified for the Selection of [timber] may be found at Port Jackson'—namely, Moore—but they wish to provide him with an assistant. The carpenter of the *Glatton* is 'not qualified for the Service being old and Infirm', so they suggest that Thomas Weeks, present carpenter on *Dido* be appointed to the *Glatton* 'and employed upon this Service he being properly qualified to give the assistance required'. By June, drawings of the Frame Timbers had been submitted for a 98, 74, and 38 gun ship, 'for the purpose of providing the Timber at New South Wales',[110] and a letter is written to King (which he apparently did not receive), informing him that the plan to regularly convey convicts and to return home timber has been approved, and directs him to 'take such steps as shall appear to you most adviseable for preparing Timber of the description required, and in the manner recommended by the Navy Board (11 June 1802)'.[111]

By March 1803, the *Gazette* noted that the *Glatton* was ready for loading.[112]

> Mr Moore has received the Governor's instructions to provide a quantity of the best timber that can be procured for shipbuilding. He has already been out to survey and make choice of the wood; and on Monday next a number of carpenters and labourers will begin the work. The trees are to be hewed according to the scale, and put on board His Majesty's ship *Glatton*, to be conveyed to England.—Red and other gums, string and iron bark, mahogany, and other hard woods will be selected in preference to any other.

March must have been the month for timber. No doubt because of the *Glatton*'s arrival, Governor King was now well-primed about the needs back home, for he also gave specific instructions about timber to John Bowen, sent that month to form a settlement on the Derwent.

> You will also inform me whether the general timber in that country is fit for the purposes of being sent to England for the construction of King's ships, particularizing, as far as you are able, the different species, length of trunk, and diameter; also whether it grows mostly crooked or strait, and notice the facility of getting it on board ships.[113]

Back in Sydney, Moore's exertions had moments of new discovery:[114]

> A species of wood which had not before been noticed, has recently been discovered about the Banks of the George's River. It bears a strong resemblance to the Lignum Vitae, used in sheaves and pins for Blocks. Mr Moore has received his Excellency's Instructions to examine it; when should it answer the above purposes, a quantity will be sent to England by His Majesty's ship *Glatton*.

A further report about this discovery followed:[115]

> Mr Moore's report of the new-discovered wood, stated in our last to have a resemblance to the Lignum Vitae, has confirmed our account of it, and a quantity is accordingly to be sent home by the *Glatton*.
>
> A quantity of timber, fit for ship-building, is now laying in the Dock-yard, ready to be put on board His Majesty's ship *Glatton*. It consists wholly of Mahogany and Iron-bark, and is hewed out agreeable to the scale dimensions.

A week later, the *Gazette* announced that the *Glatton* intended to sail on the 24th April, and that the loading had begun.

> A quantity of timber mentioned in our last, has been received on board the *Glatton* during the last week, and every expedition is used in compleating the complement intended to be shipped for England.[116]

The next issue announced that she was ready to sail,[117] but by the 24th she remained in Sydney.[118] On the following week, she continued to be loaded with timber, including the newly discovered species, with a hint that her departure would be delayed further.[119]

> On Thursday last 55 Pieces of Lignum Vitae or Dye-wood, were received on board His Majesty's Ship *Glatton* for England.
>
> The quantity of ship timber received by the *Glatton*, on Friday amounted to 120 heavy pieces. She will continue to take in as long as she may remain here.

The same *Gazette* that announced Thomas Moore's appointment as Surveyor of Timber, also published a list of the timber that Moore had placed on the *Glatton*, and commented once more that she still remained.[120] She finally departed at the end of May.[121]

Writing to Lord Hobart in May, King includes a summary of the timber placed on the *Glatton*, prepared by 'Master Builder and Actg. Purveyor of Timber':[122]

> NUMBER of Pieces of Timber (with the dimensions) for Ship building etc. Sent in His Majesty's Ship *Glatton*.

> 162 Pieces of Timber from 12 Feet length 12 Inches depth 12 Inches width to 29 Feet length 24 Inches depth 17 Inches width.
> 15 " Lignum vitae from 6 1/2 feet to 18 feet.
> 6 Grind Stones.
> 2 Casks Iron Ore.
> 20 D°. Bark.

In sending the timber on the *Glatton*, King refers to an earlier letter from Hobart requesting various species of Australian Timber, in which it is clear that the Navy Board is behind these requests.[123] He complains that he did not have Hobart's letter (29/8/1802) six months earlier, so that the specific timber requested could have been gathered ready for loading, but promises it will be ready for the next ship.[124] In another letter of the same day he elaborates further:

> I am sorry I was not previously possessed of instructions respecting the timber, as I should have had sufficient to load that ship. We have got as much as possible during the *Glatton's* short stay, and if it answers no better purpose it will serve as good samples of what we shall get and send by the first ship after the *Glatton*, as gangs of men shall be kept for that purpose alone. As all this timber is to be looked out and sized to particular dimensions according to the Navy Board plans, which will require much of the attention of one person of trust and confidence, I have fixed on the master boat-builder, who is every way equal to that business; and as he will have much to do in regulating the people's labor, &c, who are at that particular work, I beg to suggest the propriety and advantage of his having the extra allowance of 5s. a day for doing that duty, as long as obtaining timber from this country shall be considered an object, which I apprehend will depend on its being found equal to the use it is intended for, as in that case any quantity can be sent from hence; and I have no doubt but the return of that article will greatly do away the expences of the colony, when the difference between sending convicts in transports is calculated and the expence of sending them in King's ships is so much

lessened by the timber they will carry back, as it will be my duty to keep men preparing timber that there may be as little detention as possible when the ships arrive.[125]

He then speaks of some provisions being already made to have vessels suited for the gathering of the timber in readiness for future ships, including the survey of the hulk *Supply*. The survey team, which included Thomas Moore, reported that

> if she is Cut down to her Bends, that her Bottom may be usefully Converted to the purpose of bringing Timber for Construction from the different parts of this Harbour to Sydney, as well as for many other useful Colonial, and Public Services.[126]
>
> By those means, and our timber carriages, I have no doubt that the value of timber sent from hence for construction, and the saving of sending convicts, &c, by the men-of-war, will greatly reduce the expences of this colony to the nation. An estimate of the value and utility of the timber received from hence I respectfully hope will be forwarded to me by your Lordship's application to the Navy Board, as that now sent by the *Glatton*, for the reasons stated in the enclosures, can only be regarded as samples; still the value and utility of it would be a guidance to your Lordship as well as to me.[127]

King's disappointment at not having heard from the Admiralty earlier and so not being able to have the requested timber ready, also had consequences for the *Glatton*. Colnett, who outranked King, wished to hurry on home, especially given his desire to be available for the war.

> I beg leave to Submit to your Excellency that as you did not Receive the Orders until I Anchored at this port that were Intended and expected from my Lords Commissioners of the Admiralty would have reached you some time back, the delay it would occasion to wait until a Cargo of Timber is Cut, when Considered with the Quantity of Provisions that would be Expended, having been only Victualled for Twelve Months, out of which Seven Months are expired, and the report of a War making it necessary to take Two Valuable Ships under

Convoy that are now ready for Sea, would it not be advisable, for the Benefit and forwarding His Majesty's Service, to take on Board what Timber is now ready and proceed to England, as it will be giving you Time to prepare a Cargo for the next Ship. [...] If this meets your approbation, and your Opinion Coincides with mine, I propose Sailing on the 24th Day of April.[128]

By return letter on the same day, King agrees with Colnett's proposal:

Had I Received any Orders or Instructions of What was Wished by Government previous to Your Arrival I should most Certainly have Employed a Number of Men in preparing Timber to put on Board the *Glatton*, but as I only Received the Orders and Plans by that Ship, altho' not a moment is lost in procuring what Timber we are able, Yet it would require some months to Cut down and bring to this Place Sufficient Timber to load the *Glatton*. And as I observe by My Lords Commissioners of the Admiralty's Letter to Lord Pelham, that they Request the Convicts may be employed in preparing the Timber in the manner proposed by the Navy Board, previously to the Arrival of the *Glatton* that her detention may be of as short a duration as possible. I agree with you that it will be more Conducive to the Interest of His Majesty's Service, for the Reasons you have Stated, that the *Glatton* should not wait for a full Cargo of Timber, which I shall do my utmost to procure by the Arrival of the next Ship. The Timber that is now fallen shall be prepared and brought down as fast as possible; I hope every thing will be Completed by the date you mention, at least, no exertion of mine shall be wanting.[129]

With the *Glatton*, King's report to Sir Evan Nepean, Baronet Secretary to the Admiralty, included one from Thomas Moore on the colonial timbers sent with her.[130] King's covering letter calls Moore 'a very Respectable Officer (who has served long in this Colony with reputation and Esteem)'.

Sir, From the Anxiety your Excellency has Shewn to procure as much Timber from this Country as can possibly be obtained for naval purposes, to send on Board HM Ship *Glatton*, and Conceiving it my Duty in Consequence of your Excellency's having Appointed me Purveyor of Timber, to afford you every Information in my Power; I now take the liberty to Acquaint you with the different kinds of Timber in this Country, and which appears to Me to be Most durable and Most Useful—The Timber that has been Shipped on Board the *Glatton* is of different Qualities, but such I trust will give Satisfaction When inspected into—the Reason that there has been such a small Number of long pieces put on Board arises from the lowness of the Raft-Port, which put me under the Necessity of Reducing them to such lengths as would go down her Hatchways—there may be had Timber of different Kinds in this Colony, such as the Iron Bark, the Stringy Bark, the Mahogany Blue Gum and Box— all, or any of which will answer for Line of Battle Ships, to the length of 60 or 70 feet in the Trunk—this in my Opinion, is far more durable than English Oak; and will answer for Beams for first Rates—Keels, Kelsons and Sternposts—as well as other occasions—and may be had in abundance—with quantities of Knees of different Sizes—and all such I flatter Myself will be found well calculated for Naval Purposes.—

Some of the Short Timber put on Board the *Glatton* is not so good as I could wish— but owing to the Shortness of time—I was obliged to send it in the state it was in.

The Timber of this Country when Green will not stand to be moulded—and when it is Necessary to bring it to a proper Scantling it should be cut down Six Months or More.[131]

Once again, we can notice how highly Moore praises Australian timber. Against the centuries old English prejudice in favour of the English oak for ship-building, he is prepared to say that the timber of his new home 'is far more durable than English Oak; and will answer for Beams for first Rates'.

Whilst the *Glatton* was in Port Jackson, relations between Colnett and King were somewhat strained by an incident in which Thomas Whittle's son was mistreated whilst on board. Amidst the interchange over this incident, several other points of contention between the two are revealed.[132] King tells Colnett that no more timber would be put on board after 9th May, and asks him to inform his carpenter that King has received no official notice that the carpenter has permission to collect timber in NSW, as he had claimed.[133]

Amongst other issues, Colnett questioned the quality of the timber placed on board. Colnett had informed King that his carpenter had 'represented to me that a number of the logs received lately can be of no use in ship-building'.[134] King made his own inquiries of the carpenter and informed Colnett that 'he says the timber is all very fit for ship building, except the box, which does not run crooked; but it will do well for straight work, such as scarfing for keels, stern posts, &c'.[135] In return, Colnett sent King a letter from his carpenter, which he takes as denying 'whatever he said to you'.[136] King returns this letter, written after their conversation, inscribed on the back with the testimony of 'two officers of veracity' contradicting what the carpenter now claims, along with a copy of his original letter for comparison.[137] At the same time, King wonders 'what motive [Colnett] had for casting such an indirect censure on myself and the officers of this colony as that contained in your letter on the 9th instant, therein quoting your carpenter's doubtful information'. Of course, as the colony's purveyor of timber, Thomas Moore was also one of the 'officers' brought into ill-repute by the comments of the *Glatton*'s carpenter.

After a delay long enough to fracture an already broken relationship between the two men, the *Glatton* sailed.[138] Eventually, her cargo of timber would receive good report from the Navy's Master Shipwright, who, although finding problems with some of the wood, was nevertheless prepared to say of the rest that:[139]

> the several kinds of Wood may be used for the Frames of Ships &c, as the greater part of it is compass, and as we have no doubt of its durability, we are of opinion the Importation of it may answer the intention of Government, particularly at this time when the present scarcity of Oak Timber of the growth of this Country, may render it necessary.

As a further 'down side', a letter of the same day notes that the hardness of the wood not only causes additional expence of files, and frequent whetting of the saws, but requires twice the amount of labour.[140]

Not to be caught short again, once the *Glatton* had departed, King threw his efforts into preparing the next load.

> HIS EXCELLENCY has intrusted Mr Moore to keep a gang of men constantly employed in procuring such Timber as he may consider to be best adapted to Naval purposes. It will be deposited in the Dock Yard, and sent Home as opportunity may serve.[141]

The concern for timber led to the proclamation of a general order on the subject, in which the NSW system of *martelage* is clear, for the order applied to both private and public lands:[142]

> The great consumption of timber, and the requisition made by Government for as much as possible being reserved for the use of the Navy, the following regulations are to be observed by all and every of His Majesty's subjects resident or stationed in the territory, masters of ships, and all others:—
>
> Timber in this colony includes she and swamp oaks, red, blue, and black-butted gums, stringy and iron barks, mahogany, box, honeysuckle, cedar, lightwood, turpentine, &c, the property of all which, and every other kind of trees fit for timber, or likely to become so, lies in the proprietor of the land, either by grant or lease, excepting timber fit for naval or other public purposes, which those authorized by the Governor may mark, cut down, and remove in and from any situation, public or private.
>
> Any person cutting down, barking, damaging, or destroying any timber or trees fit, or likely to become fit, for shipbuilding, buildings, masts, or mechanical purposes, without the permission of the proprietor or of the Governor, if on any of the Crown lands, will be answerable to the laws provided in that behalf, and according to the local situation of the inhabitants of this colony.
>
> This regulation is not to preclude the inhabitants from getting such fuel from fallen woods as they can remove with

wheelbarrows or carts drawn by one horse, excepting fuel requisite for Government uses. Masters and commanders of ships will be informed by the Naval Officer where they may procure fuel for their ships; and those who may obtain the Governor's or proprietor's permission to cut down and remove timber fit for the foregoing purposes, or for sale at any other port, are to pay a duty of three pounds sterling to the treasurer of the Orphan Fund for every thousand solid feet taken on board, of which they are to give notice to the measurer (John Thompson) as often as they receive it, and before it is hoisted into the ship, on pain of forfeiting five pounds sterling for each neglect on conviction before two magistrates.

This regulation commences from the 26th day of June, 1803.

By August King reports his readiness for the next ship:[143]

> I have the honour to enclose a return of the timber now ready to be shipped on board the first ship that arrives for that purpose. A number of convicts, with timber carriages and boats, are kept employed cutting down and squaring timber to be sent to England when an opportunity offers.

By September he is awaiting the *Calcutta*:[144]

> The *Calcutta* not being yet arrived I have every hope of having a complete cargoe of ship timber ready to send by her, as a great quantity is now collecting, which requires the exertions of a great proportion of the convicts at public labor, altho' procuring it is now much facilitated by the construction of a proper vessel to transport it from different parts of the harbour to Sydney ready for being shipped.

Several months later, Moore had 'a great quantity of timber' collected, ready for loading into the *Calcutta*, but King still had bitter memories of his altercations with Colnett.

> A great quantity of timber is now collected, ready for the *Calcutta*, which we are in hourly expectation of seeing. I hope to have a compleat load ready for her on her arrival; and I hope the captain will be better disposed towards us than Captain Colnett [of the *Glatton*] was.[145]

The timer is still waiting in October:[146]

> We continue adding to the great stock of very fine timber for ship-building, to load the *Calcutta* or any other vessel when they may arrive.

Lieut.-Gov. Collins wrote to King from Port Phillip on 5th November 1803, singing the praises of Daniel Woodriff, Captain of the *Calcutta* as a man entirely suitable for the expedition.[147] The *Calcutta* arrived in Sydney on 26th December[148] and, upon loading her, King signalled his intention to keep the supplies coming:

> I have the honour to enclose an invoice of the timber and plank put on board the *Calcutta*, being as much as that ship could take, which I hope will be found very useful in His Majesty's dockyards; and altho' it is not certain whether any King's ships may be sent here during the war, yet I shall keep a certain number of people collecting timber for the first conveyance to Europe.[149]

Perhaps even moving ahead one step further than his predecessor, King is not only concerned to supply dockyards at home, but he is keen to promote the ship-building potential of NSW. It seems he has big plans for the dockyard under Moore's direction.

> In order to form some opinion in how short a time a vessel could be built, one of 59 tons [the cutter *Integrity*] burthen was laid down in September, 1802, and launch'd in January, 1804; and altho' there was much interruption in the work, yet the average was only four carpenters' labour for thirteen months, and one pair of sawyers twenty weeks exclusive of the labour in getting the timber. We have only two men that can be called ship carpenters,[150] the rest being rough house carpenters and 'prentice boys. I have stated this circumstance to show the time it has taken with the people we have to build that vessel, which is extremely well put together and strong, and for her first voyage is gone to Basses Straits and the Derwent. If thirty shipwrights and caulkers could be collected at the different ports, and sent here with two good assistants from the King's yards, I make no doubt that a 38–gun frigate might be built in less than two years of the best materials; but it would be necessary to

send iron and copper work, with cordage.

When the *Calcutta* had arrived in NSW, it had carried a letter to Thomas Moore from his friend, naval captain Henry Waterhouse. Having earlier furnished advice to the Navy about the question, Waterhouse could now report that 'some of the woods of N.S. Wales, I believe will shortly be an object of attention to Government'.[151]

A matter of weeks before the *Calcutta* was due to depart, on 4th March 1804, 140 marines and seamen were landed from her for potential military action in the famous 'Irish Uprising', when 233 rebels were defeated at the battle of Rouse (Vinegar) Hill. Although those from the *Calcutta* did not, in the end, see any action, as an officer in the Loyal Sydney Association, Thomas Moore would have been amongst the 28 soldiers and about 47 armed civilians under Major Johnston's command who marched and jogged from Sydney ten hours through the night, to then pursue and capture the rebels in an operation lasting from 11am to 4pm on Monday 5th.[152] Soon after receiving the Governor's thanks for their services during the uprising, the *Calcutta* departed Sydney on 16th March 1804.[153]

By the end of 1804, King appears to be working hard towards improving the colony's export potential. In particular, he asks for the permission to allow vessels to trade with China and England, but specifies that this should only be for 'three vessels of not more than two hundred tons each and built within the limits of this territory and its dependencies'. The extra advantage of this move will be that this will give 'employment to so many artisans and their families, promote ship-building and raising sailors, which will give the increasing numerous youth in these settlements the means of acquiring trades to prevent them from pursuing the same paths their unfortunate parents have trod in'. In addition, there are political advantages, for the colonial vessels could engage in the risky trade of British goods in the Spanish and Portugese colonies of the Americas.[154]

In the same letter he reflects upon the colonial timber most recently sent:

> Whether the ship timber sent from hence by the *Calcutta* may have determined the utility of that measure being perservered in I have not yet learned; but should it be considered an object the greatest quantity can be procured.[155]

When King appointed Thomas Moore 'surveyor of timber throughout the colony for naval purposes', he recommended him for a rise in salary. Unfortunately, when the *Calcutta* had arrived, she brought some bad news in this regard. Although several were favoured with various salary increases, Moore was not amongst them. Immediately, King pleaded his case:

> The master boat-builder, who has built two decked vessels and is beginning a third, exclusive of every other work incident to a person in his active situation, has made known to me his disappointment in not finding himself included in the advance. Could his pay be increased to 10s. a day I humbly conceive it would be securing the zeal and services of a very valuable man to this colony. He has selected and collected all the timber sent by the *Glatton* and *Calcutta*. I made an application by the former ship to the same purport as this, which I respectfully submit to your Lordship's consideration.[156]

In August 1805, another load was shipped to England on board the *Sydney*,[157] and the quality is deemed to be improving.

> The whole of the ship timber procured by the convicts at public labour, under the inspection of Mr. Moore, consisting of 160 pieces, estimated to contain above 4000 solid feet consigned to the Navy Board, has been shipped on board the *Sydney*. This is the best and most valuable collection of timber ever sent from the Colony, being for the major part well calculated for the most important uses in ship building.[158]

Three months earlier, Thomas Moore had been involved in an accident in which his leg was broken.

> Last Thursday evening Mr. Moore, Master Builder, had the misfortune to be overturned in a chaise, and, we are extremely

concerned to state, had his leg broke by the fall.[159]

By September, however, he was well enough to supervise the convicts loading timber onto the *Sydney*.[160] It must have been the year of broken legs, however:

> On Friday last a lascar belonging to the *Sydney* unfortunately had his leg broken in stowing the Government timber on board that vessel. He was immediately ordered to be received into the General Hospital, where every possible attention is paid to his recovery.[161]

Just before the *Sydney* had arrived, Governor King wrote his report on the present state of the settlement. Perhaps with King's grand plans in view, Moore's position is now described as 'Boatbuilder and Shipwright':

> Boatbuilder and Shipwright.—Has the charge of the dock-yard and the artificers, laborers, & c, in that department. His employment is building and keeping in repair the Government Colonial vessels, boats, and small crafts. He has been much employed in selecting ship timber for England, and attending to the repairs of such King's ships as are stationed or occasionally arrive, and is a most useful and necessary officer.[162]

The following year, that old friend of New South Wales, Sir Joseph Banks, asked some questions about building ships in New South Wales, having heard of the colony's excellent timber, partly through the *Sydney*'s cargo, but also from her own Australian re-fit:

> Will it be necessary to enact anything relative to the registration of ships built in New South Wales, either by an act of Government there or on their arrival in England, if furnished with proper certificates, or do the present navigation laws attach upon His Majesty's territories there as soon as they are declared to be colonies? Timber costs nothing there, and ship timber of excellent quality is believed to exist on the coast, not far to the north of our settlements. Ships will in consequence be soon built there, notwithstanding the high price that labor must for some time continue to bear. If the masts sent Home

and fixed in the *Sydney* prove good—and we are told that she herself has a   [blank in original]   mast standing in her cut in that country—the probability of ship-building becoming a trade there will be much increased.[163]

5. Moore and Australian Timber beyond Trafalgar

When Pitt was restored to power, he replaced St Vincent with Lord Melville, who managed to strike a deal with the Timber Trust, marking a turning-point in the timber crisis.[164] This enabled the supply of enough timber to furnish necessary repairs to the fleet, war-weary and battling the serious problem of dry rot, to bring about the victory of Trafalgar in 1805. However, even after Britain regained her mastery of the seas at the cost of Nelson's life,[165] 'the need to blockade enemy ports throughout Europe imposed a great burden on British ships'.[166] 1806 introduced 'a fresh challenge for the Royal Navy', when Napoleon introduced a concerted effort to 'outbuild Britain at sea by creating new fleets in allies' dockyards', and 'if Britain was to maintain its naval strength, a regular supply of top quality, reasonably-priced timber was essential'.[167]

Canada furnished much of the necessary timber in this decade. The freight costs made the South Seas supplies almost unviable, and it seems that not much timber returned from Australia after the *Glatton*, *Calcutta* and *Sydney* for some time. During Commissioner Bigge's visit to the colony, in 1820 he asked questions of Thomas Moore about the timber of New South Wales, asking Moore to draw upon his experience from his time at the dockyard.[168] Even as the Bigge Commission was under way, the Naval Board was giving instructions (21 July 1819) to their own Purveyor, Mr Byam Mart, to proceed to Van Dieman's Land, New South Wales, and New Zealand on board the HMS *Dromedary*, Captn. Skinner, to acquire timber samples, and 'to enter into the most rigid investigation, and amply to report thereon'.[169] The *Dromedary* arrived in early 1820, and departed laden with timber towards the end of that year, Mart's mission accomplished.[170] His report was printed in the *Sydney Gazette* in January 1826.

Other loads of timber had departed for England in the meantime. In 1823, for example, Thomas Moore's step-son, Andrew Douglas White, spent six months with the Moores at Liverpool. He left in August on the *Surry*, which was laden with timber,[171] although this may have been commercial, rather than naval.

In 1826, when reflecting upon the visit of the *Dromedary* five years previously, the *Gazette* is bouyant about the future for Australian timber exports, proclaiming that: 'the wood of the Country, and the surrounding islands, will afford a much more extensive scope for the enterprising speculatist than has yet been done, every one at all acquainted with its extreme value, will most readily acknowledge'.[172]

Mart's report is then printed, telling of his visit to Van Dieman's Land and NSW. The report allows the speculation that Mart may have had dealings with Thomas Moore, previously his counter-part in the colony, for Mart knew that the stringy-bark and iron-bark were in 'easy access in the districts about Liverpool, as it could be floated down the river, and taken in at Botany-bay'. The Liverpool district had also supplied two iron-barks for the *Dromedary*. Even after his move to Liverpool in 1809, Thomas Moore continued to act for the dockyard in surveying ships,[173] perhaps he continued an interest in the 'purveying' of timber as well. The fact that he was the one examined by Bigge, and probably consulted by Mart, suggests that his wisdom, if not his expertise and energy, were still useful to the Navy in regard to Australian timber.

But whether or not Moore maintained an active interest in naval timber, his life in Liverpool continued to be touched by the international situation. The war that began in 1793, just after Thomas left his homeland, continued on until Trafalgar (1805), and then Waterloo (1815)—where his step-son Andrew served in the Royal Engineers. The end of the war with France released vast amounts of capital into the empire, as well as freeing many

CHAPTER 5 ~ *Thomas Moore: S/Purveyor of Timber* [95]

educated men who were formerly officers in the Army and Navy, such as Andrew, who eventually found his way 'home' to the great joy of Thomas and Rachel. More negatively, the enormous numbers of demobilised soldiers and sailors added to the increase in British crime and this, in turn, led to an increasing number of convicts being transported to NSW to be dealt with in one way or another by Thomas Moore and his fellow NSW magistrates.[174] Thus, Moore lived the latter part of his life in the shadow of the French wars. Leaving for Australia in 1792, just before the outbreak of hostilities in 1793, he no doubt avoided the worries of the press-gangs under which other merchant seamen lived. As England readjusted to peace after Waterloo, he dealt with many of the sad consequences of the peace, assigning and disciplining convicts as he went about his duties as magistrate of Liverpool.

But it was probably during the dockyard years when international affairs had a more positive influence on him. Then he could have the thrill of potentially making a difference to a serious crisis situation. As he criss-crossed the colony, marking trees, finding crooked timber, felling and shaping mast timber, and readying the supplies for the next British vessel, he knew that timber was needed to keep the Royal Navy afloat and fighting. And, out in the wilds of the colonial bush on the other side of the world, Thomas Moore could take some quiet pride in the fact that he had been appointed 'Surveyor of timber throughout the colony for naval purposes'.

Notes

1. 'Mr Thos. Moore is appointed to the place of master boat-builder, in the room of Mr Daniel Paine, commencing on the 2nd instant'; Government and General Orders, 13th Sept 1796 (Enclosure), Hunter to Portland 12 Nov 1796, *HRA* I.1, 698.
2. Surveyor and Purveyor are both used for this position in the sources although the two can be distinguished; as in Albion, *Forests*, 212—but without explanation. I suspect that the term 'purveyor' is the older term, and that it had overtones of the system of pre-emption of timber (see below), whereas 'surveyor' was more neutral. If so, it is interesting to notice that, despite the official announcement using 'Surveyor',

when Thomas Moore referred to himself, he used the term 'Purveyor'; see King to Hobart, 9 May 1803, Enclosure 11 (9 May 1803), HRA 1.4, 105: 'Actg. Purveyor'; and King to Nepean 9 May 1803, Enclosure: Moore to King (13 May 1803), HRA 1.4, 265: 'having appointed me Purveyor of Timber'.
3. Government and General Order, 7 May 1803; HRA 1.4, 340 and HRNSW V.107; = Col.Sec. 6037 SZ 991, p.17. Also published in SG 15/5/1803.
4. Albion, Forests, 54, 95, 321 (quotation), 427.
5. Geo III to Phillip 25/4/1787, PRO CO 201/1: f.40. See Paine, App.1, 67. Cf. Russell, Thomas Moore, 3.
6. For the story of the Dockyard, see Russell, Thomas Moore. Hunter writes of the urgent need of repairs to the boats of the settlement soon after his arrival; Hunter to Portland, 21/12/1795, HRA I.1, 549; but the need was recognized as early as December 1788, when Robinson Reid, carpenter of the Supply, erected a boatshed on the eastern shore of Sydney Cove; see Russell, Thomas Moore, 4, who cites Collins, Account, I, 40.
7. Knight & Frost, 'Introduction', xiii.
8. Albion, Forests, 96. The warnings came through books (in 1766, 1787), and a series of 17 official reports between 1783–1793; pp. 135, 430, 453, 439.
9. Crimmin, 'Search', 86 n.9. Cf. Albion, Forests, 20, 45.
10. 'By the 1840s ships were reaching the ultimate size that could safely be built in timber, and there was already an embarrassing shortage of good shipbuilding timber in Western Europe', Kemp, 'Shipbuilding', 789–797.
11. Albion, Forests, 95.
12. Paine, App. 2, 73. For a fuller account of the entire problem, see Albion, Forests, who deals with crooked timber on pp. 5–9, 19, 21, 80–120 (esp. 99, 112, 114, 116), 225–6, 393–4, 400, 406. See also Russell, Thomas Moore, 9–11.
13. Canby, History, 66.
14. A number of factors were involved. See Crimmin, 'Search', 114–115: 'In the contest between naval and military power, Napoleon's victorious armies in the Adriatic between 1806 and 1809 put it out of the power of the Royal Navy to control the essential timber on which British naval pre-eminence rested ultimately and for which it had paid large sums. The vulnerability of seapower thus stands revealed: dependent on supplies outside its control, though, in theory and popular belief, after Trafalgar "commanding the sea", yet only one year later unable to gain access to the commodity which would enable it to continue to exert that command. Nevertheless, in a wider context this military menace was almost incidental. The real problem was the lack of financial and commercial facilities, the logistic difficulties, the problems of handling bulk cargoes, and the inadequate amounts of the right sort of shipping capacity. In wartime these handicaps could not be overcome'.
15. Canby, History, 72.
16. Albion, Forests, 317–318.
17. Albion, Forests, 317.
18. Albion, Forests, 46. Incidentally, Middleton was a prominent Anglican layman, associated with Samuel Marsden through the London Missionary Society; Yarwood, Marsden – Survivor, 86.
19. Crimmin, 'Search', 83; referring to Albion, Forests and, 46.
20. For this paragraph, see Albion, Forests, Ch. 8, and 47, 55ff., 59.
21. Albion, Forests, 58. Timber costs: 1793–1802: £20 to £21 per ton; 1803: £34.10; 1805: £36—the maximum price ever.

22. Albion, *Forests*, 74, 245, 319–324.
23. Albion, *Forests*, 46, 245, 317–24.
24. Albion, *Forests*, 46, 319.
25. For this paragraph, Albion, *Forests*, 321, 323, 365, 379–81, 393. For the history of shipbuilding in Bombay, see Wadia, *The Bombay Dockyard*.
26. This is not surprising, him being from the merchant marine. Advances in design were found in the East India Company, the Merchant Marine, and foreign navies, long before the Royal Navy adopted them; see Albion, *Forests*, 80. If trained at Sunderland, as I suspect he was, Moore would also be well-used to working with different timbers (see p.13, above). When the cutter *Integrity* was launched in February 1804, her innovative design gave Moore some public notoriety; SG 11/12/1803, 5/2 and 15/2 1804, cf. *HRNSW* V.338, 610. Moore also began the work on the brig *Portland*, eventually launched in 1816 as the *Elizabeth Henrietta*; see Russell, *Thomas Moore*, 9, 25, 27. The keel of this vessel can be seen on the stocks in Edward Dayes' 'A View of Sydney Cove' (1804, from another of 1802), now reproduced on the covers of *Journal of Daniel Paine* and Russell, *Thomas Moore*. From this picture, this vessel appears to be 'wall-sided'. Contrast the diagrams of the 1790s vessels found in Russell, *Thomas Moore*, 6, 8.
27. Paine, *Journal*, 73.
28. Paine, App.2, 74 = PRO, ADM 106/2229:222–4; 30 Mar 1802.
29. Crimmin, 'Search', 84–85. Crimmin's essay explains the reasons for this failure.
30. Crimmin, 'Search', 87.
31. Crimmin, 'Search', 84. See Albion, *Forests*, Chapter 9.
32. Albion, *Forests*, 346; cf. 304, 365; 400–401.
33. Phillip to Dundas, 19 Mar 1792, *HRA* I.1, 337.
34. Knight & Frost, 'Introduction', xviii.
35. Hunter to Under-secretary King, 1 May 1794, *HRNSW* II. 214.
36. Estensen, *George Bass*, 36–37; *Matthew Flinders*, 44–45.
37. Knight & Frost, 'Introduction', xix.
38. Knight & Frost, 'Introduction', xvii.
39. Instead, it was almost certainly Thomas Moore who properly deserves the honour of being 'the pioneer of shipbuilding in Australia'; so Russell, *Thomas Moore*, 3.
40. Russell, *Thomas Moore*, 7.
41. Knight & Frost, 'Introduction', xxi.
42. Hunter to Portland, 25 Oct 1795, Encl.: Return of Civil Establishment; *HRA* I.1, 537–538. Hunter to Portland, Despatch 20, per *Britannia*, Encl.: Return of the Civil Establishment, 20th Sept 1796; *HRA* I.1, 665. Hunter to Portland, 12 Nov 1796, Order dated 13 Sept 1796, *HRA* I.1, 698.
43. Hunter to Portland, 12 Nov 1796, Order dated 18 July 1796, *HRA* I.1, 696.
44. Hunter to Portland, 21 Dec 1795, *HRA* I.1, 549.
45. Paine, *Journal*, 22.
46. Collins, *Account*, I.381.
47. Hunter to Portland, 30/4/1796, *HRA* I.1, 568. Knight & Frost, 'Introduction', xx–xxi nn. 32, 33.
48. The Martyrs were Thomas Muir, Rev. Thomas Fyshe Palmer, Maurice Margarot, William Skirving, and Joseph Gerrald. See Clark, *History* I.100–101; Estensen, *George Bass*, 61–64.
49. Estensen, *George Bass*, 36–37.
50. Estensen, *George Bass*, 64.

51. The Scottish Martyrs touch upon the Thomas Moore story as well. Another person who associated with this group was Surgeon John White, Rachel's former master and lover, and the father of Andrew Douglass White, Moore's beloved step-son. George Bass also enjoyed the company, who married Henry Waterhouse's sister, Elizabeth, who later cared for Andrew during his school days in England. A good case can also be made that Thomas Moore took over some of the farms originally occupied by the Martyrs, see Scott, 'Scottish Martyrs' Farms'.
52. Estensen, *Matthew Flinders*, 55, drawing upon Flinders, *Narrative*, 1, and Paine, *Journal*, 1. The two adventurers had embarked on their first journey on 26 Oct 1795 (p.53). In time, Thomas Moore would also build a boat for Flinders (p.212).
53. Paine, *Journal*, 38–39.
54. His interest in a sawmill may place him at the leading edge of technology, certainly for someone trained in a conservative British Naval yard. Although they had been operating in Europe before the 17th century, and America since 1623, Britain was extremely conservative, introducing sawmills only in the late 18th century. Even by 1860, half the timber in the dockyards was still converted by hand. Albion, *Forests*, 70, 102, 103, 147, 233, 269.
55. See Paine, *Journal*, 22ff.
56. NSW Archives, 2/8286, pp. 7–8; Paine, *Journal*, 24.
57. Knight & Frost, 'Introduction', xx.
58. Hunter to Portland, 12 Nov 1796, Order dated 8 Dec 1795; HRA I.1, 683 = Paine, App. 1, doc. 1, 68.
59. E.g. Albion, *Forests*, 111, and see index. Stamping a serial number was part of the contract checking system, and so presumably would be unnecessary in Australia; see p. 72.
60. Hunter to Under Secretary King, 20 Aug 1796, HRA I, 1, 587–88. As we shall see below, Collins had actually called Moore by the term 'ingenius' some years before, after his ship-building exploits at Dusky Bay.
61. Albion, *Forests*, x, xi.
62. Frost, *Convicts and Empire*, summarised in Hughes, *Fatal Shore*, Ch. 2; Cf. Russell, *Thomas Moore*, 3.
63. Fletcher, 'Sydney Town', 7. The many observations made on timber by early arrivals shows how much this need was on the agenda; e.g. Pickersgill on Cook's voyage 5 May 1770 (*HRNSW* I.1, 215); on Norfolk Island (I.2, 126, 187, 429); on NSW by Phillip (I.127–8), Ross (I.172–3), an officer (I.222), on the Nepean (I.306, 710), etc.
64. Albion, *Forests*, 180–181.
65. Crimmin, 'Search', 112.
66. Crimmin, 'Search', 113. Crimmin does not mention Australia, but the argument holds here as well.
67. Albion, *Forests*, 15–16, 30–33, 399.
68. Albion, *Forests*, 33, 361, 364.
69. Crimmin, 'Search', 85.
70. Russia had a similar system.
71. For this paragraph, see Albion, *Forests*, 60–63, 322.
72. 'In an area hitherto untapped for naval stores the customary contract could hardly apply and the Board employed agents, first to look for timber, hemp and other articles, and then to negotiate suitable terms', Crimmin, 'Search', 85. Parliament had denied *martelage* in England, yet an Act of 1729 virtually imposed it on English

colonies. Originally American leases did not have reservation of timber to the crown, but the 1729 Act corrected this, causing affront to the colonists. See Albion, *Forests*, 230, 232, 250, 254–5, Ch. 6.
73. Albion, *Forests*, 290.
74. Governor Hunter's Instructions, 23 June 1794, item 10; *HRA* I.1, 523–524.
75. Hunter to Portland, 12 Nov 1796, Order dated 8 Dec 1795; *HRA* I.1, 683.
76. Whilst Administrator, Captain Paterson also permitted the *Experiment* to take cargo of timber to India, but this was mahogany and cedar, clearly sent in the hope of future trade, not in the interests of the naval timber crisis. Paterson to Dundas, 21 Mar 1795, *HRA* I.1, 491: 'I have permitted the master of the *Experiment* to take with him a cargo of mahogany and cedar of this country, in the hope that if it should prove valuable in India it may be of advantage to his Majesty's interest in any future intercourse with that country which may be directed by Government'. Given the previous shipment on the *Gorgon*, Russell, *Thomas Moore*, 14, is not strictly correct in citing that of the *Glatton* as 'the first shipment', unless he meant the first *under Thomas Moore's supervision*.
77. Phillip to Dundas, 19 Mar 1792, *HRA* I.1, 337.
78. Phillip to Sec. Stephens, 16 Nov 1791, *HRA* I.1, 304; Cf. Phillip to Nepean, 18 Nov 1791, *HRA* I.1, 308. Once the samples had arrived in July, they were then tested for their qualities. Sec. Stephens to Gov. Phillip 21 July 1792; Received by Lieut.-Gov. Grose 16 Jan 1793, *HRA* I.1, 368: 'The specimens of the timber of New South Wales which you sent in the *Gorgon* have been received, and trials will be made of their qualities'.
79. For the next several paragraphs, see Robinson, 'Thomas Moore', 4–8.
80. Nicholson, *Log of Logs*, 425.
81. King to Dundas, 19 Nov 1793, Enclosure: Raven to King, 2 Nov 1793, *HRNSW* II. 95.
82. Begg, *Dusky Bay*, 71, 132.
83. Robinson, 'Thomas Moore', 6, citing the journal of Robert Murry, extracted in Begg, *Dusky Bay*, 206.
84. King to Dundas, 19 Nov 1793, Enclosure: Raven to King, 2 Nov 1793, *HRNSW* II.95.
85. Collins, *Account*, 1.270. Cf. King's comments (above).
86. Crimmin, 'Search', 109.
87. See Crimmin, 'Search', 94, cf. 105.
88. Albion, *Forests*, 100, 80–81.
89. Navy Board to Sec. of Board of Admiralty, 26 May 1802, PRO, ADM 106/2229, p.388, = Paine App.2, doc. 8, 83–84.
90. E.g. *SG* 4/3/1804.
91. See lease James Redman/ Mary Marlborough/ T. Moore, and the Schäffer lease on 'the Vineyard', one of first in NSW, both now held in Moore College Library; as well as the lease governing Moore's 470 acres in the Bulanaming district (Hunter, Land Grant to Thomas Moore, 5 Oct 1799 [ML: R. Wardell papers, MS A 5330, item 6]). Governor King later judged that the phrase 'that may grow hereafter' was preventing people from planting 'exotic' trees, such as the oak, to the detriment of future generations. He therefore modified the wording of the lease to make an exception of exotic trees planted by the lease holder, which could be reserved for their own use, or, should they choose not to use the timber, with the Government taking first offer at a fair valuation. See Government and General Order printed in *SG* 7/7/1805; and Gov. King to Earl Camden, 20 July 1805, *HRNSW* V.659.

92. SG 17/7/1803.
93. Cited from Russell, *Thomas Moore*, 10.
94. Russell, *Thomas Moore*, 7.
95. Hunter Return of Labour, 1797, *HRNSW* III.337, = Paine App. 1, doc. 3, 68. The seasoning shed— used for planks and deals which, unlike masts which were kept in ponds, had to be kept out of the weather (Albion, *Forests*, 63)— is probably that seen to the right of the vessel on the stocks in Edward Dayes', 'View of Sydney Cove— 1804', that is now printed on the covers of *Journal of Daniel Paine* and Russell, *Thomas Moore*.
96. Hunter to Under Sec. King, 22 Mar 1802, *HRNSW* IV, 728–733.
97. See Paine, App. 2, docs. 1–3, 77–78.
98. Ex-Gov. Hunter to Under Sec. King, 22 Mar 1802, *HRNSW* IV, 728.
99. Ex-Gov. Hunter to Under Sec. King, 22 Mar 1802, *HRNSW* IV, 729. He is referring to the *Portland*, which commenced building in 1800, and was eventually launched in 1816 as the *Elizabeth Henrietta*; see Russell, *Thomas Moore*, 9, 25, 27.
100. Ex-Gov. Hunter to Under Sec. King, 22 Mar 1802, *HRNSW* IV, 729.
101. Ex-Gov. Hunter to Under Sec. King, 22 Mar 1802, *HRNSW* IV, 730.
102. H. Waterhouse, Description of damage and repair to *Reliance* in 1797, PRO CO 201/1: f.f.245–6, = Paine, App. 1, doc. 5. Cf. Ex-Gov. Hunter to Under Sec. King, 22 Mar 1802, *HRNSW* IV, 730.
103. Waterhouse, 'Memorandum on the Timber of New South Wales', ca. March, 1802, = Paine, App.2, doc. 4, 78–81; cf. Ex-Gov. Hunter to Under Sec. King, 22 Mar 1802, *HRNSW* IV, 731.
104. Waterhouse, 'Memorandum', Paine, App.2, 79; cf. Ex-Gov. Hunter to Under Sec. King, 22 Mar 1802, *HRNSW* IV, 731–732. To avoid the necessity of extremely tall straight trees, the practice of 'made-masts' had been in use for some time, see Albion, *Forests*, Ch. 7.
105. Ex-Gov. Hunter to Under Sec. King, 22 Mar 1802, *HRNSW* IV, 732. The same year, Hunter published *Remarks on the Causes of the Colonial Expense* (London, 1802).
106. Ex-Gov. Hunter to Under Sec. King, 22 Mar 1802, *HRNSW* IV, 733.
107. See King to Hobart, 9 May 1803, Enclosure 12: Account of the Produce of N.S. Wales as Exports, *HRA* 1.4, 106, quoting from Hobart's General Letter No. 2, 29 August 1802.
108. Board of Admiralty to Home Secretary, 4 April 1802, PRO CO 201/23: ff.171–2 = Paine, App. 2, doc. 7, 83. After speaking of having ordered the *Glatton* to be prepared to convey Convicts to NSW, the letter then proceeds: 'As it is highly expedient from the Scarcity of Timber in this County that every opportunity should be taken for procuring Timber for His Majesty's Dockyards, and as we have reason to believe that Supplies to any extent may without difficulty by [sic] obtained from New South Wales, it is our intention that the Ships to be employed in conveying the Convicts thither should bring home as much Timber as they can conveniently contain; ..', adding that they have therefore enclosed instructions to the Governor 'by the first Opportunity to employ the Convicts under his direction in preparing the Timber in the manner proposed to the Navy Board previously to the arrival of the *Glatton*, that her Detention there may be of as short duration as possible'.
109. Navy Board to Secretary of the Board of Admiralty, 26 May 1802, PRO ADM 106/2229, p.388, = Paine, App. 2, doc. 8, 83–84.
110. Navy Board to Under Sec. of State, 11 June 1802, PRO CO 201/23: f.305, = Paine

CHAPTER 5 ~ Thomas Moore: S/Purveyor of Timber [101]

App.2, doc. 9, 84.
111. Secretary of War to Governor King, 29 Aug 1802, PRO CO 202/6: ff.54, = Paine, App. 2, doc. 10, 84.
112. SG 19/3/1803.
113. King to Hobart, 9 May 1803, Enclosure 3: Instructions to Lieut. Bowen 28 Mar 1803, HRA 1.4, 152. In 1805, Paterson reported the discovery of a sassafras near Port Dalrymple, more fit for boats than others he had previously seen; Paterson to King, 21 Feb 1805, HRNSW V.555.
114. SG 26/3/1803.
115. SG 2/4/1803.
116. SG 10/4/1803.
117. SG 17/4/1803.
118. SG 24/4/1803.
119. SG 1/5/1803.
120. SG 15/5/1803.
121. SG 22/5/1803: 'Sailed on Tuesday for England, His Majesty's Ship *Glatton*, with the *Greenwich* and *Venus* whalers'.
122. King to Hobart, 9 May 1803, Enclosure 11 (9 May 1803); HRA 1.4, 105. The full invoice listing types and dimensions of timber was sent to Nepean, see King to Nepean, 9 May 1803, Enclosure 2, HRA 1.4, 253–258.
123. 'As the Name of each Species is stated in the List, the Navy Board's opinion on the best Woods (and any other observations) to be sent in future will be as strictly attended to as Circumstances will admit'.
124. King to Hobart, 9 May 1803, HRA 1.4, 106.
125. King to Hobart, 'Marine', 9 May 1803, HRA 1.4, 145–146.
126. King to Hobart, 'Marine', 9 May 1803, Enclosure 4: Survey of the Hulk Supply, HRA 1.4, 154. The survey was conducted by Js. Colnett, Wm. Kent, Wm. Scott, Thos. Wickey, carpenter of HMS *Glatton*, Jno. Coldwell, carpenter of HMS *Buffalo*, and Thos. Moore, Master Builder, Port Jackson.
127. King to Hobart, 'Marine', 9 May 1803, HRA 1.4, 145–146.
128. King to Nepean, 9 May 1803, Enclosure 1(a): Colnett to King, 7 April 1803, HRA 1.4, 252.
129. King to Nepean, 9 May 1803, Enclosure 1(b): King to Colnett, 7 April 1803, HRA 1.4, 253.
130. King also enclosed a request to the Commissioners of the Navy for payment for work done on, and for stores supplied to, the *Glatton*, the *Porpoise*, the *Buffalo*, and the *Lady Nelson*, and apprising the Commissioners of the delay at receiving orders, the timber samples placed on the *Glatton*, and his intention to make ready timber for the next vessel. He also requests a report on the timber sent by the *Glatton*. King to the Commissioners of the Navy, 9 May 1803, HRA 1.4, 269.
131. King to Nepean 9 May 1803, Enclosure: Moore to King, 13 May 1803, HRA 1.4, 265.
132. Issues such as the amount of beef delivered to the ship, advice given or not given by Colnett to King, the supply or not of indents, whether or not Colnett has insulted King and the colony, whether or not King's Secretary had betrayed Colnett's confidences; disputes over purser's receipts, Colnett's failure to dine with King nor furnish an explanation for this action, Colnett refusing to take individual receipts for convicts landed, a deficiency of supplies landed, etc. King later attributes Colnett's 'unofficer-like conduct' to his refusal to grant 100 acres at King's Island to

Colnett; and to his refusal to grant 'a free pardon to a female convict for life, who had never left the *Glatton* or the captain's cabin'; King to Hobart, 20 Dec 1804, *HRNSW* V.525, note *, and King to Banks,—Dec 1804, *HRNSW* V.529. King's refusal to allow a meeting of freemasons from the colony, the *Glatton*, and the *Buffalo* may also be an additional factor in the friction; see *HRNSW* V.106, 150, 451.
133. King to Nepean, 9 May 1803, Enclosure 13: King to Colnett, 9 May 1803, *HRA* 1.4, 278–279. Recall that the Navy Board had wanted him to act as Moore's assistant, see above, p. 79.
134. King to Nepean, 13 May 1803, Enclosure 12: Colnett to King, 9 May 1803, *HRA* 1.4, 278.
135. King to Nepean, 13 May 1803, Enclosure 15: King to Colnett, 10 May 1803, *HRA* 1.4, 281.
136. King to Nepean, 13 May 1803, Enclosure 16: Colnett to King, 11 May 1803, *HRA* 1.4, 281.
137. King to Nepean, 13 May 1803, Enclosure 17: King to Colnett, 11 May 1803, *HRA* 1.2, 281.
138. *SG* 22/5/1803: 'Sailed on Tuesday for England, His Majesty's ship *Glatton*, with the *Greenwich* and *Venus* whalers'.
139. Master Shipwright, Woolwich Dockyard, to Navy Board, 9 March 1805, PRO ADM 106/1791= Paine, App.2, doc. 22, 94–95.
140. See Paine, App.2, doc. 23, 95–96.
141. *SG* 12/6/1803.
142. Government and General Order, 21 June 1803, *HRNSW* V.156–157. *SG* 26/6/1803.
143. King to Nepean, 7 Aug 1803, *HRA* 1.4, 370.
144. King to Hobart, 17 Sept 1803, *HRNSW* V.221. Prior to leaving England, her Captain had requested the equipment needed 'to procure and load timber', including some 'timber measures', presumably for the procurement of crooked timber; see Captn. Woodriff to Nepean, 22 Nov 1802, *HRNSW* IV.910.
145. King to Sir Joseph Banks, Sept 1803, *HRNSW* V.229.
146. King to Hobart, 31 Oct 1803, *HRNSW* V.247.
147. Collins to King, 5 Nov 1803, *HRNSW* V.247.
148. King to Collins, 30 Dec 1803; Shipping Return 30 June—31 Dec, *HRNSW* V.317, 288, cf. 281 and 312.
149. King to Hobart, 1 Mar 1804, *HRNSW* V, 337–338. The second extract is also found in Paine, App. 1, doc. 10.
150. Thomas Moore, Master Builder of the King's Dockyard at the time, was one of these. I am unsure of the other.
151. Henry Waterhouse to Thomas Moore, 20th October 1804 (Moore College, Waterhouse Papers).
152. See Yarwood, *Marsden—Survivor*, 95–97.
153. For the Governor's vote of thanks for the *Calcutta's* services, see *SG* 11/3/1804. For the departure, *SG* 18/3/1804; Shipping Return, 31 Dec 1804, *HRNSW* V.534.
154. King to Hobart, 20 Dec 1804, *HRNSW* V.526.
155. King to Hobart, 20 Dec 1804, *HRNSW* V.527. King has added the note: 'A quantity is now collecting for the next opportunity'.
156. King to Hobart, 1 Mar 1804, *HRNSW* V.340.
157. The arrival of the *Sydney* was announced in *SG* 25/8/1805, and her departure for Norfolk Island and Van Dieman's Land in *SG* 6/10/1805.

158. *SG* 22/9/1805.
159. *SG* 26/5/1805.
160. *SG* 22/9/1805.
161. *SG* 22/9/1805.
162. [King, by handwriting], Present State of His Majesty's Settlements on the East Coast of New Holland, called New South Wales, 12 Aug 1806, *HRNSW* VI.139. According to Russell, *Thomas Moore*, 15, Moore was appointed master shipwright in 1801.
163. [Joseph Banks, by handwriting], Some Observations on a Bill admitting the Produce of New South Wales to entry at the Customs-house of the United Kingdom, 7 July 1806, *HRNSW* VI.108.
164. Albion, *Forests*, 323–4, 381.
165. Canby, *History*, 72.
166. Crimmin, 'Search', 83.
167. Crimmin, 'Search', 84.
168. Moore was questioned by Bigge on 2nd February 1820, and then again at Liverpool on 8th April. See Russell, *Thomas Moore*, 11 & 13.
169. *SG* 9/1/1826.
170. The Navy Board requested Samuel Marsden to travel with this vessel, given his good relations with the Maoris. It arrived in the Bay of Islands on 20 Feb 1820, and returned to Sydney on 25 Nov 1820, Marsden's third New Zealand voyage. Marsden, *Samuel Marsden*, 146.
171. *SG* (Supp) 7/8/1823: 'Mr WHITE, being about to proceed to England in the *Surry*, requests claims to be presented'. *SG* 21/8/1823: 'On Sunday sailed for England, the ship *Surry*, Captain Powers. Her cargo consists of timber, the produce of Australia'.
172. *SG* 9/1/1826.
173. On 30th April 1810, just months after his retirement, Macquarie also involved him in a military Board of Survey into the Dockyard; Russell, *Thomas Moore*, 25. He also returned to survey several ships across the next years.
174. Atkinson, *The Europeans In Australia*, 1.345. Whereas the prior average annual number of convicts was about 500, in 1815 1074 convicts arrived and from 1818 onwards the number was never less than 2000 (with the single exception of 1823).

[104] *Thomas Moore of Liverpool: One of our Oldest Colonists*

CHAPTER 6

A MAN, A CHURCH, A COLLEGE[1]

Thomas Moore and St Luke's Liverpool

THIS YEAR, MOORE COLLEGE IS celebrating its 150th year. On 1st March, 1856, Moore College opened its doors for the first time, with three students, here in Liverpool. Fifty years ago, the 100th anniversary of Moore College was celebrated at St Luke's Liverpool. And today, St Luke's is the host of the first public celebration of Moore College's 150th year. This is entirely appropriate and fitting, because our founder, Thomas Moore, ties together your church and our college.

As our text today, I have selected Psalm 116:12. The older versions read: 'What shall I render unto the Lord for all his benefits towards me?'. The NIV reads: 'How can I repay the Lord for all his goodness to me?'. Or, to say the same thing like a 21st century Aussie might put it: 'What shall I give back to God, since he has given so much to me?'

This was the text that Rev Richard Johnson, our first chaplain, chose to speak on at the first Christian service in NSW on 3rd February 1788, just after the First Fleet landed.

Thomas Moore was not there on that occasion, since he first arrived in Australia in 1792 and only settled here in 1796. But, soon after he settled here, he was married by Richard Johnson and he probably attended his church for some years.

Perhaps the memory of Australia's first sermon filtered down through that congregation, and perhaps this text was famous enough to touch the imagination of Thomas Moore as well.

For, towards the end of his life, two different people quoted Thomas Moore as saying something similar to the words of our Psalm.

Bishop Broughton, the first and only Bishop of Australia, wrote that Thomas Moore wanted to leave his estate to the benefit of the Church, 'in gratitude to God who had given him all'.[2] Now that sounds a little like our Psalm, doesn't it?

The second person who reported something similar is Arthur Lukyn Williams, who was the third Principal of the College while it was in Liverpool, and also associated with St Luke's during that time. While he was Principal (1878–1884), he tried to collect stories of Thomas Moore from the old people who still remembered him at that stage. In one such story, he said:

> [Moore] must have been a queer old fellow; while he was dying, he was asked if he would not leave something to his nephew, but he replied: "No, God gave it all to me, and I shall give it all back to Him".[3]

Lukyn Williams might have taken these words as the words of 'a queer old fellow', but then again, they also sound like the words of our Psalm: What shall I give back to God, since he has given so much to me?

Moore College has been in Newtown since 1891.[4] But before that it was here in Liverpool, down near where the hospital is nowadays. It was a rather grand building in 1865,[5] but 10 years before that, it began in the old home of Thomas Moore.

A portrait of Thomas Moore has survived, painted by Mr William Griffiths in 1840 towards the end of Moore's life.[6] At this very moment it is packed in a crate at the College in Newtown. You may have also seen another smaller portrait of his head and shoulders,[7] but apparently this was 'bodgied up' by a photographer from the larger picture,[8] so that means there are not two portraits, but only one. It has been described as a gloomy portrait,[9] but, in fact, close inspection—or the right kind of photography—reveals its true colours.

Up on the wall, behind Moore's left shoulder, there is a small picture of Thomas's wife Rachel. You have seen her before, of course, because after she died, Thomas erected a memorial for her in your church. Even though her husband has left only one portrait, this means that Rachel has left two—the one in the picture, and the marble relief here on your wall.

The text of the St Luke's memorial describes a lovely, godly Christian woman.[10] This description may have surprised some of the companions she had in her younger days. For Rachel Moore began her life in Australia as Rachel Turner, a convict. She was sentenced to transportation for 7 years for stealing some household goods from the family she worked for as a servant. She arrived in NSW on board the Transport *Lady Juliana*, part of the Second Fleet.[11] So, if she began as a convict, when did she become a godly Christian woman?

Richard Johnson, the man who preached Sydney's first Christian sermon, on Psalm 116:12 (our text), also preached to the women convicts of the *Lady Juliana* after she arrived. He spoke passionately about the love of God and about how Jesus died on the cross for our sins, and how that means we can now be forgiven for everything. After their long voyage in extremely trying conditions, and as they were about to begin a tough life in a land far from home, many of these women were moved to tears as they heard Johnson preach the gospel of forgiveness.[12] Now, Rachel would have been amongst Johnson's hearers. Was she touched by this gospel of free forgiveness on that day? We don't know.

When she landed, she became the servant of the Surgeon John White. In time and in accord with the common practice of the day, she also became his mistress, and bore him a son, Andrew Douglass White—who is now buried with his mother in Pioneer Park here in Liverpool.

We don't really know when her faith in Christ blossomed. But there are several reports of her Christian service here in St Luke's, and especially her real gift of hospitality. Rachel and Thomas would take visitors to St Luke's back to their home and feed them and entertain them long into the evening.[13] Her 'constant attendance at the house of God' and her 'devotion to family prayers', as mentioned in the St Luke's memorial, shows her clear desire to soak up the goodness of God, and her service of others shows her response to God's goodness in very practical ways.

Now, we don't get much of an impression of what Rachel looked like from the rather formal marble relief here in the church, and her picture in the oil painting is not the main feature and so is relatively small. But nevertheless, it is clear enough for us to see the kindly features of her face, and even her laughing eyes. It is a face that matches the surviving words of people who held Rachel in great affection.

There is little doubt that it was Thomas who composed the words now carved to her memory here at St Luke's.[14] So, that means that we can also learn a bit about him. Although such memorials may have a tendency to some reverent exaggeration, the memorial tells us that, when he buried his wife, Thomas was a man who felt that he had been loved by her, and who had found her to be a long and faithful Christian companion.

From reading his Bible, Thomas Moore would have known that the man who finds a good wife finds a good gift from God. We can imagine him turning to Psalm 116:12 as he remembered Rachel, and saying: 'What can I give back to God in return for him giving Rachel to me?'.

What about Thomas himself? What can we know about him?

We don't know much about his early years. He probably came from the northeast of England, near Durham, or in Northumberland. But he was 30 years old when he first arrived here, and so far nothing else is really known about him before that time.[15] He arrived in 1792 as the ship's carpenter on the *Britannia*, and was involved with her crew in various adventures in these waters before settling here in 1796 and marrying Rachel in 1797. It is likely that they both attended Richard Johnson's church while they lived in Sydney.[16]

For thirteen years he used his carpentry skills as the Master

CHAPTER 6 ~ *A Man, A Church, A College* [109]

Boat Builder at the King's Dockyard, which was on the western side of what we now call Circular Quay.

His relationships with our early governors varied quite a bit. He was friends with John Hunter, who was also an evangelical Christian.

He also got on well with Governor King. King's daughter-in-law was a bit like Rachel: she seems to have earned a reputation for being a remarkable Christian woman. She and her husband, Admiral King, lived near St Marys (the suburb), where they attended church. Their son Robert Lethbridge King would become the second Principal of Moore College while it was still at Liverpool (1868–1878), and while he was here he also had some associations with St Luke's.[17]

But Governor Bligh was a different story. In 1808, NSW had its famous 'Rum Rebellion' in which Governor Bligh was relieved of his position and a rebel government was installed for over a year. It is one of the colourful facts of Thomas Moore's life, that he was one of those who signed the request for Governor Bligh to be arrested. Consequently, Moore was on Bligh's 'hit-list'—a list he wrote of those who were not permitted to leave the colony, presumably in the hope that they could be punished when Bligh regained his power.

But, as our history books tell us, that never happened. Instead, he was replaced by Governor Lachlan Macquarie. Over their time in NSW, Governor and Mrs Elizabeth Macquarie became close friends with Thomas and Rachel Moore. The Moores even became the guardians of Lachlan jnr., just in case anything happened to his parents during their time in NSW. Governor Macquarie and his wife Elizabeth often stayed with the Moores when they visited Liverpool over the years, and even when they returned to England the Governor and Thomas continued to correspond with each other.[18]

During Macquarie's Governorship, Thomas Moore prospered. In 1809 he and Rachel moved from Sydney to a large grant of land on the south bank of the beautiful George's River. By the time they moved, Thomas had already built a house there, and they called their property 'Moore Bank'. The place where their house was can still be found in Whelan Ave, Chipping Norton, and the view down the river towards Liverpool is almost the same as it was in their day.

On 7th November 1810, Governor Macquarie and his party arrived at Moore Bank early in the morning, picked up Thomas Moore and then proceeded to tour the area to find the site of a new town, which he called Liverpool. In the years following, Macquarie gave Thomas Moore a great deal of responsibility in the town. He laid out the streets, had oversight of the building of many of the public buildings, he took on all the many and varied duties of the resident magistrate, he was interested in the school, the orphans of the area, banking, the aborigines, and he performed many other civic duties across the next 30 years. Moore gained a lot during this time and he became one of the colony's major landholders and became very wealthy. But when he asked, what can I give back to God for all he has given me? One answer would have been that he clearly gave his time, his energy and his money to making his town a better place to live.

And then there was his church.

St Luke's was such an important part of Thomas's life, that it appears in Griffiths' oil painting peeking through the window.

St Luke's has had a long association with Moore College. Most recently, in the last twenty years 14 young people have gone from here to Moore College to be trained for the ministry of the gospel and, of course, there are some who have joined us this year.[19] There have also been a succession of Moore College students joining St Luke's as catechists, and our graduates have been here as curates and rectors. We can hope and pray that your church and our college might continue to have a strong and mutually beneficial association across the years to come.

But the relationship between the Church and the College hasn't always been a good one. In fact, for the first 35 years of the College's existence—that is, the whole time it was here at Liverpool—the minister of the church was not really a friend of the college. The College under men like William Macquarie Cowper, William

Hodges, Robert Lethbridge King, and even Arthur Lukyn Williams, was clearly evangelical. That is, committed to living by and preaching the gospel of Jesus Christ as God's gracious revelation to a lost world. The Rev Charles Priddle, on the other hand, was known as a 'Puseyite', a 'Tractarian'; that is, someone who wanted the Anglican Church to be more like the Catholic Church.

But St Luke's did not begin with that flavour of churchmanship. From the beginning, it seems, Liverpool was a place with a great deal of evangelical Christianity, and it was a place with a great deal of missionary interest—and Thomas Moore was clearly in these circles.

In Thomas Moore, St Luke's and Moore College share the same founder. Governor Macquarie was a great builder and our oldest surviving church buildings date to his day. In 1816 Moore added his own energies to those of the newly arrived Chaplain John Youl to get a Church built in the new town. By the end of 1816, the parsonage (a home for the minister) was completed. The builder was Nathaniel Lucas, the man whose gravestone now stands against the outside wall of St Luke's. On 7th April 1818, Governor and Elizabeth Macquarie and their 4 year old Lachlan, Rachel and Thomas Moore, Rev and Mrs Youl, and the architect Francis Greenway, were all present at the laying of the foundation stone for the church. Nathaniel Lucas was again appointed to be the builder, but sadly, after a drunken binge, his body was found in the mud of the George's River, apparently having taken his own life. James Smith took over and the church began to take shape. The first service was held on 18th October 1819, but at that stage the church only had a roof and four walls. It would not be completely finished until 1824, another 5 years on.

Thomas Moore was involved with the building of St Luke's across the entire period of its construction. And more importantly, up until he died he was also actively engaged in supporting the work of the gospel around Liverpool and beyond, and he served upon the St Luke's committee. He was a founding member of the Bible Society a member of the Benevolent Society, and the

Protestant Committee, concerned for the relief of the poor, the sick, the orphans. And he was concerned for Christian education.

He was also involved in Liverpool's missionary concerns. He took an active interest in Marsden's mission to New Zealand, which had several strong links to people in Liverpool. There is a letter from Samuel Hassall, in which we learn that Mr Moore had been trying to persuade him to go to New Zealand as a missionary. Thomas Moore was apparently involved in setting up Church Missionary Society in NSW[20] and was also active in the Wesleyan Auxiliary Missionary Society. And we could go on.

When we consider the life of Thomas Moore, there are many ways of answering the question of Psalm 116:12. What did he give back for all the good that God had given him?

He gave back untold amounts of practical care and concern for his town and society. But even more importantly he gave his time and energy to support the work of the gospel in his own town, in his own country, and beyond into mission fields overseas.

And then there is his final gift to the work of the gospel. When he died on Christmas Eve 1840, he had left his entire estate to further the work of Christ in this land. A major portion of that estate went towards founding a college for the training of clergy. And through the ministry of Moore College, for 150 years the good news of Jesus Christ has been proclaimed to the nations.

'What shall I give back to the Lord, for all he has given to me?'

Remember Thomas Moore's dying words as reported by Arthur Lykyn Williams: 'God gave it all to me, and I shall give it all back to him'.

We have all benefited from Thomas Moore's generosity. We at St Luke's. We at Moore College. We, the people of Sydney, and, indeed, Australia.

But, if it was God who gave everything to Thomas Moore, then it is not ultimately Thomas Moore who should be thanked. Through this man, many good things have been given to us; but each one of those things has been given to us by God himself.

As we remember Thomas Moore, and as we celebrate 150

CHAPTER 6 ~ *A Man, A Church, A College* [113]

years of Moore College, there is a question that we should all be asking. What shall *we* give back to God for all his goodness towards us?

Notes

1. The original version of this essay was a sermon preached at St Luke's Liverpool, 5th March 2006, as the first public event in the Sesquicentenary Celebrations of Moore College.
2. Broughton to Coleridge, 25th Feb 1839.
3. From the Moore College magazine, *Societas* 1937, p.18. Williams was 25 when he became principle, and so when sharing these reminiscences, he would have been about eighty four. He died in Cambridge on 6th October 1943. See Loane, *Centenary History*, Ch. 4.
4. As we celebrate the sesquicentenary, increased student numbers and the subsequent overcrowding of the Newtown site have forced the College to seriously consider whether it is time to move again, for only the second time in its history.
5. For the picture, see Loane, *Centenary History*, facing p.68.
6. For further discussion, see ch. 9 in this volume 'The Griffith Portrait'.
7. This is the portrait usually used to accompany information on Moore. It appears facing p.16 in Loane, *Centenary History*, and is used on several websites and in the Liverpool City Library pamphlets on Moore.
8. I owe this information to Bishop Donald Robinson.
9. Robinson, 'Thomas Moore & Early Life', 167 (3).
10. St Luke's Memorial to Rachel Moore: 'The Tablet of Mrs Thos Moore, who departed this life on the 13th day of November 1838, aged 76 years. She was the most affectionate, and virtuous wife, a tender mother, and ever kind to the poor. She was united to her husband for 42 years, during which time she was a constant attendant at the house of God and a strict observer of family prayer, and died in peace. "Sickness and sorrow mingle here, Each heart with tenderness is moved, Ere long we'll be resumed again, and raised to nobler ends above".'
11. For a colourful account of the journey of the *Lady Juliana* and of some of her occupants, see Rees, *The Floating Brothel*.
12. Collins, *Account*, 100, mentions that his sermon drew 'tears from many of these unfortunates, who were not yet so hardened as to be insensible to truth'. Macintosh, *Richard Johnson*, 51–52, suggests that this may have been one of the occasional results of Johnson's preaching that was recorded because it was exceptional.
13. Governor Macquarie, G.W. Walker, Bishop Broughton and Sarah Felton Matthew all comment on receiving such hospitality.
14. When this address was given, I had not discovered the documents in the Sydney Diocesan Archives, which contain several expressions of affection for Rachel from Moore's pen. See ch. 8, 'Liverpool and the Lash' for more details. Thomas was clearly proud of the words on the memorial, for he sent a copy of them to his brother William in England. William, in turn, liked them so much that he asked permission

to use them himself: 'The Copy of the Tabulet you have erected to the memory of your dear Wife I have shewn to many of my friends, they think the composition very beautiful and evidently speaks the mind of him who has lost so valuable a Treasure— I should if it meets your approbation like to have it inscribed on the stone now erected to the Memory of my Daughter in South Church Yard'; William Moor to T. Moore, 24 Dec 1839, SDA 0851CH, Item 6, doc. 35.

15. When this address was given, I had not discovered the documents that reveal Moore's origins more exactly. See further ch. 3, 'Birth Announcement'.
16. Others have also made this assumption. It remains only a good guess, however, as long as positive evidence is lacking. As a step towards such evidence we can draw attention to the fact that the 'civil and military officers' and a fair number of the merchants and the trading community attended the 11am service in William Cowper's day (see Cowper, *Autobiography and Reminiscences*, 16, 64), which may reflect a pattern set up under Johnson. As Master Boat Builder at the dockyard, Moore was one of the civil officers.
17. See Loane, *Centenary History*, Chapter 3.
18. A collection of Macquarie's letters to Moore have survived (SDA 0853CH, Item 4).
19. Denise Nicholls, Lyn Yap, Leanne Burns, Stuart Gyngall, Patrick Larrea, Peter Flower, Connan O'Shea, Thomas Bielenburg, Jason Ramsay, Steve Grey, Mark Ramsay, Phil Riley, Tim St Quinten, Thora Judge.
20. I say 'apparently' because, although this is the claim of Boyce, *Thomas Moore*, I have been unable so far to verify the claim from the CMS archives. Moore's name does not appear on any of the early committees, but it may be that he was involved at a more preliminary level.

CHAPTER 7

THOMAS MOORE'S BOOKSHELF
A Preliminary Examination

Part A: A List of Books the Property T. Moore, Esq.

The List

In the Sydney Diocesan Archives, amongst the papers of The Trustees of the Estate of the Late Thomas Moore, there is an exercise book which contains a 'List of Books the Property T. Moore Esqre'.[1] It is undated, but, since it is in his own handwriting, this catalogue was probably compiled by Moore himself with a view to the disposal of his property after his death.[2]

The Books

Thomas Moore died on Christmas Eve, 1840. Moore's Will was opened on the same day as his funeral (29/12/1840), and William Grant Broughton, Bishop of Australia, Alexander McLeay, Colonial Secretary to NSW, and Robert Campbell, businessman and merchant, found themselves appointed as trustees.[3] John Layton was instructed to take charge of the Liverpool residence and its property, until arrangements were made to dispose of it. On 21 January 1841 the Trustees 'instructed Mr John Blackman Auctioneer, to advertize the sale of the Household furniture, Books, Plate &c at the residence of the late Mr Moore, on the 1st February next'.[4] On the same day, Mr Kerrison James was commissioned to proceed to Liverpool and bring 'all Deeds, Instruments and Papers relating to the Estate, to be deposited in the Bishop's Registry office: which was accordingly done'.[5] Evidently there was a case of books amongst this material, packed up by John Layton.[6]

In the closing weeks of January, Mary Ann White, the widow of Moore's stepson Andrew, informed the Trustees that some of the contents of Moore's Liverpool home belonged to her, and she was granted permission to retrieve these items. As the Trustees' minute puts it:

> Mrs M.A. White, having represented to the Executors that certain articles at the residence of the Late Mr Moore, are her property, Resolved, that the same be delivered up to her upon her identifying them, and signing a receipt therefor.[7]

As we shall see below, quite a few of the books in Moore's possession probably once belonged to Andrew, so presumably these could have been taken by Mrs White (nee McKenzie) when she retrieved the items considered her property.

The sale of Moore's effects took place at his residence on the 1st February 1841, realizing £341.10.3, exclusive of charges.[8] The day following the sale, the Trustees attended court for the proving of the Will,[9] and probate was granted by the Supreme Court on 14th April.[10] As far as the books were concerned, some at least were not disposed of at that time, since an entry in the Trustees' Minute Book as late as 1844 shows that 'auctioneer Blackman reports the sale of some books owned by Thomas Moore, £3.9.1'. Given the apparently small amount remitted on this occasion,[11] however, presumably most were either sold previously with the rest of his effects, or retained by the Trustees for some other purpose.

The Books and the Man

What can we learn from Moore's bookshelf? One of the first difficulties that presents itself is the ownership of the books. Were they all his? Thomas was predeceased by his step-son Andrew Douglas White, who was educated at Charterhouse, before becoming an officer in the Royal Engineers in time to serve at the Battle of

Waterloo. The subject matter of a number of the listed books quite clearly connects them to Andrew, rather than Thomas. Presumably they had been on Moore's bookshelf since at least the time of Andrew's death in November 1837. If they came to Thomas at that time, then the list would have been compiled after that date. There is no way of knowing, however, whether they had been on Moore's shelf since Andrew's arrival back in the colony.[12]

Irrespective of how long they have been on the shelf, the presence of Andrew's books brings an added complication. Because some of the books were his, we have little way of knowing how many other books belonged to him, rather than to Thomas. In other words, this is not a 'pure' collection of Thomas Moore. On the other hand, however, many other books most certainly represent Thomas's interests. So, although the bookshelf was eventually labelled 'books the property T. Moore Esq.', it clearly blends the interests of two men.

Another difficulty arises when we ask what can be learned about a man from the books on his shelf? It is not easy to make judgements about a person from what is found in their library. A person of broad interests or education may have such a range of reading matter, that almost nothing specific can be learned about their own views, beyond the fact that they had a broad range of reading matter! However, although a person may possess a book that is entirely different to his or her interests and attitudes, it is also reasonable to assume that at least some, if not many, of the books on a person's bookshelf bear some relationship to their special interests. This is probably true all the moreso for a private collection from early nineteenth century Australia. In addition, if the library has been carefully listed, as in the case at hand, it may even more closely represent their owner's interests, especially if we can assume that some some books may have already been culled, and those listed represent the treasured remainder. A collection is usually made on the basis of some underlying principle, or principles, and so it is a reasonable assumption to seek to discern the 'mind' behind a bookshelf[13]—although we should repeat the usual caveats that any such judgements must remain more probable, than certain.

A further fascinating question arises when we ask what eventually happened to these books.[14] Did they eventually leave the colony, or did they remain in circulation in Sydney? If so, have any of them survived in any of our various libraries? In particular, since the Trustees knew that Thomas Moore's Will looked to a future college to train Protestant youth in the principles of the United Church of England and Ireland, how many of the books on Moore's shelf were deemed suitable to this purpose, and so set aside to form the core of the library of what would become Moore College? Another route to the same end would have been via the Sydney Diocesan Library, begun by Bishop Broughton, one of the first Trustees of Moore's Estate, which eventually also found its way to Moore College.[15] Unfortunately, the kind of detective work required delays answering this question until another time.

The present task consists mainly of identification. What follows, therefore, in Part 2, is a description and brief general analysis of Thomas Moore's bookshelf. To explain my procedures: Each book is listed in the same order as found in Thomas Moore's exercise book. I have added page numbers, and assigned a number to each book on the list, after the pattern 'page.item on page' (i.e. 2.4 = page 2, fourth item). The initial heading for each book is a transcription of the short title used on Moore's list, which is then followed by the identification of the book in full.[16] The original date of publication is cited, unless this has been too difficult to discover, even though Moore may have owned a later edition. Further comments are added where relevant, necessary, or interesting, but there is a fair degree of randomness in the comments, arising as they do from the book itself, its history, or from its author. This inquiry is a 'preliminary examination' because these comments are made more from 'circumstantial' evidence about the authors, rather than from a detailed examination of the contents of the books themselves.

To provide some further points of connection with the wider world, I have also compared Moore's list with several other lists—

again, rather randomly generated. The list of books sent out with Australia's first chaplain, Rev. Richard Johnson, shows the kind of books thought useful for the evangelical cause in a penal colony.[17] Similar concerns may be discerned in the list of books circulating in English prison libraries in the late 1830s and into the early 1840s.[18] A book listed here gives it a place within the reform agenda,[19] and closely associates it with the Religious Tract Society[20] and so, with the evangelical movement, and with a society of which Moore was a known supporter.[21] The Bray collection, now housed in Moore College Library, was brought to Australia in 1809 by Chaplain Samuel Marsden to form the core of the Port Jackson Lending Library,[22] although, being donated, it probably represents concerns broader than Marsden's evangelicalism. I have also noted when a book was offered for sale in two (randomly selected) Sydney newspaper advertisements, one for a list of 'valuable books' on sale in December 1824;[23] the other placed by James Tegg in December 1838. This may give some indication of a work's currency amongst the readers of the colony. Moore's older books have also been compared with Jeake's catalogue,[24] and with Green's list of best- and steady-sellers for the period 1530–1729,[25] and other indications of a book's reputation have been gleaned from a variety of sources wherever they have come to light.

The ultimate reason for commenting upon the various books, of course, is to attempt to draw some conclusions about the intellectual life of their owner. After providing some classification of the bookshelf, Part 3 therefore attempts to draw some lessons about the man who once listed its contents. Since I have commented at some length on most of the titles, Part 2 has become rather lengthy. Those readers who prefer a 'direct', rather than a 'scenic', route, may perhaps like to skip the details of Part 2 and go immediately to the observations and conclusions of Part 3. Those who take the journey through the details will, of course, have a far richer experience, perhaps something akin to standing in the Liverpool study, with St Luke's framed in the window, and 'browsing' through the books collected by Mr Moore.

Part B: The Books Identified

1. Page 1: [Heading:] Books – English & French[26]

1.1 *D'Oyly & Mants Bible 3 Vol*

The Holy Bible ... with notes ... taken principally from the most eminent writers of the United Church of England and Ireland ... prepared and arranged by the Rev. George D'Oyly ... and the Rev. Richard Mant, etc.

This was an annotated version of the Authorised Version of 1611—what might be called a 'study Bible' today—with notes prepared by George D'Oyly and Richard Mant. It was known as the 'D'Oyly and Mant's Bible', as here in Moore's list.

Rev. George D'Oyly (1778–1846), educated at Cambridge, was a well-known preacher and theologian in his day, as well as a biographer. He served as an admirable parish priest, as the Rector of Lambeth, Surrey, and Sundridge, Kent, from 1820–1846.[27] He was involved with societies active in mission, serving as treasurer for the SPCK, and a member of the London committee for the SPG. He was also a promoter of King's College London.

As for his co-writer, Richard Mant was ordained deacon in 1802, and detained in France during the war (1802–1803), then priested. He went on to become successively Bishop of Killaloe (1820–23), and of Down and Connor (1823–48)—a stronghold of, mainly Presbyterian, Protestantism—to which Dromore was also later added, although he prepared these notes before being consecrated.[28] Richard Mant went on to produce a prayer book on a similar plan (1820).

The three-volume edition owned by Moore would be that published by Rivington in 1826, or Cambridge University Press in 1830, subsequently promoted by the Society for Promoting Christian Knowledge.

1.2 *Lempriere's Dictionary*

John Lempriere, *A Classical Dictionary* (1788). It was greatly enlarged in the second edition (1797) and by 1815 had run to nine editions with further editions to follow (1818, 1828, 1832, 1833, 1838, 1843, 1888).

Lempriere (1765?–1824) was a classical scholar, who taught in various schools, did some translation (Herodotus), was the vicar of Abingdon (1800–1811), and wrote biography. His dictionary, his most famous work, listed all the proper names mentioned in ancient authors, and the value of coins, weights, and measures used among the Greeks and Romans, as well as providing a chronological table.[29]

This was a useful book for anyone seeking an education in the classics. Andrew could have used this book during his education at Charterhouse. If it was Thomas's book, it was not published in time to be used by him at school, even if the classics were part of an ordinary grammar school education, and even if he had attended the Lesbury School where his uncle, James Moor, was the teacher. He could, however, have purchased it at a later date, in the quest for self-improvement that he most certainly appears to have embarked upon. His booklist also contains Plutarch's *Lives* (3.11), and some notes have survived from 1822 which show that Thomas was drawing out life lessons from figures from the ancient world, some of them dealt with by Plutarch.[30] Lempriere certainly would have been useful during such reading projects.

1.3   Milton's History of England 2 vol

John Milton, *The History of Britain, that part especially now call'd England, from the first traditional beginning, continu'd to the Norman Conquest. Collected out of the antientest and best authours by John Milton* (1670).

John Milton (1608–1674), famous for his *Paradise Lost* and *Paradise Regained*, completed his *History* in 1669, although it was written long before.[31] Milton can be (and has been) classed as a Puritan, but not easily. 'His fanatical piety, scriptural convictions, and commitment to Protestant England are indeed essentially puritan, but his theological opinions (Anti-Trinitarianism, Arminianism), his consistent acquiescence in traditional Anglican practices [...], and his Humanist learning and delight in poetry and music suggest that the label "puritan" is as inadequate now to describe John Milton as it was in the seventeenth century'.[32]

There was A *History of England* amongst the books circulated to prisoners, which may well have been Milton's.[33] Milton's *Works* were on sale in Sydney in 1824 and 1838.

1.4   Blair's Sermons 3 vol

Hugh Blair, *Sermons on Various Subjects* (1777).

An account of Blair's life (1718–1800) can be found in *Sermons*, written by James Finlayson DD, 'A Short Account of the Life and Character of Dr. Hugh Blair' (1826). After Blair was appointed to Edinburgh's High Church in 1758, he retained this charge for the rest of his life. He was also a professor of rhetoric and belles lettres in the University of Edinburgh. He was a member of the intellectual society which flourished in Edinburgh at that time, a member of the 'Poker Club' with David Hume, A. Carlyle, Adam Ferguson, Adam Smith, Robertson, and others. He was an intimate friend of Henry Dundas, later Lord Melville. His sermons enjoyed popularity for a long time. Strachan, the publisher, declined the first volume, but Blair showed it to Samuel Johnson who liked it and so Strachan bought it, and by 1794, they had gone to the 19th edition of the first volume of sermons, and the 15th of the second. In 1801 a five volume edition was published, including an account of Blair's life, and another new edition appeared in 1807. The sermons were translated into many other languages and reprinted throughout the nineteenth century.

There were 5, 4, and 3 volume editions. If Thomas Moore's 3 volumes were a complete set, then this would identify them as the new edition published by T. Cadell of London (1822), or that of Thomas Tegg of London (1824, 1825, 1827, 1834).

In the history of preaching, Blair's were landmark sermons. They were carefully composed, and 'they are the best examples of the sensible, if unimpassioned and rather affected, style of the moderate divines of the times'.[34] Leslie Stephen, who is not very fond of eighteenth century preaching in general, is rather more damning of Blair:

> As the century went on, the eloquence became feebler, for all the warmth of sentiment had passed to the side of Wesley and Whitefield. A preacher in the land of Knox obtained a great popularity, and the sermons of Hugh Blair may represent the last stage of theological decay.[35]

Leslie's description of Blair's sermons portrays them as essays from the professor of rhetoric, rather than sermons; in which commonsense argument is replace by the feeblest of platitudes; the morality is summed up as respectability; philosophical reasoning is virtually absent; and any theology that appears is mere window dressing.[36] Despite such comments, Leslie has to admit that Blair's sermons were very popular in his own day and beyond. A two volume set was on sale in Sydney in 1824 and 1838.

1.5. Treatise on Cattle by Lawrence

John Lawrence, *A General Treatise on Cattle, the Ox, the Sheep, and the Swine, comprehending their Breeding, Management, Improvement, and Diseases* (1805).

1.6. Treatise on Horses by do

John Lawrence, *A Philosophical and Practical Treatise on Horses and on the Moral Duties of Man Towards the Brute Creation* (2 vols.; 1796–8; ²1802, with additions; ³1810 with large additions).

1.7. New Farmers Calendar

John Lawrence, *The New Farmer's Calendar, a Monthly Remembrancer for all kinds of Country Business, comprehending all the Material Improvements in the New Husbandry with the Management of Live Stock, by a Farmer and Breeder* (1800; ²1801, with considerable additions). *The Farmer's Pocket Calendar* is an abridgement of this work.

John Lawrence (1753–1839),[37] the author of these three books (1.5–7), began to write for the press in 1787. He insisted on the duty of humanity to animals. 'The Horse,' Lawrence wrote, 'is endowed with such as we are compelled to denominate qualities of mind; namely, perception, consciousness, memory, free will; in these originate love, hatred, fear, fortitude, patience, generosity, obedience, a limited sense of justice. He reasons: he therefore possesses an immortal and imperishable soul.' His treatise on land management (1801) and his *New Farmer's Calendar* advocated the painless killing of animals for food. His life-time concern for humane treatment of animals led to him being consulted before parliament introduced the bill against cruelty to animals (1822).[38] He was influential in his day, his *Treatise on Horses* running to three editions, but his name was almost forgotten until Mr E.B. Nicholson, *The Rights of Animals* (1879) republished some chapters.

These three books can probably be taken to show Thomas Moore's Christianity being applied to his main farming interests: horse and cattle breeding.

1.8 The Life of Hy Longden/ Late of Sheffield

Henry LONGDEN, *The life of H. Longden ... and other documents, compiled from his own Memoirs. To which is affixed a funeral discourse by W. Bramwell* (Liverpool, 1813, 1815, 1821, 1822, 1831).

Henry Longden (1754–1812), was born in Sheffield, Yorkshire. As an apprentice razor maker, he was a wild youth, who earned fame as a champion prize fighter, before running away to join the army at the age of twenty. He was brought back by his father to complete his apprenticeship, and then to enter his father's business. In 1776 he married and was converted, joining the Mulberry St Chapel, where, within a few years, he began to preach. This book narrates the life of this Methodist minister—including a rather detailed account of his last days and hours—whose prosperous business enterprises enabled him to be generous to good causes, before giving himself to evangelism and philanthropy after his retirement.[39] Did his spirit of philanthropy inspire Thomas Moore in his own generosity?

1.9 Buchan's Domestic Medicine

William Buchan, *Domestic Medicine: Or, A Treatise On The Prevention And Cure Of Diseases By Regimen And Simple Medicines. With An Appendix Containing A Dispensatory For The Use Of Private Practitioners* (1769; rev. ^{8}1784).

By the 16th edition (1798) an extended title reflected the additional material:

... To which are added, observations on the diet of the common people; recommending a method of living less expensive, and more conducive to health, than the present.

With later additions to come: '*to which are added some important observations concerning sea-bathing, and the use of mineral waters*' (18—?).

William Buchan (1729–1805) was an amateur doctor in his village before being sent to Edinburgh to study Divinity. Once there, however, he switched to medicine, and, after graduating, practiced in Yorkshire and Sheffield, settled in Edinburgh (1766), then moved to London (1778). Apart from this volume, he published other medical tracts.[40]

Buchan's *Domestic Medicine* was the first of its kind in English, and was an immediate success, running to 19 large editions, with 80,000 copies sold in his lifetime in Great Britain alone. It was translated into all European languages and continues to be re-edited and copied. It was on sale in Sydney in 1838.

1.10 Discourses by Dr Andrews

Lancelot Andrewes (1555–1626), *Three Learned, And Seasonable Discourses. Sacriliege A Snare. Of The Right Of Tiths. Of Episcopacy* (1647).

Cambridge educated, Lancelot Andrewes (1555–1626) was ordained in 1580 and was soon chaplain to Whitgift and to Queen Elizabeth. Although refusing two bishoprics under Elizabeth, he had a rapid rise under James I, being successively Bishop of Chichester (1601), Ely (1609) and Winchester (1619). He took part in the Hampton Court conference (1603–04) and in 1607 he was one of those appointed to produce the Authorised Version. As well as being an eminent prelate and writer (although mostly published after his lifetime), he was regarded highly as a preacher, being called 'an angel in the pulpit', and managing to fascinate Queen Elizabeth. Just like John Tillotson would be regarded as the best example of the new style, Andrewes was regarded as the most distinguished of the old style, 'with their Greek and Latin quotation, plays upon words, and minute analyses of the text'.[41]

Amongst his published works there are several volumes of *Sermons*, but Moore's description is clearly to Andrewes' *Discourses*, which identifies this as the 1647 volume dealing with Sacrilege, Tithes, and Episcopacy.

Andrewes appears to have been one of Bishop Broughton's heroes, for he spoke of erecting a statue of him and of Ridley at the entrance to his proposed theological college in Sydney.[42] Was Moore reading Andrewes with the Bishop's encouragement?

1.11 Sturms Reflections 2 vol

Christopher Christian Sturm, *Reflections For Every Day In The Year On The Works Of God, And On His Providence In The Regions Of Nature, And In The Government Of The Universe* (1790).

According to George Long's *Penny Cyclopaedia* (1842), Christopher Christian Sturm (1750–1786), pastor and preacher at Magdeburg then Hamburg, was renowned for his piety, his poetry, and his practical writings for adults and children.[43] Written in German in 1785, the work translated as *Reflections* went through many editions, which, according to Long, shows that it 'has been very popular in England'.

Reflections was circulated amongst English prisoners.[44] Moore owned a three volume set, the last of which is listed below (2.7). A three volume set of Sturm's *Reflections* was amongst the books advertised for sale in Sydney in both 1824 and 1838.

1.12 Hymns by Wesley

Hymns and Sacred Poems (1739) was the first collection of hymns published by John and Charles Wesley. The second came in 1740, and the third in 1742, which was then published in various editions.

Some hymns were circulated amongst the prisoners, but the name of Wesley is not specifically mentioned in their connection. Although the *Sydney Gazette* of December 16th 1824 does not list them amongst the 'valuable books' for sale, the front page contains another advertisement, 'Wesleyan Hymn Books for sale, very neat and cheap'. In 1838, however, Wesley's Hymn Books are explicitly advertised.

1.13 Euler on Vessels

Leonhard Euler (1707–1783), a swiss mathematician who wrote the first complete book on differential calculus, also wrote this work, *A Compleat Theory of the Construction and Properties of Vessels with Practical Conclusions for the Management of Ships made Easy to Navigators* (1776; new edition 1790).

1.14 Peate's Lectures

Although the identification of this volume has been difficult, it could be the syllabus of a course of fourteen lectures delivered by the almanac-maker and long-time editor of 'The Gentleman's Diary, or Mathematical Repository', Thomas Peat (1708–1780). The lectures were delivered at Nottingham about 1743, on mechanics, hydrostatics, optics, pneumatics, astronomy, and the use of globes. The syllabus was published possibly the year after, as *A Short Account of a course of mechanical and experimental philosophy and astronomy*, etc.[45]

1.15 Lessons in Humble Life

Although there were other volumes dealing with 'humble life', that is, life in humble circumstances, this title is most probably that of Elizabeth Frank of York, *Lessons for Young persons in*

Humble Life, etc. (York, 1808; ²1809). By Moore's death this book had run into the 10th edition (1836). It was originally published just in time for Andrew's schooling at Charterhouse, and perhaps it was one of his volumes.

There is a book using the same short title as Moore's, presumably also Frank's volume, on the Milbank Prison list.[46]

2. Page 2

2.1 Berens abridgmt of Waldo's Liturgy

Edward Berens, *Lectures on the Liturgy of the Church of England ... arranged and slightly abridged from the Commentary by P. W.* (Oxford, 1821).

Edward Berens (?1777–1859) was archdeacon of Berkshire 1832-1855. Behind Berens' *Lectures* lies Peter Waldo, *A Commentary, Practical and Explanatory, on the Liturgy of the Church of England, by a layman* (1772).

2.2 Bishop Man[n] on the Gospels

Isaac Mann (1712–1788), was Bishop of Cork and Ross from 1772–1788. Amongst other devotional and liturgical writing, he produced *The Four Gospels, And The Acts Of The Apostles; With Notes Explanatory And Practical, For The Use Of Families And Schools* (Dublin, 1781; London, 1783; new edition 1836).

A single copy of this volume was brought to NSW by Richard Johnson, which suggests that it was considered useful for the Chaplain himself, rather than for distribution.

2.3 Berens Village Sermons

This short title could refer to any of several volumes of Edward Berens' sermons: *Eleven Village Sermons On The Chief Articles Of Faith And The Means Of Grace* (1820, ⁷1824); *Sixteen Village Sermons on some parts of the Christian Character* (1822); *Six Village Sermons on some of the Relative Duties* (1822); *Twenty-six Village Sermons* (1836).

Edward Berens (see 2.1) was a popular and voluminous author for his day. These sermons were preached in the parishes of Shrivenham and Englefield in the County of Berkshire, where he later served as Archdeacon.

2.4   Conversations on Philosophy

Jane Haldimand Marcet, *Conversations On Natural Philosophy; In Which The Elements Of That Science Are Familiarly Explained, And Adapted To The Comprehension Of Young Pupils* (1819). The book was evidently popular, being republished in many editions across the next thirty years.[47]

Anonymously, Mrs Marcet wrote two enormously popular books cast in the form of conversations 'between Mrs B and the long suffering Emily and Caroline'. *Conversations on Chemistry* (1806) and *Conversations on Political Economy* (1816). Their success inspired her to continue this approach to discussing science in understandable terms with *Conversations on Natural Philosophy*. She also went on to write in a similar vein, *Conversations on Evidences of Christianity* (1826), *Vegetable Physiology* (1829), the *History of England* (1842) and *Language for Children* (1844).

2.5   Bishop Burnet on the Reformation 3 vol

Gilbert Burnet, published his *History of the Reformation* over a thirty-five year period (vol. 1: 1679; vol.2: 1681; vol. 3: 1714). Some publications have a title that shows that this was particularly meant *for the use of students at the universities and candidates for the Holy Orders.*

Gilbert Burnet (1643–1715),[48] originally from Aberdeenshire, Scotland, was involved throughout his life in the controversies between the English and Scottish churches. Amongst other posts, he was professor of Divinity at Glasgow (1669) and Bishop of Salisbury (1689). He was a representative of broad church views in politics and doctrine.[49]

This volume was circulated to prisoners.[50]

2.6 Wells' Geography of the Old / New Testament

Edward Wells, firstly wrote *An Historical Geography of the New Testament*, published in 1708 (^{2}1712, ^{3}1718), followed by 3 vols. on the OT: *An Historical Geography of the Old Testament* (1711–1712). These two works were then combined into two volume work found on Moore's shelf, *An Historical Geography Of The Old And New Testaments* (1801, then 1809 and 1819, with 'a new edition published by Rivington in 1828, and then SPCK in 1835).

Edward Wells (1667–1727) was regarded as one of the most accurate geographers of his time. He wrote other works apart from his *Historical Geography*, several of which show that he wrote against dissent.[51]

2.7 Sturms Reflections (1)

This is evidently the third volume in the set referred to above (1.11).

2.8 Recreations in Mathematics 4 vols

Jacques Ozanam, wrote his *Récréations mathématiques et physiques* in 1696, which was rendered into English as *Recreations Mathematical and Physical* (1708), and eventually expanded into *Recreations in Mathematics and Natural Philosophy* (4 vols.; 1803, 1814). Other editions, continued to be published to the end of the 19th century. Ozanam had also published a course in mathematics of special interest to 'a man of war' (1693) and a work on fortifications (1694). If this military theme also came into *Recreations*, it may have been one of Andrew's books, but, then again, mathematics was also essential for the ship builder.

2.9 All Religions & Ceremonies

Thomas Robbins, *All Religions and Ceremonies, in two Parts. Part 1: Christianity, Mahometanism, and Judaism. To which is added a Tabular Appendix, by Thomas Williams. Exhibiting the Present State of the World as to religion, population, religious toleration,* government, &c. Part 2: A View of the History, Religion, Manners and Customs of the Hindoos, by William Ward. Together with the religion and ceremonies of other pagan nations (1823).

This was a compilation of ceremonies of non-Christian religions by the dissenter, Thomas Robbins (1777–1856), of Hartford, Connecticut, who was also one of the earliest missionaries in the western Ohio district.[52]

2.10   Bp Hall's Contemplations 2 vol

Joseph Hall's, *Contemplations On The Historical Passages Of The Old And New Testaments* ran to 8 volumes, published over the course of almost fifteen years (1612–1626). From his later pen came a two-volume *Contemplations on the New Testament* (Vol. 1: 1628; vol. 2:1661), followed by *Contemplations on the Life of Jesus* (1679). Because Thomas had '2 vol' of contemplations, this suggests that he only had a partial set of *Historical Passages*, or, more likely, that he owned the *Contemplations on the New Testament*.[53]

Bishop Joseph Hall (1574–1656) was a famous puritan and prolific writer. His mother, Winifred Bambridge was a strict puritan, and when Joseph was 15 a puritan divine, Mr Pelset offered to educate him for the ministry. Instead, his father sent him to Emmanuel College, Cambridge. He first made a reputation as a writer of satire (1597), calling himself the first English satirist, by which he must have meant 'of the Latin model'. In 1597 Whitgift and Bancroft ordered his satires to be burned, together with books by Marston, Marlowe, and others, due to their licentiousness, but days later Hall's work was reprieved. After taking Holy Orders and going to Halsted, Suffolk (1601), he composed the first of his meditations, then the second volume, which attracted the attention of the Prince of Wales, who asked to hear him preach and then appointed him his chaplain (1608), before he went to Waltham, where he preached three carefully prepared sermons each week. In 1617, now dean of Worcester, he was summoned to accompany King James to Scotland to defend the Five Articles of Perth, part of the king's attempt to introduce some ceremonies and the liturgy of the episcopal church, which Hall did, despite being known as not a very zealous assistant. Fond of Calvinistic theology, in 1618 he was one of the English deputies at the Synod of Dort, taking a well-received conciliatory line, before returning to find the same issues brewing in the Church of England, to which he applied his same conciliation. In 1627 he became bishop of Exeter, but was kept under Laud's watchful eye, in view of him being thought too favourable to Calvinistic teaching. Leaning to the puritans and the low church party, Hall maintained a delicate balance of keeping the government happy, but practicing a relatively soft policy towards puritans. He wrote defending episcopacy by divine right, accepted William Laud's revisions, and subsequently entering into controversy with, amongst others, John Milton. After becoming bishop of Norwich, he was imprisoned for a time for high treason, before retiring to write devotional treatises until his death in 1656.[54]

As a theological writer, Joseph Hall has been positioned between Andrewes and Jeremy Taylor. His *Contemplations* are devotional, rather than exegetical. *Contemplations on OT and NT* was owned by Jeake, amongst those circulated to the prisoners at Wakefield prison,[55] and a five volume set was on sale in Sydney in 1838.

2.11 Bingleys Travellers [?]

Although the second word is difficult to read, it is longer than 'Travels' (cf. 4.2), and appears to be 'Travellers'. William Bingley (1774–1823), was a naturalist and Church of England clergyman.[56] Between 1819 and 1822 he published a series under the title page 'Modern Travels', being condensed accounts from modern writers of the various continents, which then became the 6 volume *Modern Travels through Every Important Country of the Old and New Continent* (1823). The longer form of the second word, however, identifies this volume as: *Biographical Conversations on Celebrated Travellers Comprehending Distinct Narratives of their Personal Adventures* (1819).

2.12 Paley's Theology

William Paley, *Natural Theology, Or, Evidences Of The Existence And Attributes Of The Deity: Collected From The Appearences Of Nature* (1794; ^{6}1803).

William Paley (1743–1805), Archdeacon of Carlisle, was famous for this work of apologetics. He also agitated against the slave trade (1789), and was keenly interested in the role of the law, writing a tome on the magistracy (^{3}1838).[57] This book was amongst those circulated to prisoners.[58] His *Works*, noted to include *Natural Theology*, were on sale in Sydney in 1838.

2.13 Pearces Sermons 4 vols

Zachary Pearce, *Sermons* (1778) 4 vols.

Educated at Trinity College, Cambridge (1710), Zachary Pearce was inducted into the parish of St Martin's in the Field, where he was introduced to Queen Caroline. She liked Pearce, ordered him to preach before her, offered him preferment but died before she could help him in this. He became successively Bishop of Bangor (1748) and of Rochester (1755), with the deanery of Westminster.[59]

Moore had the four volume set of his *Sermons*, published in 1778.

2.14 A Treatise on the Police of the Metropolis

Patrick Colquhoun, *A Treatise on the Police of the Metropolis, explaining the Various Crimes and Misdemeanours which are at present felt as a pressure upon the Community, and suggesting Remedies for their Prevention, by a Magistrate* (1795; ^{7}1806).

Patrick Colquhoun (1745–1820) moved to London in 1789, and when the police system was reconstructed in 1792, through the endeavours of Henry Dundas, was appointed one of the new justices. He was a metropolitan police magistrate for the next 26 years (1792–1818), during which time he wrote tracts on trade, liquor traffic, poor relief, and police questions.[60]

This book suggests the appointment of a public prosecutor, the extension of the jurisdiction of stipendiary magistrates to the city proper, and the employment of convicts in productive labour. The work attracted the attention of government, even of the king, and went through several editions. The seventh edition proposed the establishment of a board of commissioners of police for the whole of London. The University of Glasgow awarded him a LLD for this work.

Since Thomas Moore was a magistrate in NSW, a colony founded to deal with the results of the English legal system, such topics would obviously have been of interest to him. With his interest in Law reform, charity, education for the poor, savings banks, and British colonies, Colquhoun could have even provided something of a role model for Moore, who displayed the same concerns at the other side of the world.

3. Page 3

3.1   Kelly's Astronomy

Patrick Kelly, *A Practical Introduction to Spherics and Nautical Astronomy; being an attempt to simplify those ... Sciences. Containing ... the discovery of a projection for clearing the lunar distances in order to find the Longitude at Sea; with a new method of calculating this ... problem* (1796).

Patrick Kelly (1756–1842), was a mathematician and astronomer. The first part of this book offers Kelly's attempt to simplify, and the second a selection of the chief propositions used in, nautical astronomy. Kelly also contributed 'the commercial and mathematical department' in D. Steel's, *Shipmaster's Assistant* (compare item 5.10, below).[61]

This work was published in 1796, the year Moore left the sea to become the Master Boat Builder of the colony. Perhaps its relevance to him lay in him moving towards becoming a ship owner at this time, or perhaps some 35 years associated with the sea had left him with an abiding interest in its associated arts.

There was an *Introduction to Astronomy* circulated amongst prisoners, which may have been Kelly's.[62]

3.2   Cottage Economy

William Cobbett, *Cottage economy* (1822).

William Cobbett (1762–1835)[63] was a writer with a colourful and controversial career. After serving in the army, he emigrated to Philadelphia, where he opened a bookshop (1796), selling violent loyalist literature, including the 'life of Thomas Paine'. His pamphleteering soon caused him trouble, and he left for England in June 1800. Since his fame preceded him, he was received warmly by the government party, but his writing would eventually cause him grief in England as well. Although he was not a great thinker, reacting mainly from 'feeling',[64] he nevertheless became the leading journalist for parliamentary reform. His *Cottage Economy* was one of many other writings displaying his bent as a 'moralist'.

3.3   Military Monitor 2 Vol

This could have been the American publication, *The Military Monitor and American Register. (Containing a correct record of the events of the war between the United States of America and the United Kingdom of Great Britain and Ireland. Declared on the 18th day of June, 1812)*. Volumes 1 and 2 of this weekly magazine were published from August 1812 through to 1814, and Moore's volumes were possibly the bound collection issued at the end of the year, as was the custom with other magazines at the time.

These were published at the time that Andrew received his commission, so his interest in military campaigns would have been high. They could therefore have been his own, or perhaps those of a step-father closely following things of importance in the young man's career.

3.4 Johnsons Dictionary

This would be the famous *English Dictionary* of Samuel Johnson (1709–1784), which he began in 1747, and published in 1755.[65] Tegg had a copy on sale in Sydney in 1838.

3.5 Methodist Magazine

There was an American publication by this name from 1818 to 1828, which was then continued as the *Methodist Magazine and Quarterly Review* (1830–40).

There was, however, an earlier English *Methodist Magazine* from 1798 to 1821, which contined the *Arminian or Methodist Magazine* begun by John Wesley (thus, vols. 21–44).

Moore does have a few American items on his shelf, but given the English connections of himself and also of the evangelicals and Methodists in the colony it seems more likely that it would be the English magazine.

3.6 Toons Magistrates Manual

William Toone, *The Magistrate's Manual: or, a Summary of the duties and powers of a justice of the peace, etc.* (1813). A 'second edition with very considerable additions' was published in 1817, and reprinted in 1821. The 'fourth edition, with considerable additions' appeared in 1828.

From a reference in Moore's Account book, we know that he purchased this volume for £2–12–6 from Mr Moffitt, Stationer, when he was on one of his many trips to Sydney, on 16th April 1835,[66] so his copy would have been the fourth edition.

3.7 Psalms of David by I[c]. Watts

Isaac Watts (1674–1748), *The Psalms Of David: Imitated In The Language Of The New Testament, And Applied To The Christian State And Worship* (1828). There is another edition in 1832.

Watts[67] grew up in a dissenting family, with his father being in prison for his religious opinions when Isaac was born, and later forced to hide in London for two years (1685). Isaac's early facility in poetry prompted a physician to offer to sponsor him to university, but he preferred to stay amongst the dissenters. By 1698 he was assistant pastor to the chapel at Mark Lane, and by 1702 he was pastor. He quickly found himself unequal to the task of sole minister, and employed an assistant. He was a very popular writer. At the beginning of the century, Calvin had laid a firm embargo on the use of music except metrical psalms, but this had already been broken by the obscure hymns of Mason, Kead, Barton and others. But 'the poetry of Watts took the religious world of dissent by storm. It gave utterance, till then unheard in England, to the spiritual emotions, in their contemplation of God's glory in nature, and his revelation in Christ, and made hymn-singing a fervid devotional force'. The success of Watts' hymns approached that of his new version of the Psalms. Even by the early years of the nineteenth century, the annual output of Watts' hymn books was still about 50,000.

His *Hymns* were published in 1707 (^{2}1709), and his *Psalms of David* in 1719. As time went on they were often bound together, giving a total of about 600 pieces in all. He also produced the first children's hymn book, *Divine Songs*, later renamed *Divine and Moral Songs*, which ran through 100 editions by the middle of the nineteenth century.

Watts was unfortunately caught up in the Arian controversy of this period. He was at the meeting at Salter's Hall, Exeter (1719), where he voted with the minority—as did Foster (see 9.1). Some say the last two years of his life he adopted a Unitarian position, but the relevant writings were destroyed by his literary trustees, Doddridge and Jennings, so it is impossible to be sure. Apart from this controversy, his theological position has been described as being a milder Calvinism.

3.8   Edmondsons Sermons

Jonathan Edmondson had two volumes of sermons: *Short Sermons On Important Subjects, Designed As A Companion For The*

Pious Of Every Denomination (1808). *Short Sermons on Important Subjects*, with sermons on the nature and operations of the Holy Spirit, which were combined and translated into Tamil in 1831 as *Five Sermons on the Nativity, the Crucifixion, the Resurrection, &c.*

Jonathan Edmondson (1766/7–1842) was converted at an early age and graduated M. A. with the idea of ordination into the Church of England. A member of a Methodist Society, he entered the itinerancy in 1786 and exercised an active circuit ministry for fifty years until ill health forced him into retirement. He was Secretary of the Wesleyan Methodist Missionary Society 1814–15 and President of Conference in 1818.[68]

3.9   *Evangelical Magazine*

The *Evangelical Magazine* published twenty volumes between 1793 and 1812, when it ceased publication. It then appears to have become *The Evangelical Magazine and Missionary Chronical*, which was published from 1813–1822, and began with volume 21.[69] G. Burder was its editor for a time.

Since this is listed as a separate item, it probably consists of a set or sets bound together, as was the custom of the day. Although the short title would be appropriate at any stage, if it indicates strictly that Moore owned magazine(s) from the earliest run, this would mean that he was reading this magazine, and presumably of evangelical sympathy, prior to 1812.

3.10   *Life of Mr Fletcher*

John Fletcher of Maddeley (1729–85), with Benson, strove to keep Methodism within the Church of England. In the Arminian-Calvinist dispute, he was a champion of Arminianism against the likes of A.M. Toplady. He was recognised increasingly as a saint in his lifetime and his reputation grew posthumously, exemplifying John Wesley's teaching on Christian Perfectionism.[70]

By Moore's day, there were two books written on Fletcher's life. In 1804, his friend and co-labourer Joseph Benson published *The

Life of the Rev. John W. de la Fléchère (1804). However, given that Moore's short title used the English version of Fletcher's name (and there were French titles on the shelf), his book was most probably the popular version of Fletcher's life penned by John Wesley himself, *A Short Account of the Life and Death of the Revd. John Fletcher* (1786). This version was also amongst the books circulated to the prisoners.[71]

3.11   Plutarchs Lives

Plutarch gained a wide influence due to the translations of him of the Renaissance, including Sir Thomas North's translation of the *Lives*. Rousseau was influenced by him. His influence diminished somewhat in the amongst 19th century scholars.[72]

Plutarch's Lives were amongst the books circulated to the prisoners at Wakefield.[73] Langhorne's *Plutarch's Lives* (8 vols) was advertised for sale in the *Sydney Gazette* on 30 December 1824 (as well as a 4 volume *Modern Plutarch*), and in 1838.

3.12   Life of Christ

Although writing *Lives of Christ* became, in time, a boom industry, at Moore's time there was a limited—but nevertheless substantial—number to choose from; for example, a *Life of Christ* was written by Christopher Sutton (1604), Valentin Weigel (1648), George Whitehead (1668), Jeremy Taylor (1678), John Parker (1704), Samuel Clark (1790), Joseph Milner (1808), James Gall (1825?), Edward Johnstone (1835), Thomas a Kempis (ET published by John Wesley, 1837), and John Fleetwood (?1837).

The *Life of Christ* 3 vols by Jeremy Taylor was on sale in Sydney 1838.

3.13   Don Quixote V–1–3–4

Miguel de Cervantes Saavedra (1547–1616), *The History And Adventures Of The Renowned Don Quixote*.

Many editions of Cervantes' classic were published in the late eighteenth and early nineteenth century. Since Moore's bookshelf contained volumes 1, 3, and 4, the edition in his possession needs to have (at least) four volumes, of which there were several: the third edition (London: T. Osborne, 1785); the fourth edition and the fifth edition (London: W. Strahan, 1770 and 1782); the Smollet translation, which included a life of Cervantes (Glasgow: Chapman & Lang, 1803); the edition of Mary Smirke's translation, embellished with engravings from pictures painted by Robert Smirke (London: T. Cadell & W. Davies, 1818). If Moore had mislaid volume 5 as well as volume 2, then his set could have been the five volume Cooke's edition (London: C. Cooke, 1799), which was also re-issued in four volumes (London: for C. Cooke, by Brimmer, 1801).

A four volume *Don Quixote* with coloured plates is amongst the 'valuable books' advertised for sale in the *Sydney Gazette* on 30 December 1824, as well as Miss Lennox's *Female Quixote*. In 1838 Tegg advertised a 2 volume copy, with plates by Cruickshank, as well as one abridged for children.

3.14 Miscellanies in prose & verse

Since it was quite common to publish 'miscellanies in prose and verse', it is impossible to identify this book with any certainty. Although there are other similar titles, those containing the exact expression as Moore's short title include: William King, *Miscellanies in Prose and Verse* (1709); Jonathan Swift, *Miscellanies In Prose And Verse* (1711); Richardson Pack, *A new collection of Miscellanies in prose and verse* (^{2}1725); Anna Williams [and] Samuel Johnson, *Miscellanies in prose and verse* (1766); E.A. Dutton (ed.), *Divine, Moral, And Historical Miscellanies, In Prose And Verse*, etc. 3 vol. (1761–63); Hester Chapone (Mulso), *Miscellanies in Prose and Verse. By Mrs. Chapone ... To Which Is Added, The Temple of Virtue, A Dream: Published By James Fordyce* (1775); Thomas Chatterton, *Miscellanies in prose and verse; by the supposed author of the poems published under the names of Rowley, Canning, &c* (1778); Milcah Martha Moore, compiler: Benjamin

Franklin, *Miscellanies, Moral and Instructive, in Prose and Verse; Collected from Various Authors, for the Use of Schools, and Improvement of Young Persons of Both Sexes* (1787); Francis Garden, *Miscellanies in Prose and Verse; including remarks on English Plays, Operas and Farces, And on a Variety of other Modern Publications.* (^{2}1792); [Author?], *Miscellanies, Moral And Instructive, In Prose And Verse* (1796); Isaac Wilson, *Miscellanies in Prose and Verse (etc.)* (1829).

3.15 Siblys Astronomy

Ebenezer Sibly (d. 1800) devoted himself to medicine and astrology.[74] He is still famous for the natal horoscope he cast of the United States, published in 1787 and still cited. He was a freemason, and his *The Celestial Science of Astrology* (1780) is important for masonic astronomy. He also published, *Uranoscopia: or the pure language of the Stars unfolded by the motion of the seven erratics, etc* (1780?), and *A New and Complete Illustration of the Occult Sciences. Or, the Art of foretelling future events and contingencies* (1790). None of his works, however, have 'astronomy' in the title, and so if Moore was referring to one of Ebenezer's works, he would have had to have mistaken astrology for astronomy.

On the other hand, Ebenezer's brilliant brother Manoah (1757–1840),[75] a linguist and Swedenborgian preacher, published a translation of Placidus Titis under the title *Astronomy and Elementary Philosophy, translated from the Latin of Placidus de Titus [sic] ... to which are added, introductory notes and observations, with a concise method of judging horary questions ... the whole carefully revised by M. Sibly* (1789). He also revised Whalley's translation of Ptolemy's Quadripartus, which could conceivably be summarised as 'astronomy'; *The Quadripartite; or, four books concerning the influenceof the stars* (1786).

3.16 Life of Mr Whit[e]field

George Whitefield has been described as an 'Anglican clergyman and Methodist preacher'.[76] He was a member of Wesley's Holy

Club in Oxford, found personal assurance of salvation in 1735 and was ordained in 1736 after which his preaching was met with instant success and attended by great crowds of listeners. He began preaching out of doors in 1739 and encouraged the Wesleys to do the same. He continued preaching in England and America for the next thirty years. His friendship with Jonathan Edwards and the Tennent brothers in America strengthened his Calvinistic convictions which eventually led to a break in his friendship with the Wesleys, and the eventual division of Methodism into Wesleyan (Arminian) and Calvinistic branches. Grundy comments that 'throughout his life it was he, rather than the Wesleys, who was the archetypal Methodist in the public mind'.

George Whitfield wrote his own memoirs, and the life of this famous eighteenth century preacher of the evangelical revival also attracted several other biographers.

John Gillies published *Memoirs of the Life of the Rev. G. Whitefield* in 1772, and this work went through several editions in Moore's lifetime (1798, 1801, 1811, 1812, 1837, 1838).

George Whitefield's own, *An Authentic Memoir Of The Life Of The Late Rev. G. Whitefield* was later published and distributed by the Religious Tract Society. This not only accounts for it being distributed amongst the prisoners,[77] but, given Moore's involvement with this group, it probably identifies this as the volume on his shelf.

4. Page 4

4.1 James's Russia-Poland &c 2 vol

John Thomas James, *Journal Of A Tour In Germany, Sweden, Russia, and Poland, During The Years 1813 And 1814* (1816), subsequent editions in 2 vols.: 1817 and 1819).

John Thomas James (1786–1828), was educated until he was twelve at Rugby, where his father Thomas was headmaster, then switching to Charterhouse (1794–1804). After graduating from Christ Church, Oxford, he went abroad, visiting the courts of

Berlin, Stockholm, St Petersburg; and then Moscow, Poland and Vienna. On his return, he published *Journal of a Tour.* In 1816, he studied painting in Italy, returned and took Holy Orders. He wrote on Theology and Art (1825, 1826, 1827), before being appointed to the Bishopric of Calcutta to succeed Heber. He arrived January 1828, but by August he had died at sea whilst on a voyage for his health.[78]

4.2   Hollands Travels

In his mature years, Sir Henry Holland (17881873) was a physician to royalty, including to Queen Victoria, and one of the best known men in London society. At the beginning of his career, immediately after graduating MD from Edinburgh, he had travelled in Europe for a year and a half (1812–1813), the account of which he published in 1815: *Travels in the Ionian Isles, Albania, Thessaly, Macedonia, &c, during 1812 and 1813* (1815; ²1819). He maintained an interest in travel and continued to make long tours up until his last days.

4.3   Fall of Jerusalem

Henry Hart Milman, *The Fall Of Jerusalem: A Dramatic Poem* (1820; ⁶1831).

After an Oxford education, Henry Hart Milman (1791–1868) was elected the professor of poetry at Oxford, to be succeeded by Keble. He published *The Fall of Jerusalem* in 1820, which forcibly depicted the conflict between Jewish conservatism and new truth. In 1827, he delivered the Bampton Lectures, in which he addressed the evidence for Christianity from the character of the apostles. These lectures were rather unoriginal. Three years later, however, he wrote *The History of the Jews* (1830), which has been described as 'epoch-making', and which spread so much consternation amongst the orthodox that the series of which the book was the first number ceased publication. Amongst the opponents were Bishop Mant, and John Henry Newman. Milman went on to become the dean of St Pauls Cathedral.[79]

4.4 Stebbings Sermons V, 2, 4

There were three generations of Stebbings with the name Henry;[80] two of them preached at Gray's Inn and had published volumes of sermons.[81] Since Moore had vols. 2 and 4, we are looking for at least a 4 volume work, although I have been unable to discover one.

The elder Henry published *Sermons on Practical Christianity* (1759, ²1760) 2 vols.

Henry Stebbing (1687–1763) was well known as a controversial champion of Church of England orthodoxy. He wrote against George Whitefield, Benjamin Hoadly, Bishop of Bangor, and especially against Warburton. His *A Caution against Religious Delusion. A Sermon On The New Birth: Occasioned By The Pretensions Of The Methodists* (1739) took on the Methodists in general, and in *Christianity Justified upon the Scripture Foundation* (1750), the Deists. He was chaplain to the king (1732), archdeacon of Wiltshire (1735), Chancellor of Sarum (1739), and rector of Redenhall in Norfolk (1748–1763).

Henry Stebbing (1716–1787) was the son of the above, also a preacher at Gray's Inn in the place of his father. His sermons were published, in turn, by his son—the third Henry Stebbings, a barrister under the title: *Sermons on Practical Subjects. To Which Is Prefixed Some Account Of The Character Of The Author, By His Son Henry Stebbing* (1788–1790), 3 Vols.

There was also a Henry Stebbing (1799–1883) born in Norfolk to a different family, who was a poet, historian, editor of *the Athenaeum* and about 30 volumes of 'Sacred Classics' (on sale in Sydney, 1838). He was also a preacher, being a moderate churchman with leanings towards evangelicalism.[82] He published several volumes of sermons, although one is definitely too late for Moore's interest (*Sixteen Sermons*, 1862), *Sermons* (1833) and *Sermons on the Resurrection* (1835), are within his time frame.

4.5 Appletons Sermons 2 Vol

Although Jesse Appleton published several individual sermons, there was no collection published under this title. There are,

CHAPTER 7 ~ *Thomas Moore's Bookshelf* [145]

however, two works by Jesse Appleton, both titles containing 'sermons', but both rather unnaturally short-titled by that word.

Jesse Appleton, *Lectures Delivered At Bowdoin College And Occasional Sermons* (1822).

Jesse Appleton, *The Works Of Rev. Jesse Appleton ... Embracing His Course Of Theological Lectures, His Academic Addresses And A Selection From His Sermons: With A Memoir Of His Life And Character* (A. S. Packard, ed.; 1836–37). 2 vols.

Since Moore lists his copy being '2 vols.', this would identify it as a copy of Appleton's *Works*. If this is the volume, it would have arrived in Moore's possession fairly late in his life.

Jesse Appleton (1772–1819),[83] a Congregationalist minister, became second president of Bowdoin College, Brunswick, Maine, in 1807. Attempting to instill what he called 'piety' into Bowdoin students, he served in that office until his death, probably from tuberculosis, in 1819. His appointment came after ten years of service to a Hampton, New Hampshire, parish. A 1792 graduate of Dartmouth College, Appleton was an experienced teacher and orator; his Bowdoin College addresses were collected and printed in 1820. Appleton married Elizabeth Means, they had three daughters and two sons who survived infancy. Their daughter, Jane, became the wife of Franklin Pierce (Bowdoin 1824), fourteenth president of the United States.[84]

4.6 *Regulations, & Orders for the Army*

Thomas was a member of the Militia, in his early days of Sydney at least. These bodies were also governed by published regulations, such as *Regulations under which the several Corps of Local Militia in Great Britain are to be assembled for training and exercise in the year 1810* (1810). Moore's short title, however, specifically mentions the regular army, which published many sets of *Regulations & Orders*, and so it is most likely that this book belonged to his step-son Andrew, of the Royal Engineers. The volume closest to Moore's short title was *General Regulations and Orders for the Army* (1811), published just before Andrew received his commission, and probably most useful for him from that time on.

4.7 Lives of Hale, Hammond

This was the 1806 republication of two earlier works: John Fell, *The Life of Hammond* (1661, ²1662), and Gilbert Burnet, *The Life and Death of Sir Matthew Hale* (1682).

Educated at Eton and Oxford, Henry Hammond (1605–1660) was ordained in 1629, and in 1633 took the living of Penshurst, Kent, where he supervised the education of his nephew, William Temple. In the Civil War he assisted the king against parliament, and spent a period of exile in Oxford, and was imprisoned in 1647, although his opponents held him in high esteem. He was kindly and benevolent, 'from his youth spent much of his time in secret devotion', and practised self-denial almost to the point of asceticism. He wrote the preface to *The Whole Duty of Man* and was clearly familiar with its author. Fell's *Life of Hammond* has been called 'one of the most charming pieces of biography in the language'.[85]

When his parents died early, Matthew Hale (1609–1676) was brought up under the guardianship of puritan Anthony Kingscote. After studying law, he was involved in several high profile trials and became a prominent judge, Lord Chief Justice of England, and counsel for Archbishop Laud. Elected to parliament in 1654, he spoke in favour of subordinating the single person to the parliament, but this was over-ruled by Cromwell's argument that there ought to be a Protector. As a member of the committee for religion, he advocated the old ecclesiastical polity against presbyterianism, yet he also attempted to introduce a bill for comprehension of presbyterians. He was friendly with Richard Baxter, as well as other divines such as Tillotson, Ussher, Wilkins, and Seldon. 'Hale remained throughout his life attached to his early puritanism. He was a regular attendant at church, morning and evening, on Sunday, and also gave up a portion of the day to prayer and meditation, besides expounding the sermon to his children'. He was an extreme anti-ritualist, did not tolerate music, objected to singing, and practised strict plainness in dress. He was strictly orthodox, yet impatient with the subtleties of the theologians.[86]

Hale and Hammond was amongst those circulated to the prisoners.[87]

4.8   Bowdlers Selections

Thomas Bowdler, *A Short Introduction to a Selection of Chapters from the Old Testament for the use of the Church of England Sunday School Society in Swansea* (1822), reprinted as *Select Chapters from the Old Testament with Short Introduction* (1823).

Thomas Bowdler (1754–1825) was born to a pious mother, Elizabeth, who wrote *Practical observations on the Book of Revelation* (1800). He trained as a doctor, but came home after a period of travel with a strong aversion to his profession. He settled in London, where he became acquainted with Bishops Hinchcliffe and Porteus, Mrs Carter, Mrs Chapone, and Mrs Hannah More. Characteristic of this circle, he got involved in charity work, and prison reform. His nephew, John, was also an evangelical, associated with the Clapham sect and a writer for the Christian Observer under the pseudonym 'Crito'.[88]

In 1818 he edited the *Family Shakespeare*, which omitted expressions that could not be read with propriety in the family—his name thus giving rise to the expression 'to bowdlerize'. He also prepared a version of Gibbon's *History of the Rise and Fall of the Roman Empire* (1826) along the same lines, which he completed just before his death. Applying similar principles to the OT, his *Select Chapters from the Old Testament* (1822), omitted passages deemed to be of an immoral or irreligious nature.[89]

Selections was amongst those books circulated to prisoners.[90]

4.9   The Whole Duty of Man

Moore had two books with this title on his shelf (see also 6.11). These may have been duplicate copies, but it is also possible that he had two different volumes by the same short title, in which case one could have been an important 'enlightenment' work and the other one promoting Christian piety.

The enlightenment volume was that by the German jurist, Samuel, Freiherr von Pufendorf (1632–1694), best known for his defence of natural law, *The Whole Duty of Man according to the Law of Nature* (1698). In this work, Pufendorf departed from the medieval theological approach and based natural law on man's existence as a social being, arguing that every individual has a right to equality and freedom. He then derived his views of civil, penal and constitutional law from this notion. The eighteenth century saw a great number of editions of Pufendorf's works, with John Locke and J.-J. Rousseau recommending that they be be read by young people.[91] Pufendorf would bring 'leading edge' thinking to Moore about issues of relevance to his role as magistrate in a new colony (i.e. law, society, equality, freedom, and civil, penal, constitutional law).

The popular Christian book of this title was one of those eventually distributed by the Religious Tract Society, namely: *The Practice Of Christian Graces, Or, The Whole Duty Of Man: Laid Down In A Plaine And Familiar Way For The Use Of All, But Especially The Meanest Reader: Divided Into XVII Chapters, One Whereof Being Read Every Lords Day, The Whole May Be Read Over Thrice In The Year, Necessary For All Families: With Private Devotions For Several Occasions* ... (1658).

This anonymous work was the first of a series of devotional books eventually collected together in a volume of *Works* (1687). Although disputed,[92] the authorship has traditionally been ascribed to Richard Allestree (1619–1681), in collaboration with Bishop John Fell. Allestree took arms for the king during the English Civil War and served under Sir John Biron (1641). He later took holy orders and became censor of his college, Christ Church, Oxford, being expelled by the parliamentarians in 1648. Afterwards he became Canon of Christ Church and DD (1660), regius professor of divinity at Oxford (1663–79), and provost of Eton College (1665).[93]

The volume spawned a stream of other works in a similar style, including *The New Whole Duty of Man* (1747, 1808, 1819). On the other hand, in a letter in the *Daily Advertiser*, George Whitefield attacked a work of this name, provoking a subsequent interchange.

This book was on Green's list of best-sellers. Chaplain Richard Johnson brought 2 copies of *The Whole Duty of Man* as he commenced his ministry in NSW, and it was also circulated in UK prisons.[94]

4.10   Edmon[d]sons Scripture Views of the Heavenly World

Scripture Views of the Heavenly World (1835) is another work by Jonathan Edmondson, the Methodist preacher discussed above (3.8). Given its date, it appears Thomas's careful preparations for his own death, and perhaps Rachel's, included some reading on the Christian's blessed hope.

4.11   Flavels Mystery of Providence

Mystery of Providence (1677), was written by John Flavel (?1630–1691), an English Dissenting minister, who was ejected from Dartmouth in 1662, but continued to minister there secretly. Amongst his many other works, he published *Husbandry Spiritualised* (1669), and *Navigation Spiritualized* (1677), presumably both of interest to Moore, although not on his shelf. These, along with *Mystery*, were published in a volume of *Select Works* appearing in 1823 and 1834.[95]

4.12   The Book of Nature &

The phrase 'book of nature' appears as part of quite a number of titles. In several of these the phrase could be legitimately taken as the short title, such as George Sikes, *The book of nature translated and epitomiz'd* (1667), or *The Book of Nature, a Poem*, sometimes attributed to William Mason (1771).

Perhaps Moore's ampersand (&) indicates a much longer title, such as that by Jan Swammerdam, *The Book of Nature, or the History of Insects: Reduced to Distinct Classes, Confirmed by*

Particular Instances, and Illustrated (1758); or William Jones, *The Book Of Nature; Or, The True Sense Of Things, Explained And Made Easy To The Capacities Of Children*. Part 1 (1788), and Part 2 (1792), which ran to 12 edtions by 1824, and continued to be published well beyond then, including in an edition by the SPCK.

William Jones (1726–1800) was a life-long friend of Bishop George Horne, both were students of John Hutchinson. His vicarage in Nayland became the centre of a circle which afterwards expanded into the high-church party of the early 19th century. Jones was one of the most prominent churchmen of his day, and part of a group that forms the link between the non-jurors and the later Oxford school. He spoke against the Methodists.[96]

Another longer title is that of John Toogood, *The Book Of Nature: A Discourse On Some Of Those Instances Of The Power, Wisdom, And Goodness Of God* (3rd ?1798; 4th 1802). Appended to this volume was a dissertation on 'the duty of mercy, and sin of cruelty to brutes'.

Although continuing to practice as a medical doctor, John Mason Good had a prodigious literary output. His *The Book Of Nature* (1826; ³1834) 3 vols, resulted from three courses of lectures delivered at the Surrey Institution in 1811–1812, which can be classified under biology, botany, and animal economy. Although growing up in a congregationalist household, he became a Socinian (=unitarian) from the time he settled in London (1784) but was later converted to evangelical Christianity. He had met Samuel Marsden in January 1808, after he had begun to have serious doubts about his unitarianism, and was impressed by Marsden's character of life.[97] At a later time, he frequently acted as Marsden's advocate in important circles in England. In his later years he was keenly attached to the evangelical cause, active in the Church Missionary Society, and corresponded with Marsden about the mission to New Zealand.[98]

W. Hutton, *The Book of Nature Laid Open, in a popular survey of the phenomena of the universte* (²1821) a work of physics, or natural philosophy.

CHAPTER 7 ~ *Thomas Moore's Bookshelf* [151]

The astronomical work by John Stewart, the traveller, *The Book of Nature ... London, in the 7000th year of Astronomical History, from the Chinese Tables* (?1818).

There was a *Book of Nature* circulating at Wakefield prison.[99]

4.13 *Observations on the Conversation [sic] &c of St Paul*

G. Lyttelton, *Observations On The Conversion And Apostleship Of St. Paul. In A Letter To Gilbert West, Esq.* (1747, and subsequently more than 14 editions).

Baron George Lyttelton (1709–1773) was a politician with family connections with William Pitt and the Grenvilles. He was a man of 'strong religious convictions and respectable talents'. He enjoyed at one time a considerable reputation as an author, but is regarded as never being original.[100] Gilbert West (1703–1756) was an author and poet, who is said to have influenced the religious views of both Pitt and Lyttelton.[101] This may explain why Lyttleton addressed this work to him. It was a work of apologetics, and was frequently attached to West's *A Defence Of The Christian Revelation* (1748, 1785) and to Sherlock's *Proofs Of Christianity* (1769).

This would be the *Letter to Gilbert West* that circulating at Wakefield prison.[102]

5. Page 5

5.1 *A Selection from Bp Horns Commentary on the Book of Psalms*

George Horne, *Commentary On The Book Of Psalms. Selections. A Key To The Book Of Psalms* (1798).

This was the shorter version of Horne's, *A Commentary On The Book Of Psalms. In Which Their Literal Or Historical Sense, As They Relate To King David, And The People Of Israel, Is Illustrated; And Their Application To Messiah, To The Church, And To Individuals, As Members Thereof, Is Pointed Out: With A View To Render The Use Of*

The Psalter Pleasing And Profitable To All Orders And Degrees Of Christians (1771). 2 vols.

George Horne (1730–1792), spent most of his life in Oxford, firstly as a student, then as president of Magdalen College (1768), and Vice Chancellor of the university (1776). He was made dean of Canterbury in 1790, but suffered from bad health, becoming Bishop of Norwich in June 1790, shortly before dying in 1792. Like many earnest clergy of the day, Horne was charged with Methodism, but he was distinctly what would be called now a High Churchman. He protested publicly against those who learn their theology from Whitefield and Wesley, rather than from the great divines of the Church. He nevertheless had a great deal of sympathy for the Methodists, and would not forbid John Wesley from preaching in his diocese.[103]

His *Commentary on the Psalms* (1771) occupied about twenty years of his life. Containing the text of the authorised version, the *Commentary* was partly exegetical and partly devotional. It set forward the clear principle that most of the Psalms are messianic and so they could not be understood without reference to the Messiah.

The influence of the *Commentary* was extended by others 'borrowing' from it. John Gillies' edition of the Psalms for the Church of Scotland extracted Horne's 'notes devotional and practical' (1786, 1796, 1798), and Richard Mant transferred Horne's preface almost *en bloc* to his annotated Book of Common Prayer.

The *Commentary on the Psalms* was amongst those circulated to the prisoners at Wakefield prison was probably his.[104] His *Discourses* (2 vol.) were being sold in Sydney in 1824 and his *Commentary* in 1838.

5.2   The Lives of Hooker – Herbert & Sanderson

Izaak Walton, *The Lives Of Mr Richard Hooker, Mr George Herbert And Dr Robert Sanderson*. There were also several later editions, such as those of 1824 and 1825.[105]

CHAPTER 7 ~ *Thomas Moore's Bookshelf* [153]

Famous among fishermen for his *The Compleat Angler*, Isaak Walton (1593–1683) published a *Life* of John Donne (1640), Sir Henry Wotton (1651), Richard Hooker (1665) and George Herbert (1670), all four of which were published together in 1670. His *Life of Robert Sanderson* followed in 1678.[106] Eventually, all five *Lives* were collected together (e.g. 1825, 1854), but the edition on Moore's shelf was that containing only Hooker, Herbert and Sanderson published in 1819.

Richard Hooker (1554–1600), 'while not departing significantly from the essentials of Reformed theology, Hooker's positions directly challenged some of the other positions of the puritan movement. he was perhaps the first to argue that the Elizabethan settlement was not merely a compromise of the time but the ideal form for the Church of England. He criticized overemphasis on preaching and placed greater emphasis on the sacraments and on liturgical prayer and ceremonies, in many ways anticipating the views that would later be expressed by bishops such as William Laud'.[107]

Educated at Cambridge, George Herbert (1593–1633) was a classical scholar and accomplished musician. He attracted the notice of Lancelot Andrewes, the Bishop of Winchester. He defended the established church and declared himself against puritanism early in his career, although this work was not published until thirty years after his death. After being a public orator, he was ordained deacon (1626) to a parish in Huntingdonshire, then Wiltshire, where he was priested (1630). He wrote a lot of his poems here, sadly dying of tuberculosis only three years later. His wife took his manuscripts, which were later burned when the parliamentary forces set fire to the house they were in.[108]

Robert Sanderson (1587–1663) was an episcopalian who remained Calvinist in his soteriology throughout his life, despite being urged to modify his position by various Arminians. He was a chaplain to Charles I, on the recommendation of Laud. In 1642 he became the regius professor of divinity at Oxford, but did not take it up until 1646. He refused to take the covenant and was ousted from his seat in Oxford (1648), also being seized and held hostage for a puritan minister for a time. At the Restoration he was reinstated to Oxford, before becoming bishop of Lincoln for three years (1660–1663). He was the moderator of the Savoy Conference, and he contributed to the revision of the Book of Common Prayer. The 'Prayer for all Conditions of Men' and the 'General Thanksgiving' have been ascribed to him, probably wrongly, but the second Preface ('It hath been the burden ...' was certainly his.[109]

This book was amongst those circulated to prisoners, as were the separate *Lives* of Hooker and Herbert.[110]

5.3 A Summary of the Principal Evidences of the Christian Revelation (2)

Beilby Porteus, *A Summary Of The Principal Evidences For The Truth And Divine Origin Of The Christian Revelation. Designed Chiefly For The Use Of Young Persons* (1800; then 1801, and by 1835 it had reached its 15th edition).

After being educated at Christ's College, Cambridge (1752) and ordained in 1757, Beilby Porteus (1731–1809) attracted notice through a university sermon he preached in 1761, and in the following year was appointed domestic chaplain to Thomas Secker, Archbishop of Canterbury, then rector of Lambeth (1767), and chaplain to George III (1769). He was Bishop of Chester 1776–87; and of London 1787–1808. Porteus supported the rising Evangelical party in both Sees, although not identifying himself with their more Calvinistic doctrines. He was sometimes called a Methodist, but he was strict in enforcing Church principles, and refused to call himself by any party name. He was a friend of Hannah More, worked against slavery, supported the Sunday schools, instituted a fund for poorer clergy, he was an early patron of the Church Missionary Society, and joined the British and Foreign Bible Society as Vice President.[111]

5.4 Family prayer for every day

There were many books of family prayers, but three best suit Moore's short-title:

Family Prayers for Every Day of the Week compiled from the Authorised Forumularies of the Reformed Episcopal Church of England and Ireland (1824), by one 'Clericus'. The same year, Lady Lucy E.G. Whitmore produced her *Family Prayers for Everyday of the Week, selected from various portions of the Holy Bible* (1824). The year after these two came *Family Prayers for Every Day of the Week* (1825), by Henry William Powlett (1797–1866), Baron Bayning.

Although nothing with Moore's short title is on the prison lists, family prayer itself was certainly encouraged (presumably with a future application!), with *The Duty of Family Prayer* being found amongst those circulated to the prisoners at Wakefield prison.[112]

5.5 The Claim of the Estab^{sd} Church

There were several works published which suit this short title. Several were sermons, such as that of Robert Housman (?1816) and William Hodgson Cole (1827), and also the eight sermons making up G. Faussett's Bampton Lectures in 1820.

Robert Meek's, *The Claims of the Established Church of England to the attachment and conformity of the Christians of this country* (SPCK, 1836), was possibly published too late to attract Moore's interest, as was David Monypenny, *The Claims Of The Established Church Of Scotland On The Country, To Promote Its Extension In The Present Crisis: Considered And Enforced On Legal And Constitutional Principles* (1837).

The best candidate, in terms of its popularity at least, would be that of John Bowles: *The Claims Of The Established Church: Considered As An Apostolical Institution, And As An Authorized Interpreter Of Holy Scripture* (1815, 1817; new edition: 1821, 1828; new edition: 1830).

John Bowles (1751-1819), was 'a campaigning barrister active in High Church causes such as relief for the Scottish episcopal church in the 1790s, the SPCK and church education'. In this work he charged that the Protestant Church had set up their authority as the infallible guide to the Scripture as had Rome, with even worse consequences. Alluding to the Unitarian movement of the 1770s and 80s, Bowles laid the blame at the feet of the advocacy of private judgement and *sola scriptura*.[113]

5.6 Baxters Sts Rest

Richard Baxter, *The Saints Everlasting Rest, Or, A Treatise Of The Blessed State Of The Saints In Their Enjoyment Of God In Glory: Wherein Is Shewed Its Excellency And Certainty; The Misery Of Those That Lose It; The Way To Attain It, Assurance Of It; And How To Live In The Continual Delightful Fore-Taste Of It, By The Help Of Meditation / Written By The Author For His Own Use, In The Time Of His Languishing, When God Took Him Off From All Publick Employment, And Afterwards Preached In His Weekly Lecture* (1649; published by RTS in 1831). This was sometimes (e.g. 1814) bound with his 'A Call to the Unconverted'.

Richard Baxter (1615–1691)[114] was a prominent pastor and author, who did much to shape 17th century Puritanism by his powerful personality and writing. He never accepted any denominational label, and is best described as a puritan Arminian. His theology was influential in the next generation of non-conformists. *The Saints Everlasting Rest* was a best-selling volume, according to Green, with 12 editions by 1729. It was owned by Jeake, amongst the books circulated to prisoners,[115] and on sale in Sydney in 1838.

5.7 Cottage Sermons

There are two possibilities here. Charles Davy, the Curate of Hampstead Norris, Berks., published, *Cottage Sermons; Or, Short Discourses Addressed To Plain People; Being Principally Designed For The Use Of Pious Cottagers, And Those In Humble Life, Etc.* (1823, 1837).

But given Moore's connection with the Religious Tract Society, it more probably their publication: George Burder, *Cottage Sermons ... Short And Plain Discourses, Etc.* (3 vol.; 1826–28). George Burder (1752–1832)[116] was brought up by a mother who was converted by George Whitefield's ministry. He himself was much affected by the preaching of Romaine and Whitefield, and, in fact, he reported George Whitefield's last two sermons for the press in September 1769. He was an engraver by trade, who took to preaching in 1776 after being noticed by Fletcher of Madelay and encouraged to do so. He had no education for the ministry, but was ordained to a congregation at Lancaster (1778), while also travelling to preach in England and Wales. He then pastored a congregation at Coventry (1783), there initiating Sunday Schools (1785) and encouraging involvement in foreign mission. In 1799 he suggested forming the Religious Tract Society. After moving to Fetter Lane, London (1803–32), he became the secretary of the London Missionary Society (1803–27), of which he was a founder (1795). He was also a founder of the British and Foreign Bible Society (1804). These impeccable qualifications show him to be firmly part of the evangelical revival. He edited various devotional works, including a version of Bunyan's *Pilgrim's Progress* for children and his *Holy War*, and theological works (such as several abridgements of John Owen), collected hymns to supplement those of Isaac Watts (as was the pattern at this time), and served as the editor of the *Evangelical Magazine.*

After previously publishing several volumes of *Village Sermons* (1797, then seven more volumes until 1820), and *Sea Sermons* (1821, see below 6.12), Burder published *Cottage Sermons* (1826) with the Religious Tract Society, containing 24 of his own sermons and another eleven abridged sermons from Joseph Milner.

This book circulated amongst the prisoners at several facilities.[117]

5.8   Enfields Speaker

William Enfield, *The Speaker, Or, Miscellaneous Pieces, Selected*

From The Best English Writers, … To Which Is Prefixed An Essay: On Elocution (1774).

William Enfield (1741–1797),[118] divine and author, received his earliest instruction under Rev. William Hextall, a dissenting minister. He was himself ordained to a congregation of protestant dissenters in Liverpool, then Warrington (1770) and Norwich (1785). He was an influential writer and a persuasive preacher. *The Speaker*, which was re-published every couple of years, contained instruction on elocution.

5.9   *Memoirs of the Manner Of the present Ages*

There is apparently no book published under this title, but if Moore's short title refers to the subtitle, it would be the novel by Captain Thomas Ashe, *The Liberal Critic, or Memoirs of Henry Percy. Conveying a Correct Estimate of the Manners and Principles of the Present Times* (1812), 3 Vols.

Captain Thomas Ashe was a sort of literary Jack-of-all-Trades, and author of some twenty works on various subjects. He was of an Irish family, and died in poverty about 1831.[119] John Arden's radio play, Poor Tom, Thy Horn is Dry (2003), based upon Ashe's own *Memoirs*, depicts the Captain as a soldier, clerk, tradesman, teacher, sailor, murderer, embezzler, explorer, impersonator, writer of political propaganda, hack journalist, plagiarist, blackmailer and more.[120]

The *Liberal Critic*, of which apparently only one copy survives (in the British Library),[121] was a satire told through the mouth of Henry Percy. The reviewer in *Monthly Review* was critical of this work:[122] 'A self-named *Liberal Critic* here makes a dull story the vehicle for conveying his opinions on religion and politics; and he attacks both the established clergy and sectaries with an intemperance which must prevent us from acquiescing in his assumed title. Some parts of the work are offensive to delicacy, and it is throughout occasionally ungrammatical and vulgar'. There is much in the book to distress its readers at the time. The novel is critical of orthodox Christianity, university education, and the established Church and its practices. While explicitly attacking 'enthusiastic', quietistic, and evangelical Christianity at various points, the novel endorses a religion based on the contemplation of nature, and the worship of a non-Trinitarian God, not solely through Jesus Christ. This Unitarian perspective places this book at loggerheads with most of the other Christian books on Moore's shelf.

Why would Moore have this novel on his shelf? The hero of the novel, 'Henry Percy' was connected to the ducal family hailing from Alnwick, Northumberland, many of whom had shared our hero's name. This was the same area in which Thomas grew up and in which many of his family still resided. Perhaps this 'local interest' may partially account for his possessing this work, although the hero never actually travels to this area and little is said about it.

Perhaps there was more to it as well. Although the book is cast as a novel, Ashe explicitly distances himself from the usual task of the novel to provide destraction, aiming to 'correct and strengthen the judgment, to enlarge the faculties of the mind, and to raise the soul to a free and generous way of thinking'.[123] Even though Moore would probably disagree that the end of such a process ought to be Unitarianism (as the novel suggests), he would certainly have shared the aim of improvement through reading and thoughtfulness about life, the world, and God. The book sits nicely within the broad eclectic collection on Moore's shelf, which suggests a thoughtfulness that is not afraid to think along with those of alternative viewpoints.[124]

5.10   The Elements & practice of Rigging And Seamanship 2 v.
Partly based upon Jacques Bourdé de Villehuet's "Le manœuvrier", David Steel's, *The Elements And Practice Of Rigging And Seamanship*, etc. (2 vols.; 1794), became a standard work amongst shipwrights. It contained detailed instructions and diagrams relating to rigging, masts and remasting, and a glossary of all the relevant terms.

5.11 A Collection of Voyages

In an age of seafaring, it is not surprising that there are a number of possibilities for this title. Probably the most famous was that of the two Churchill's:

Awnsham Churchill (d. 1728) and John Churchill (fl. 1695), *A Collection Of Voyages And Travels: Some Now First Printed From Original Manuscripts, Others Translated Out Of Foreign Languages … To Which Are Added Some Few That Have Formerly Appear'd In English, But Do Now For Their Excellency And Scarceness Deserve To Be Reprinted. In Four Volumes. With A General Preface, Giving An Account Of The Progress Of Navigation From Its First Beginning To The Perfection It Is In Now, &C* (1704).

The Churchills were booksellers on Paternoster Row. They put together their collection in 1704, selling the 4 volume work to subscribers. John Locke was involved in this collection. Two more volumes came out in 1732, when the first 4 were also re-issued. The third edition, dated 1744–46, also had six volumes, and another edition was put out by Thomas Osborne in 1752, whose two further volumes became vols. 7 & 8 of Churchill.[125]

Kerr's volume is a little broader than suggested by Moore's short title: Robert Kerr (1755–1813), *A General History And Collection Of Voyages And Travels, Arranged In Systematic Order: Forming A Complete History Of The Origin And Progress Of Navigation, Discovery And Commerce, By Sea And Land, From The Earliest Ages To The Present Time* (1816).[126] Kerr compiled the first ten volumes of this eighteen volume work.[127]

There were several collections of particular interest to someone in Australia. The first, a translation from Constantin de Renneville's compilation, told the story of the Dutch East Indies:

A Collection Of Voyages Undertaken By The Dutch East-India Company: For The Improvement Of Trade And Navigation …: Together With An Historical Introduction, Giving An Account Of The Rise, Establishment And Progress Of That Great Body/Translated Into English, And Illustrated With Several Charts (1703).

The second set of books included the voyages of William Dampier:

A Collection Of Voyages: In Four Volumes ...: Illustrated With Maps And Draughts: Also Several Birds, Fishes, And Plants, Not Found In This Part Of The World: Curiously Engraven On Copper-Plates (1729).

The third also focused upon the southern hemisphere:

Charles de Brosses, *A Collection Of Voyages To The Southern Hemisphere* (1788).

The fourth was devoted to the great South Seas navigator, so inspirational to future sea-farers, Captain James Cook:

A Collection Of Voyages Round The World, Performed By Royal Authority: Containing A Complete Historical Account Of Captain Cook's First, Second, Third And Last Voyages ...: To Which Are Added Genuine Narratives Of Other Voyages Of Discovery Round The World ... Including The Substance Of The Most Remarkable And Important Travels And Journeys, Which Have Been Undertaken At Various Times To The Different Quarters Of The World, The Whole Comprehending A Full Account Of Whatever Is Curious, Entertaining, And Useful ... / Compiled From The Authentic Journals Of Several Principal Officers And Other Gentlemen ... Who Sailed In The Various Ships (1790).

Amongst the books circulated to prisoners, there are quite a few *Voyages*, including *Cook's Voyages*,[128] which was also on sale in Sydney 1838.

6. Page 6

6.1 New South Wales Calendar for 1836

The *New South Wales Calendar & General Post Office* Directory was published from 1832. The title of this work is self-explanatory, but, as with the other calendrical material (cf. 6.9; 7.10; 8.12) on the bookshelf, we can ask why this year was of particular note for Thomas. Nothing especially stands out, however, apart from his name appearing in the directory, and a description of his Liverpool home as the house 'most particularly worthy of notice' in the midst of a town which 'has a straggling appearance, but, on the whole, very clean and pleasant' (p.20). But both these items have regularly appeared since the 1832 Calendar, so perhaps the presence of this volume on the shelf is simply random.

6.2 A Guide to the Receiving the Lord's Supper

Theophilus Dorrington, *A Familiar Guide To The Right And Profitable Receiving Of The Lord's Supper* (1695, ²1698, ⁷1718).

Theophilus Dorrington (d. 1715) was the son of a non-conformist, who was educated for ministry amongst the dissenters, began with them, and then deserted them. In 1698 he took Holy Orders in the established church, taking out an MA from Oxford in 1710. The other devotional work he wrote was *Family Devotions for Sunday Evenings* (1693–1695), 4 vols. The *Familiar Guide* was also translated into French (1699), and by 1718 had run into 7 editions.[129]

This book was on Green's list, with 7 editions by 1729. Green suggests that this handbook was meant especially for godparents to give to their godchildren.

6.3 Young Man's first Compoⁿ

I have been unable to locate this book. It is a good guess that this would have been one of Andrew's old schoolbooks. Amongst the papers in the Sydney Diocesan Archives, there are two of Andrew's exercise books from 1805, probably kept by Moore for sentimental reasons, in which he is practicing his writing in an excellent, clear, strong hand.[130] Perhaps this *First Composition* was used by him about the same time?

6.4 French Grammar

There were many French grammars in the 18th and 19th century and Moore's shelf contains three (cf. 10.6, 7). These could have been from Thomas's own schooldays, if French was taught at his Uncle's school in Lesbury, and if he attended there, but it seems far more likely that these books belonged to Andrew, who probably studied it at school before serving in France for the battle of Waterloo and then for some years after.

6.5   Horns manual of prayer For the afflicted

Thomas Hartwell Horne (1780–1862), was a biblical scholar, a bibliographer and a polemicist. He was educated at Christ's Hospital, for two years a contemporary of Samuel Taylor Coleridge, who gave him private instruction for the summer vacation in 1790. He published *A Brief View of the Necessity and Truth of the Christian Revelation* (1800; 1802), and soon after joined the Wesleyan Methodists and continued with them many years. In 1818 he published his *Introduction to the Critical study and Knowledge of the Holy Scriptures*, his chief work, for which King's College, Aberdeen, awarded him an honorary MA, and which passed through several editions.[131] Bishop Howley ordained him for ministry in London, and in 1832, he published his *Manual for the Afflicted*.

6.6   Standing Orders By Col Pasley

The brilliance of Charles William Pasley (1780–1861) meant that he advanced rapidly in the Royal Engineers. During the Napoleonic wars he was Europe's leading demolitions expert and specialist in siege warfare. After active service at various historic battles, an injury changed his direction, so that he devoted the rest of his life to founding a complete science of military engineering and to the thorough organization and training of the corps of Royal Engineers. He became the head of the newly created school of military engineers at Woolwich in 1812, the year Andrew received his commission. Amongst a number of works arising from his military interests, he published a volume of *Standing Orders* which contained a complete code of military rules for the duties of all army ranks.[132] He was one of the great military thinkers of this era, and, as a leading and innovative Royal Engineer, who, if he was not one of Andrew's teachers at the academy, would most certainly have been one of the inspirational figures in his world.

6.7 Nelson's Direction

Robert Nelson, *Instructions For Them That Come To Be Confirmed: By Way Of Question And Answer. With Prayers To Be Used Before And After; Also, Directions To Be Observed During Confirmation* (1774).

As a young man, Robert Nelson (1656–1715) was tutored by George (later, Bishop) Bull, of whom he would eventually write a *Life* (1713). About 1690 he became a non-juror (400 clergy who refused the oath of allegiance to William III and Mary II after the 'glorious revolution' of 1688–9) and began the religious writing for which he is known. He was an active supporter of various charitable causes and societies, including the SPCK and SPG when they were founded, as well as 'the Associates of Dr. Bray', a society which especially aimed at providing parochial libraries'.[133] He left the nonjurors in 1710 and took the sacrament. He became known for his religious writings, some of which were distributed by the SPCK.[134]

Six copies of Nelson's Directions arrived in NSW with Richard Johnson.

Did this volume originally belong to Andrew, used during preparation for his confirmation. Or was it used by Thomas and Rachel with any godchildren they may have had?[135]

6.8 Doddridges Rise & Progress

Philip Doddridge, *The Rise And Progress Of Religion In The Soul: Illustrated In A Course Of Serious And Practical Addresses, Suited To Persons Of Every Character And Circumstance: With A Devout Meditation Or Prayer Added To Each Chapter...* (1745).

Philip Doddridge (1702–1755), the non-conformist divine and celebrated hymn writer, was ordained to the Castle Hill church in Northampton in 1730 and remained there for his life. Doddridge included John Wesley, George Whitefield and the Countess of Huntingdon in his circle of acquaintances. This book on Moore's shelf, *The Rise and Progress of Religion in the Soul* (1745), was that through which Wilberforce was converted.[136] It is also listed amongst the books advertised for sale in the *Sydney Gazette* in 1824 and 1838, and amonst those circulated to prisoners.[137]

6.9 Directory & Almanac for 1835

The title is self-evident, but, as with the other calendrical material (cf. 6.1; 7.10; 8.12), was this year of particular interest to Moore, or has the volume simply survived accidentally?

6.10 A Supplement to the Essay Upon the numbers of Danial & St John

George Burton, *A Supplement To The Essay Upon The Numbers Of Daniel And St. John, confirming those of 2436 and 3430, mentioned in the Essay; from two numerical prophecies of Moses and our Saviour* (1768).

George Burton (1717–1792) was the rector of Elveden (1740) and Heringswell, Suffolk (1751). He was the younger brother of Philip, whose daughter married George Horne, Bishop of Norwich.[138] He published treatises on biblical chronology (1766–87).

This book was a supplement to his previous book, *An Essay Towards Reconciling The Numbers Of Daniel And St. John, Determining The Birth Of Our Saviour, And Fixing A Precise Time For The Continuance Of The Present Desolation Of The Jews; With Some Conjectures And Calculations, Pointing Out The Year 1764, To Have Been On Of The Most Remarkable Epochs In History* (1766, ²1769).

The supplement to this work was published in London in 1768, it has been suggested that it may have also been issued as part of the second edition of *An Essay* published in 1769. According to a near contemporary, Rev. George Ashby (1724–1808), Burton cleared nothing up, and 'nor could he ever make himself intelligible to, or convince, a single person'!

By carefully noting that this was *A Supplement*, Moore's short title indicates that he only had the separate publication, that is, the version put out in 1768.

6.11   The Whole Duty of Man

See the discussion above (4.9).

6.12   Sea Sermons

Sea-farers have always felt rather vulnerable and in need of extra help from 'the gods'. There is a long history of English sermons published to help meet this need, stretching from the early days of printing down to at least a century after Moore's death, through Richard Marks (1843), Alfred M. Lorrain (1851), and Thomas Spurgeon (1895) in the late nineteenth century, down to Leslie Dixon Weatherhead (1953) in the twentieth.

There are three published early enough to be in Moore's possession. Henry Valentine, *Foure sea-sermons, preached at the annuall meeting of the Trinitie Companie, in the parish church of Deptford* (1635). Henry Valentine was the vicar of the Deptford church at the time of his preaching, the location of one of the Navy's principal dockyards. The Navy was also served by James Ramsay, Vicar of Teston, *Sea Sermons; Or, A Series Of Discourses For The Use Of The Royal Navy* (1781). In the early nineteenth century, the Religious Tract Society published George Burder, *Sea Sermons; Or, Twelve Short And Plain Discourses For Seamen* (1822)—(see above 5.7).

If Thomas's book dated to his own sea-faring days, then he would have had either Valentine or Ramsay. If he acquired his copy more recently, perhaps out of nostalgia for his seafaring days, or more likely because of some present interest in Christian ministry to sea-farers (probably through the Bethel Union), then Burder would be the most likely one, especially given Moore's connections with the RTS.

Sea Sermons was amongst the books distributed to the prisoners at Northampton County Gaol.[139] There were so many ex-seamen in the prisons at this time. Once the wars with the French were over, naval and military personnel were cashiered, only to add to the incidence of crime. This, of course, also had a spill over for the convict population of NSW, and so this book would be useful for Thomas for the purposes of distribution.

7. Page 7

7.1 Instructions for the better understanding of the L^{ds} Supper

Thomas Wilson, *A Short And Plain Instruction For The Better Understanding Of The Lord's Supper: With The Necessary Preparation Required For The Benefit Of Young Communicants, And As Such As Not Well Considered This Holy Ordinance, To Which Is Annexed The Office Of The Holy Communion, With The Proper Helps And Directions For Joining In Every Part Thereof With Understanding And Benefit* (1733).

Educated at Trinity College, Dublin, Thomas Wilson (1663–1755), became the Bishop of Sodor & Man, where he exercised a strong ministry in a church with many troubles. His conscientious ecclesiastical discipline, later praised by the leaders of the Oxford Movement, Keble (who dedicated sixteen years to writing Wilson's *Life*) and Newman, was not particularly Anglican, but can be paralleled from contemporary presbyterian or anabaptist records. His ministry was open to, and well received by, many non-Anglicans, including Roman Catholics, dissenters, and quakers. He had an interest in foreign missions, writing an essay on the conversion of the Indians in 1740, being an early advocate of SPG and SPCK, and his association and support of Count Zinzendorf (who he met in 1738) and his Moravian brethren, even resulted in him being invited to fill a vacancy in the Moravian church.[140]

Bishop Wilson adopted the scheme of Thomas Bray and began to establish parochial libraries in his diocese, which led to the provision of materials in the manx language. Wilson's *Principles and Duties of Christianity* (1707) was the first book to be published in manx, and it was soon followed by *A Short and Plain Instruction* ... (1733) and other works. When Chaplain Richard Johnson arrived in NSW, he brought 100 copies of this book with him (as well 12 of Wilson's *Instructions for the Indians*).

7.2 Watts' Psalms & Hymns

Isaac Watts, *An Arrangement Of The Psalms, Hymns And Spiritual Songs* (^{4}1805, new edn. [G. Burder] 1806, 1812). For more on Watts, see above (3.7). His *Divine and Moral Songs* was on sale in Sydney in 1838.

7.3 Wreath of Friendship

There was a novel by this name: *The Wreath of Friendship; or, a Return from India. A novel, in a series of letters* (1790) 2 vols., but, given the paucity of novels on Moore's shelf, this is probably more likely to be the book edited by Bernard Bowring, *The Wreath of Friendship; a token of regard ...*, and/or its second part, *The Keepsake for the Young: an annual present. Illustrated, etc. Being pt. 2 of "The Wreath of Friendship* (1835?).

Given the title of part 2, was this also a book given to Andrew in his youth?

7.4 A Weeks preparation for receiving the Lords Supper (2)

Gregory Bedell, D.D, *A Weeks Preparation Towards A Worthy Receiving Of The Lords Supper: After The Warning In The Church For The Celebration Of The Holy Communion: In Meditations And Prayers For Morning And Evening For Every Day Of The Week: Also Some Meditations To Live Well After Receiving The Holy Sacrament* (1679; ^{11}1687). It was later accompanied by: *The Second Part Of The Weeks Preparation For The Sacrament. Consisting Of Soliloquies, Prayers, Hymns, Ejaculations, Thanksgiving And Examination, For Sunday Evening, After The Celebration Of The Holy Communion. As Also For Morning And Evening On Every Day Of The Week*

Following. Together With Directions To Lead An Holy Life (1686). This was re-published in 1716, and a 'new' version published in 1785. It is one of Green's 'best-sellers', having 40+ editions by 1729, and 11 of the second part.

7.5 Marine Dictionary

William FALCONER, *An Universal Dictionary Of The Marine*, more popularly known as *Falconer's marine dictionary* (1769, 1771, [4]1780, 1784). This was re-issued in revised form as: *A new universal dictionary of the marine: being, a copious explanation of the technical terms and phrases usually employed in the construction, equipment, machinery, movements, and military, as well as naval, operations of ships: with such parts of astronomy, and navigation, as will be found useful to practical navigators: illustrated with a variety of modern designs of shipping, etc: together with separate views of the masts, yards, sails and rigging: to which is annexed a vocabulary of French sea-phrases and terms of art, collected from the best authorities/ originally compiled by William Falconer, now modernized and much enlarged by William Burney* (1815).[141]

Although interested in literature from an early age, William Falconer (1732–1769) spent time at sea in the merchant marine and Royal Navy. Several of his poems caught the attention of others who encouraged him in his writing. His dictionary, written in 1769 and well spoken of, apparently described 'retreat' as a French manouevre 'not properly a term of the British marine'! Falconer went down off the Cape of Good Hope in the *Aurora*.

It is probably a safe assumption that Moore would have used this dictionary—the standard work of the day—during his seafaring days, and so his would be one of the older editions.

7.6 An Alarm to unconverted Sinners

Joseph Alleine, *Alarme To Unconverted Sinners... Whereunto Are Annexed Divers Practical Cases Of Conscience Judiciously Resolved* (1671).

Joseph Alleine (1634–1668) was ordained as an associate of George Newton at Taunton (1654), and ejected in 1662. After remaining there and preaching illegally, he was imprisoned for Evangelical preaching (1663–1664 and again in 1665). In 1664 he wrote a treatise urging others to illegal preaching.[142] Because of the ardency of Alleine's pastoral life, his imprisonment, and his early death, he became a hero to many amongst the English dissenters and the New England Puritans.

Alarme was sometimes published under the title *The Sure Guide to Heaven*. In 1673 and 1703, it had forwards by Richard Alleine and Richard Baxter. It was reprinted regularly, esp. throughout early 19th c. on into 1978, and translated into other languages. It became a classic of puritan devotion, and was then picked up by the Methodists.[143] These associations, as well as its drive towards conversion, indicate that this book can be regarded as part of the central armoury of the methodist/ evangelical movement.

This book was on Green's best-seller list, and amongst those circulated to prisoners.[144]

7.7 A Letter concerning the Lives Of Churchmen & Dissenters

John WHITE, *A Letter to a Gentleman dissenting from the Church of England, concerning the lives of Churchmen and Dissenters. Wherein Dr. Watts's book, An humble attempt towards the revival of practical religion among Christians, so far as relates to this subject, is largely examined, etc.* (1743, ²1745).

John WHITE, B.D. (1685–1755), was a Fellow of St. John's College, Cambridge. His letter received three responses from a 'dissenting gentleman', M. Towgood (1807, 1809, 1811).

7.8 Communion with God

This was a favourite topic amongst the 17th century divines, whose works continued to be published into the 18th and 19th centuries, amongst them are several which would yield the short-title used by Moore.

Samuel Annesley LL.D., Minister of St. Giles', Cripplegate,

Communion With God. In Two Sermons Preach'd At Pauls, Etc. (1655).

William Strong, Preacher at Westminster Abbey, *Communion With God In Ordinances, The Saints Priviledge And Duty* (1655).

John Owen, *Of Communion With God The Father, Son, And Holy Ghost, Each Person Distinctly, In Love, Grace, And Consolation; Or, The Saints Fellowship With The Father, Son, And Holy Ghost Unfolded* (1657). John Owen, *A Vindication of some Passages in A Discourse concerning Communion with God, from the exceptions of W. Sherlock* (1674). Cf. William Sherlock, Dean of St. Paul's, *A Discourse Concerning The Knowledge Of Jesus Christ, And Our Union And Communion With Him, Etc.*

Matthew Barker, *A Discourse Of The Right Way Of Obtaining, And Maintaining Communion With God*, in *A Continuation of Morning-Exercise Questions, etc.* (1683).

Matthew Henry, Nonconformist Minister, *The Duty of a Christian, or, Directions For Daily Communion With God. In Three Discourses, Shewing How To Begin, How To Spend, And How To Close Every Day With God* (^{3}1715), which was published by the Religious Tract Society (1836) and so finds its way amongst the books circulated to prisoners.[145]

Robert Hall, of Arnsby, of the Northamptonshire Association, *The Privilege and Duty of Communion with God, considered in a circular letter from the Baptist Ministers, assembled at Spalding, June 2, 3, and 4, 1789, etc.* (1789).

7.9   Robertson's Charles the 5 1 – 3 & 4 v.

William Robertson, D.D., *The History of the Reign of the Emperor Charles V, etc.* (1769), 3 vol. Although the first edition (1769) only had three volumes, the second edition (1772) ran to four. A new edition (1777) then apparently went back to three volumes in the Irish release, but four in London. The sixth, corrected, edition (^{6}1787) had four, as did subsequent editions which appeared in rapid succession across the course of the next half century (^{7}1792, ^{8}1796, ^{9}1798, ^{10}1800, ^{11}1806, ^{14}1817, ^{15}1821, 1825, 1827). It was translated into French, Italian and Russian (vol. 1).

7.10 British Imperial Calendar for 1835

This series ran from 1810 to 1972, after which it became known as the 'Civil Service Year Book' (1974+), since the book listed all the civil servants in the realm. As with the other calendrical material on Moore's shelf (cf. 6.1; 6.9; 8.12), we can ask whether he bought/kept this particular year for a purpose, or was it accidental?

8. Page 8

8.1 The Christian Hero

Sir Richard Steele, *The Christian Hero: An Argument Proving That No Principles But Those Of Religion Are Sufficient To Make A Great Man* (1701, [2]1701, 1709, [3]1710, 1711, [7]1722, [8]1727, [9]1741, 1755, 1792, 1802, 1837).

In 1700, Richard Steele (1672–1729), fought a duel in which his opponent was left dangerously wounded. This made a serious impression on Steele, leaving him with a life-long dislike of duelling. This incident was also partly connected to his *Christian Hero*, first published in April 1701, with a second and enlarged edition by July of the same year. Upon its publication, he was ostracised by his companions amongst the Tower Guard, 'for his declarations as to Religion'.[146]

8.2 Rippons selections of Hymns

A Selection Of Hymns From The Best Authors (1787). This collection by Baptist Minister, John Rippon, D.D. (1751–1836),[147] went to more than 25 editions, being published practically every couple of years, until well into the late 19th century. The sub-title told of its purpose: '*intended to be an appendix to Dr. Watts's Psalms and hymns*'.

8.3 Wesleys Moral sacred Poems

John Wesley, *A Collection Of Moral And Sacred Poems From The Most Celebrated English Authors* (1744), 3 vols.

8.4   Hervey's *Meditations* (1)

Whilst at Oxford, James Hervey (1714–58)[148] was greatly influenced by the Oxford Methodists. He was one of John Wesley's students at Lincoln College Oxford, studying Hebrew at his suggestion, and a member of the Holy Club. After taking Holy Orders he was curate in London for a year with Mr Kinchin, another Oxford Methodist. After another curacy in Devon (1740), where he began his 'Meditations amongst the Tombs', he became incumbent of Weston Favell, Northants (1743). When he died, his funeral sermon was preached by 'the ablest of all the evangelicals, William Romaine'.

He was an early critic of John Wesley's 'irregularities', and published works commending Calvinism—see especially his most famous work, *Dialogues between Theron and Aspasia* (1755), a defence of the doctrine of imputed righteousness, which drew down upon the works of John Wesley. Wesley, in turn, wrote against one of his books, arguing that its defence of imputed righteousness would lead to antinomianism. His writings were exceedingly popular for a long time.

Hervey's *Meditations and Contemplations* were originally published in two volumes, one of which, or, more likely, a later combined edition, has found its way onto Moore's shelf. The first volume (1745–46) contained 'Meditations among the Tombs', 'Reflections on a Flower Garden', and 'A Descant upon Creation'; the second (1747), 'Contemplations on the Night', Contemplation on the Starry Heavens', and 'A Winter Piece'. The *DNB* writer comments: 'These were filled with truisms and flowery language and yet admired by educated persons, probably due to Hervey's sympathy with the principles of the evangelical revival, and partly due to his true appreciation of the beauties of nature—rare at the time'. By 1791 his *Meditations* had reached a 25th edition.

His *Meditations* are also amongst the books advertised for sale in the *Sydney Gazette* in 1824 (as well as his *Theron and Aspasia*) and in 1838, and amongst those circulated to prisoners at Wakefield prison.[149]

8.5 A System of Practical Arithmetic

This book is impossible to track down, since there were at least 20 volumes published in England alone across the course of Moore's life, that could accurately receive the short-title he has used here: Hutton (1764), Eadon (1766), A. & J. Birk (1766), Dyer (1770), Sadler (1773), Hedley (1779), Taylor (1783), Eadon's new version (1794), Wiseman (1798), Buchanan (1798), Joyce (^{2}1808), Pearson (1825), Young (1833), Crossley and Martin (1833), Shakerley (1839), and others not mentioned.

If Moore's copy was from his own school days, then it would be Sadler, Hedley, or Taylor (from this list). If it was from Andrew's, then Joyce would be the most current at that time.

Prisoners were also circulated with arithmetic books.[150]

8.6 The Guardian (1) [??]

This could be the single volume binding of copies of the paper, containing the writings of Richard Steele, Joseph Addison and others, *The Guardian in one Volume, with notes and indexes* (1829).

However, a two-volume work called *The Guardian* amongst those circulated to prisoners[151] leads me to suggest that this work was part of the moral reform agenda.

This would therefore probably dismiss the comedy by Abraham Cowley (1650), or the novel by Stephen Penton, *The guardian's instruction, or, The gentleman's romance written for the diversion and service of the gentry* (1688). Penton's title suggests it is almost diametrically opposed to the reform agenda, in which reading for distraction was commonly pitted against reading for 'useful knowledge' and so for renovation of life.

The same author, however, later published another work which seems much more amenable to reform: *New instructions to the guardian shewing that the last remedy to prevent the ruin, advance the interest, and recover the honour of this nation is I. a more serious and strict education of the nobility and gentry, II. to breed up all their younger sons to some calling and employment, III. more of* them to holy orders, with a method of institution from three years of age to twenty one* (1694). This work would clearly be of interest to those with a high regard for education as the means to moral and societal reform. Since Moore apparently shared many of these ideals, this book would also have been of interest to him. It may have even been one of the sources of his inspiration towards educational benefaction.

8.7   Village Conversation [?]

This title is very difficult to read but the best option for the transcription would be *Village Conversation*. This probably receives confirmation from the volume by that name amongst those circulated to prisoners.[152] Three books could go by that short-title: Sarah Renou, *Village Conversations, or The Vicar's Fire-side* (2 vols.; 1815 & 1816); George Davys (Bishop of Peterborough), *Village Conversations on the Liturgy of the Church of England* (1820, 1821, 1829, 1831); and Richard Whateley (Archbishop of Dublin), *Village Conversations in Hard Times, &c* (1831), an evangelistic work. If the singular is significant, this would point to one of Davys' other works, *Village Conversation on the Catechism* (1827).

8.8   A New Manual of Devotions

A New Manual Of Devotions, In Three Parts. Part I. Containing Prayers For Families And Private Persons. Part II. Containing Offices. ... Part III. ... (^{2}1713). By 1826 this volume had reached its 30th edition).

Richard Johnson brought with him twelve copies of a *Manual of Devotions*, presumably this work.

8.9   The free Thinker

The notion of 'free thinker' or 'free thinking' appears in a number of book and magazine titles.

Eubulus. *A letter to the Free-thinker; with some remarks upon his conduct* (1718).

Honest free-thinker. *The touchstone: or paradoxes brought to the test of a rigorous and fair examination, for the settling of dubious points to the satisfaction of* ... (1732).

Ambrose Philips, *The free-thinker.* ... (1722–23). 3 vols. Also editions from 1733, 1739, 1740.

The Christian free-thinker. Or an epistolary discourse concerning freedom of thought. In which are contained observations on the lives and ... (1740).

Country gentleman.. *The political free-thinker, being an impartial and dispassionate enquiry into the grounds of our foreign and domestic broils, and particularly of* ... The second edition. (^{2}1745).

Free-thinker. *The free-thinker's answer to his friend the Quaker's letter* (1755).

A Political Freethinker's Thoughts on the Present Circumstances (1795).[153]

Amongst the valuable books for sale in the *Sydney Gazette* of 30 December 1824, there is found the 3 volume *The Freethinker.*

8.10 Directions for a Devote [sic] & Decent behaviour in the public Worship of God

Directions for a devout and decent behaviour in the public worship of God; more particularly in the use of the Common Prayer, appointed by the ... A new edition, corrected (1758; ^{24}1766; new edn, corrected and enlarged: 1778).

8.11   The Practical Navigation [?]

Although the transcription of the second word is not secure, this is the best fit and is probably correct. In this case, the book would be that of the compass-maker John Seller, (fl. 1658–1698) with the lengthy title:

Practical navigation: or, An introduction to that whole art Containing 1. Several definitions in geometry, astronomy, geography, and navigation. 2. A new and exact kalender, shewing the suns declination and true place, for 60 years. 3. And an almanack of the moon for eight years. 4. The calculation of triangles, both plain and spherical, and their application in navigation. 5. *The form of keeping a journal, or sea reckoning.* 6. *Several useful tables, as tables of meridonal parts; latitudes and longitudes of places, &c.* 7. *The original invention of the mariners compass.* 8. *A discourse of the variation, and the natural causes thereof.* 9. *The description and use of the most necessary instruments in navigation, as the cross-staff, quadrant, azimuth compass, &c. the inclinatory needle, to find the latitude of a place without observation of sun or stars.* 10. *With an appendix, shewing the secret virtues of the load-stone* (1669).

8.12   The Literary & Historical Register

This has not been easy to identify.

The Historical, Political, And Literary Register, Containing An Account Of Every Public Transaction And Remarkable Production Necessary To Illustrate The History, Literature, Or Public Amusements Of The Year 1769. To Be Continued Annually (1770). When Volume 1 was issued, in both London and Dublin, it ran to almost 500 pages and was divided into sections on various topics: state papers, historical state of Europe, judicial articles, theatrical register, poetry, anecdotes, antiquities, and miscellanies. It also contained a complete diary of London theatrical and operatic performance for the year. Despite the promise of the final part of the title, the British Library catalogue questions whether this was the only volume issued.

Another publication sounds closer to Moore's short title: *The Museum: Or, The Literary And Historical Register.* This was first published on Saturday March 29, 1746. The British Library Catalogue lists the series up to Saturday, September 12, 1747.

If either of these publications are what Moore had on the shelf, it would be interesting to know why they had significance, given that, by his time, they both concerned a long distant day (cf. 6.1; 6.9; 7.10).

9. Page 9

9.1 Fosters Discourses 2 Vols

James Foster, *Discourses On All The Principal Branches Of Natural Religion And Social Virtue* (1749, 1752), 2 vols.

The son of a dissenter, James Foster[154] (1697–1753) began preaching in 1718. At this time the dissenters were tending towards Arianism, and it was agreed to make a statement of orthodoxy at Salter's Hall, Exeter (1719). Two of Foster's friends were expelled, and he took the side of the non-subscribers and offended the congregation. In 1720 he argued that the doctrine of the Trinity should not be regarded as essential, and implies that his own views were Arian. He was, however, converted by reading the writings of John Gale against infant baptism, and was baptised by Gale in London. After 1728 he became known as an eloquent preacher and controversialist. He replied to Matthew Tindal's work (1731), and entered into controversy with Henry Stebbing the elder (1735). He published four volumes of sermons (1744) as well as separate sermons.

His *Discourses in all the Principle Branches of Natural Religion and Social Virtue*—which appeared in the same decade as David Hume's *Essays* and Montesquieu's *L'Esprit des lois* —had two thousand subscribers.

9.2 The Shipbuilders Repository

Anonymous, *The Shipbuilder's Repository; or, A Treatise on Marine Architecture. Wherein are Contained, the Principles of the Art, with the Theory and Practical Parts fully explained; And every Instruction required in the building and completing a Ship, of every Class, from the forming of the Draught, to the launching into the Water. Calculated to the Capacity of young Beginners: Compiled and digested in a Manner entirely new, and laid down different from what has hitherto appeared on the Subject. The whole being intended as A Complete Companion for those Naval Architects, desirous of attaining a Competent Knowledge of that important Art* (1788).[155]

CHAPTER 7 ~ *Thomas Moore's Bookshelf* [179]

This was published just about the time Moore would have been completing his apprenticeship. It would have been useful for him as ship's carpenter on the *Britannia* and Master Builder at the King's dockyard.

9.3 2 Bibles

9.4 5 Testaments

Perhaps these (9.3 & 4) need no further introduction, but it is worth noting the numbers here. As a member of the Bible Society, Moore would have been involved in distribution of Bibles and Testaments to his local area. Perhaps the multiple copies here are the remainder of his 'distribution stockpile'.

9.5 2 Prayer Books

Were these for distribution too? Or did Rachel and Thomas have one each?

9.6 6 Odd Books

After carefully listing the titles of the other books in his possession, it seems strange that Moore would not bother to do so with these. Amongst those advertised in the *Gazette* in 1838 was 'Odd Volume', by Seymour and Cruikshank, i.e. *The Legend of the Large Mouth and other Tales [The Odd Volume]*. But this seems out of character with the rest of his books, and why would he have had six copies? An alternative suggestion would be that these are books associated with the Order of Oddfellows. There were many of these, each with the word 'odd' in the title.

9.7 Lot of Old Magazines, Maps &c.

Although it is impossible to identify these magazines with any certainty, they may be the unbound issues of *The Evangelical Magazine*, or the *Methodist Magazine*, if the titles listed previously refer to bound editions. Of course, they could also be completely different magazines. If the identity is unclear, their presence suggests that Moore was a regular reader, keeping up with some kind of specialty interest, whether in a weekly, fortnightly, monthly, or quarterly fashion.

The maps may be reminiscent of his seafaring days, or his times in the bush gathering timber as Master Boat Builder, or S/Purveyor of Timber. They could also have belonged to Andrew from his days in the Royal Engineers, but perhaps his maps are those listed at 11.10.

156

French Books

9.8   Art Militaire 2 Vol

There are two possibilities here.

Marie Henri François de Carrion-Nisas, *Essai Sur L'histoire Générale De L'art Militaire, De Son Origine, De Ses Progrès Et De Ses Révolutions, Depuis La Première Formation Des Sociétés Européennes jusqu'à Nos Jours* (1824, 2 Vols. [An Essay on the General History of the Military Art, of its Origin, its Progressions and Revolutions, since the First Formation of European Society until our Days]

Colonel Carrion-Nisas's book is a general work, published fairly late in Andrew's career. On the other hand, de Vernon's work is more in line with Andrew's specialty (an Engineer), and was published early enough to used during his training and in the early part of his active service.

Simon-François Gay de Vernon, *Traité Élémentaire D'art Militaire Et De Fortification À L'usage Des Élèves De l'École Polytechnique Et Des Élèves Des Écoles Militaires* (1805), 2 vols. [An Elementary Treatise on the Military Art and on Fortification for the Use of the Students of the Polytechnical School and the Students of the Military Schools]

CHAPTER 7 ~ *Thomas Moore's Bookshelf* [181]

9.9   Traites De Fortification Souteraine

C.-L. Gillot, *Traité De Fortification Souterraine, Ou Des Mines Offensives Et Défensives* (1805). [Treatise on Subterranean Fortifications, or on Offensive and Defensive Mines]

This was a collection of verbal reports from C.-L. Gillot, a captain of the corps of the imperial guard; of his experience with the (military) mines, edited by Denis Simon Magimel. Dealing with subterranean fortifications, this was clearly a work of interest to a military engineer like Andrew.

9.10   Principes De La Strategie

Charles, Archduke of Austria, *Principes de la stratégie, développés par la relation de la campagne de 1796 en Allemagne: Tome 1. Renfermant les principes, et leur application sur un Théâtre de guerre supposé. Tome 2. Renfermant la première période de la Campagne de 1796* (original French, 1818; republished in paperback, 2006). [Principles of Strategy, developed by the Account of the Campaign of 1796 in Germany: Volume 1. Containing the Principles, and their Application in a Theatre of Assumed war. Volume 2. Containing the first Period of the Campaign of 1796]

Charles, Archduke of Austria (1771–1847), third son of Leopold II, was Commander of the Austrian army (1796–1812). This was translated from the German by Antoine Henri de Jomini (1818), 4 vols. The fourth volume is a collection of maps and plans to accompany the text. Moore lists one volume here, and the other three at 10.3. Once again, the military nature of this book tends to suggest it was Andrew's.

9.11   Pousse Des Terres

This short title evidently referred to another engineering work, but there are several possibilities.

Gaspard-Clair-François-Marie Riche de Prony (1755–1839), *Recherches Sur La Poussée Des Terres Et Sur La Forme Et Les Dimensions À Donner Aux Murs De Revêtement* (1802). [Research into the Thrust of Soils and into the Form and the Dimensions to give to covering Walls]

Six years later, Mayniel, the chief of the battalion of the guard, wrote on the same topic: *Traité Expérimental, Analytique Et Pratique De La Poussée Des Terres Et Des Murs De Revêtement* (1808). [Experimental, Analytical And Practical Treatise on the Thrust of Soils and on Covering Walls]

Alexandre-Jean-Maximin de Label, comte de Lambel, a director of fortifications, added to this body of work with his *Applications Du Principe Des Vitesses Virtuelles À La Poussée Des Terres Et Des Voûtes* (1822). [Applications of the Principle of the Virtual Velocities for the Thrust of Soils and of Vaults]

Although this latter work would no doubt be interesting and useful to Andrew, one of the earlier two are probably more likely his, since they were published just before he did his training.

9.12   Bousmard Fortification

H.J.B. De Bousmard, *Essai General De Fortification Et D'Attaque Et Defense Des Places, Dans Lequel Ces Deux Sciences Sont Expliquees Et Mises L'une Par L'autre A La Portee De Tout Le Monde* (1797–1799), 3 vols. [General Essay on Fortification and on Attack and Defense of Places, in which these two Sciences are Explained and Placed Side by Side So that Everyone Can Understand]

Bousmard was a French military engineer, who emigrated to Prussia after the French Revolution. There is a 4th volume sometimes listed, but that volume was dated 1804 and was by a different publisher, while volume 3 of the set indicates that it was the 3rd and last volume (stated at end of text in volume 3).

The three volumes were on Moore's bookshelf, this one and the other two listed separately (see below at 10.12). The subject matter would suggest quite clearly that these volumes belonged to Andrew, officer in the Royal Engineers.

10. Page 10

10.1 Jomini Operations Militaires 8 vol

Antoine Henri de Jomini (1779–1869), *Traité Des Grandes Opérations Militaires Contenant L'histoire Critique Des Campagnes De Frédéric II Comparées À Celles De L'empereur Napoléon, Avec Un Recueil Des Principes Généraux De L'art De La Guerre.*(2nd edn. 1811–1816) 8 vol. [Treatise on Large Military Operations containing the Critical History of the Campaigns of Frederick II compared to those of the Emperor Napoleon, with a Collection of the General Principles of the Art of War]

Jomini was one of the two celebrated 19th century war theorists (with Clauswitz).

10.2 Histoire De Marlborough 3 vol.

Madgett & Dutems, *Histoire de Jean Churchill, duc de Marlborough, etc.* (1806). [History of John Churchill, Duke of Marlborough]

Although composed principally by Madgett, this book was edited and enlarged by J. F. H. Dutems. Sir Winston Churchill, writing a biography of his ancestor John, commented that this work 'is of special interest because it was written by the direction and under the supervision of Napoleon, whose appreciation of Marlborough as a soldier was profound'.[157]

An English *Life of Marlborough* was circulated amongst the prisoners at Wakefield.[158]

10.3 Principes De La Strategie 3 vol.

These are the remaining volumes of the set referred to above (9.10).

10.4 Histoire Dufence

It this is an accurate transcription (which may not be the case), it seems to be incorrect (ie. Should it be 'de la defense'?), and I have not been able to discover any title that corresponds to it. If it does concern defence, it would obviously be of interest to Andrew's military engineering.

10.5 Lecons Francaises De Litterature Et De Morale 2 vol

M. Noel & M. de la Place, *Lecons Francaises De Litterature Et De Morale*. 2 vols. [French Lessons from Literature and Morals]. I have not been able to discover the original publication date of this volume, but it was in its sixth edition by 1813, so would have been available for Andrew's schooling.

10.6 Grammaire De Restaut

Pierre Restant (1696–1764), *Abrégé de la langue francoise (ou grammaire francoise) contenant les principes généraux du discours, avec quelques règles de syntaxe & d'ortographe pour servir de préparation à l'étude du Nouveau rudiment & de la Méthode latine. A l'usage des colleges et des pensions* (1748). [Abridgement of the French Language (or French Grammar) containing the General Principles of Discourse, with whatever Rules of Syntax and Orthography to enable Preparation for the Study of the New Rudiment and the Latin Method]

10.7 Levizac French Grammar

Jean-Pont-Victor Lacoutz, abbé de Lévizac, *A Theoretical And Practical Grammar Of The French Tongue, In Which The Present Usage In Every Part Of Syntax Is Displayed And All The Principal Difficulties Explained* (1815).

10.8 Consideration Sur La Revolution 3 V

There are several 'Considerations' on the revolution. Is it the political work on the revolution in France and policy throughout Europe, M.E Brandes, *Considerations Politiques Sur La Revolution Francoise* (1791) [Political Considerations on the French Revolution]. Or is it the post-humous publication of Germaine de Staël-Holstein (1766–1817), Madame La Baronne de Stael, *Considerations Sur Les Principaux Evenemens De La Revolution Francoise* (1818). 3 vol. [Considerations on the Principle Events of the French Revolution]

10.9 Campagne En Sax 2 vol

The French army were involved in two major campaigns against Germany, one in 1806, the other in 1813. Although both were written about, the 1813 was referred to as 'Campagne *de* Saxe', whereas several works wrote of the 1806 action, using the expression *en Saxe*. If this clue is sufficient, this book on Moore's shelf was probably one of these discussions of the earlier campaign, and could have been one of Andrew's texts from his military training just after its publication.

Campagne de la grande armée en Saxe, en Prusse et en Pologne en l'an 1806 et l'an 1807, ou recueil des bulletins et de toutes les pièces officielles relatives à cette guerre avec la Saxe, la Prusse et la Russie, jusques et y compris les derniers traités de paix avec ces différentes puissances (1807). [Campaign of the Grand Army in Saxony, in Prussia and in Poland in the year 1806, or collection of the bulletins and all the official pieces relating to this war with Saxony, Prussia and Russia, up to and including the last peace treaties with these different powers]

Campagne des armées françaises en Prusse, en Saxe et en Pologne... en 1806... On y a joint des notices biographiques sur ceux qui ont péri dans cette mémorable campagne... Cet ouvrage est orné de vingt portraits... On y a joint le plan de la bataille d'Iéna (1807) 4 vols. [Campaign of the French Armies in Prussia, in Saxony, and in Poland in 1806. It brings together biographical notes on those who perished in this memorable campaign ... This work is adorned with twenty portraits ... It brings together the plan of the battle of Lena].

Campagnes des armées françaises en Prusse, en Saxe et en Pologne, commandées en personne par S. M. l'empereur Napoléon Ier, en 1806 et 1807, ou Recueil complet des relations officielles, suivi des traités de paix de Tilsitt et d'une explication géographique de ces traités (1807). [Campaigns of the French Armies in Prussia, in Saxony and in Poland, commanded personally by H.M. the Emperor Napoleon I, in 1806 and 1807, or Complete Collection of the Official Accounts, following the Peace Treaty of Tilsitt and a Geographical Explanation of this Treaty].

10.10 Dictionaire Des Sieges Et Batailles 3 vol

Although there were some more recently published 4 and 6 volume dictionaries of sieges and battles, this three volume work is probably the older one by Jean-François de La Croix, (de Compiègne), *Dictionnaire historique des sièges et batailles mémorables de l'histoire ancienne et moderne, ou Anecdotes militaires de tous les peuples du monde.* (1771), 4 parts in 3 volumes. [Historical Dictionary of memorable Seiges and Battles of Ancient and Modern History, or Military Anecdotes of the Peoples of the World].

10.11 Traites Complet de Fortification 2 vol

Gaspard Noizet-de-Saint-Paul, *Traité Complet De Fortification* (1792; 3rd 1818), 2 vol. [Complete Treatise on Fortification].

10.12 Bousmard Fortification (2)

These are the other two volumes of De Bousmard, *Essai General* (see above, 9.12).

10.13 Campagne De Russie

This campaign also naturally attracted the attention of writers. On the Russian side, Dmitry Petrovich Buturlin wrote *Histoire militaire de la campagne de Russie en 1812* (Paris, 1824) [Military History of the Russian Campaign in 1812], and Count Roman Sotyk, *Napoléon en 1812. Mémoires historiques et militaires sur la campagne de Russie* (1836) [Napoleon in 1812. Historical and Military Memoirs on the Russian Campaign].

Amongst French authors, there was Napoleon himself as part of his *Ouevres* [Works], Louis Philippe, Compte de Ségur, *La Campagne de Russie: Mémoires du Général Cte de Ségur* (1825) [The Russian Campaign: Memoirs of General Count of Ségur], and Eugène Labaume, *Relation circonstanciée de la Campagne de Russie; ouvrage orné des Plans do la Bataille de la Moskwa, et du Combat de Malo-Jaroslavetz. (Itinéraire de la marche du quatrième corps, etc.)* (^{3}1814) [Detailed Account of the Russian Campaign; etc].

This graphic eyewitness account of the 1812 campaign by Eugene Labaume (1783–1849), who would write several volumes about the Napoleonic wars, went into its third edition by 1814, and would go on to at least three more in French by 1820. It was translated into English in 1815 and was also later published in America. The volume's evident popularity makes it a good candidate for being the one on Moore's catalogue.

11. Page 11

11.1 Lettres sur La Guerre De Russie

L. V. D. P., i.e. L[e] V[icomte] D[e] P[uibusque], *Lettres sur la Guerre de Russie en 1812, sur la Ville de St. Pétersbourg, les mœurs et les usages des habitans de la Russie et de la Pologne* (1816). [Letters on the Russian War in 1812, on the Town of St Petersburg, the Manners and Customs of the Inhabitants of Russia and Poland].

This is another account of the campaign, beginning the year Andrew received his commission (1812).

11.2 Deletanvilles French Dictionary

Thomas Deletanville, *A New French Dictionary, In Two Parts: The First, French And English; The Second, English And French: ... To Which Is Prefixed, A French Grammar,* ... (1771). Then 1779; 'carefully revised by Mr. Des Carrières ' in ³1794; 2 vols.

11.3 Le Avventure Di Telemaco Figliuolo D'Ulisse 2 vol

This is an Italian title (1735) of the French novel, *Les Aventures de Telemaque, fils d'Ulysse* (written in 1693–4, published 1699), by Francois Salignac de la Mothe Fenelon (1651–1715). Fenelon had been a missionary to the French Protestants, and eventually became Archbishop of Cambrai. *The Adventures of Telemachus, son of Ulysses* was a severe attack on the divine absolute right of the French monarchy. Despite enraging Louis XIV, it was popular enough to continue in publication well into the nineteenth century. In 1838 it was being sold in Sydney in an edition of French Classics.

11.4   Amores De Borleau 3 vol

I have not been able to identify this book.

11.5   P.[etit] Care^{a}me De Missillon[159]

Jean-Baptiste Massillon, *Sermons de M. Massillon, Évêque de Clermont, Ci-devant Prêtre de l'Oratoire, l'un des Quarante de l'Académies Françoise. Petit Carême* (1745). [Sermons of Mr Massillon, Bishop of Clermont, previously Priest of the Oratory, one of the Fourteen French Academies. Minor Fast].

Jean Baptiste Massillon (1663–1742) was a renowned preacher, who became the Bishop of Clermont, France (1717–). He was noted for his gentle persuasiveness and preference for moral questions, rather than doctrinal. His works were first published in 1745 by his nephew, and they retained great popularity across the eighteenth and nineteenth century. Amongst those sermons cited as his masterpieces, there are the sermons on the Prodigal Son, on the small number of the elect, on death, for Christmas Day, and for the Fourth Sunday in Advent, and *Petit Carême*, a sermon which he delivered before the young king Louis XV in 1718.

Selections from Massillon was on sale in Sydney 1838.

11.6   Siecle De Louis 14 5 Vol

François Marie Arouet de Voltaire, *Le Siècle de Louis XIV* (1733). [The Age of Louis XIV].

This book was written by that voluminous French writer[160] and champion of the Enlightenment, Voltaire.

The eras of both Louis XIV and Louis XV were still of general interest in the early 19th century. Amongst the books advertised for sale in the *Sydney Gazette* on 30 December 1824, there is *Life of Louis the XIV* (2 vols.) and *Life of Louis XV* (4 vols.).

Voltaire, in his native France, fought for civil rights, freedom of religion and the right to a fair trial. Such values were also gained with a struggle in the new colony of NSW. Thomas Moore was involved in this struggle.

11.7 Emile De L'Education 3 Vol.

This is the controversial work of another enlightenment thinker, John Jacques Rousseau, published the year that Thomas Moore was born, *Émile Ou De L'éducation* (1762) [Émile, or On Education].

The work was almost immediately condemned by the French parliament, censured by the theology faculty at the university and refuted by those who thought they knew better.

Rousseau's *Works* in which *Émile* occupied three volumes, are amongst the 'valuable books' for sale in Sydney in 1824.

11.8 Cattipaedia &c

This title has been difficult to locate. Strictly, the title speaks of being 'against child-rearing', or 'against education', but it is possibly an abbreviated slogan word for being against infant baptism. Infant baptism was (and remains), a hotly disputed subject, and presumably there were some works which used this term in relation to its opposition, even though the term is apparently not widely known in the literature of our day. I have found, for example, a work by John Humfrey (1621–1719), *Animadversions And Considerations Upon A Sheet, Printed For Francis Smith, Containing A Confession Of The Faith Of Several Catapædobaptists, Whose Names Are Thereunto Subscribed. As Also The Absurdities Of The Doctrine Of Arminianism, Free-Will, And General Redemption; And That It Is A Popish Doctrine; And Their Objections Briefly Answered* (1679).

The book on Moore's shelf obviously dealt with more than the objection to infant baptism (Note: '&c'), so it, too, could have been dealing with other issues such as those enumerated in Humfrey's title. John Humfrey (16211719) was ejected in 1662, came to London and gathered a congregational church.[161]

Amongst others, John Tombs, an Anglican with Presbyterian views of government, was a constant opponent of infant baptism.

Amongst his many writings on the subject, there is one that comes close to Moore's short title is; *Anti-pædobaptism* (1652). This was further expanded twice: *Anti-pædobaptism, or, the second part of the full Review of the Dispute concerning Infant-Baptism: in which the invalidity of arguments inferring a duty from a positive Rite of the Old Testament concerning a positive Rite of the New, by reason of analogy between them, is shewed; and the argument against Infant-baptism, from Christ's institution ... is made good against the writings of Mr. Stephen Marshall, Mr. Richard Baxter, etc* (1654); The third part (1657) replied to twenty-three contemporary writers.[162]

Another close title is that of John Goodwin, Vicar of St Stephen's Coleman street, *Cata Baptism or New Baptism, waxing old, and ready to vanish away. In two parts. ... An answer to a discours against Infant baptism, published not long since by W. A(llen) under the title of, Some Baptismall Abuses, briefly discovered, etc* (1655)

On Green's list of best-sellers, with some 7 editions by 1729, Daniel Featley's polemical work against Baptist theology may have been part of the other side of the controversy, given its similar title: *katabaptistoi ... the Dippers Dipt* (1645).

11.9 D'Anvilles Atlas

This is the *Atlas Générale* (circa 1740) [General Atlas] by Jean Baptiste Bourguignon d'Anville (1697–1782), who was perhaps the greatest geographical author of the 18th century, greatly improving the standards of map making. Most of his maps were made for the individual customer, and, based on careful research, he left blank what was not known, making his maps look empty compared to the highly-embelished ones of his predecessors.[163] In otherwords, this was a revolutionary atlas, put together to suit the new mood of Renaissance/Enlightenment learning. Accuracy was now becoming a virtue.

11.10 Maps &c

As with the previous listing of Maps, these could have been Thomas's or Andrew's (see 9.7).

Part C: Some Comments upon the Books the Property of T. Moore Esq.

The first observation should be on the extent, breadth, and depth of this bookshelf. In extent, with 138 separate entries representing more than 220 volumes, this is quite a substantial private library.[164] It is all the more remarkable for being in the possession of a man said to be uneducated, who lived in a pioneering town in New South Wales—although we ought to remember that it also contains Andrew's books, the educated military officer. In subject area, the library has breadth, covering all of the areas that could be regarded as necessary for a good education, especially in those circles for which reading had the 'hygenic' function of moral reformation.[165] In depth, although the bookshelf contains one or two novels, and some manuals for practical use, on the whole it consists of substantial works dealing with the serious topics suitable to such a purpose.

1. Andrew's Books

Before this catalogue can be utilised to gain some understanding of the intellectual world of Thomas Moore, it is necessary to isolate his volumes from those originally belonging to Andrew.

Given that Andrew served in France at Waterloo and for some years after (until 1818), and that most of the French volumes focus upon military concerns, especially military engineering, it seems most likely that all of the volumes at the end of the list under 'French Books' originally belonged to the step-son so dear to Thomas Moore, who had achieved success as an officer in the Royal Engineers. Here we find several resources for learning and using the French language (10.5, 10.6, 10.7, 11.1). Amongst the books on military engineering (9.9, 9.11, 9.12, 10.10, 10.11, 10.12), and the related geography/topography (11.9, 11.10), we also find books on strategy (9.8, 9.10, 10.3), and military history, both french and english (10.1, 10.2, ?10.4, 10.9, 10.10, 10.13, 11.1), which is, of course, another vehicle for understanding strategy, as well as some volumes on French History more generally (10.8, 11.6).

Andrew's books are often 'leading-edge' volumes from the 'great ones' of the period. The fact that he was reading books on military thinking produced by the enemy (at that time) indicates that the Royal Engineers were taught to 'know thy enemy', in order that the French military 'science' could then be countermanded and overcome.

The only book described as a novel that has been clearly identified amongst Andrew's books (11.3),[166] was really a political tract, rather than the kind of novel associated with the 'reading for distraction' looked down upon by the moral reformers. There is only one volume of sermons, Massillon's *Petit Carême* (11.5), and even this may have been more of political/historical interest to Andrew, given that it was preached to the young Louis XV.

As well as those showing 'leading-edge' thinking in his own field, several other books may hint towards Andrew dabbling amongst the radical thinkers of the time: the *Considerations* on the Revolution (10.8), Fenelon's novel against the divine right of the monarchy (11.3—but why did he have the Italian version?); the writings of Voltaire (11.6) and Rousseau's radical essay on education (11.7).[167] Andrew's father, Surgeon John White, during his time in New South Wales associated with the 'Scottish Martyrs',[168] as did others with links to 'radical' thought, such as Daniel Paine,[169] Thomas Moore's predecessor at the dockyard, and the 'Enlightenment man' George Bass.[170] Andrew was received into White's family when he went to England and was cared for by Elizabeth Bass (nee Waterhouse). Perhaps there was a radicalism in these circles which he may have picked up?

As well as the 'French Books' which fairly clearly seem to have belonged to Andrew, there are other books on the early pages of the list that may have belonged to him. Some of these reflect his own interests: the army's General Regulations (4.6), Pasley's Standing Orders (6.6), Military Monitor (3.3). Other volumes specifically aimed at young persons were probably also his, possibly given to him by his step-father in the interests of his moral and Christian upbringing: Porteus (5.3), evidences for young persons;

Preparation for confirmation, Nelson (6.7); Wilson's helps on the Lord's Supper (7.1), and perhaps Dorrington's (6.2); Frank's *Lessons in Humble Life* (1.15), and Bowring (7.3). Others reflect the kind of education that he would have received at Charterhouse, which no doubt included something of the classics (Lempriere, 1.2; Plutarch, 3.11), arithmetic (8.5) and mathematics (Ozanam, 2.8), French Grammar (6.4), and Natural Philosophy (2.4, ?4.12).

Perhaps some come from an earlier stage of his education. The *First Composition* (6.3) nicely accompanies several exercise books from 1805 containing Andrew's own practice handwriting exercises, executed in a beautiful, flowing hand, which Thomas retained amongst his own papers.[171] This retention of Andrew's work speaks of the affection between the two, and of Thomas's sentimental memory of his step-son's early steps towards adulthood. In fact, it is interesting to reflect upon the fact that Moore retained these books, rather than Mary Ann. This could be because Moore paid for Andrew's schooling and possibly also his military commission. But it was more likely for sentimental reasons, given the strong emotional ties that existed between the two men throughout Andrew's days.

2. Moore's Books

Thomas Moore began his working life as a ship's carpenter, became the Master Boat Builder of the colony, then moved to farming and business, also serving as a magistrate for the last thirty years of his life. Thomas had reading matter dealing with each of the various aspects of his 'professional' life, except perhaps his business interests, much of it of a high level and at the 'leading-edge'.

His seafaring and shipbuilding days were served by: Euler (1.13); Peate's lectures (1.14); Steel (5.10); Falconer's Dictionary (7.5); the *Shipbuilder's Repository* (9.2); volumes on travels and voyages (5.11) and possibly some of the Maps (9.7).—which may also date to his days as Purveyor of timber. He also appears to have dabbled in navigation, as shown by *Practical Navigation*

(8.11), and Kelly's work on astronomy for the purpose of navigation (3.1). Other works on astronomy may have also served this purpose, such as M. Sibly's rendering of ancient astronomy, or, if it was his brother Ebenezer, astronomy-cum-astrology (3.15), and, similarly, Stewart, if indeed this work was on Moore's shelf (4.12). Navigation and sea travel may have aroused an abiding interest in Almanacs and Calendars (6.1, 6.9, 7.10; cf. 6.10, 8.11 and 8.12).[172] Mathematics was important for both ship's carpentry and navigation (Ozanam, 2.8). His interest in the sea would also partly explain his interest in *Sea Sermons* (6.12).

Whether in his role as a prominent civil officer in Sydney, or a pioneer of Liverpool, let alone his own domestic concerns with family and servants, Buchan's *Domestic Medicine* (1.9) was probably of much practical use. However, since, in the absence of a properly qualified surgeon, ship's carpenters could be called upon to act in their place, this book may also go back to Moore's earliest days.

After settling in the colony of New South Wales, Moore was increasingly occupied by his farming interests, especially when he retired from the dockyard and settled on the George's River in 1809. Although he may have been helped by Cobbett's focus on domestic life (3.2), and perhaps Good's *Book of Nature* (4.12), and although the Almanacs and Calendars (6.1, 6.9, 7.10; cf. 6.10, 8.11 and 8.12) were also useful to the farmer, his farming concerns come through most clearly in the three volumes by Lawrence (1.5–7). Lawrence's commitment to the humane treatment of animals was also echoed by Toogood, if Moore had his book (4.12). Since Lawrence argued from a belief that animals had souls, his books on Moore's shelf may also indicate that Thomas was seeking to put his Christian faith into practice in his daily tasks of animal husbandry.

In 1826 Thomas Moore went on public record saying that in the early days of the colony magistrates did not know much about the law.[173] His bookshelf has at least two works to help him in this role. Colquhoun (2.14) was a leading-edge thinker about the British criminal justice system and its consequences. Colquhoun also illustrates the wider role the magistrates could and did have in political reform. Like Colquhoun Moore was also involved in many broader social issues, including those instrumental to NSW moving from a penal colony towards nationhood. We also have independent evidence of him buying the new edition of Toone (3.6),[174] which indicates he was keeping professionally up-to-date, whether by choice or as a requirement of the Governor. Beyond these two volumes, Hale (4.7) would have provided a model of a prominent legal man of Christian conviction, and if he owned Pufendorf (cf. 4.9, 6.11), he would be thinking about justice in company with an important enlightenment thinker.

However, although active in New South Wales society and in political reform, Moore's shelf shows almost no interest in the radical/loyalist political debates being discussed in Britain after the 1790s, as a comparison with *The Political Writings of the 1790s* (ed. Claely) shows.[175] Politics was certainly included in *Literary & Historical Register* (8.12), and Cobbett (3.2) was an important figure in reform, but the particular work of his owned by Moore leaned more towards moral, than political, reform. Certainly there is the slight hint of enlightenment interests amongst Moore's books (e.g. the accurate Geography of Wells, 2.6; the presence of Plutarch, 3.11; perhaps Pufendorf, 4.9, 6.11; and perhaps the Free Thinker, 8.9), but not much truly radical thought. We should remember that he moved in the same Sydney circles as John White, Rachel's former lover and the father of his beloved Andrew, and so the 'revolutionary' circles of those early days may have been as familiar (or moreso) to him as they were to Andrew. He certainly was involved in the reform agenda, both political and moral, in the infant colony of New South Wales. But his bookshelf does not speak loudly of these concerns.

Moore's booklist, in fact, reflects more of a moral reformer. In these circles, education was itself regarded as 'hygienic', for the whole reason for reading was the improvement of life. This belief can be found as part of such movements as those to introduce libraries into prisons, or amongst troops at war, or into every parish, or the rise of the public libraries, Schools of Arts, Mechanics Institutes, and Literary Institutes in Australia, as elsewhere.[176]

Despite the fact that Bishop Broughton described Moore as 'unlettered' and 'destitute of literary accomplishments',[177] this bookshelf questions that attribution. Moore came from a family with education on the agenda, since his uncle James was the schoolmaster in Lesbury, under whom he could possibly have had a basic education. His interest in education is clear from him paying for Andrew's time at Charterhouse, to his founding and support of the Liverpool school, his financial support of other schools and teachers, through to his long-term concern for a tertiary college which, through his legacy, eventually issued in Moore College.

His bookshelf is clear evidence that this interest in education included his own. Broughton's remark can almost certainly be taken to mean that he had no *university* education, and probably also that he had no secondary education in one of the prominent English schools. In this regard, Moore's library is similar to that of the many *autodidacts*,[178] forced to embark on a self-education through their position of dissent from the Church of England (which had something of a stranglehold on formal education), or for some other reason. Moore's original craft as a shipwright suggests that he had taken the path of an apprenticeship instead—although the books related to this pursuit show a very high level of learning was involved in this trade as well.[179] But despite his lack of formal education, his bookshelf covers the range of topics of interest to a gentleman of his time. But not just the gentlemen. As a product of the Enlightenment movement's ideal of equality based on natural law, created the presence of 'free-floating intellectuals' as one of the achievements of the 'embourgeoisement of society'.[180] The range and variety of topics to be read for moral reform is an expression of the late eighteenth century shift towards *extensive* reading (as opposed to intensive, with focus upon a small set of works, such as the Bible).[181] Such topics were regarded as important for the moral reform thought to come through reading, which no doubt explains why a similar breadth of topics can be found on the lists of books distributed in english prisons.

Moore has books of relevance to a broad general education, touching on the classics (Lempriere, 1.2; Plutarch, 3.11); Natural Philosophy (2.4; 2.8, ?4.12); Mathematics (1.14, 2.8, 3.1) and Arithmetic (8.5); French Grammar (6.4); and literature (Johnson's Dictionary, 3.4; Miscellanies, 3.14; Milman, 4.3; Don Quixote, 3.13). He had an interest in history, including ancient (1.2, 3.11), English (1.3), Reformation (2.5), that of Charles V in Europe (7.9), and had a personal connection with the present struggles with France through his work, his finances and his stepson.[182] The *Literary and Historical Register* (8.12) may also reflect the same historical interest, as may the almanacs and calendars (6.1, 6.9, 7.10, cf 8.11), and perhaps Burton on biblical chronology (6.10). There was also the usual interest in travels and voyages (*Voyages*, 5.11; Bingley, 2.11; James, 4.1; Holland, 4.2).

His christian reading matter was broad, written by or about Anglicans (D'Oyly/Mant, 1.1; Blair, 1.4; Andrewes, 1.10; Berens, 2.1; 2.3; Mann, 2.2; Burnet, 2.5; Wells, 2.6; Bingley, 2.11; Paley, 2.12; Pearce, 2.13; Milman, 4.3; Stebbing, 4.4; *Directions*, 8.10; James, 4.1; Hammond, 4.7; Hale, 4.7; Allestree, 4.9, 6.11; Hooker, Herbert, and Sanderson, 5.2; Porteus, 5.3; Davy, 5.7; Wilson, 7.1; White, 7.7); some broad church (Burnet, 2.5), some old High (?Nelson, 6.7), some (early) High church (Jones, 4.12; Horne, 5.1; Bowles, 5.5); Puritans (?Milton, 1.3; Hall, 2.10; Hale, 4.7; ?Baxter, 5.6; Alleine, 7.6); dissenters (Flavel, 4.11; Enfield, 5.8; Doddridge, 6.8; Alleine, 7.6; Foster, 9.1; Watts, 3.7, 7.7; cf. 5.7; the Congregationalists; Burder, 5.7 and Appleton, 4.5; the Baptist, Rippon, 8.2), sometime dissenters (Dorrington, 6.2), and writers against dissenters (Herbert, 5.2; White, 7.7; cf. Wells, 2.6), Methodists (Wesley's hymns, 1.12, 8.3; *Methodist Magazine*, 3.5; Edmondson, 3.8, 4.10), methodist influenced or flavoured (Hervey, 8.4; Horne, 6.5), and writers against methodism (Stebbing, 4.4; Jones, 4.12), as well as Anglicans with Methodist/Evangelical commitments or sympathies (Fletcher, 3.10; Whitefield, 3.16; Porteus, 5.3; Bowdler, 4.8; Horne, 5.1); There were authors and works well-known in evangelical circles (Alleine, 7.6; ?Good, 4.12; 4.9, 6.11[183]; Stebbing, 4.4; Doddridge, 6.8; Burder, 5.7, 6.12; Hervey, 8.4; Foster, 9.1; *Evangelical Magazine*, 3.9, cf. 5.7; Whitefield, 3.16; Bowdler, 4.8; Porteus, 5.3).

Much the same breadth is found in his many volumes of sermons, which show Moore's desire to nurture his faith from expositions from preachers of many different persuasions and periods, including those of some reputation. Blair (1.4), from the 'old school' of 'moderate divines'; Andrewes from the old style Anglicans (1.10); Berens (2.3), Pearce (2.13), Stebbing (4.4) and Foster (9.1) were Anglican, as were Davy (5.7) Valentine & Ramsay (6.12) if they were on Moore's list; the Methodist, Edmondson (3.8); the Congregationalist, Appleton (4.5); and the Evangelical/Methodist Burder (5.7, ?6.12). Sermons were evidently read in Sydney with sufficient demand to create a market, for, in 1824, amongst the 'valuable books' advertised for sale in the *Sydney Gazette* there were several volumes of Sermons and Discourses, by Blair, Sludden, Russel, Mason, Robertson, Horne, Prince, Allison, Sturm.

Moore has some serious works of Theology on his shelf, such as Paley (2.12), Foster (9.1), and Flavel on Providence (4.11). He appears to have an interest in heaven, owning Edmondson on the Heavenly world (4.10), Alleine (7.6) and Baxter's *Saints Rest* (5.6). More generally, his books represent a variety of theological positions. His shelf included Calvinists (Hall, 2.10; Watts, 3.7; Sanderson, 5.2; Hervey, 8.4; Whitefield, 3.16) and Arminians (Milton, 1.3; *Methodist Magazine*, 3.5; Fletcher, 3.10; Baxter, 5.6; possibly attacked in *Cattipaedia &c*, 11.8; Hervey, 8.4, wrote against the Arminianism of John Wesley). On the other hand, he also possessed a full-blown commendation of Unitarianism (5.9), as well as several with an Arian/Unitarian 'suspicion', 'reputation', or 'past experience' about them (Milton, 1.3; Watts, 3.7; Good, 4.12; Foster, 9.1; Bowles specifically wrote against it, 5.5), and possibly also a Swedenbourgian (M. Sibly, 3.15).

Despite the variety, however, this is the library of an evangelical Anglican.

The basic Anglican shape of his piety is reflected in various liturgical helps (2.1. 6.2. 6.7, 7.1, 7.4, 7.8). The concern for proper preparation for the Lord's Supper was also a feature of the Puritan/Methodist/Evangelical trajectory.

There is a very close connection between Puritanism and Methodism/Evangelicalism. Samuel Johnson described Methodism as 'a new kind of Puritanism'. English Puritanism of the 16th and 17th Centuries had a passionate concern for personal experiential faith, which undergirded its political, ethical and religious impulses. Both Samuel and Susanna Wesley came from Puritan Stock, despite their conversion to High Church Anglicanism, and Susanna ordered her family life 'according to a careful "method", with set times for teaching her children, prayer and meditation, and keeping a spiritual journal'. She read Puritan authors, especially Richard Baxter. After 1738, John Wesley rediscovered his Puritan heritage, and the English Puritans are most represented in his *Christian Library*. He strongly identified with the Puritan clergy ejected from the church in 1660–1662. He used Baxter's *Reformed Pastor* as a manual of pastoral practice for his preachers. He derived his Covenant Service by transforming an individual act of devotion derived from Puritans Joseph and Richard Alleine to a communal.[184]

This is the shelf of a man whose piety was shaped by the Bible. The D'Oyly & Mant's 'study bible' (1.1) was not simply for reading, but it was meant principally to facilitate understanding. Since Moore's 3 volume copy was only available since 1826, we have a picture of a man who was still studying his bible in the final years of his long life. Other aids to the careful study of Scripture include Well's Geography (2.6), Mann's Commentary (2.2), and the large amount of sermonic and devotional material. Amongst the devotional books, we find evidence of the practice of daily reflection upon God and his word: such as Sturm's *Reflections* (1.11), Hall's *Contemplations* (2.10), *The Whole Duty of Man* (4.9, 6.11); Bedell (7.4); *New Manual* (8.8).

The emphasis on personal devotion, both public and private,

is clear from Moore's books (D'Oyly & Mant, 1.1; Sturm, 1.11 and 2.7; Mann, 2.2; Wells, 2.6; Doddridge, 6.8; Hervey, 8.4; Hall, 2.10; [Allestree], 4.9 and 6.11; Horne, 5.1; Alleine, 7.6; Burton, 6.10; the prayer books, 9.5; Dorrington, 6.2; the *New Manual*, 8.8; *Directions*, 8.10; *Communion with God*, 7.8. He owned a copy of Alleine's *Alarme*, which was a classic of Puritan and then Methodist/evangelical devotion (7.6).

Family prayer was a particular feature of the puritan/methodist/ evangelical trajectory, and Moore had several resources here to assist him in the prayers that we know went on in his household (Mann, 2.2; *Family Prayer*, 5.4; Bowdler, 4.8; ?wreath of Friendship, 7.3; *The Whole Duty of Man*, 4.9, 6.11; *New Manual*, 8.8), beyond those which he probably bought for Andrew's benefit.

Moore had more than a fair share of hymn books and Christian poetry: Wesley (1.12; 8.3), Rippon (8.2), Watts (3.7; 5.7; 7.2), were all situated outside Anglican circles as could be expected at this time. Moore was an active supporter of the Wesleyan Auxiliary Missionary Society, and his multiple hymnbooks may reflect his 'methodist tendencies', since 'the stress on hymn singing' was often seen as a trait of the methodists.[185]

As for missionary interest, his shelf included works from those who were themselves active in mission or in missionary societies, and works aimed to equip readers for their own missionary task (Robbins, 2.9; Whitefield, 3.16; Porteus, 5.3; Edmondson, 3.8; Appleton, 4.5; J.M. Good, 4.12; Burder, 5.7; Nelson, 6.7; Wilson, 7.1). Both the *Evangelical* and *Methodist Magazines* (3.5, 3.9) would also foster missionary interests.

The presence of the *Methodist* (3.5) and *Evangelical Magazine* (3.9) is also good evidence of his own predilections towards this end of the theological spectrum, on the assumption that, whereas a book might outline a particular viewpoint which can be read by friend or foe, a magazine indicates that its subscriber wishes to keep regular contact with what it stands for. We have evidence from letters that Moore regularly received the newspapers from England, indicating that he liked to 'stay in touch'. This is also indicated by his 'lots of old magazines' (9.7), and, in particular these two magazines show that Moore was interested in regular offerings from the Evangelical/Methodist camps, which helps to situate him as an insider to these movements.

Bibles, Testaments, and Prayer Books, were, of course, staples of evangelicalism, and were handed out or sold by the Bible Society and the Religious Tract Society. Richard Johnson originally came to NSW armed with 100 Bibles, 100 Prayer Books in two sizes, and 400 Testaments in various sizes. The presence of several copies of such volumes on Moore's shelf may be a remnant of his active support of the Bible Society and of the Religious Tract Society.[186]

It is a little strange that Moore does not list a copy of Bunyan's *Pilgrim's Progress*, or, indeed *Foxe's Book of Martyrs*, part of the staple reading diet of evangelical homes at the time, and both amongst the books distributed amongst prisoners.[187]

The booklist does, however, reflect the Puritan-Methodist-evangelical concern for moral reformation. Within the 'moralist' framework, the power of example for good or ill is almost axiomatic. On the negative side, Bowdler's *Selections* (4.8) epitomizes the fear that a mere exposure to 'immorality', even in the Scriptures, will lead to an immoral outcome. But the power of positive example is represented more frequently. Such examples need not be found only within the Christian ambit, for they are also furnished from the classical world, in Plutarch's *Lives* (3.11), or from the romantic hero Don Quixote (3.13). Christian circles furnished the majority, however, starting with the *Life of Christ* himself (3.12), through those of Hale & Hammond (4.7), a Churchman and a Puritan; those of churchmen Hooker, Herbert and Sanderson (5.2); the Methodist, Longden (1.8), the Anglican-Methodists Fletcher (3.10) and Whitefield (3.16). Other authors on the list also provided models, even if they were not the subject of a *Life*, such as Wilson (7.1), whose moral reforms were spoken of highly in Anglican circles.

Although Christian ministers are in good supply here, the Christian laymen such as Steele's *Christian Hero* (8.11), Hale (4.7), the campaigning lawyer Bowles (5.5), and the legal reformer

Colquhoun (2.14) would have provided welcome models for Moore. Some on the list were involved in the kind of philanthropy Moore himself was known for (Porteus, 5.3; Bowdler, 4.8; Nelson, 6.7; and Wilson, 7.1, especially through promoting libraries along the Bray scheme). Moore's own involvement in philanthropic endeavours may be represented on his bookshelf, if the Odd books (9.6) are indicative of his membership in the Oddfellows, and if the Bibles, Testaments and Prayer Books are indicative of his involvement in the Bible Society and/or Religious Tract Society. If Penton's later work (8.6) was on Moore's shelf, it would have provided him with an impetus to view education within the grand vision of imparting the principles of moral reform to the next generation. This sounds strangely prophetic of one of the major aspects of Moore's life and the cause to which he committed his legacy.

If reading was the key to moral reformation, then not only does the mere existence of this library speak of Moore's moral agenda, but such volumes can be regarded as at the core of a library collected for that purpose. At the other end of the scale, however, were the novels, which were part of the 'reading for distraction' that the moral reformers despised. Moore's shelf had only a few works which could be called 'novels'. Don Quixote (3.13) and Steele's *Christian Hero* (8.11), however, could be regarded as exemplary tales, encouraging Romantic moral heroism. The *Wreath of Friendship* (7.3) may have been another novel. Captain Ashe's, *Liberal Critic* (5.9), is the only work definitely in the 'trashy' category, according to one reviewer at the time of publication. This could have been on the shelf due to nostalgia, since it purported to speak with the voice of Henry Percy, the namesake and distant relative of several dukes and earls from Moore's home district in Northumberland. On the other hand, as a novel with moral reform in view, even if that reform was to be derived from a Unitarian belief system, it could find a clear place amongst the library of a reformer, for it was a novel which purported to have a serious purpose.

Does this booklist provide a window onto Moore's own ministry and mission? He owned several evangelistic works (Edmondston, 4.10; Alleine, 7.6; Baxter, 5.6; Doddridge, 6.8; perhaps *Village Conversations*, 8.7) useful for distribution, as were the Bibles and Testaments and perhaps the Prayer books (9.3–5). Apart from the famous apologetic work from Paley (2.12), other volumes also served the apologetic purpose, such as Porteus (5.3), Lyttelton (4.12), ?Stebbings (4.4); Foster (9.1); possibly Burton's work on Daniel, since the prophecy of Daniel played a large part in apologetics at the time (6.10); and possibly Robbins' treatment of other religions (2.9). *Sea sermons* (6.12), probably reflects Moore's continued interest in the sea and seafarers, and he could have been involved in the Bethel Union, set up to provide ministry to such people. Horne's *manual of prayer for the afflicted* (6.5) is a definite aid to ministry. Since it was published late in Moore's life, he may have used it for his own concerns, or as part of his care for Rachel in her old age, as well as for others. Is the presence of Enfield's *Speaker* (5.8) an indication that Moore may have preached from time to time? If so, presumably at St Lukes, or on the Methodist circuit.

Part D: Thomas Moore's Bookshelf: Some Preliminary Conclusions

The 'List of Books the Property T. Moore Esq.' shows books owned by Thomas Moore and his step-son Andrew White. Those clearly belonging to Andrew are in French and largely concerned with his profession, military engineering, for which he was evidently well educated. They may also show a slight leaning towards enlightenment thought, 'radical politics', and only a slight interest in religion.

From Thomas Moore's books we can construct a profile of a man who was keen to be educated, both in the broad sense of the word, and specifically about his professional activities, whether seafaring, ship-building, farming, or acting as magistrate.

Although there is only slight evidence of an interest in political reform and Enlightenment thinking, the major strength of the library is in Christianity. Moore's books indicate that he was a man of piety, who fed his faith on the study of Scripture, aided by sermons from a variety of sources, Bible study aids, and some serious theological works. Although his piety seems to have been within an Anglican framework, he also engaged with the thought of dissenters and even Unitarianism finds a place on his shelf. Nevertheless, the balance and focus of his books seems to indicate that he stood within the Puritan/ Methodist/ Evangelical trajectory. Not only does this seem to have determined his piety, and shaped his concern for moral reformation, but it also fostered an interest in mission and ministry to others.

This preliminary exploration has therefore enabled a small beginning in the task of uncovering the intellectual and 'heart' history that lay behind the life and actions of Mr Moore of Liverpool, 'much esteemed for his piety and charity'.

Notes

1. List of Books the Property T. Moore, Esq. (SDA: The Trustees of the Estate of the Late Thomas Moore, 0853CH, Item 5).
2. As Moore neared the end of his life, it is clear that he took a number of steps with regard to the later disposal of his property. See, for example, not only his careful, long-term decisions in regard to his Will and its Codicil, but also other items he prepared to make the Trustees' job a little simpler, e.g. T. Moore, Memorandum to Trustees & Executors, 21 Dec 1837 (SDA: 0853CH, Item 15, doc. 17). On 10th December 1829, he had pasted into his rent book, a list of the 'Plate' found in his residence (SDA 0884CH, Item 6a). Just months before he died he appended a note, 'counted all the above and found all correct, T.M.', (28 May 1840). Presumably this was for the same purpose, and listing his books may have been another such step.
3. Trustees Minute Book 1, p.1; Loane, *Centenary History*, 177. See further, [ADB], 'McLeay, Alexander (1767–1848)'; Newman, 'Campbell, Robert (1804–1859)'; Cable, 'Broughton, W.G. (1788–1853)'.
4. Trustees Minute Book 1, p.3, entry for 21 Jan 1841.
5. Trustees Minute Book 1, p. 2, entry for 21 Jan 1841.
6. When looking for a lost plan of Liverpool, Layton wrote to Kerrison James asking him 'to have the goodness to look in the Case of Books, as I remember throwing every think of the kind that I discovered on the premises after the sale, into that Case'; J. Layton to K. James, 7 Jan 1842, SDA 0851CH, Item 8, doc. 1.
7. Trustees Minute Book 1, p.4, entry for 30 Jan 1841. Mary Ann appears to have been

rather concerned to ensure she got what she considered belonged to her. After the death of Andrew, notwithstanding the fact that his Will distributed his estate amongst those he considered his family, she wrote to the English relatives of his father, John White, asking them if 'the Family will readily give it up in her favor without the trouble and expence of its being paid in the Court of Law', Anne Lorack to Rachel Moore, 11 Aug 1838 (SDA 0853CH, Item 11, Doc. 10).
8. *Trustees Minute Book*, p.5.
9. *Trustees Minute Book* 1, p.5: '2 Feb. 1841, 'The Executors of the late Mr Moore attended this day at the Supreme Court, Sydney, and proved the Will and Codicil'.
10. *Trustees Minute Book* 1, p.10.
11. *Trustees Minute Book* 1, p.58, entry for 12 Nov 1844. Although direct comparison is difficult for all kinds of reasons, it might be worth noting that the total value of Jeake's library of 2100 volumes was £141.05.07 on 1 June 1681, and £145–05–11 on 2 Oct 1690; Hunter, Mandelbrote, et al, *A Radical's Books*, 318–319, which was regarded as 'a substantial sum' (p.xxix).
12 I have not pinpointed Andrew's arrival back in the colony, but it was in the earliest 1830s. *Thomas Moore's Account Book 1828–1840*; SDA 0885CH, Item 6, shows that Thomas was still sending Andrew letters in 1830 (entry for 15/4), and that his stepson had arrived in Sydney by 1833 (27/3, and beyond).
13. For a similar attempt to discern an intellectual profile from a list of books in an earlier private collection, see Hunter, Mandelbrote, et al, *A Radical's Books*. For an Australian private collection, the library of Rev. Thomas Hattam Wilkinson, Rector of Canberra and a number of Sydney parishes 1840–1870, now housed as a special collection in Moore College library, can be considered to show 'the interests of a clergyman of the last half of the nineteenth century'; Robinson, 'Anglican Libraries: Moore', 72.
14. Cf. the discussion about 'the fate of [Jeake's] library in Hunter, Mandelbrote, et al, *A Radical's Books*, lx–lxiv.
15. The SDL eventually found its way into the Moore College collection in 1959; see Robinson, 'Anglican Libraries: Moore', 71.
16. These identifications have been made through online/electronic resources of EEBO, ECCO, NSTC; the catalogues of COPAC, the British Library, Cambridge University, Trinity College Dublin, Library of Congress, Bibliothèque National De France, Moore College Library, State Library of NSW, Bibliothèque Nationale de France, worldcat.org, as well as Amazon.com, biblio.org, abebooks.com, and several other websites of specialist antiquarian booksellers, and other material available through the search engines www.google.com and www.yahoo.com. I have performed some checking of details where books have been available to me, and I have also consulted Wing, *Short Title Catalogue 1640–1700*. Despite some obvious limitations in this method, the end results have been, nevertheless, sufficient for this 'preliminary examination'.
17. See Mackintosh, *Richard Johnson*, 105–106.
18. I have referred to two reports, the 4th report of 1839, and the 7th report of 1842, since the booklists of these two reports are accessible on the web. See, respectively, http://www.institutions.org.uk/prisons/info/prison_report_1839.htm (23/12/2006); http://www.institutions.org.uk/prisons/info/prison_report_1842.htm (26/12/2006).
19. Note: 'Nearly all of the most intelligent and zealous chaplains [...] agree in considering a library a very useful instrument of good in a prison', 1842 Prison Report.
20. Note the 1842 Prison Report, where the compiler notes that 'The Chaplain [of Gloucestershire prison] purchases such as he thinks proper out of the Society's list'.
21. *Thomas Moore's Account Book 1828–1840*; SDA 0885CH, Item 6, 12/11/1835: 'Paid Mr Moffitt for Tracks for Mr Sadler, £4–18–9'; 30/11/1835, Paid Subscription to Religious Tract Society, 2 years to January 1836 £4'.
22. Robinson, 'Anglican Libraries: Moore', 71. It consisted of 71 volumes, see Moore

College Library Catalogue. As it happens, although there is some overlap of authors, none of these books are found amongst Moore's.
23. SG on 30 December 1824.
24. Hunter, Mandelbrote, et al, *A Radical's Books*.
25. Green, 'Sample'.
26. '& French' is crossed out in pencil, as is the later listing of French books on pages 9ff. Note that square brackets, [], enclose my own descriptive comments or queries.
27. DNBA 1.836; DNB 5.1324.
28. See the brief biographical sketch in Swanzy, *Succession Lists*. See also DNB 12.981–983.
29. DNB 11.911–912.
30. The Memorandums began on 8 April 1822, and they include lessons drawn from Cyrus, Antigonus, Pericles, etc. Thomas Moore, *Memorandums & Occurrences* (SDA: 0884CH, Item 5).
31. DNBA 2.2039–40; DNB 13.471–488.
32. Dyton, 'Milton, John (1608–74)'.
33. See 1842 Prison Report, Wakefield, Kendal, Derbyshire, and Norwich. The histories of England by Pinnock and Goldsmith also appear, listed by their names.
34. DNB 2.622–623.
35. Stephen, *History*, 2, 346.
36. Stephen, *History*, 2, 347.
37. DNB 11.706–708.
38. 'Lawrence', DNB 11.707.
39. Methodist Archives Biographical Index, http://rylibweb.man.ac.uk/data1/dg/methodist/bio/biol.html (11/4/07); source: Revd. T. Alexander Seed, *Norfolk Street Wesleyan Chapel, Sheffield* (1907), 107–111.
40. DNBA 1.379; DNB 3.180–181.
41. DNB 1.401–405; DNBA 1.55.
42. Broughton to Coleridge, 28th December 1844.
43. *The Penny Cyclopædia of the Society for the Diffusion of Useful Knowledge*, http://books.google.com/books?id=HGt_tlAq1R8C&pg=PA169&lpg=PA169&dq=%22christopher+sturm%22&source=web&ots=QyIcdQRlt9&sig=gOR0bIEvUN8tp_kiljhBmw3JRNQ (12/4/07).
44. See 1839 Prison Report, Lancaster Castle, Milbank.
45. DNB 15.625.
46. See 1839 Prison Report.
47. For digital copies, see http://www.lib.msu.edu/digital/Exhibit1/Books/MARCET.htm (14/4/07), and http://www.openlibrary.org/details/conversationsonn00marciala (14/4/07).
48. DNBA 1.403–404; DNB 3.394–405.
49. One of his later relatives, however, George, was an evangelical, serving as curate for Henry Venn (1759); Wood, 'Burnett, George'.
50. See 1839 Prison Report, Lancaster Castle; and 1842 Prison Report, Wakefield.
51. DNB 20.1138–39.
52. His diary is now on http://www.questia.com.
53. DNB 8.959–964.
54. *The Life of Bishop Hall* is included in the later editions of *Historical Passages*, written by James Hamilton (1780–1835). John Jones, Perpetual Curate of Cradley, Worcestershire, also wrote *Bishop Hall, His Life And Times: Or, Memoirs Of The Life, Writings, And Sufferings Of The Right Rev. Joseph Hall, D.D., Successively Bishop Of Exeter And Norwich, Etc.* (London, Buckingham [printed], 1826). Peter Hall (1802–1849), a divine, edited Bishop Joseph Halls works (1837–1839). See also DNBA 2.1285; Webster, 'Hall, Joseph (1574–1656)'.
55. See 1842 Prison Report. His *Works* and *Life* were circulated at Lancaster Castle, see 1839 Prison Report.

CHAPTER 7 ~ *Thomas Moore's Bookshelf* [207]

56. *DNB* 2.517.
57. *DNB* 15.101–107.
58. See 1839 Prison Report, Lancaster Castle; and 1842 Prison Report, Northamptonshire.
59. *DNB* 15.596–597.
60. *DNBA* 1.615; *DNB* 4.859–861.
61. *DNB* 10.1245.
62. 1839 Prison Report, Milbank.
63. *DNB* 4.598–601. For his lesser known writings, see the list at http://www.pickering chatto.com/index.php/pc_site/major_works/william_cobbett_selected_writings.
64. So, Brinton, *English Political Thought*, 61–73, esp. 62.
65. *DNB* 10.919–935.
66. 16/4/1835: 'Paid Mr Moffitt for Magistrate Manuall', *Thomas Moore's Account Book 1828–1840*; SDA 0885CH, Item 6.
67. All information here from *DNB* 20.978–981.
68. See also Vickers, 'Edmondson, Jonathan (1766–1842)', 107.
69. After volume 30 (1822) there was a new series published from 1823–1858 (36 volumes), a ten volume third series (1859–1868), a 21 volume fourth series (1869–1892), and in 1893 a fifth series was launched. An index to the first 24 volumes was published in 1817.
70. *DNBA* 1.1030; Forsaith, 'Fletcher, Rev. John William (1729–85)', 124.
71. See 1839 Prison Report, Lancaster Castle, and 1842 Prison Report, Wakefield, Derbyshire.
72. *OCD* (rev. ^{3}2003, ^{3}1996, 1949), 1201.
73. See 1842 Prison Report.
74. *DNB* 18.185.
75. *DNB* 18.185.
76. Grundy, 'Whitefield, George (1714–1770)', 392.
77. See 1842 Prison Report.
78. *DNBA*, 2. 1574; *DNB* 10.654–655.
79. *DNB* 13.448–451.
80. *DNB* 18.1010–1011.
81. *DNB* 18.1010–1011.
82. *DNB* 18.1011–1012.
83. Personal information, including Appleton's sermons, is available in the Jesse Appleton Collection. http://library.bowdoin.edu/arch/archives/jag.shtml (28/7/06).
84. http://library.bowdoin.edu/arch/mss/jag.shtml (28/7/06).
85. *DNB* 8.1126–1130.
86. *DNBA* 2.1278; *DNB* 8.902–908.
87. See 1839, Milbank, cf. Lancaster Castle had the separate *Life of Hale*; 1842 Prison Report, Wakefield.
88. Railsback, 'Bowdler, John'.
89. *DNBA* 1.301; *DNB* 2.952–954.
90. 1839 Prison Report, Milbank.
91. [Enc.Brit.^{15}], 'Pufendorf'.
92. See, for example, 'Hammond', *DNB* 8.1128.
93. *DNB* 1.324–325; *DNBA* 1.42–43.
94. 1839 Prison Report, Milbank; 1842 Prison Report, Wakefield.
95. Wallace, 'Flavel (Flavell), John (1627–1691)', 1.98; *DNBA* 1.1023.
96. *DNB* 10. 1065–66
97. Marsden, *Memoirs*, 45–46.
98. *DNB* 8.110–111. See Marsden, *Memoirs*, 118.
99. 1842 Prison Report.
100. *DNB* 12.369–374.
101. *DNB* 20.1241.

102. 1842 Prison Report.
103. *DNBA* 2.1480; *DNB* 9.1250–1251.
104. See 1842 Prison Report.
105. These works can now be found in e-form at http://anglicanhistory.org/walton/index.html.
106. *DNB* 20.730–734.
107. Bremer, 'Hooker, Richard (1554–1600)', 1.130; see also *DNB* 9.1183–1189.
108. *DNB* 9.636–639.
109. McGee, 'Sanderson, Robert (1587–1663)', 1.227; see also *DNB* 17.754–755.
110. 1839 Prison Report, Lancaster Castle; 1842 Prison Report, Wakefield.
111. *DNBA* 3.2426; *DNB* 16.195–197.
112. See 1842 Prison Report.
113. Nockles, *Oxford Movement*, 64 n.66 and 107.
114. Spurr, 'Baxter, Richard (1615–1691)', 1.19–21.
115. 1839 Prison Report: Lancaster Castle; 1842 Prison Report: Derbyshire, Norwich.
116. *DNBA* 1.393; *DNB* 3.294–295.
117. 1839 Prison Report: Lancaster Castle; 1842 Prison Report: Kendal, Wakefield, Northamptonshire.
118. *DNBA* 1.934; *DNB* 6.787–788.
119. Olphar Hamst, in " Notes and Queries," fourth series, vol. ii. p. 340, 1868, cited in connection with Ashe's residence on the Isle of Man at http://www.isle-of-man.com/manxnotebook/manxsoc/msvol24/p122.htm (16/4/07). See also http://www.british-fiction.cf.ac.uk (16/4/07).
120. http://web.ukonline.co.uk/suttonelms/jarden.html (20/4/07).
121. I have fortunately been able to read the microfilm copy held in the Australian National Library.
122. *Monthly Review*, 2nd ser. 72 (Nov 1813): 327. www.british-fiction.cf.ac.uk/reviews/libe12-19.html (17/4/07).
123. Ashe, *Liberal Critic*, 219.
124. This is, of course, speculative. Another possibility could be that Moore began as a Unitarian, but was somewhere converted to Christianity—following the pattern of Dr Mason Good, whose book may have been on his shelf (see 4.12), and Foster (9.1).
125. *DNB* 4.307–308.
126. For other similar books on voyages, see http://www.easternwoodlandindian.com/index_files/page0022.html (26/12/2006).
127. *DNB* 11.64.
128. 1842 Prison Report: Kendal, Derbyshire.
129. *DNB* 5.1155–1156.
130. SDA 0884CH Items 2 and 3 (both 1805).
131. *DNB* 9.1257–1258.
132. *DNB* 15.439–442.
133. The library brought back to Australia in 1809 by Samuel Marsden to form the Port Jackson Lending Library was donated by 'the Associates of Dr Bray'. It now forms the 'Bray collection' in Moore College Library.
134. *DNB* 14.210–212.
135. We know of one, at least. Rachel was the godmother to another Rachel Moore, daughter of J.J. Moore. See *Thomas Moore's Account Book 1828–1840*; SDA 0885CH, Item 6, entry for 14/1/1839.
136. Dykes, 'Doddridge, Philip (1702–51)', 98; *DNBA*, 1.807.
137. 1839 Report: Milbank, Lancaster Castle; 1842 Report: Kendal, Wakefield, Derbyshire, Gloucester, Nottinghamshire.
138. *DNBA* 1.411; *DNB* 3.456.
139. See 1842 Prison Report.

140. *DNB* 21.610–613.
141. This edition has been recently republished: *Falconer's New Universal Dictionary of the Marine* (Chatham Publishing, 2006), an improvement on *The Old Wooden Walls ... being an abridged edition of Falconer's celebrated Marine Dictionary* (Ed. & arr. Claude S. Gill; London: W. & G. Foyle, 1930).
142. *DNBA* 1.39; Wallace, 'Alleine, Joseph (1634–1668)', 1.3.
143. See the 1794 edition: 'London: printed by G. Paramore; sold by G. Whitfield, and at the Methodist preaching-houses in town and country, 1794'.
144. 1839 Prison Report: Lancaster Castle; 1842 Prison Report: Kendal, Wakefield, Nottinghamshire.
145. 1842 Prison Report: Derbyshire.
146. *DNB* 18.1017–1025.
147. See further *DNB* 16.1204–1205.
148. Vickers, 'Hervey, Rev. James (1714–58)', 156; *DNB* 9.733–735.
149. 1839 Prison Report: Lancaster Castle; 1842 Prison Report: Kendal (his *Works*), Wakefield, Derbyshire.
150. 1839 Prison Report: Milbank has a volume short-titled 'arithmetic'.
151. 1839 Prison Report: Lancaster Castle.
152. 1842 Prison Report: Wakefield.
153. See Claeys, *The Political Writings of the 1790s*, Vol. 4; http://www.pickeringchatto.com/index.php/pc_site/major_works/the_political_writings_of_the_1790s (17/4/07).
154. *DNBA* 1.1052; *DNB* 7.494–495.
155. For a facsimile edition, published by Jean Boudriot (1992), see: http://www.amazon.com/Shipbuilders-Repository-1788-Limited-Facsmile/dp/B000KIVBOQ/sr=1-7/qid=1166857703/ref=sr_1_7/105-5427445-1759658?ie=UTF8&s=books. For an extract from the book, see the transcription by Lars Bruzelius of its explanation of shipbuilding terms at http://www.bruzelius.info/nautica/Etymology/English/Repository(1788)_p443.html (23/12/06).
156. After this line in the original, the books are crossed out with a pencil cross through each section/ page. 'French Books' is Moore's heading.
157. http://www.maggs.com//AU3800.asp (23/12/06).
158. See 1842 Prison Report.
159. The 'a' is written above the 'e'.
160. For a list of his works, see http://efts.lib.uchicago.edu/efts/VOLTAIRE (28/12/06).
161. *DNB* 10.235–237.
162. *DNB* 18.930–931.
163. Cf. http://www.davidrumsey.com/maps462.html (26/12/2006); http://experts.about.com/e/j/je/jean_baptiste_bourguignon_d'anville.htm (26/12/2006).
164. Hunter, Mandelbrote, et al, *A Radical's Books*, xiv-xv, observe that, although relatively few personal libraries have survived from 18th c. England, the most famous of which being that of Samuel Pepys (3500 vols.), several catalogues from this period have survived, besides Jeake's (2100 vols.), including that of Richard Baxter (1500 vols.), T. Hall (1000 vols.) and T. Teakle (333 vols.). The list of books belonging to enlightenment surgeon and explorer, George Bass, had only 90 titles; Estensen, *George Bass*, 65–66.
165. See Gribben, 'Introduction', 1–4, and Horde, 'The Library', 19–42. Since both evangelicals and utilitarians of the middle classes agreed that 'improving' literature was necessary for the working classes, works deemed to be suitable to this aim stocked the emerging public libraries and were propagated by such bodies as the Society for the Diffusion of Useful Knowledge; see Lyons, 'New Readers', 332–335. The American Tract Society published pamphlets on proper reading methods within this framework, see those reproduced in Nord, *Faith in Reading*, Appendix, 161–163.

166. Item 11.4 may prove to be another.
167. If item 11.8 was 'against education', then this too may find belong to the enlightenment discussion about education, but this remains speculative while the book remains unidentified.
168. For his friendship with T.F. Palmer, a Unitarian minister, see Chisholm, 'Editor's Introduction', 14–16. Although they were associated less than two months, he gave Palmer a house and four acres of land, and took documents to England on his return which resulted in the publication of Palmer and Skirving's narrative; Chisholm, 'Editor's Introduction', 15–16.
169. 'There was then close links between non-conformism in religion and radicalism in politics, and Paine's subsequent career shows that he possessed this latter cast of mind', Knight & Frost, 'Introduction', xviii, xxiii–xxiv. For Paine mixing with the Scottish Martyrs, see *Journal*, 24, 30.
170. Chisholm, 'Editor's Introduction', 16. Estensen, *George Bass*, 61–65, who calls Bass 'Surgeon and Sailor of the Enlightenment'.
171. SDA 0884CH, Items 2 & 3.
172. On 3/1/1829 he 'paid 7–16 for Almanack', *Thomas Moore's Account Book 1828–1840*; SDA 0885CH, Item 6.
173. This was in a libel action reported at length in *SG* 20/12/1826. A lack of legal training was the norm for magistrates at the time, and, in our early days, even Judge-Advocates (such as David Collins) knew little of the law.
174. 16/4/1835: 'Paid Mr Moffitt for Magistrate Manuall', *Thomas Moore's Account Book 1828–1840*; SDA 0885CH, Item 6.
175. Claeys (ed.), *Political Writings of the 1790s*. The list of pamphlets collected here includes two of Moore's authors, John Bowles and William Paley, but not the works he possessed. http://www.pickeringchatto.com/index.php/pc_site/major_works/the_political_writings_of_the_1790s.
176. See Lyons, 'New Readers'; Gribben, 'Introduction'; Horde, 'The Library'.
177. Broughton's Latin Oration, *SMH*, see Robinson, 'Early Life', 165.
178. See Lyons, 'New Readers', esp. 335–344. Autodidacts were often associated with radicalism.
179. This is further endorsed by the reputation Thomas Moore gained as an excellent ship builder.
180. Wittmann, 'Reading Revolution?', 287.
181. Wittmann, 'Reading Revolution', 285.
182. Moore was indirectly involved in the Napoleonic wars, officially, through his position as S/Purveyor of Timber in the colony seeking timber for naval uses; and personally, through the purchase of some of the '3% Consols' (i.e. bonds) sold by the Home Government to help finance the wars.
183. Despite Whitefield's opposition.
184. For this paragraph, see Newton, 'Puritanism', 285; and Monk, 'Puritanism and Methodism', 173.
185. Yarwood, *Marsden. Survivor*, 202.
186. 12/11/1835: 'Paid Mr Moffitt for Tracks for Mr Sadler, £4-18-9'; 30/11/1835, Paid Subscription to Religious Tract Society, 2 years to January 1836 £4'; *Thomas Moore's Account Book 1828–1840*; SDA 0885CH, Item 6.
187. Foxe: Kendal House of Correction, see 1842 Prison Report. Bunyan: Lancaster Castle & Home District (1839 Report), Wakefield, Nottingham, Kendal (1842 Report).

CHAPTER 8

LIVERPOOL AND THE LASH

The Magistrate Thomas Moore[1]

As part of the celebrations marking 150 years of Moore College, tonight we remember the college's benefactor Mr Thomas Moore of Liverpool.[2]

The life of Thomas Moore can be divided nicely into three distinct phases. First, the thirty years prior to 1792 when he arrived in Australia as ship's carpenter on the *Britannia*. Until this sesquicentenary year we have known nothing about this phase of Moore's life, but some recently uncovered letters in the Diocesan Archives have enabled the discovery of Moore's English place and family of origin. Having intrigued you with this declaration, we are not going to look at this phase of his life tonight.[3]

The second phase was between 1796 and 1809, when Thomas Moore was the Master Boat Builder at the King's Dockyard on the western side of Sydney Cove, roughly where the Museum of Contemporary Art now stands. In 1970, Donald Robinson carefully described much of what can be known of Thomas Moore's life during this period, which is certainly full of great interest and intrigue.[4] But having assured you of how interesting phase 2 of Moore's life is, we are not going there either.

Tonight I want to focus on some aspects of what we might call the 'mature Thomas Moore'. Phase 3 begins in 1809, when Thomas retired from the Dockyard after 13 years service, now aged 47.

He and his wife Rachel then moved to the house he had built on the banks of the George's River, aptly named 'Moore Bank'. The site of Moore's house is now commemorated as 'Thomas Moore Park' in Chipping Norton, and its name, of course, survives in the suburb we still call Moorebank.

In 1810, Moore accompanied Governor Lachlan Macquarie when he selected the site for a new township, which Macquarie named Liverpool. That same year, Macquarie had also appointed Thomas Moore as the resident magistrate for the district—a position he would hold for the next thirty years, right up until the time that he died on Christmas Eve, 1840.

This is the phase of Thomas Moore's life we will be dipping into tonight, under the title, 'Liverpool and the Lash: The Magistrate Thomas Moore'.

Liverpool and the Lash

You cannot really speak of a magistrate in early NSW without mentioning the lash. NSW was founded as a penal colony and, since the transportation of convicts only ceased in 1838,[5] two years before he died, Thomas Moore only ever knew NSW as a penal colony. As a magistrate, he was entrusted with the onerous duty of checking offences against the convict code. In NSW convicts were 'assigned servants', but their masters had no right to use the lash to discipline them.[6] If they offended, it was the magistrates who heard the cases and dispensed whatever punishments were deemed necessary.

The penal environment in earliest NSW was, as a whole, severe. 'The principal weapon in eighteenth-century English criminal law was the death penalty, or at least the threat of it. Some 200 offences carried the death penalty.'[7] Although the English courts often commuted death sentences, NSW criminals under sentence of death were far more likely to go to the gallows. It underlines the severity of this era, to note that after execution the condemned criminal's body was then dissected and placed on public view.[8] Such were the times.

Not being permitted to administer the death penalty, for the NSW magistrates it was the cat-o-nine tails—also known as 'the three sisters'—which was the weapon of choice.[9] There is no doubt that NSW magistrates made very good use of the lash, and 'flogging was the symbol of the system' for them and for us.[10] If you wanted to avoid a flogging, you were far safer to be a convict in England or America. NSW magistrates ordered about five times more floggings than their English counterparts.[11] In 1830, in the Massachusetts State Prison, ten lashes were considered a severe punishment, while at the same time in NSW male convicts received an average of 44 lashes each. Indeed, if you wanted to keep your back unscarred, you were better off being a slave in America, where the legal limit was the biblical 39 lashes, whereas in NSW it was 100.[12]

This was certainly the dirty side of Thomas Moore's job as magistrate at Liverpool. The lash was his to dispense, in these harsh times and in a system of overly-intense policing,[13] and overly-severe punishment. Some magistrates rightly earned a reputation for being far more severe with the lash than others.[14] Some magistrates, such as Chaplain Samuel Marsden, may have earned this reputation.[15] Marsden may have had it unjustly thrust upon them, but have it he did.[16] As far as I have been able to discover, Thomas Moore did *not* have a reputation for being severe in his punishments.[17]

The memory of the severity of punishments in the early days had grown to almost legendary proportions at a later time.[18] But it was not only the severity of punishments handed down by NSW magistrates that was a concern. A series of events in the early 1820s originating with the Parramatta bench led to a local inquiry at the initiative of Governor Brisbane, and then to the matter being tabled before the House of Commons in London in April-May 1826.[19] The issue here was not so much the *severity* of the punishments, but their *illegality*. It was not deemed proper in British law to punish a prisoner in order to illicit a confession, or to gain information; nor to have an indefinite sentence hanging over their head; nor to have a repeated punishment. Yet a practice of such things had grown up in certain parts of the colony, especially between 1815 and 1823, and especially at Parramatta. But the Parramatta magistrates were not the only ones who were named in the 1826 *Return* that was submitted to the House of Commons. Unfortunately our own Mr Moore was caught up in the bad press. For the Liverpool bench, with Thomas Moore as the senior magistrate, had one of its cases named in that submission to Parliament; a case of ordering punishment in order to illicit further information about the crime.

Even at the time, there was a fair degree of understanding shown towards these cases. The *Sydney Gazette* was proud (in fact, almost self-righteously so) of having stirred up the issue so much that it was eventually heard by the House. And yet, despite its strong stand against these punishments, the *Gazette* could proclaim at the same time that the magistrates were operating within a system that they had inherited, and that they had unconsciously fallen into these errors. By the end of the year, a libel action had arisen out of the whole sequence. It is interesting to note what Thomas Moore had to say when he was called as a witness in the libel action. Despite one of his own judgements being named in the English Parliament as being illegal, he could look back and say that the magistrates 'had not much reference to law in those times', that is, they were acting in ignorance.[20]

The libel action at the end of the year also flushed out some other cases that the colony itself regarded as inappropriate. In this context, another case was named in which Moore was on a bench that dealt rather severely with a prisoner.[21] Without taking this any further, it seems that whatever strategies we have previously had to invoke to redeem the good name of Samuel Marsden, we may also have to invoke in favour of Thomas Moore—at least in these two cases.

But we have gathered here tonight not to bury Moore, but to honour him, so let me quickly pass over these few cases, to speak of the wider duties attached to his office. For as magistrate, Thomas's duties extended to far more than dispensing the lash at Liverpool.

The Duties of a Colonial Magistrate

By the time the office of Justice of the Peace arrived with the First Fleet,[22] it had already acquired important and powerful duties across four and a half centuries of existence in England, and over one hundred years in other colonies.[23]

In England, the Justices of the Peace were usually country gentlemen, who had the time needed to fulfil the many duties.[24] Due to their various responsibilities, the country magistrates were virtual rulers of their districts.

Perhaps this is why Thomas Moore has been called 'the king of Liverpool'. In NSW the magistrate not only dealt with judicial matters in court, but he was also the agent of civil government in his district. He was responsible for the assignment of convicts as servants; he organized musters of convicts and other inhabitants; drew up jury lists (after the introduction of trial by jury), organized and presided at public meetings, presented petitions on behalf of the inhabitants to the appropriate authorities in Sydney' and carried out many other non-judicial functions.[25]

The Government records for 1816 give us a good sample of the duties that Moore was called upon to fulfil as magistrate. At this time the number of convicts being transported to NSW was increasing, and so one duty Moore frequently engaged in was the assignment of the convicts to those who would act as their masters. The convicts were usually sent by water to Parramatta, then by land to Liverpool. In 1816 he distributed 25 convicts from the *Ocean* in February,[26] and 10 more to be reassigned from the government gangs,[27] 30 from the *Guildford* in April,[28] 9 from the *Atlas* in June,[29] 15 from the *Elizabeth* on October 11th,[30] and a further 20 from the *Mariner* on October 18th,[31] two becoming his own servants,[32] and then the final 17 to be assigned came from the *Surry* on boxing day.[33]

He supervised the police and hired and fired government employees. And there were other bureaucratic duties of the kind that has occupied public servants for centuries. He submitted quarterly reports of births, deaths and marriages for the district. So, for example, Thomas recorded for the first quarter of 1816, that there were four children born (3 boys and 1 girl), 2 deaths (4 year old Mary Ann Jackson; and convict Stephen Kilfod, slain in a quarrel).[34] In the second quarter, Liverpool was quite productive, with 9 births (5 girls; 4 boys); and convict John Brocklehurst died.[35] In the third quarter, the boom continued with 10 births (8 girls; 2 boys) and since no-one died, I guess life was a bit safer.[36]

Thomas Moore was also the supervisor of public works in Liverpool from 1810 to 1823,[37] during which time he oversaw the construction of the public buildings in Liverpool, including the parsonage and Church building for St Luke's.

The power of the magistrate, could, of course, be abused, and there were many examples of NSW magistrates who used their position corruptly. Thomas Moore, however, was known for exactly the opposite. Take for example, the testimony of Mr G.W. Walker who visited the Moores in 1836:

> Thomas Moore is a magistrate, and an active promoter, by his influence and example, of the welfare of the community.[38]

But the magistrates in Early NSW had an importance beyond their local district. The status and power of this position was important in terms of the move towards a free Australia.

The Move Towards a Free Australia

NSW began as a penal colony and took fifty years to become a free society. If we had to nominate 'the one point at which the transition from penal colony to free society was complete, the grant of a partly-elected legislature in 1842 would be the date to choose'.[39] This means that Thomas Moore died before the struggle towards free society was complete. This is a pity, because Thomas Moore was one of the few magistrates who had been amongst those working towards this goal.

On the whole, the NSW magistracy sought to block the introduction of the institutions of a free society. The majority of magistrates were Exclusives, that is, those who wished to exclude ex-convicts from full membership in 'respectable society'. Their rival was the Emancipist faction, made up of those who had once been convicts themselves, and others who sympathised with their cause. This group argued that once a person had served their time, they ought to be restored to the full range of English liberties.

The issue that came to symbolise the Emancipist struggle was the provision of trial by jury in the courts. This became the symbol of freedom for all Englishmen. For those who could see a little further into the future, such as W.C. Wentworth, the struggle towards trial by jury was also a step towards having the full representative government that would enable NSW to say at last: 'we are free'.

Now where was Thomas Moore in all of this? Even though the magistracy was dominated by Exclusives, who were resisting this move towards freedom, the evidence suggests that Thomas Moore stood against his brother magistrates and threw his weight behind the Emancipist cause.

We should remember that Thomas Moore had good reason to be sympathetic to the emancipists, as he was actually married to an ex-convict. Rachel Moore had originally come to NSW 'at His Majesty's pleasure' on a 7 year sentence for theft. They had married in January 1797, the year after Thomas was appointed Master Boat Builder. The Romantics amongst us might like to go along with the theory that Rachel was one of the reasons he decided to leave the sea and settle in NSW. Certainly, it seems that Thomas doted on Rachel for the 42 years they spent together and valued her Christian faith, her love and companionship throughout that period. Whenever Thomas sat down to eat a meal, he had a very strong reason for supporting the Emancipist cause sitting across the table from him.

Thomas also received his original 1810 commission as a magistrate from Governor Macquarie,[40] who in many ways began the struggle towards free society with his active and public pro-Emancipist policies. In fact, Moore was actually one of the Governor's friends. Macquarie often enjoyed the Moore's hospitality at Liverpool. In case anything happened to him and Lady Macquarie while they were in the colony, the Governor also appointed Thomas and Rachel to be the guardians of Lachlan junior. When Macquarie was about to leave the colony, there was some suggestion that Thomas would take the voyage to England with him, and Rachel was one of only two emancipist women who attended Macquarie's farewell ball. After Macquarie had left, he continued his friendship with the Moores by mail. This friendship with Macquarie is another of Thomas Moore's strong associations with the pro-emancipist cause, as is his support of the later reforming governor Richard Bourke.[41]

And there are other indications as well. The supposed lack of suitable people to serve on a jury was an oft-used argument against the proposal for trial by jury. In 1819, well before the campaign for trial by jury had got under way strongly, we find Moore writing to Sir John Jamison, a leading supporter of the move towards free society, and listing the number of settlers around Liverpool who would make suitable jurymen.[42] The following year he expressed his views to Commissioner Bigge, on the convict system and made suggestions for reform.[43] In 1825, he adds his signature to a letter in support of trial by jury for the colony.[44] In 1827 it was Thomas Moore who requested the sheriff to convene a meeting to petition the King and both Houses of Parliament for Trial by Jury and a House of Assembly.[45]

We could further explore Moore's involvement in the wider political movements of the colony, but perhaps our sample so far is sufficient to demonstrate that Thomas Moore used his position as magistrate, not just to do good in his local area, but also to bring about a society that valued freedom for all its members.

But there is one last aspect of this third phase of Moore's life. As he worked towards the benefit of his local district and of the wider society, Thomas Moore operated with an even larger vision.

The Gospel Promise of the World to Come

When Thomas Moore fulfilled his many and varied duties as a magistrate, he did so as a Christian man, clinging to the gospel promise of the world to come.

Now, it is always a difficult thing to look into someone's heart, and especially difficult to do so when they are someone from the past. There are good indications, however, that Moore was motivated by Christian convictions and that he was firmly associated with evangelical Christianity.

The best indications of Moore's faith also come from this third phase of his life in which we are dabbling tonight. It is difficult to know whether he came to Australia already converted, or whether he was converted after arriving here, perhaps through the ministry of Rev. Richard Johnson.

Now, I know I previously said that I was not going to tell you anything about my discoveries about his early years. Well, I am about to go back on that promise. I will tell you something after all—I can't resist! Thomas Moore grew up in Northumberland, in a village called Lesbury. Here his family attended the local Church of England. His ancestors came from Holy Island, famous for the decorated Lindesfarne Gospels. This was also an area in which there was a strong Wesleyan presence, and indeed, John Wesley himself had preached in the district a number of times. So there are several possible Christian influences in Phase 1 of Moore's life.

The same goes for Phase 2. When Thomas was Master Builder of the Dockyard, presumably he joined the Governor and other civil and military offices in attending Richard Johnson's Church. Here he would have sat under many a gospel sermon preached by this fine evangelical servant of God, who also christened his stepson and married Thomas and Rachel.

After moving to Moore Bank—the time our third phase begins—Moore may have ridden to Parramatta to attend St Johns, where he would have sat under the ministry of another evangelical, the Rev Samuel Marsden. Once services began in Liverpool schoolhouse, he was no doubt there to hear Marsden preach again. When St Luke's Liverpool was completed—under his supervision, we should add—he and Rachel were members of that congregation for the rest of their days, under the ministry of more evangelicals, such as John Youl, Robert Cartwright and Richard Taylor.

But so far we have simply discussed various Christian aspects in his environment that could have influenced Thomas. Do we have any evidence that they actually did?

We know of his involvement with, and generous financial support of, several organizations associated with the Christian cause, such as the Benevolent Society and the Temperance Society. Although this support could have simply resulted from Moore's generous philanthropic spirit, his membership of the Bible Society speaks more strongly of his Christian convictions. When the Bible Society was founded in 1817, Thomas Moore was on the original committee.[46] This was an active committee, with members taking responsibility for doorknocking the homes in their area to offer the gift of a Bible or a Testament. In this penal society, the thought of the local magistrate appearing on your doorstep with a stack of Bibles in his hand is rather amusing, but, of course, it is also a delightful picture of the evangelical commitment of Mr Moore.

In our continued search after Moore's inner convictions, we can also listen to the testimony of others. From as early as Phase 2 and throughout Phase 3 reports can be found into Moore's good character. At the end of his life, the death notice published in the paper draws attention to the fact that 'Mr Moore was one of our oldest Colonists and much esteemed for his piety and charity'.[47]

Thomas and Rachel's home also had a reputation for its piety. There are several reports of the hospitality of the Moores. One such report tells of the Moores taking some visitors to St Luke's home after the morning service and entertaining them throughout the day and long into the evening.[48] On the tablet erected in St Luke's Liverpool to Rachel's memory, she is remembered for being 'a constant attendant at the house of God, and a strict observer of family prayer'.[49]

There is also a delightful story told by the Quaker, Mr. G.W. Walker, who, during his tour of New South Wales, visited the Moores on the 13th September 1836. As he put it:

> Went by coach to Liverpool, a town of some importance in New South Wales, containing at that time 500 inhabitants.

> 9 mo. 16—We breakfasted with Thomas Moore and his wife, the oldest inhabitants in Liverpool, having been the first to locate themselves in what was a wilderness. Thomas Moore is a magistrate, and an active promoter, by his influence and example, of the welfare of the community. After reading the Scriptures my companion had some appropriate counsel to offer, under the renewed feeling of gospel love, which was well received.[50]

At this time, Liverpool was a centre of keen missionary interest, and Thomas Moore mixed in these circles. But once again, we have more than circumstantial evidence. There is a suggestion that he may have been involved in some capacity in the early stages of setting up the Church Missionary Society in NSW.[51] Be that as it may, he was certainly a committee member for the Wesleyan Auxiliary Missionary Society.[52] We also have a letter from 1818, in which Samuel Hassall—grandson of the famous Tahitian missionary, Rowland Hassall—told his brother James that: 'Mr Moor [sic] of Liverpool for some time past has been using all his influence to prevail on me to go to New Zealand'.[53] Evidently Moore was leaning on Samuel to follow in his grandfather's footsteps by joining the (Wesleyan?) mission in New Zealand.[54] Surely this missionary interest speaks of a strong commitment to the gospel of Jesus Christ.

But do we have anything about his faith from his own mouth? Until recently, the answer would have been 'no'.[55] However, in this sesquicentenary year our Diocesan Archives have yielded some treasures that help us towards hearing about the faith of Thomas Moore from Thomas Moore himself.

Two years before he died, Thomas appears to have renewed contact with his family of origin in England. A letter from his brother William shows a warm Christian fellowship between the two brothers, with William evidently responding to things that Thomas has told him about his spiritual life and about how God had blessed him during his time in NSW.[56] Here we hear Moore's voice indirectly.

Perhaps we get a little closer with another discovery. Amongst the papers in the Archives, there is an exercise book entitled: 'A List of the Books the property Thomas Moore, Esq.' —a record of the books on Moore's bookshelf.[57] On the assumption that a man's bookshelf tells us something about the man, what can we learn here? Amongst books on a wide range of topics, the core of this library is solidly Christian and, in fact, evangelical. As well as 2 Bibles, 5 Testaments, and 2 Prayer Books, we find works of Christian biography (including on Wesley, Whitefield, and Hooker), a *Life of Christ*, the Hymnbooks of Watts and of Wesley; a history of the Reformation; books on Liturgy; devotional material and family prayers; copies of the *Evangelical Magazine*; William Paley's *Theology*; and numerous collections of printed sermons. This looks like the bookshelf of a man who was keen to regularly nurture his Christian life from the study of God's word. In addition, Moore also possessed Lawrence's two works on Horses and Cattle, both of which attempted to articulate a Christian approach to animal husbandry. Even though the ideas in Lawrence's books may sound rather odd to us today, the fact that they were on Moore's shelf is a very good indication that he seriously sought to translate his faith into his two main farming activities. His devotional life extended to the practicalities of his everyday business: horse breeding and cattle breeding.

These newly recovered treasures also take us beyond such indirect evidence, for there are a number of documents that come from Moore's own pen, and amongst this material, we find several occasions when he expresses his Christian convictions for himself.

For example, in February 1823 Andrew Douglas White visited Thomas and Rachel. Andrew was Rachel's son, from an alliance with Surgeon John White to whom she had been assigned when she first arrived in the colony. When she married Thomas, he also took on responsibility for her infant son and, from all accounts, he doted on the boy throughout his life. In 1823 Andrew, now a Lieutenant in the Royal Engineers and a veteran of the Battle of Waterloo, spent about six months with the Moores at Liverpool.[58]

When he left again in August, Thomas and Rachel evidently

saw him on board, and watched the vessel sail out of Port Jackson. As the last item in a list headed 'Occurrences', Moore recorded a rather emotional account of Andrew's arrival and departure, and here we find his Christian faith poking through:[59]

> 1823
>
> February 7th: Our dearly beloved Son Andrew arived [sic] at 8 oClock P:M: at Liverpool N:S:W: to our Great Satisfaction
>
> August 17 Sailed our dearly beloved Son Andrew to England in the Ship *Suray* Capt. Powers and got Clear of the Heads of Sydney Port Jackson at 2 P:M: May the Almity God bless him and keep him from all Sin and dangers and return [?] him safe to fond parents once more, Amen.

Thomas's Christian faith also comes to the fore around the time of Rachel's death in 1838.

Several letters survive from friends offering Thomas consolation at the loss of Rachel. For example, the Christian Judge, Willliam Burton, wrote from Sydney the following day offering to come to Liverpool to be with Thomas if only Thomas said he wanted him there.[60] His letter brings the comfort of the gospel to his bereaved Christian brother, thus indirectly testifying to Thomas's faith:

> It is some consolation, and I do not doubt will be so received by you, that our Heavenly Father in this as in all things has mercifully disposed his dispensations; and has permitted you to lay the wife of your bosom in her grave before it has been his will to call you to Himself; You will now at least be spared the pain of Her remaining behind you to struggle with pain and illness -: Yours is indeed the lot to mourn for her loss, but I trust, and do not doubt that your mind is so happily trained under God's grace, that you will not sorrow as one without hope for Her who is dead in the Lord.

Several things written by Thomas himself show that he certainly did not grieve without hope, but he mourned for Rachel with a clear hold on the gospel promise of the world to come. These testimonies are found in rather strange places; strange, but showing that, in a literal way, Thomas carried his hope with him into his ordinary, everyday life.

In an exercise book in which he kept record of his daily expenditure, his records of moneys spent is interrupted by the entry for 13th November 1838:[61]

> My Dear Wife departed this life at Quarter past Seven oClock in the Morning, and I hope and trust that the Almity God has sent her Gardin Angle to Conduct her passed therunto to his Heavenly Kingdom where I hope to meet her again to praise the Lord to part no more forever Amen.

On the back cover of his rent book, Thomas had inscribed three other items relating to Rachel's death.[62] There was the newspaper obituary, published a week after Rachel died:[63]

> Death
> At Liverpool on the 13 November 1838
> Mrs Rachel Moore after a long protracted Illness
> the beloved Wife of Thomas Moore Esquire J.P. aged
> 76 years, She died [in] peace, Much and deservedly lamented.
>
>   Oh then this Moral let the Soul retain
>   All thoughts of happiness on Earth are Vain

The rent book also contains some words intended for her tombstone, but which apparently never made it to the headstone on Rachel's grave that can be read today in Liverpool's Pioneer Park:[64]

> Engraved on her Tomb stone
> Take Sacred Earth all that my Soul holds Dear –
> Take that Blest Gift that Heaven did give –
> Who can grive too much what time shall end
> our Morning for so dear a friend –
> Farewel my best beloved Farewel
> We only part to meet again –

And, finally, there were some words composed for a tablet in her memory:

> The Tablet of Mrs Thomas Moore
> Who departed this Life on the 13 day of November
> 1838 Aged 76 years. She died in peace, and [was] buryed
> In Liverpool Churchyard burying Ground
>
> Reader she was the Most Affectionate of Gods creatures, correct in all her duties; She led a Life of unassuming Virtue and practical piety; She was the Comfort and Solice of her Husband for 42 years; And a blessing to the poor—He who places this marble to her Memory, wood indeed be the most Wretchard of Husbands did he not feel the Christins hope of meeting in a better World; Her whom he has lost in this.

It is also interesting to notice that these words never found their way to the tablet that can be read today in St Luke's Liverpool.[65] Although the sympathies are similar, this tablet reads slightly more formally, with the loss of some of the sense of the feelings of her bereaved husband and Moore's hope of the world to come has also been slightly muted:

> The Tablet Of
> Mrs Thos Moore
> who departed this life on the
> 13th day of November, 1838
> aged 76 years
>
> She was the most affectionate and virtuous wife, a tender mother, and ever kind to the poor. She was united to her husband for 42 years, during which time she was a constant attendant at the house of God, and a strict observer of family prayer and died in peace.
>
> > Sickness and sorrow mingle here,
> > each heart with tenderness is moved.
> > ere long we'll be resumed again,
> > and raised to nobler ends above.

In these testimonies, we can hear a man taking his hope from the gospel promises.[66] He looked for the day when he would meet his beloved Rachel once again.

His daily expenditure book contains two more testimonies to his beloved wife. On the day of Rachel's funeral, Thomas wrote:

> Nov 16 1838 My Dear Wife was Intered in the Liverpool Burial Ground in ~~M~~ our Valt, A Sorrowful day for me.[67]

By the end of the month, Moore had received the bill from the funeral director, which he regarded as somewhat high. Combining his persona as the money-making business man with that of the devoted husband, he wrote in his expenditure book:

> Receved from Mr Hoskings my Dear Wifes Funeral expenses and the amount is high little expenses £130 pounds—altho high I will paid it for her as the last tribute of affection.[68]

The day of Rachel's funeral, Thomas had spoken with Bishop Broughton about his long-standing desire to leave his fortune to the Church, now that there were no close relatives with a higher claim upon it. According to his Expenditure book, the day before he received the bill for the funeral, he travelled to Sydney to visit his friend Judge Burton, and there he altered his Will in favour of the church.[69] And, of course, these alterations he made to his Will are what enable us to gather together tonight to celebrate 150 years of the college that still bears his name.

By the time Thomas Moore died, he had amassed a great deal of wealth through his land, his business and banking dealings, his breeding of cattle for Sydney's meat market, and his breeding of fine horses, not to mention his rents and mortgages. Why did he sign all of this wealth over to the Church of England?

The testimonies of Moore's faith, which we can now hear from his own mouth, as it were, add strength to a report of the motives behind his generosity that we already knew about. The May 1937 issue of *Societas* included an article by the third Principal of the College, Arthur Lukyn Williams.[70] In his time the College was still at Liverpool, and Lukyn Williams had made a point of talking to the elderly folk of Liverpool to collect their memories of Thomas Moore. Because of one story, Thomas Moore struck Principal Williams as rather odd:

> [Moore] must have been a queer old fellow; while he was dying, he was asked if he would not leave something to his nephew, but he replied: "No, God gave it all to me, and I shall

give it all back to Him."

This echoes another report from Bishop Broughton, who said that Thomas Moore gave his fortune to the church, because he was moved 'in gratitude, as he very becomingly expressed himself, to God who had given him all'.[71]

SO, WHAT HAVE WE LEARNED about Thomas Moore, Esq., from the third phase of his life, when he was magistrate of Liverpool. He actively used his position to bring about the good of his local community. He also worked more broadly to bring greater freedom to his nation. But he also lived, worked and died with the broadest of all hopes in view. As an evangelical Christian, Moore had believed the gospel promise of the world to come.

Tonight we celebrate his generosity to us, through the foundation of our College.

Notes

1. The original form of this address was delivered at the Thomas Moore Dinner, 28th October 2006, the 'grand finale' of the year's sesquicentenary celebrations.
2. Despite the fact that Judeo-Christian culture and institutions 'shaped the colonial civil order until the 1860s, and did so with the consent and co-operation of the migrants themselves' (Shaw, 'Judeo-Christianity', 29), detailed study of this shaping has received little attention. In 2000, Prof. Brian Fletcher observed that 'the religious beliefs and pursuits of free persons considered as a group have not received the attention they deserve. While the response of convicts to efforts to arouse their faith has been the subject of a major study [i.e. Grocott, *Convicts*], no attempt has been made systematically to examine the relationship between free persons and the churches', Fletcher, 'Christianity and free society', 94. Thomas Moore came to the colony in its infancy and lived out his days as it grew towards maturity. He lived and died as a free settler and, in his own quiet way, had a remarkable influence in the development of the colony. It is also apparent that he was also a man whose religious convictions were a major driving force in his life. Thus, a study of the Thomas Moore's contribution towards Christianity in early colonial Australia provides one case study towards the project desired by Brian Fletcher.
3. See ch. 3, 'Birth Announcement'.
4. Robinson, 'Thomas Moore & Early Life'.
5. Neal, *Rule of Law*, 155.
6. Neal, *Rule of Law*, 36, 49–50.
7. Neal, *Rule of Law*, 12.

8. E.g. *SG* 9/11/1816, 'the three unhappy criminals' who had been condemned to death for the murder of John Miller, 'underwent their sentence at the usual place of execution, and after remaining an hour suspended, their bodies were given up for dissection'.
9. Severity of punishment 'cannot be measured by the number of strokes alone; type of instrument and vigour of application also make a difference [...] The cat o nine tails, each tail knotted, wounded the buttocks and backs of convicts [...] A "good" flogger would draw blood at the fourth or fifth stroke [...], more quickly if the back were freshly scarred from a recent flogging'; The psychological effects should also not be ignored; Neal, *Rule of Law*, 50–51.
10. Neal, *Rule of Law*, 52.
11. 'On average, one out of every four convicts was flogged in 1835, although this would have to be discounted for repeat floggings; the average number of lashes per flogging was 46. Magistrates ordered 7,103 floggings that year to a population of 27,340 male convicts (female convicts were not flogged). By way of a rough comparison with a contemporary free society, there was an average of 234 court-ordered floggings per year over the period of 1811–1827 in England', Neal, *Rule of Law*, 49–50. Although 'that year' in this quotation makes these figures apply to 1835, Neal later says that these figures were for the period 1830 to 1837, not just the year 1835 (p. 156). I have therefore estimated my 'five times' by 7,103 /7 = approx. 1000 per year.
12. Neal, *Rule of Law*, 42.
13. See Neal, *Rule of Law*, Chapter 6.
14. Douglass was named in the 1826 *Return* to the House of Commons as using more of the punishments deemed illegal, than other magistrates in the colony; see *SG* 26/9/1826. Hannibal McArthur was known to be severe, according to W.C. Wentworth, in a libel action McArthur had taken against the editors of *The Monitor* (see below, note 21): 'I myself happen to know nothing of his magisterial conduct, the rumour is so current of his severity, that the circumstances of his awarding five hundred lashes, I am convinced, would surprise no-one'; 'His whole magisterial career, short as it was, was distinguishable for the extreme of harshness' (*SG* 20/12/1826).
15. Marsden's pattern of severity apparently began after the Irish rebellion of 1800, when Judge Advocate Richard Atkins and Marsden gave Paddy Galvin 'the barbarous punishment' of 300 lashes, in an attempt to ring information from him about hidden weapons. This incident was immortalised in the literature of the day, in the eyewitness account of Joseph Holt, who was forced to witness the flogging of the Irish rebels, narrating his description of the infliction of 300 lashes on Maurice Fitzgerald and then on 'Paddy Galvin, a young boy about twenty years of age'. (See the various accounts in Sheehan, 'Identity of Richard Rice'). In the official records, Fitzgerald was sentenced to 500 lashes (*HRA* I.2, p.650). The total number of lashes meted out was 8,400 amongst 16 men, of whom five were to receive 1000 each (*HRA* I.2, 651). What made it easier to inflict such an extreme number of lashes is the employment of one Richard Rice, a left-hander, to assist John [William] Jonson, the Hangman from Sydney. With the prisoners' 'armes pulled around a large tree and their breasts squeezed so that the men had no power to cringe or stir', and one right and one left handed flogger, 'they stood at each side and I never saw two trashers in a barn move there stroakes more handeyer than those two man killers did', says Joseph Holt. (This is the version in *True Patriots All*, see Sheehan, 'Identity of Richard Rice', 124, and 125.)
16. Historians such as M.H. Ellis and C.M.H. Clark depict him as 'harsh and brutal in the extreme'; Loane, *Hewn From The Rock*, 13, who provides a more sympathetic portrayal

of Marsden. Marsden clashed with Governor Macquarie over emancipists. In 1810 he refused to work with two emancipists as a trustee of the Parramatta Turnpike. Trouble smouldered away between the two men, and in 1817 Macquarie blamed Marsden for an anonymous attack upon him. When he wrote to Earl Bathurst, he said that Marsden was the harshest and most severe of all the magistrates of the colony; Loane, *Hewn From The Rock*, 14. When Commissioner Bigge brought his inquiry to NSW, he tended to find in Marsden's favour in regard to the convict system and emancipist issue, and he applauded Marsden's valuable service as a magistrate. He did, however, comment that Marsden's sentences were more severe than those of his colleagues; Loane, *Hewn From The Rock*, 15; drawing upon Yarwood, *Samuel Marsden* (1968), 22.

17. When the 1826 *Return* was published (see *SG* 26/9/1826), the *Gazette* exclaimed 'we must confess our astonishment to find some names in the [offending, presumably] Magistracy of which we never dreamt before'. Given his generally good reputation, was Moore one of the ones causing 'astonishment'?

18. For e.g., the *Sydney Gazette* explained 'we lift up our hands and voices against many of the punishments in the days of yore, which were awful in the extreme: we can just remember them, and that's all'; *SG* 25/9/1826. Cf. Hassall, *In Old Australia*, 2, who claims that the convict days were not as dark as some like to make them out to have been.

19. See the summary in *SG* 26/9/1826.

20. The action is reported at length in *SG* 20/12/1826. A lack of legal training was the norm for magistrates at the time, and in our early days, even Judge-Advocates (such as David Collins) knew little of the law.

21. In February 1822, Moore was the senior magistrate on a bench of six, which handed down one month's solitary confinement, 500 lashes, and transportation to Port Macquarie for the remainder of his original sentence (which turned out to be life), to James Straiter, an elderly shepherd assigned to Hannibal McArthur, another magistrate. He received 300 of the lashes assigned, due to a special order of the same bench. After the House of Commons report named the NSW cases of illegal punishment, the *Monitor* expressed surprise that Straiter's case was not listed, mentioning only Hannibal McArthur in connection with the illegal punishment, even though he was not on the bench. He then successfully sued the editors. During the libel action, according to the *Sydney Gazette*'s rather full reporting (20/12/1826), Moore was named in another case in which 100 lashes were awarded. Witness Lewis Solomon told of the 1821 case where Hannibal McArthur had his servant tried before Moore for taking too long to arrive, blaming a restive horse. Although this sounds a lot to our sensitive modern ears, at least this was the legal limit. See Neal, *Rule of Law*, 42.

22. McLaughlin, 'The Magistracy and the Supreme Court', 92.

23. McLaughlin, 'The Magistracy and the Supreme Court', 93; for documentation, see n.7.

24. McLaughlin, 'The Magistracy and the Supreme Court', 91.

25. McLaughlin, 'The Magistracy and the Supreme Court', 94.

26. Circular re distribution of convicts per "Ocean"; Col. Sec. 6004; 4/3494 pp.336–8 (5th February 1816).

27. Circular re convicts forwarded to Liverpool for distribution; Col.Sec. 6004; 4/3494 p.374 (16th February 1816).

28. Circular re distribution of convicts per "Guildford"; Col.Sec. 6004; 4/3494 pp.463–5 (15th April, 1816).

29. Circular re convicts landed from the "Atlas"; Col.Sec. 6005; 4/3495 pp.60, 61 (29 June 1816).

30. Col.Sec. 6005; 4/3495 p.181 (11th October 1816).
31. Col.Sec. 6005; 4/3495 pp.203, 205 (18th October 1816).
32. James Burridge, and James Luxford.
33. Col.Sec. 6005; 4/3495 p.409 (26th December 1816).
34. Quarterly Report (1/4/1816); Col. Sec. 2/8301, p.17.
35. Quarterly Report (1/4/1816); Col. Sec. 2/8301, p.18.
36. Quarterly Report (1/4/1816); Col. Sec. 2/8301, p.19.
37. For the permission requested and granted for Moore's resignation from this position, see T. Moore to Goulburn, [19th] May 1823; and Goulburn to T. Moore, 18 Oct 1823 (SDA 0853CH, Item 9, docs. 1 and 2).
38. Backhouse, *Life of Walker*, 253.
39. Neal, *Rule of Law*, 58. 'This achievement crowned the political struggles of the 1820s and 1830s. Other points on the continuum had been the growth of the Emancipist group, the New South Wales Act of 1823 granting a nominated council, the development of a free press in the 1820s, the battles over the jury issue, the growth in the number of free immigrants in the 1830s, and the decision to cease transportation in 1838 thus ending convictism as the defining feature of social and political life in the colony'.
40. The original Dedimus Potestatem appointing him to this position is now in Sydney Diocesan Archives, 0852CH, Item 7, doc. 2.
41. I am yet to discover his relationship with the other pro-emancipist governor, Brisbane.
42. Moore to Jamison, 3 Feb 1819, Bigge Report, Appendix, p.2445 (Mitchell BT Box 18).
43. Moore to Bigge, 28 Mar 1820, Bigge Report, Appendix, pp.4051–6 (Mitchell BT Box 21).
44. Liverpool Bench; 2 Oct 1825, Enclosure to T. Brisbane's Despatch, No 94, Oct 25, 1825; (Despatches From Gov. NSW—Enclosures, 1823–26, p.219; Mitchell A1267–10).
45. Moore to Mackanass, 16 Jan 1827 (Wentworth papers; Mitchell A758, p.78).
46. Thompson, *Australia*, 34–35.
47. S(M)H 28/12/1840; SG 29 Dec 1840.
48. Havard, 'Mrs Felton Mathew's Journal', 123.
49. Tablet erected to the memory of Rachel Moore, St Luke's Liverpool, NSW.
50. Backhouse, *Life of Walker*, 253.Cf. Boyce, *Thomas Moore*, 10.
51. Boyce, *Thomas Moore*, 9. The claim is repeated in [*Australian Encyclopedia*[2]], 'Moore, Thomas', 145. He does not appear anywhere in the early documents of CMS NSW, but he may have been involved in some preliminary stage.
52. Loane, 'Moore, Thomas', 255; Dickey, 'Moore, Thomas', 266. He was appointed to the (Wesleyan) Missionary Committee in Parramatta in 1825 (SG 7/10/24), 1829 and 1836 (*The Australian* 9th October 1829 and *SG* 9th October 1836—presuming that 'T. Moore' refers to him on both occasions.) In 1825 he was the largest individual subscriber to WAMS (SG 17/2/1825), and his Account Book 1828–1840 SDA 0885CH, Item 6, shows donations on 24/8/28,12/8/29, 13/12/32, 18/12/33, 21/12/33, 18/12/33, 21/12/38, 11/2/40.
53. S.O. Hassall to Rev. J. Hassall, Sept 19, 1818; Hassall Correspondence, vol. 4, p. 656 (ML A1677–4).
54. The Moores also supported the Wesleyans in the colony. Moore donated land to build the first Methodist church in Liverpool, Freame, *Early Days*, 36. Both Thomas and Rachel were subscribers to the construction of Wesleyan chapels: e.g. *Sydney Gazette* 23/11/1827, 3f: Mrs Moore, Liverpool, subscribes to Richmond Wesleyan Chapel.
55. 'Our knowledge of Moore's character is derived entirely from incidental references to his activities, and from occasional remarks made by others about him. We have nothing from his own pen,' Robinson, 'Thomas Moore & Early Life', 183 (21).

56. William Moor to T. Moore, 24 December 1839 (SDA 0851, Item 6, doc. 35).
57. 'List of Books the Property Mr Thomas Moore, Esq.' (SDA 0853CH, Item 5). For an analysis, see ch. 8 in this volume, 'Thomas Moore's Bookshelf'.
58. This has previously been spoken of as his return to Australia; see Robinson, 'Thomas Moore & Early Life', 186–187 (24–25), drawing upon Rienits, 'Biographical Introduction'. In February, the *Sydney Gazette* announced his arrival from England, via Hobart, on the *Morley*, *SG* 13/2/1823. It was, however, simply a fleeting visit for a matter of about 6 months, for the *Gazette* also announced his departure in August, on board the *Surry*. *SG* (Supp) 7/8/1823: 'Mr WHITE, being about to proceed to England in the *Surry*, requests claims to be presented'. *SG* 21/8/1823: 'On Sunday sailed for England, the ship *Surry*, Captain Powers. Her cargo consists of timber, the produce of Australia. Passengers: W.B. Carlyle, Esq., R.N. late surgeon Superintendent ship *Morley*, M. Price, Esq., R.N. late surgeon Superintendent ship *Brampton*; Leslie Duguid, Esq; Mr L.W. Dickson; Mr McKinstry; and Lieut. A.D. White'.
59. T. Moore, 'Occurrences', SDA 0884 CH, Item 5.
60. W. Burton to T. Moore, 14 Nov 1838; SDA 0853CH, Item 11, doc. 11. Moore also received consolatory letters from Rev. Robert Cartwright (R. Cartwright to T. Moore, 27 Nov 1838, SDA: 0851CH, Item 6, doc. 26), and Esther Taylor (E. Taylor to T. Moore, 20 Sept [1839], SDA: 0851CH, Item 6, doc. 32).
61. Note on Rachel's Death, 13 Nov 1838, *T. Moore's Account book, 1828–1840*; SDA 885CH, Item 6.
62. T. Moore, Notes on Rachel's Death, rear cover of Rent Book; SDA 0884CH, Item 6b.
63. Cf. *S(M)H* 21/11/1838: 'At Liverpool, on the 13th instant, Mrs Rachel Moore, after a long protracted illness, the beloved wife of Thomas Moore, Esquire, J.P., aged seventy six years. She died in peace, much, and deservedly, lamented. "Oh then this moral let the soul retain—All thoughts of happiness on earth are vain"'.
64. The present inscription simply reads: 'Sacred to the memory of Rachel Moore, the beloved wife of Thomas Moore Esq., J.P., who died 13th November 1838, aged 76 years'.
65. This is an almost exact copy of the tablet erected in St John's Parramatta by Governor R. Bourke to his wife Jane, who died on 7/5/1832. Apparently Moore copied it to use as something of a model for Rachel's tablet.
66. On his bookshelf, Thomas had several volumes focusing on the life to come. See 'Thomas Moore's Bookshelf' ch. 8 in this volume.
67. T. Moore, Entry on Rachel's Funeral, 16/11/1838; *T. Moore's Account book, 1828–1840*; SDA 885CH, Item 6.
68. T. Moore, Entry on Rachel's Funeral expenses, 29/11/1838; *T. Moore's Account book, 1828–1840*; SDA 885CH, Item 6.
69. T. Moore, Entry on Will alteration, 28/11/1838; *T. Moore's Account book, 1828–1840*; SDA 885CH, Item 6:

> Went to Sydney to alter my Will
> [...]
> Deeds to Sydney to be made out to the Deed of Gift to the Church.

70. Williams, 'Moore College 1878–1884'. For some biographical details, see Loane, *Centenary History*, Chapter 4.
71. Broughton to Coleridge, 25 February 1839.

Thomas Moore of Liverpool: One of our Oldest Colonists

CHAPTER 9

PORTRAIT OF THE LATE THOMAS MOORE, ESQ.

IN THE SUMMER OF 2005–2006, while almost everyone at Moore College was enjoying a well-deserved break, Thomas Moore embarked on a journey of his own. Moore College was founded on the wealth of his Estate. Although the College has been operating at Newtown since 1st August 1891, it began its life in his old home in Liverpool, NSW.[1] As Moore's most recent voyage began, the College, overcrowded on the Newtown site, was in the midst of serious discussions about moving for the second time in its history. It was also poised on the edge of its sesquicentenary. Perhaps Thomas had heard about the 150th, and so the man who originally arrived in Sydney from England by the ship *Britannia* in 1792, once again crossed the sea for Sydney in 2005. Only, this time, Thomas was just a portrait of his former self and his ship, the *Santa Annabella*, sailed from Lyttelton, New Zealand.

In 1998, with the permission of the Dean and Chapter of St Andrew's Cathedral, Sydney, the

Portrait of the Late Thomas Moore, Esq.
Artist: William Griffith(s), 1840.

portrait had been loaned to the Southland Museum & Art Gallery, Invercargill, NZ. Just over two hundred years prior to this little excursion, Thomas Moore had made his first trip to the land of the long white cloud. He was amongst the small sealing party left by the *Britannia* in Dusky Sound from October 1792 until September 1793. While his crewmates collected sealskins, he became the first European to build a house in New Zealand, and, when that record was set, he proceeded to be the first European to build a ship from New Zealand timber.[2] In view of these connections with the South Island, Southland Museum borrowed the portrait for their 'In Hodges Wake' exhibition. When that was over, they hung it in the museum's dedicated Dusky Sound Gallery.[3] They had agreed to return the large oil painting 'when requested to do so by the Chapter'.[4]

If the Cathedral ever forgot about the open-ended loan arrangement, Moore could have been left pining in Fiordland forever. But thankfully, when it came time to close the Dusky Sound Gallery, Southland arranged for his journey home.

Although Thomas's home-sickness might have been almost over, his imminent arrival sent some in Sydney into a flurry of activity. Prior to hanging in Invercargill, Thomas had hung in the Chapter House of St Andrew's Cathedral for about forty years.[5] At the end of 2005, Phillip Jensen, the present Dean, could not remember why the portrait had been at the Cathedral, and suggested that it be delivered to where it properly belonged: the College.

This was, after all, where it had come from. In 1961, when the expanding College opened its new dining room,[6] the portrait was taken out of the old dining room, which was destined to become a class-room, and sent to the Cathedral.[7] The removal required the disassembly of the windows and their brick surrounds in order to get the large frame out.

In this rather small room, Thomas Moore had hung ceiling to floor for many, many years. Donald Robinson remembers the portrait hanging in 'the old dining room', for 'as long as I can remember'—which takes us back to his boyhood days at the

College in 1937. But the painting was already there by 1914, when F.B. Boyce wrote his pamphlet *Thomas Moore, An Early Australian Worthy*: 'A large oil painting of him, taken in his later days, is at Moore College'.[8]

In 1975, Bishop Robinson speculated upon the path the portrait had taken to get there.

> His trustees inherited a huge portrait of him, [...] and they did not know what to do with it. I think it probably went to the St James property in Sydney which Moore's trustees owned, and then it went to Moore College when the College moved to Newtown.[9]

After Thomas had died on Christmas Eve, 1840, and was buried on the 29th, the Trustees of his Estate (Bishop W.G. Broughton; merchant Robert Campbell; colonial secretary, Alexander McLeay) began to set his affairs in order. On 21 January 1841 they 'instructed Mr John Blackman Auctioneer, to advertize the sale of the Household furniture, Books, Plate &c at the residence of the late Mr Moore, on the 1st February next'.[10] On the same day, Mr Kerrison James was commissioned to proceed to Liverpool and bring 'all Deeds, Instruments and Papers relating to the Estate, to be deposited in the Bishop's Registry office: which was accordingly done'.[11] Presumably the portrait may have also been amongst the property transported from Liverpool to the St James property. If so, this would confirm Robinson's guess, and indicate that the painting was hidden in the bowels of St James from 1856 to 1891.

Three features of the painting may have worked against its public display. From the beginning, it was not regarded by some 'in the know' as being well-executed. After a display of the artist's works in 1847, which included the painting of Moore, an art critic from the *Sydney Morning Herald* commented that it was 'deficient in both drawing and effect'[12]—although others were more complimentary.[13]

Its second 'problem' was its appearance. In 1970, when Donald Robinson wrote on Thomas Moore's early days, he referred to 'the gloomy full-length portrait which hung for many years at Moore College and now hangs in the Cathedral Chapter House'.[14] Being in the rather dark, formal style of the day, does not help the painting in this respect. The same *Herald* critic accused the painting of reminding him of Conrad the Corsair, an allusion not only to Lord Byron's work by that name, but to the rather dramatic and gloomy illustrations that accompanied it.[15] On closer inspection, however, Moore's portrait has its own colour and delight.

The third factor is its size. This comes out in the various comments already noted: It was a 'large' oil painting of him; His trustees did not inherit just a portrait, but a 'huge' portrait of him; In the old dining-room, it hung 'floor to ceiling'; The removal required the disassembly of the windows. It hung 'above the stairway' in Chapter House. In 1968, the size of the painting was taken into account in a quotation for its cleaning and restoration resulting in the figure of $100, which may sound rather paltry by today's standards, but at the time required something of a slight cough and apology.[16]

Its size has also been a noted factor in the latest chapter of its life. When Elisabeth Arnett, Personal Assistant to the Principal, received news of its impending arrival at Moore College, she made arrangements in case it arrived when she was away on holiday. She left a message with College Reception:[17]

> In the first week of January a parcel containing a painting from a museum in New Zealand will be delivered to the College. When you take delivery of it you might like to pass [it] onto Michael Hill [the Acting Principal] to store in his office, or place it in my office if Michael is not here.

When this 'parcel', that could so easily be 'taken delivery of' and 'passed on' and 'stored' in one office or another, subsequently arrived, the three men the deliverer had requested to assist the unloading turned into another four or five—with nearly as many more 'advisors' offering all kinds of 'helpful' suggestions. This crate was big! And if windows had to be demolished when it first left Newtown, if it was going to return, the College would now have to lose its doors! And so the crate was left outside while the College had a collective think about its future.

Before the good oil left for New Zealand, the then Dean, Boak Jobbins, had also commented on the disadvantage brought by the portrait's size. In explaining why the Chapter was not in favour of permanently removing it from Australia, Dean Jobbins noted:

> Moore himself is of significance here not only to the theological college named after him but also to the district of Liverpool: both groups would like access to the portrait from time to time, though I suspect neither is willing to care for it permanently, particularly when they note its size.[18]

Passing over the fact that Dean Jobbins said nothing about the 'interest' of the Cathedral here, his comments proved strangely prophetic when, fresh off the boat from New Zealand and still just as large as ever, Thomas Moore was almost turned away from his own College. Although nobody dared to ask whether we find another 'St James' to bury it for another thirty-five years, other questions were asked. Perhaps due to his size, questions were asked about 'who really owns this portrait', and where should it really belong? Should it be sent back to the Cathedral? Or, should it be received into the College about to celebrate 150 years under Moore's name? (Apparently nobody thought of sending it back to Liverpool, where it could no doubt adorn the walls of the Thomas and Rachel Moore Education centre at Liverpool Hospital, which now stands on the site of the old house). If these questions are too difficult to answer—is there another country with a museum needing a huge, gloomy portrait for an indefinite loan?

What more can be known of this portrait? Robinson described it as depicting Thomas Moore as:

> an obscure figure, standing with his hand resting on a table, St Luke's Liverpool visible through an open window, and on the wall of the room a portrait of the bonneted Mrs Moore, inoffensive but respectful, if not always so respectable as her husband.[19]

The latter allusion is to Rachel's convict past, which received comment from Bishop Broughton, when he said:

> His wife had been, I believe, once a prisoner of the Crown and not of very good character: however, from the time that I first saw her she was an inoffensive old person and behaved with the greatest respect, and therefore I never thought it necessary to go back into former histories: not always a pleasant inquiry even in the best of places; and *here* peculiarly ticklish and dangerous.[20]

Although not the main focus of the canvas, the portrait of Rachel is important not only for those with an interest in Moore and his family, but also because it is apparently the only portrait of a Second Fleet convict to have survived. Not content with this fame, Rachel has actually left behind two depictions, for she is also memorialised in marble on the wall of St Luke's Liverpool, in the tablet Thomas erected to her memory. In stark contrast to the rather severe and highly stylised features of the marble, her portrait in the background of the oil painting shows a woman of soft features, with friendly, laughing eyes. Whatever technical blemishes the painter may have committed, in this depiction of Rachel, he seems to have captured the same warmth of character that is so often spoken of affectionately in the surviving sources.

St Luke's Liverpool presumably appears in the portrait because of the importance of this place to the Moores. Thomas Moore had superintended the building of this Francis Greenway Church, built between 1818 and 1823, as part of Governor Macquarie's grand building programme. Thomas and Rachel were present at the laying of the foundation stone in 7th April 1818, and twenty years later St Luke's was the venue for their funerals. When the first service was held on St Luke's Day, 18th October, 1819,[21] St Luke's was already their Christian home, in which they continued to play an active part. Thomas served on the St Luke's committee.[22] They were renowned for their hospitality, receiving guests into their home after the St Luke's service and entertaining them on into the evening.[23]

In front of the window, the desk is bedecked with some books, papers and writing implements, and other objects. Assuming that a stylised portrait depicted something of the person in the features it included, then these speak of Moore's love of reading, and his use of the pen. Perhaps the books represent the substantial intellectual resource that he had collected into his personal library, and his interest in education.[24] Perhaps the writing materials illustrate his many business affairs, or his role as a magistrate, or the administration of his farming interests, or perhaps even the correspondence involved with his well-known generosity as a benefactor.

Under the portrait is what looks to be a leather armchair, speaking of a man who is comfortable in his study. And in front of the hour-glass, perhaps telling of a man who needs to carefully watch his time due to his many interests and activities. Is that a pipe that can be seen on the desk (I am not sure)? And if so, what does this tell us? A man who enjoyed a moment to puff, relax, and to mull over the day?[25]

For a long time towards our end of the portrait's life, the artist was unknown. In New Zealand, the portrait was exhibited with display notes attributing it to an unknown artist.[26] This is a little odd, however, since Donald Robinson had made inquiries in the late sixties and discovered the name of the artist.[27] Perhaps this was never widely known, or perhaps forgotten during the period of exile in the Chapter House.

This 'gloomy' portrait, entitled 'Portrait of the Late Thomas Moore, Esq.', was amongst those displayed at the Society for the Promotion of the Fine Arts in Australia Exhibition (1847). This was the venue for our critic from the *Sydney Morning Herald* to damn it, along with another by the same artist of Judge William Burton. Burton was a friend of Moore's, and the judge involved in drafting his Will in favour of the Church and the future College. As noted already, to our critic, both portraits were

> deficient in both drawing and effect. If the likenesses be correct, the paintings remind us of Conrad the Corsair. We forebear to say more.

On the other hand, the same critic praised the artist's two crayon portraits of George Suttor, Esq, and an unidentified lady, also on exhibition. Although many of the artist's crayon works were destroyed in a 1854 fire, several of his portraits of people in mid-nineteenth century Sydney have survived:[28] Elizabeth Rouse and Richard Rouse (both 1847 crayon); the miniatures of Marsden, Bobart and clerk in the famous depiction of the three-tiered pulpit which hung for years at St John's Parramatta; Mrs Elizabeth Hassall, wife of Rowland, probably 1842; Rev. William Walker, Wesleyan Missionary to Black Town, 1842; Captain Sadleir, probably 1850; and Mrs Sadleir, nee Cartwright; then Sir W.W. Burton, c. 1844, a crayon and watercolour, then an oil; the auctioneer Patrick Hayes and members of the pioneering Paton family.

Several of these people are familiar figures to the district of Liverpool. This may have something to do with a family connection. The name of the artist was William Griffith (or Griffiths) who after a period of professional training in France, came to Australia on the same ship as Susan Duffus. Soon after arrival, the pair married[29] and, according to the usual story, eventually set up home in George, then Marsden Sts Parramatta, where Susan conducted a school, and William opened a portrait practice and conducted art classes.[30] Susan Duffus came to Australia with her sister and brother-in-law, who was the Polish Count Lucien de Broel Plater, and the Count's brother Ferdinand.[31] The Duffus clan were following another brother who had already come to Australia, the Rev. John Duffus, and they initially settled in his district.[32] After arriving in the colony in October 1838,[33] John Duffus supplied ministry to St Luke's Liverpool, Thomas Moore's congregation, until 1845.[34]

When was the portrait of Thomas Moore painted? In 1914, Boyce generalised to 'in his later days'.[35] In 1968, Donald Robinson was wondering about its painter, and guessed that it was painted in the 1830s. By his Havard lecture of 1975, Robinson had learned the painter was W. Griffiths, and suggested it was 'painted in [Moore's] last years'.[36] At the risk of stating the obvious, in this pre-photographic period of history, the painting had to have been painted by the time Moore died on Christmas

Eve, 1840, which sets the limits on one side. The other is also clearly set for us, since Griffith(s) only arrived in Australia in 1839. Not only does this mean that Moore's portrait was quite likely one of the first that Griffith painted once he was set up in Sydney, it also means that there was a limited window of opportunity in which the portrait could have been painted.

We can, in fact, reduce this window even further. A letter uncovered recently in the Sydney Diocesan Archives reveals new information about the 'Portrait of the Late Mr Thomas Moore, Esq.' On the 24th March, 1840, Bishop W.G. Broughton wrote a letter to Thomas Moore in which he urged his Liverpool friend to have a portrait painted, and he commended Griffith(s) to him:

> Some time ago you may perhaps remember I was speaking to you of sending to England the portrait of yourself which you have in your parlour, in order that a copy might be taken by some good artist, with a view to its being preserved in this country. Lately I have heard that a gentleman named Griffith has arrived who is a skilful painter and that he has settled at Liverpool. Give me leave therefore to ask you whether you will permit your picture to be taken by him. This would be by far more satisfactory to your friends than having a copy made of the other which is not a good likeness.[37]

This letter unearths a previously unknown fact about Griffith, that in early 1840, he was living in Liverpool, where his new wife had her family connections. They must have moved to Parramatta at a later date. Being located here gave him ready access to Mr Moore in his own home, where the portrait was presumably painted.

Broughton also alludes to a previous portrait of Moore, not a good likeness. Perhaps this is the opportune time to mention yet another picture of Moore that has been in circulation for some time more recently. This 'headshot' of Thomas used to grace the walls of the Moore College Faculty Common Room until the early 1990s, when it was stolen, along with some other paintings and photographs. This was the picture of Moore published in Marcus Loane's *Centenary History of Moore Theological College* (1955), and which has now found its way onto several websites with an interest in the pioneer of Liverpool.[38] Apparently, however, this 'portrait' was produced by Dr Frank Cash, Rector of Lavender Bay (1922–61), whose son, John, is memorialised in the Cash Chapel at Moore College, Newtown.[39] An avid photographer, who is famous for his photographs documenting the construction of the Harbour Bridge, Cash apparently produced this familiar headshot by photographing the Griffith(s) painting and then 'doctoring' the photograph.[40] In other words, even though Rachel left two 'portraits' to posterity, when it comes to Thomas, since the former one alluded to by Broughton has long-since disappeared, the Griffith(s) painting is the one and only 'Portrait of the Late Thomas Moore Esq.' to have survived. We are therefore reliant upon this portrait for any knowledge of his appearance.

So when was it painted? The window can be narrowed a little further as a result of another recent discovery in the Sydney Diocesan Archives. Later that year, George Bewson [?], of Grenville College, Parramatta, wrote to thank Thomas Moore for his previous £10 donation, and to assure Thomas that, since he had put himself down as a life subscriber, 'as I feel confident it gives you pleasure to help by your patronage, and Money, God's good work, I shall only add that the Society will feel grateful for any donation you may think proper to order'. He then adds the following comment:

> I should wish much to see your "likeness" which I hear is so admirably well done, and I intend to take an early opportunity in going to Liverpool for that purpose.[41]

Already the word is out, and the crowds are flocking to see the freshly completed painting! Since Bewson wrote on 9th November, this clearly shows that 'The Portrait of the Late Thomas Moore, Esq.' was painted sometime between the end of March and early November, 1840. If it was considered to be an 'admirably well done' 'likeness' of Thomas, then what we look at in this portrait is a man who turned 78 in June of that year, and who, just six weeks after receiving Bewson's note, would pass away quietly in his own home. And I must say, on my own inspection of the portrait, despite the many adventures that he had had in his long life, for a man his age, Thomas looks remarkably well preserved!

But one question remains for us to answer: why had Broughton for some time been so keen to have a portrait of the man whom some have called 'the King of Liverpool'? His letter shows that they had previously discussed sending the poor likeness already in Thomas's possession to England, no doubt for some kind of extreme makeover! And now, just months before Moore dies and leaves his money to the Church and for the foundation of a College, Broughton is writing to him to avail himself of Griffith's services. What is Broughton's concern in all this?

The answer is there, without any ambiguity, in his letter:[42]

> I sincerely speak my opinion that the design of having your portrait preserved is worthy of immediate attention: for as your name is already connected with the establishment of the Church of England here, through the noble gift which you have bestowed upon the Cathedral, and other donations which you have made and propose to make and as I trust that the design of establishing at Liverpool a College bearing your name may be hereafter carried into effect, I am perfectly sure that our posterity will be anxious to have among them the likeness of one who has been so great a benefactor both to religion and learning.

There we have it, as the College and Cathedral authorities wondered together at the beginning of 2006, about who really owned this huge portrait (and so who should take care of it), the discussion was certainly between the right parties. Thomas Moore gave the original benefaction for the Cathedral, and (I think it is true to say) that his remains the only such benefaction the Cathedral has received.[43] And, of course, he is also the benefactor of the College, which began small at Liverpool but now overflows at Newtown.

But Broughton then adds a further piece of information which clinches the deal. Having mentioned the intended College, he goes on to say:

> In all the old institutions of the same kind in England, there is nothing that is felt as so great a deficiency as not to see the Portrait of the Founder. I do therefore hope that you will gratify us, and prevent such a deficiency occurring here by allowing Mr Griffith to paint yours.

The facts are now firmly on the table. From its very inception, this portrait was intended to hang in the College in memory of its founder.

Thomas Moore himself knew that this would only ever be a symbol. In April 1822 he had written as his 17th Memorandum 'The first portraiture of Men is their own actions',[44] and certainly there is much in this man's life for which future generations have thanked God. But the 'first portraiture' aside, the reason why Thomas Moore sat for William Griffith(s) sometime between April and November in the last year of his life, was to provide those who come to his future College with a portrait of their founder.

Thomas never made it to the sesquicentenary. Oh, he arrived in time, but unfortunately, he was too big to fit into the College without serious demolition work, so he spent the year on his side, outdoors. Perhaps there is some strange kind of parable here of the present state of the College, in which the student body is (almost) too big to fit into the buildings. Exactly one year after his arrival, when all the sesquicentenary dust had settled, he got a brief airing. On the first of February, 2007, a small group gathered around as the lid was taken off and Thomas was rolled over in his crate. Now relocated out of the weather, he lies peacefully on his back—home again at last, and awaiting re-positioning in some prominent position as the College's founder. Liverpool, Newtown, … I wonder where he is dreaming of next?

Notes

1. Loane, *Centenary History*, 92.
2. For the story and the setting, see Robinson, 'Thomas Moore & Early Life'; and Begg, *Dusky Sound*.

CHAPTER 9 ~ *Portrait of The Late Thomas Moore, Esq.* [245]

3. Gillies to Barton (Customs), 11/01/2006 (Arnett File, Moore College).
4. Marriott to Dean Jobbins, 7/8/1998 (Arnett File, Moore College).
5. In 1975, Donald Robinson observed that, 'For the last 20 years or so it has hung on the staircase in the Chapter House of St Andrew's Cathedral'; 'Thomas Moore of Moore Bank'. He recalls that it was moved to Chapter House from Moore College, presumably with the permission of the Trustees (who are the rightful owners), when the new dining room was opened in 1961; Donald Robinson, personal conversation with the author, 1st March 2006.
6. A plaque on the building housing the present dining room commemorates its opening by Archbishop Gough on the 13th May 1961.
7. Donald Robinson, personal conversation with the author, 1st March 2006. For my generation of students (1982–1985) the old dining room became the 'Bible and Missions Room', and more recently it has been turned into a residence for faculty.
8. Boyce, *Thomas Moore*, 12.
9. Robinson, 'Thomas Moore of Moore Bank'.
10. *Trustees Minute Book* 1, p.3, entry for 21 Jan 1841.
11. *Trustees Minute Book* 1, p. 2, entry for 21 Jan 1841.
12. *Sydney Morning Herald* 26/7/1847.
13. As we shall see below in a comment from George Bewson, just after the portrait was completed, he had heard many say what an excellent likeness it was. Of course, this is not the same as saying the painting was well-executed.
14. Robinson, 'Thomas Moore & Early Life', 167 (3).
15. See http://www.crcstudio.arts.ualberta.ca/streetprint/Pages/viewtext.php?s=browse&by =title&route=browseby.php&tid=210 (3/2/2007). The 1814 illustration of Conrad the Corsair can be seen at http://people.bu.edu/jwvail/byron_illustrations.html (3/2/2007). Rather than speaking of a likeness between the two persons depicted, the critic no doubt referred to the dark and dramatic style of the paintings.
16. Morton to Ashen, 28 May 1968; Morton to D.W.B. Robinson, 30 May 1968 (SDA: Cathedral Church—Dean's Correspondence [Morton]). 'He points out that a good deal of time will need to be spent on such a large canvass [sic], which in itself is in very good condition, in spite of its age'.
17. Arnett to Vickers, 15/12/2005 (Arnett File, Moore College).
18. Jobbins to Marriott, 4/8/1998 (Arnett File, Moore College).
19. Robinson, 'Thomas Moore & Early Life', 167 (3).
20. Broughton to Coleridge, 25 Feb 1839. If he had dabbled in Rachel's history, he would have found testimonies to her good character stretching from his own contemporaries way back to her trial itself. There is some suggestion that she may have been a 'fall guy' for an inner household problem. Her trial at the Old Bailey can be found at http://www.oldbaileyonline.org/html_units/1780s/t17871212-13.html. See also the comments on Rachel Turner in Rees, *The Floating Brothel*, 21–23, 136, 232.
21. See the commemorative plaque in the grounds of St Luke's; Bain, 'St Luke's', points out that this makes it the oldest existing Anglican church building in Australia. To do this he argues that St Matthew's Windsor was completed after St Luke's, even though the foundation stone was earlier; only the towers of St John's Parramatta predate St Luke's; and although the foundation stone of St James's King St is earlier, it was originally intended to be a law court. Freame, *St Luke's*, 4: 'If the date of a church is to be computed from the laying of its foundation stone, then St. Matthew's is older than St. Luke's. If, on the other hand, its age is reckoned from the date when services

were first held within its walls, then St. Luke's is the senior'. Freame has no mention of the 18th October 1819 service, although he speaks of one, attended by the Governor, on 3rd December.
22. See, for example, the advertisement for Pew rents for the following year, signed by 'R. Cartwright, Thomas Moore and H.C. Antill, Church Committee', *SG* 16/12/1824.
23. This was the experience of Felton and Sarah Louisa Mathew in 1833; Havard, 'Mrs Felton Mathew's Diary', 123. Governor Macquarie and Bishop Broughton also comment on often enjoying the Moore's hospitality.
24. See Ch. 8 in this volume, 'Thomas Moore's Bookshelf'.
25. If this is a pipe, it may have made Thomas a little unusual in evangelical circles. Smoking was certainly rare amongst the clergy. Hassall, *In Old Australia*, 193, calls the Rev Frederick Wilkinson, who served in Illawarra, then Picton, the Oaks and Enmore: 'the only clergyman that I knew of, at that time, who was a smoker'.
26. Display notes, now in Arnett File (Moore College).
27. In 1968, his inquiries led him to the *Sydney Morning Herald* 26/7/1847 and the *Catalogue for the Exhibition of Fine Arts, 1847* (Mitchell Library 706 S), which revealed the artist as W. Griffith. The *Catalogue* ascribes ownership to the Trustees of St James's Church.
28. This list has been compiled from Power Institute, 'Griffith'; Donald Robinson, File Note; Mitchell Library card index.
29. In 1916, Freame, *Early Days*, 40, wrote: 'Another sister of Mr Duffus married Mr. Griffiths, a Parramatta artist, who died in 1870. Mrs Griffiths died 20 years ago, aged 90'. Freame had apparently learned something about the Griffiths' later years, perhaps drawing upon oral history of the district, as he does in other places. Compare this, however, with the Power Institute, *Dictionary of Australian Artists*, 314: 'Nothing is known about him after this time [i.e. 1850] and he may have left the colony. One source, *Truth* of 26 January 1919, states that Griffith died in Sydney in 1870; this has not been verified'.
30. Power Institute, 'Griffith', *Dictionary of Australian Artists*, 313–315.
31. The Count and his brother were collateral descendants of Kosciusko. The third sister married Prince Lubecki; Freame, *Early Days*, 40.
32. Freame, *Early Days*, 40.
33. *SG* 18/10/1838 reported that the ship *Eden*, 419 tons, Captn George Noble, having left London 21st May and touching at the Cape of Good Hope on 29th August, had arrived, carrying amongst the passengers, 'Rev. John Duffus, Episcopalian Minister, Mrs Duffus and 5 children'.
34. 'Ecclesiastical Preferments' announced in *SG* 29/12/1838, include: 'The Rev John Duffus, BA, of Queen's College, Oxford, has been licensed to St Luke's Church Liverpool, in the room of the Rev R. Taylor, who undertakes the temporary charge of St Peter's Campbell Town, vacated by the death of the Rev. T. Reddall. [...] The Rev. John Duffus and Rev. J.C. Grylls [appointed to Port Phillip] have also been commissioned as Surrogates for granting marriage licences, under the Act of Council 7 Wm. 4, No. 6.' Duffus conducted Thomas Moore's funeral; *St Luke's Burial Register*, 29/12/1840. His time at Liverpool unfortunately ended in a breakdown and a high-profile scandal in 1845. In 1848, he moved to Ti Hihi, Mangonui, Northland, New Zealand. His daughter Elizabeth subsequently married Cecil Taylor, son of Rev. Richard Taylor, one of the better known of the CMS missionaries. Cecil had been born at Liverpool, NSW, where his father had been detained by Marsden to serve 1836–1838. Freame, *St Luke's*, 7, 20.

Duffus engaged in farming until he died in 1870. For most of these details; see http://www.airgale.com.au/duffus/pafn02 [and 03].htm (18/1/06).
35. Boyce, *Thomas Moore*, 12.
36. Robinson, 'Thomas Moore of Moore Bank'.
37. W.G. Broughton to T. Moore, 24/3/1840, SDA 0851CH, Item 6, doc. 39.
38. This is the portrait usually accompanying information on Moore. It appears facing p.16 in Loane, *Centenary History*, and is used on several websites and in the Liverpool City Library pamphlets on Moore, not to mention publicity from the College.
39. For the story of the Cash Chapel, see Cash, 'The John Francis Cash Memorial Chapel', in Loane, *Centennial History*, 206–220.
40. Donald Robinson, private conversation 1st March 2006.
41. Geo Bewson [?] to T. Moore, 9/11/[1840]. SDA 0851, Item 6, doc. 46. Bewson does not give the date on his letter, but he does say that Moore's subscription for 1840 is now due. I have assumed that he is calling for the subscription for the current year, although it is almost over. On the evidence of this letter alone, the other possibility is that he is writing in November 1839, requesting the subscription for the year to come. We know, however, from Broughton's letter of the 24/3/1840, that Moore had not sat for the portrait at that stage, which clearly dates Bewson's letter after Broughton's, i.e. November 1840. I have thus far been unsuccessful in my attempts to learn more about this Grenville College that received Moore's lifetime interest. I suspect that it did not survive long enough to be well-remembered.
42. Broughton to T. Moore, 24/3/1840, SDA: 0851CH, Item 6, doc. 39.
43. In December 1866 the first Synod of the Diocese of Sydney formed a Committee to look into the condition of the still incomplete Cathedral (original foundation stone laid: 1819). Next Synod (August 1867) it reported, amongst other things: 'a piece of land in George Street, with certain buildings thereon, had been by deed dated January 2 1839 vested in Bishop Broughton and his successors as trustee, upon trust to apply and expend the rents in and towards the building and erecting of the Cathedral then in course of construction, and, upon the completion of the Cathedral, in and towards its support, maintenance and repairs'. This was the land that Moore had donated. The Committee reported that the gross income from this property was £300 (net approx. £280), hitherto expended partly on erection, repaying SPG of £3,000 loan to Cathedral Building Fund, £1,000 for flooring and £25 towards East window inserted as a memorial to Bp Broughton. The Balance in hand was £900. Besides the offertry, the rents from these properties provided the only income for the support of the Cathedral. Johnstone, *St. Andrew's Cathedral*, 36.
44. Thomas Moore, *Memorandums & Occurrences*, Memorandum No 17, April 1822, SDA 0884 CH, Item 5.

Thomas Moore of Liverpool: One of our Oldest Colonists

CHAPTER 10

TRAINING COLONIAL CLERGY

After Moore's Will and before Moore's College[1]

This year is the sesquicentenary (150th) celebrations of Moore College. On the 1st March, 1856, just nine months after his arrival in New South Wales and in view of the pressing need for clergy in the colony, Bishop Barker opened a college in Liverpool. Why so far out of town? As Principal Barry would later say, Liverpool would never have been chosen for a college 'had not Mr. Moore's house happened to stand there'.[2] For when the interim principal, William Macquarie Cowper, arrived[3]—bringing the first three students with him from Stroud, in Newcastle Diocese—the opening chapter of the history of Barker's new college would be written in a house inherited from Thomas Moore.

Thomas Moore can be described as the leading citizen of Liverpool in those days. He had received land on the Georges River in 1809 and moved to this property, known as Moore Bank, when he retired from his position as Master Builder in the King's Dockyard. In 1810, he accompanied Governor Lachlan Macquarie on his journey to select the site of the new town, which he would be instrumental in building.[4] From Macquarie's day to the last decade of his life, he served the township in the many and varied duties of a colonial magistrate, and was a prominent member of many of the societies and causes that sought to make the town—and indeed, the colony—a better place. He also bore some responsibility for the building of St Luke's Liverpool, where he and his wife Rachel enjoyed the fellowship of God's people. It was from St Luke's that his funeral procession departed at the end of 1840.

By the time he died, Thomas Moore had become a major landholder in the Colony. His stepson, Andrew Douglas White, had died in 1837, and his wife Rachel in 1838. He had several relatives still alive in England, but they were not named as beneficiaries in his Will. For several years before he eventually died, the old man had been talking with the Bishop of Australia, William Grant Broughton, about leaving his property as an endowment for Christian work in the colony. Moore's Will instructed his trustees to apply a substantial portion of his estate to the founding of a college for the education of young men of 'the Protestant persuasion in the principles of Christian Knowledge'.[5]

Moore's Will was proved on the 2nd February 1841, but, for various reasons,[6] Moore's College did not open its doors until 1st March 1856. In the meantime, across the course of that fifteen-year period, where were the clergy of New South Wales to be trained?

At a later date, as bishops struggled to find sufficient clergy willing to work in the Australian environment, they had three main options.[7] They could recruit men trained in England and Ireland; they could ordain others after an apprentice-like situation, knowing this training was inadequate; or they could establish their own colleges, where the education of clergy would be in the hands of carefully chosen teachers.[8] In the 1840s, just after Thomas Moore died, these three strategies were also clearly present in the thinking of the only man entrusted with episcopal authority in Australia. After succeeding T. Hobbes Scott as Archdeacon of New South Wales in 1829, on 14th February 1836, William Grant Broughton was consecrated at Lambeth, to be the first (and only) Bishop of Australia. Sailing back to Australia, he took up the episcopal duties that would consume him until his death in February 1853. When he found himself a beneficiary of Thomas Moore's estate, he was the only Bishop in this land so far from 'home'. Soon he would enjoy the fellowship of Selwyn, in the new diocese of New Zealand (declared in 1841) and Nixon, in Tasmania (1842), but distance was still an impediment to frequent conversation, and until the division of the rest of his domain into Dioceses in 1847,[9] Broughton felt almost alone under the pressure of the need for clergy.

When he returned to Australia in his first flush of purple, Broughton found his vast new harvest field supplied with just sixteen clergy, and 'of these three or four are worn or wearing out with old age: and as many more do more harm than good'.[10] At this stage, he looked to the English universities to train his clergy. But perhaps an early exasperation at their inability to do so can be detected in his question to Coleridge:

> Is it really impossible to find among the young graduates in the Universities *some* duly qualified and *willing* to engage in our service? Indeed I do request you and all my friends, from regard to the interests of Divine Truth and the cause of pure Christianity, to watch every opportunity of procuring for us such assistance.[11]

Broughton had met Rev. Edward Coleridge when he travelled to England in 1834, a man who would become a dear friend of the Bishop and of his work in Australia. A master at Eton, Coleridge urged Bishop Broughton to write to him by way of every ship that left Port Jackson. Although Broughton would bewail the fact that his pressing duties meant that many ships left port without a letter, he nevertheless wrote frequently enough to enable later generations to have some access to his thinking in this crucial period of Australian history.[12] These letters help us to understand the journey from Moore's Will to Moore's College, and they provide some insight into the training of colonial clergy in this period.

The story begins with some conversations between the Bishop and Thomas Moore.

Thomas Moore changes his Will

Two years before Moore died, Broughton outlined the history of his conversations with the 'old gentleman' in a letter to the philanthropist Joshua Watson.[13] He speaks of how Rachel and Thomas had always been 'very civil and hospitable to me in my visits to their house travelling through the country', and mentioned that 'the old gentleman was always forward in contributing to the support of the Church'. Broughton had explained that Moore had 'often thrown out hints to me of his intention to make a bequest to the Church', but, because Rachel and her son Andrew were still alive, Broughton 'never encouraged the conversation, but, to say the truth, always evaded it'. When Andrew died, Moore then informed the Bishop that he was going to make a fresh Will, leaving his property for the Church of England. Because Rachel was still alive, Broughton again felt reluctant to encourage this change, but referred Moore to Mr Justice Burton to talk over the details. Once Moore had talked things over with the judge, the Will was drafted, although Broughton was not acquainted with its details at that time.

A fortnight before the letter to Watson, however, Rachel had died. On 16th November 1838, the Bishop had travelled to St Luke's Liverpool to conduct the funeral, and, after the funeral Moore told him that the Will must again be altered. On 28th November, Moore met with Burton again,[14] this time accompanied by the Bishop, 'that we might receive his testamentary dispositions, and enable him to carry them into effect'. When Moore produced his previous Will at this meeting, the Bishop was impressed with the benefactions: 'Indeed I must say the objects were all well chosen; and the entire design put me strongly in mind of the pious and humble purposes which the men of former days used to manifest, of providing for the advancement of God's glory upon earth after their own departure from it'. A new Will was then drawn up in which the entire estate would come to the service of the Church.

> Mr Moore proposes by Deed of gift to convey in trust to the Bishop for the time being, his house near Liverpool called Moore Bank, with 2000 Acres of land, to be the residence of such Bishops for ever. By a similar Deed he conveys the remainder of the Estate of 4000 Acres and upwards to provide for the augmentation of clergymen's stipends: and by another Deed he

> gives a property in Sydney which lets for £420 per ann: towards the building and perpetual support of the Cathedral Church of St Andrew in this town. The remainder of his property, real and personal, is to pass under his Will for the various uses which I have above specified; only appropriating the house in which he now resides at Liverpool to be the Site of a College, to be called St Thomas's College, as a place of education connected with the Church of England and all the land which he has in and about that town is to be devoted towards the support of the College.

Broughton was keen that Watson alert Dr Warneford to the nature of Moore's bequest, since he had already approached the famous benefactor[15] to consider something towards the endowment of the See, and did not want him to be unaware of the windfall from Moore's Will. But there were also some legal concerns in the Bishop's mind.

> There are one or two concomitant circumstances that ought to be mentioned. In the first place I believe those donations and bequests, if made in England; would be altogether void by the Statutes of Mortmain. It is generally held that those Statutes do not apply here; but the point has never yet been brought to judicial determination;[16] and it is therefore impossible to say what construction might be put upon the laws if the question of applicability should be raised, as may occur, in this very case.

The Statutes of Mortmain had been a concern for Broughton for some time.[17] Medieval law attributed to the Church a perpetual existence and so perpetual ownership of property, even though this clashed with the usual feudal understanding brought to England by William the Conqueror, in which land ownership was vested in the king. This meant that the land of religious communities was in a situation of mortmain, i.e. in the hands of dead people! In 1279, however, the mortmain statute of Edward I declared that 'no person, religious or other [...] shall buy or sell lands or tenements or receive them, or appropriate them (under pain of forfeiture) so as to cause the land to come into mortmain'. Religious bodies acquiring land before this statute continued to hold onto it by 'Saxon tenure', although some statutes of Henry

VIII enabled him to seize property previously in mortmain, and for twenty years after the death of Edward VI the statutes of mortmain were suspended. The *Charitable Uses Act 1601* permitted alienation to mortmain for charitable, but not superstitious uses. Worried by large dispositions under these provisions, a 1736 Act declared them null and void unless executed with certain prescribed solemnities and not less than 12 months before the death of the donor.

The question as to whether or not gifts for charitable purposes were prohibited by the mortmain statutes was being discussed elsewhere in the middle decades of the 19th century, i.e. around the time Moore died.[18] Despite the Bishop's concerns, however, the Statutes of Mortmain were not extended to the colonies, a point which had been reiterated by the Attorney General and Chief Justice Forbes, with recourse to the opinion of Sir William Grant, in a famous case before the NSW Supreme court on 17th June 1825.[19] These statutes were in the news later that same year, when the authority of Broughton's predecessor as Archdeacon, Thomas Hobbes Scott, to act as the King's Visitor for the Parramatta Female Orphan School was challenged. When Mr Wentworth declared that Governor King had exceeded his authority in granting freehold lands to the trustees of the school in perpetuity, declaring this contrary to the Statutes of Mortmain, the Court asked him whether he was aware that 'it has been decided that the Acts of Mortmain do not apply in the Colonies'.[20] Despite what he could have learned from the short history of the Colony itself, however, just to be on the safe side, Broughton was eager to have a legal opinion from home.

The Bishop was also concerned about Moore's surviving relatives. He had only just learned on the day after Rachel's funeral, that Moore had 'a brother and a nephew living in England', and at the meeting with Burton and Broughton the day before the letter to Watson, Moore had confirmed this to be so.

> I urged him, as strongly as I could, to leave to these relatives a suitable proportion: but he seems, on what account I know not, to have little feeling of affection for them: saying they are

not badly off, and he shall send them a few hundred pounds during his life time, which will be quite enough.

Broughton was not happy with Moore's attitude here, and was going to try to change it. But there was also another problem beyond Moore's lack of family affection:

> But the important point is that they may possibly contest the Deeds of Gift and the Will: and even if they should be unsuccessful, still our defence must cost money, which, as no one has a direct personal interest in the issue, it may be difficult to find.

These problems raised, Broughton went on to inform Watson that the residence and land was on a 21 year lease —from the Bishop's point of view, at an 'inadequate' rent—and so the bequest would be unlikely to assist Broughton himself. The Deeds and Will had been placed in the hands of Dr Kinchela,[21] a retired judge, who had been involved in a similar case in Ireland, which was then confirmed by an Act of Parliament—a copy of which Broughton would greatly love to receive from Coleridge, if at all possible.

The Will is proved

On Christmas Eve, 1840, Thomas Moore departed this life and was buried from St Luke's on 29th December, Rev. John Duffus presiding. His Will was proved the following February.

Almost immediately, Broughton turned to Coleridge to help solve his legal anxieties, writing two letters about the Will in one day.[22]

> We have recently by the death of a Mr Moore received a very valuable bequest to the Church in money and land. The entire value I do not consider less than £20,000 besides 6,000 Acres of land before given. As he directs all his personal property to be laid out in purchase of land, *the whole* would be void if the circumstance had occurred in England. But we have every reason to believe that the same law will not reach it *here*. I am about however to ask a favour of you: that is to obtain a good legal opinion (and I know you have access to the best) as to the validity of the bequest, and the course which it would be

advisable for us to pursue if it should be questioned. I purpose therefore to send a copy of the Will and Codicil to England by a friend Mr Robert Lethbridge who is returning by the *Andromache*; and he on his arrival will forward the same to you by Post: which mode of conveyance, I have reason to believe, is now abundantly cheap. Therewith I will write more fully upon that subject.[23]

The second gets straight to the point:

I beg herewith to forward to you Copies of the Will and Codicil of the late Mr. Moore, referred to in my Letter of this day, forwarded by the *Andromache*. The affair, as you will perceive, is of importance to the interests of the Church and if any attempt should be made to set aside the Will (or the Deeds of Gift referred to in the Codicil) the probability is that it would proceed upon the repugnance of such bequests and donations to the Statutes of Mortmain. My wish therefore is to obtain, through your kind agency, the best opinion and advice how we should meet that objection if it should be raised. My good friend Burton of course cannot be our counsellor; as that would be incompatible with his position as a Judge in the cause. The prevalent opinion here, as far as I am able to gather it, appears to be that the Mortmain Acts are not in force here: but the determination of that question must finally rest with our Judges: and we cannot be too well armed with arguments to fix their Honours' decision in our favour, in case it should come to a trial. I have no particular reason for deeming it probable this will be the case: but there are so many wrong-headed jealous spirits, who would consider it a triumph to deprive the Church of England of every advantage, that it is most prudent on our part to be *prepared*.

It is interesting to notice that Broughton's previous concern for Moore's bereft relatives does not resurface, being replaced by fears of those hostile to the cause of the Church of England. The Bishop goes on to ask Coleridge to seek advice on the exact wording of the Will, to ensure that it relates to the disposal of the whole of Moore's property, not just his land, for this was his memory of Moore's intention.[24]

CHAPTER 10 ~ *Training Colonial Clergy* [257]

Evidently his anxiety was not resolved quickly enough for him, for early in December 1841, Broughton reminded Coleridge of his February letter, when he was 'hoping you might be able to obtain some opinion for me as to its sufficiency against Mortmain enactments'.[25] By the end of that month his anxieties are compounded by news from Moore's surviving relatives (this time a 'sister' replaces the 'nephew' he previously mentioned).[26]

> Since my last despatch I have had Letters from England in reply to some which were written on the subject of old Mr Moore's death and disposal of his property to the service of the Church. I am therefore in hopes of receiving news from you of the arrival of the Copy of his Will which I forwarded to you via the "*Andromache,*" last February; hoping that you might be able to procure for me a hint or two as to what course it would be advisable to take if the Statutes of Mortmain were brought to bear upon us. I am sorry to learn that the old gentleman has left a brother and sister in very narrow circumstances, for whom we trusted he had made provision;[27] which indeed he might have done without at all impairing the amount of his bounty to the Church. His relatives are desirous of obtaining a copy of the Will, and the Executors here are anxious that they should have it: and therefore I shall be glad if you can send to them the Copy which you have: it being I presume of no further use to you now. If there be any reason for your wishing to retain the document may I request you to forward it to Mr Francis 5 Agnes Court Throgmorton St, Bank, who will cause a copy to be made, and return the original to you. Moore's family are in communication with Revd Archdeacon Scott, Whitfield Rectory, Hayden Bridge, Northumberland; and with the Revd George Fielding, Bishop-Auckland, through either of whom the papers might be conveyed to them: most readily I believe by the latter.[28]

By February 1842, Broughton has received a satisfactory answer to the legal questions, without reference to their particular result, although Moore's relatives are now well and truly out of view:

> Turning now to other subjects I am happy to say that your more than kind Letter of the 10th September 1841 reached me on the

28th January 1842, accompanied by the original and duplicate Case and Opinion on Mr Moore's Will. This is entirely satisfactory to us: and I beg you to accept the best thanks of myself and brother Trustees and indeed of the Church at large, for the care and attention you have bestowed upon this matter.[29]

And there is further good news in April, a testimony to the diligence of Coleridge:

The opinions on Mr Moore's Will (in original and duplicate) have also arrived safe. Indeed I am not aware that any thing whatever which you have dispatched has ever miscarried.[30]

Towards a local college

With the legal concerns settled, and the relatives somehow dealt with,[31] Broughton now had plenty of time for dreaming about the college that would come into existence in 'sixteen or seventeen years'. The extended visit of Selwyn in 1842 *en route* to New Zealand enabled the two antipodean bishops to fire one another up about clergy training. Broughton reflected upon their discussions in a letter which would prove to have a huge impact upon those at home, the so-called 'germinal letter' of 16th June 1842.[32]

The tone of the letter is enthusiastic and, despite the college being so far off, Broughton bubbles over with detail, as he unfolds his plans, inspired by the conclusion of their conversation, namely, that of:

Erecting under the immediate eye of each, a School of Divinity in which promising young men (from 18 to 23) might be trained in the knowledge of the duties of their profession, as well as initiated into the practical discharge of them. By means of such institutions, in addition to what the S[ociety for the].P[ropagation of the].G[ospel]. may be able to accomplish first, we trust that the church might be supplied with a due succession of men qualified rightly to divide the word of Truth.

He tells of how Bishop Selwyn has the resources to begin already, and then proceeds to outline the plans for his own See. The great public schools can supply the professions in England, but colonial clergy could be recruited from smaller schools.

> Assuming that there are such persons then, it would be a matter for prudential consideration whether the object proposed could be best attained by assisting them through an English university course, or by sending them to pass four or five years in an establishment here under the immediate superintendence, inspection and control of the bishop of the colony. No special recommendation of the former course, that of a home education, occurs to my thoughts excepting the superiority of advantage in point of scholarship which it must confer; but this would not appear to me deserving of so much consideration as to be set in opposition to numerous benefits attached to their being trained in an episcopal seminary here, from eighteen to twenty three, and so being habituated to the duties of their future station: while their characters and capacities would be unfolding themselves to the knowledge of him who would afterwards have to direct their services, and under whom they would be trained and disciplined to act. It is my firm conviction, that without such an Institution we cannot reasonably hope to make the impression required upon the mass of indifference, and even of worse characteristics, which new colonies must necessarily (I fear) present.

After referring again to the Bishop of New Zealand's plans, he turns to his own:

> I would therefore confine myself to my own case, and will tell you what it would be my wish to accomplish; leaving out of the question for the present whether resources can be found for the accomplishment of that wish. With a view to its futurity I think that if the colonial bishoprics fund should have resources to apply towards the permanent endowment of the See of Australia (which would certainly become necessary on my vacating it) it would be judicious to purchase the premises in which I now reside, to be the bishop's residence until the lease of the estate given by Mr More for that purpose shall fall in: in about 16 or 17 years. When that occurs, the land on

> which this house now stands or by which this is surrounded, being in the midst of the town, as by that time it will be, may be let upon building leases to great advantage; and could afford first of all, to see the bishops of Australia the means of building a see-house at Moorebank, and when that is paid for a certain annual income.

He then encloses a sketch of the land around his own house, explaining that he has already purchased a little of it (at a rather inflated price) for a church for the area, and suggests the remaining allotments also be purchased.

> The next step would be to erect a small residence for the principal of the seminary who might also be the incumbent of the church, and apartments for students; commencing with 6, and augmenting the numbers as resources should be found and as need might require. You see, my whole plan which would place such students during the period of study and until the age of ordination arrives, under my immediate direction: and if they would be chosen already imbued with general knowledge and good principles we might train them up, I hope, thro' God's blessing to be faithful and useful for the edifying of the church. The whole establishment must be conducted on principles of restricted frugality: and after the first outlay I believe the regular annual expenditure would be very trifling.

This letter reveals quite clearly that, at this stage, Broughton is dreaming dreams about an interim local college in his own Darlinghurst backyard. He clearly sees the advantages of a local college outweigh those of an education in England. With concrete plans, and even a purchase, Broughton has his eyes set on the future, and is a man in a hurry to get this college firmly established within the colony. His English friends have been asked for just two things: funding, and to supply a stream of young men fresh out of school. With a supply of the right type of men, a college under the watchful eye of the bishop would produce the clergy that Australia so desperately needed.

Just one month later, however, Broughton's tone has changed.[33]

Once again he seems rather despondent about Australia's needs for clergy. The SPG has done all that it can, but his seven years of experience has shown him that they cannot do what is needed. As an example, he speaks of his disappointment over the abilities of young Watson,[34] who had arrived with Selwyn, telling frankly of his inadequacies, and yet revealing that he has now been compelled to put him in charge of a parish of 4,000 souls. What is needed is clear:

> Without a totally different class of men to carry on the work, how is the Vineyard to be cleared of the thorns and briars by which through long neglect it has been suffered to be overrun. I firmly believe it is God's interposing providence (called into exercise by the united prayers of His Church) which can alone raise up for its aid such men as are required: for they must (if they are to do the work) be men of exemplary ability, judgment, temper, and firmness: and yet there is next to nothing (in a worldly sense) proposed for their reward.

Broughton now contemplates a different course of action, and his previous excitement about the local college seems to have faded.

> If circumstances admitted, perhaps an Institution specially appropriated to the education of such, might be as well established in England; as a central fountain from which the waters might flow to *all* the Colonies. But if so, it *must* be under the control and direction of some one versed in Colonial Church affairs. It would be a blessing indeed if the Bishop of Barbadoes could be prevailed upon to devote the residue of his days to the management of a Seminary having this object in view.

This bishop was William Hart Coleridge, Edward's cousin,[35] who did, in fact, go on to become the first Warden of St Augustine's College, only to die after some 18 months in the post. As Broughton was formulating these plans, however, he has another person in mind should Bishop Coleridge decline the invitation.

> If he would *not*, I am not sure whether it might not be a position in which I might hope with God's blessing to do more really effective service than even where I am: but I look for nothing, and seek nothing: only I would be ready to act wherever, in the

judgment of yourself and of such friends as have with you the welfare of the Colonial Churches at heart, my services might do good. My only settled persuasion is this: that a Colonial Bishop *must* be at the head of every such Institution in order to make it work well. If it be set up in England, then the Bishop presiding would form a centre to the entire ministry of the Churches in all the Colonies:[36] if there be such an Institution in each separate Diocese, then every Bishop would be the head of his own. To provide effectually for the continuance of such a ministry as is the chief want of the Churches abroad, one or other of these Plans must be had recourse to.

It seems that Broughton's thoughts have turned to home, and to a potential new ministry of his own. Nevertheless, he presents two options, here equally weighted: one English college, or a local college in each colonial Diocese. The only essential item, whatever the outcome, is to have a bishop to form the centre.

On the same day, he informed philanthropist Joshua Watson of what he had suggested to Coleridge.[37]

The real want under which we labour, I evidently see is that of clergy duly qualified by character and acquirements for their high office. The same want presses in every Colony that I am acquainted with. England, it is to be feared, cannot, as affairs are now ordered, supply that want. I therefore write most urgently and expectedly to Coleridge, to consider the practicability of establishing either one Seminary in *each* Colonial Diocese, or one Seminary in England for the common service of *all* the Colonies, in which may be trained a class of clergymen suited for Colonial service; a class such as, I do not hesitate to say, *we cannot do without.*

Having pondered his own possible move to this potential college, Broughton's thoughts begin to turn to his successor. Early in 1843, when discussing Coleridge as a potential candidate for a colonial bishoprick, perhaps South Australia, Broughton realises that his Eton friend would be perfect to fill his own shoes. Despite the English Institution now being on the agenda, however, he has not abandoned his own. When listing the things for which 'there *may*

CHAPTER 10 ~ *Training Colonial Clergy* [263]

be a fresh impulse necessary which a successor would communicate with more effect', he included the fact that: 'There is Moore's College to bring to maturity, in connexion with the King's School at Parramatta and the Grammar School at Sydney which are to be its feeders'.[38] Clearly Broughton's thoughts of Moore's College have not been entirely suppressed, and he has begun to think about assembling a local supply of students to be trained there.

Two years later, he answers Coleridge's query about what had happened with this institution:

> You ask also about Mr Moore's [estate]. His property you are aware was strictly tied up to certain uses; not leaving the Trustees any discretion but to apply it to the purposes named in the Will. One of these was the institution of a College at Liverpool (where he dwelt) but unhappily he made very slender provision for it. I have been nursing [?] the funds for that purpose: and have a small sum in hand, which may be sufficient to commence building with. But I wait the coming of Mr Formby: without whose aid I do not think it possible to carry on such an undertaking.

However, although writing as if the college at Liverpool is still an option, a couple of sentences in the same letter turn, once again, to the potential of the lot next door.

> I sent you some time since a sketch of a little College Court which if means were within my reach I should be very glad to build adjoining my own garden; which would be more convenient to me than at Liverpool (21 miles off) but the means are *not* at my command: and I shall lie upon my oars till I hear of Mr Formby.[39]

In this vast land, the 'Tyranny of Distance' has already been felt across the 21 miles to Liverpool! Of course, this would militate against ministerial training being done under the watchful eye of the bishop. When the 'sixteen or seventeen years' have reached their fullness, the bishop may be ensconced at Moore Bank, but, for the moment, he still resides in town.

By this time, Broughton's hopes appear to have become

entangled with the expectation of the arrival of Formby, who was to come on the recommendation of Coleridge. On the 8th April, 1845, however, he received a letter 'putting the matter in abeyance' and he immediately wrote to Formby, explaining the nature of the position in view.[40] Nevertheless, when the crunch came, Formby declined the bishop's invitation, much to Broughton's disappointment. Three years closer to his 'sixteen or seventeen year' goal, the Bishop of Australia was still unsure of where his clergy would be trained.

The St. Augustine's side-track

Meanwhile, things had been stirring 'back home'. Broughton's letter of 16th June 1842 has been called the 'germinal letter', because it seeded some ideas from which a series of concrete actions arose.[41] Although this letter clearly shows Broughton looking to a future college at Liverpool, capitalising upon Moore's bequest, and formulating plans for an interim college locally, the effects of this letter in England were such that the plans for colonial training were hijacked in a different direction.

The Colonial Clergy Act of 1819 provided for the creation of colonial clergy, but they could officiate in England only with the Archbishop of Canterbury's permission. This meant that those clergy who had been ordained by the Bishop of London for the colonies were reduced to second-class status—a situation that would prevail for 150 years![42] The man who would preside over the three students from Stroud when Barker opened his college in Moore's old Liverpool dwelling was the first of the Australian-born to realise the advantage of being ordained in the regular way in England. After studying at the evangelical Magdalen College, Oxford, William Macquarie Cowper —son of Rev. William Cowper, of St Philip's Church Hill—was ordained in 1834 by the Bishop of Exeter, ensuring that he would always be a first-class clergyman![43] No doubt this proved to be an asset when he followed his father to St Phillip's, and then on to become Sydney's long-standing and celebrated Dean.[44]

But despite the provisions for creating colonial clergy, where

CHAPTER 10 ~ *Training Colonial Clergy* [265]

were they supposed to be trained?

As we have seen, when Selwyn arrived in Sydney on the way to New Zealand, the two bishops had discussed the need for clergy and for their training. As part of his strategy, Selwyn went on to form his own college, and, fired up by conversations with Selwyn, and prompted by Moore's bequest, Broughton was moving in a similar direction. However, at the time a rather different attitude towards colonial colleges prevailed 'at home', as illustrated by Henry Bailey's reflections on this period, some forty years later:

> Meanwhile the Church abroad was making what efforts she could to supply herself with clergy. Bishop's College, Calcutta, had been successfully established for some years; in New Zealand Bishop Selwyn was founding a Theological College at the Waimate; and a start in the same direction was being made in Australia. But the Colonies were still in their infancy; there was as yet scarcely any provision for even secular education; the average settler was not a man calculated to take kindly to literary pursuits; and for a while at least bishops would have to turn to England for a supply of cultured and well-trained clergy to work their dioceses.[45]

For several years, there had been conversations in England about the need for training clergy for colonial service. In 1843, reflecting upon previous years, Bishop Bagot of Oxford and Mr Beresford Hope, the eventual benefactor of St. Augustine's College, stated that they had felt the need for such an institution for a long time. Rev. Charles Marriot, Sub-Dean of Oriel College, Oxford, and Dr Cotton, Provost of Worcester, both had a scheme for the founding of a missionary college at Oxford.[46] Broughton himself had previously (?1834?) raised this concern with the Bishop of London, saying that 'there was still wanting within the Church of England an institution for rearing up clergymen for the Colonies'. Despite being the Bishop responsible for the colonies, the Bishop of London gave Broughton 'no encouragement to think such a proposal could be brought to accomplishment, nor indeed could I very readily suggest whence the funds were to be derived'.[47]

By the beginning of 1843, Broughton seems to be rather enamoured with the idea of an English college, and with the suggestion that he should be its principal and Coleridge his successor in Australia.[48]

> But that which has fixed itself strongly in my thoughts is the design, which I wrote to you about last year, of having an Institution in England for the preparation of candidates for Orders in the Colonies *beyond* what the Universities may supply. The want of qualified clergymen is a serious calamity here and every where. If any such institution could be drawn together, and your able relative Bishop Coleridge would not undertake the guidance, I think that as an unworthy substitute I am might do good: and *that* would be the way in which if I *were* to leave my present charge, it would be my desire to be employed.

At the beginning of February, he returns even more strongly to the same thoughts, dissuading Coleridge from taking up South Australia in favour of succeeding him in Sydney, 'leaving me to occupy myself for the remainder of my working life in presiding over such an Institution as I have suggested the propriety nay necessity of establishing in England for training up candidates for ordination and usefulness in the Colonial Churches'.[49] By mid-month he is urgent in his plea:

> that very point on which I have written to you so often and so anxiously namely the adoption of some systematic plan *within the Church itself* to procure clergymen in sufficient numbers and suitably qualified for the Colonial Churches—lies nearer to my heart than ever. If I could have charge of that department as my recent Letters have suggested, I should be thankful to be so employed where in my opinion my services would be of use […]. *Pray* do your best to bring about under *some* suitable direction or other, the design of a Seminary in which Students may be trained for the Sacred Office in the Colonies.[50]

By this time, Broughton's germinal letter (16/6/1842) had provoked Coleridge into action.[51] By letter of 24th February, 1843, Coleridge enlisted the support of Dr Bagot, Bishop of Oxford, who on the 1st of March wrote of the need for 'the *speedy* adoption of some Institution for the training of Missionaries for our colonies'.[52] When Bagot elicited the support of the Primate, William Howley, the Archbishop argued that 'the advantages of training the Missionaries in this country, in preference to the Colonies, are, in my opinion, decisive with respect to health, morals, and efficient teaching'.[53] He suggested that there ought to be one college, and in the environs of Oxford. The Heads of Houses were not so keen and, besides, at this stage Archbishop Howley did not permit Coleridge to publicly promote the scheme for a further six months, as the SPG was in financial trouble and competition for funds was deemed to be inadvisable.[54] At the end of this embargo, the Archbishop wrote supportively on behalf of himself, the Archbishop of York and the Bishop of London,[55] and, although requesting a further period of delay, he permitted Coleridge to write a private circular to his friends, but not to request funds at this stage.

Broughton continued to encourage Coleridge's plans. In December, after a journey to Port Phillip once again pressed the need for clergy upon him, he wrote to Watson:[56]

> I am writing to Coleridge to animate him in maturing his Collegiate Institution, which, if it provides a race of competent clergymen to occupy our Colonial Churches during the next twenty years [...] will have effected more than I think any undertaking whatever has yet accomplished for the promotion of the Catholic faith throughout the world, and providing a counteracting influence against the encroachments of Rome.

By 3rd January 1844, the English college has become the only hope: 'You must not, and I am sure, for the love of God, you will not let go your design for the Colonial Institution for clergymen. It will be the one and only measure by which we can stand'.[57] In mid-year, he continues to fan the plans for 'your Colonial College' into flame.

> But after all if your Colonial College goes on (which may the Almighty grant) and we can obtain a due succession of men qualified to wage the great battle against ungodliness and sensuality, and not caring much for any more of temporalities than

an overruling Providence I trust will always provide for them, we may maintain our position, and enlarge our borders.[58]

Just prior to writing this to Coleridge, Broughton had deliberated with Cowper and Allwood about whether his presence in England may add weight to the cause of the proposed college.[59] After deciding to stay, by December he is nevertheless able to rejoice at the news of Beresford Hope's purchase of St. Augustine's monastery for the purpose of a colonial training college.[60]

One year later,[61] at the same time as sending donations from himself and Governor Gipps, and a letter of recommendation for Australia's first St. Augustine's student, Percy Smith, he mentions his attempts to help the cause of St. Augustine's in Sydney, by twice printing the college's subscription list and the names of the committee (being impressed with the list himself!). He plans to speak with the Diocesan Committee about the college, but is not hopeful of much support. As reasons for this reluctance, he cites not only the fact that those with property are often heavily in debt, but both theological and 'nationalistic' reasons as well.

Even in England 'the scheme of St. Augustine's College, in whole or in detail, was in many quarters looked upon with great disfavour'.[62] The possibility of its location at Oxford (home of the 'Oxford Movement', or 'Tractarianism', associated with Pusey and Newman) had already roused the suspicions of prominent Low Churchmen, and the criticisms of the St Augustine's proposal simply increased when the associations with its benefactor became known.[63] Beresford Hope had been one of the leading laymen of the High Church party since his youth.[64] He had stated that the Warden should 'be at the head of a Catholic and not a Protestant Seminary' and that the Fellows should be High Churchmen. In January 1845 before 'any irrevocable steps had been taken' Hope and Coleridge had laid their plans before the Archbishop and, according to Hope,

> at this interview his Grace distinctly repudiated any connection of the proposed college with the Low Church party, and recognised the college as one which should embody the views called High Church, as being the true ones of the Church of England.

> Mr. Coleridge and myself were both delighted at receiving such an assurance from his Grace, without which, I believe it is not too much for me to say, I believe we both should have felt ourselves compelled to abandon the undertaking.[65]

Thus 'it is patent that from its inception their college was to figure as a High Church institution'.[66] Although there were other reasons for the delays in Coleridge raising the appeal for St. Augustine's, as we have seen, it is also true that 'the College scheme was being denounced in certain quarters as savouring of Tractarianism, and the Archbishop thought it better that it should not step into the public arena at present'.[67]

This reputation had also travelled to Australia. Broughton himself had spoken of an article from an Oxford paper that had been reprinted in the Sydney press, 'which showed very plainly that the leaders of the puritan pack had scent of your movements, and would speedily be in full cry. When one sees what they have done in other cases, their hostility is certainly not to be despised'.[68] In view of a 'grudge' he felt the Colonial Church Society held against him,[69] he hoped that his own name being linked with St Augustine's would not make matters worse.

Mid way through January,[70] amidst his own evident delight at the progress towards St Augustine's, he expressed disappointment to Coleridge that he was unable to deliver on a promise he had previously made, 'that you should receive a joint Address to the Archbishop from myself and clergy expressive of our thankfulness for the establishment of this great Institution, with a pledge of our united confidence in the principles on which it was founded and proposed to be conducted'. He suggested that he would raise the question of his intended address at the forthcoming Diocesan Committee meeting, being dissuaded from doing so on this earlier occasion by the outspoken opposition of Cowper, one of the Diocese's leading evangelicals.

> At this time, however, my worthy friend Dr Cowper, (for worthy he is though on one point a little wrong-headed, as I formerly hinted to you) [...], began, as I was informed, to break forth

into vehement denunciations of Puseyism (of which he knows less, God save the mark, than I of Arabic); and so I found, in his then suspicious frame of mind, he would be not unlikely to take a fling at the poor College, and to interrupt that unanimity which it was my object to array on its side.

The objections raised in England were evidently also being raised in Sydney, even if Broughton did not take them seriously. In his letter of the 30th, when contemplating his airing the matter at the Diocesan Committee, he stated that some were 'taking refuge behind that easiest of all pretences, an imputation of Puseyism, as an excuse for refusing to assist'.[71] On this occasion, he was more sympathetic to what could be called the 'nationalists', even though he does not hold out much hope for support from this camp either:

> I trust however there may be some few who will display a juster feeling. There is another class, more worthy of respect, but who will probably do no more towards assisting you: I mean the persons who would give the preference to a Seminary of Divinity to be established *here*.

Now that St Augustine's was going ahead, Broughton's mind had been made up. His previous preference for a local college has been replaced by a dual system, for he adds, 'and I so far concur in their views as to admit that this would be very desirable in conjunction with St. Augustine, but not as a perfect substitute'.

While his friends worked towards the English institution, Broughton was working on the Australian side of the partnership.

St James in the Shadow of St Augustine's

St James College had a meteoric rise and fall. It opened in the St James' King St parsonage in 1845, under the incumbent, Rev. Robert Allwood.[72] Although secular students were enrolled, probably with a view to later studying at the university, St. James' was principally 'the first attempt made in Australia to train local Anglican ordinands'.[73]

The local college is mentioned in December 1844. As Broughton rejoices at the news of the purchase of St. Augustine's, he responds to Coleridge's suggestion of a local college for the training of deacons.[74]

> Another singular coincidence I will mention, which seems to shew that all things *do* work *together*, when we are sincerely and heartily devoting our thoughts in our respective stations to promote the glory of God by extending his kingdom upon earth. You urge me to prepare a place where young men qualified for the office of Deacon may find a *refugium* in case you should be able to send out to me any such. It is truly remarkable that on the Sunday before your Letter came (that is *last* Sunday) I had ordained a Deacon[75] exactly upon the terms which you suggest and had been occupying my thoughts with the Plan of a small College for Sixteen such, under a Tutor who should be their classical and mathematical instructor, and (when we can afford it) a Master who should be the theological professor: which office however I might pro tempore supply. What you say about Mr Formby falls in so exactly with what I want, that I am tempted to say again, Here is really a providential interposition. I shall write to you again about this, on or about the 15th of January when one or two Vessels are to sail for England: and will then send you a Ground Plan of my projected College, and (by way of curiosity) the pencil sketch which I had drawn out before your Letter came. The *name* even had occupied my thoughts. Corpus Christi (suggested by your brother's early memoirs of Arnold) is a very fine name if rightly understood: but the world I fear is hardly wise enough for that, and we must give none offence if we can help it. Exeter it shall be called, if *you* desire it. If not I had fixed on Pembroke Hall (of "late mine own College") with statues (or at least niches for statues) of Ridley and Andrewes on either side of the Gate. But *now* I think, if the grand scheme proceed, it must be "St Augustine's". I will say more about Mr. Formby in writing again. But *pray* keep him up to his purpose if you can.

He elaborated further on his plans for the local training of deacons in his letter of 4th January 1845, when he is once again excited about his local college.[76]

My principle purpose in now writing (next to that of letting you know particulars about the N.Z. party) is to speak a little more about a College here of candidates for the ministry. My mind is yet full to overflowing with the wonderful consummation likely to be accomplished by Mr. Hope's magnificent (magnificent because so humble and unpretending) appropriation of his worldly goods to the purchase of St. Augustine's. Should it take effect (and I will hardly allow myself to doubt) we may surely say "This is the Lord's doing and it is marvellous in our eyes." However, as to our own needs they are *so* great that nothing must stand in the way of an endeavour to train up a due and constant succession of deacons, at any rate, under my own charge. The expense is the *only* obstacle: but surely after what we have witnessed we must not be deterred by that apprehension from making the attempt. We have as you know a piece of land adjoining my present residence, purchased with *your* money. In my eagerness I gave too much for it certainly: but still in consideration of its extremely convenient position, it may be worth more to us, both now and for ever, than it could be to any others. So although I have grieved and have reproached myself for not husbanding the money better, it is not worth while to continue to do so; but to set to work in earnest upon a design which if it take root and bear fruit will be indeed as the sycamine tree planted in the midst of the sea: for a situation less likely, in a natural sense, to have given birth to any thing of the kind there could scarcely be. The plan of the College (to hold when completed 14 or 16 students) is now in the hands of an Architect to put my irregular conceptions into a workmanlike shape. In the spirit of faith I hope, and not of rashness, I shall, after my return, proceed with the work: and hope to find funds to build rooms for the *tutor*: who (if he finally determine under God's guidance to come to me) may be Mr Formby. You say he is qualified: and he is therefore wanted and will be welcome. Till something better can be done, if he be a single man, he can live in my house. Another Whytehead is not to be looked for: but a good and clever man will be at any rate a great acquisition, and he can be set immediately to work. At this moment I am placed under a most unspeakable perplexity.

By mid-year, however, he seems to be looking to St. Augustine's exclusively: 'we require (to say all briefly) Bishops Priests and Deacons. Under Providence I think Mr Hope's College and *your* College, of St Augustine may supply them all'.[77] But, when he writes in six months time, January 1846,[78] he had already been training some young men in the parsonage of St. James', King St, for some months.

> At this moment I have collected around me some eight or ten young men[79] of moderate acquirements in learning and, so far as I can judge, religiously disposed as well as of sober and correct principles. With the aid of my good friend Allwood I have been directing their course of reading since my return to settle at home for a time, three weeks ago. We give an entire day of examination in each week: and by the beginning of March it is my hope to find them so well advanced that they may be brought a little more into public observation: and from thenceforth I purpose beginning for them a course of Lectures on the 39 Articles. To be sure their scholarship is not the first rate, as such things are reckoned among *you*: but I am every day more fully persuaded of the truth of Hooker's observation (B.V.S 81) as to there being no remedy in such a case as ours, but to take into the ecclesiastical order a number of men meanly qualified in respect of learning lest the greatest part of the people should be left utterly without the public use and exercise of religion.

Broughton intended St. James' graduates to play 'second-fiddle' to the new college planned for Canterbury, as he says in the same letter:

> As many as may be required to fill the more important cures, and to uphold the credit of the Church by their superior acquirements, I trust we may look to St. Augustine to supply.[80]

This represents a change from previously. The St. James' graduates will not only be ordained to the diaconate, for this would not meet the needs of Australia. They will also be priests, even if second-rate priests!

> My position is very trying and painful. Such is the scarcity of clergymen that I cannot open several Churches: nor provide for the regular service in those which have been opened except by myself fulfilling the entire duties of a parochial minister as often as there is any sickness in our body; which is the case just now. I have often meant to explain, in reply to an expression of wonder which once preceded from you that I had not recourse to a re-establishment of the order of *Deacons*, that such a step would do me little or no good. In the large populous parishes I would gladly have deacons, if it were in my power assisting the priests: but we have not, even in the largest parishes, a Stipend for a second clergyman. In the country parts where there is so great a distance between one clergyman and the next, a Deacon would for obvious causes be less effective. In order to supply even imperfectly the wants of so many parishes, and to render each clergyman competent to discharge the duties in which he can hardly obtain the help of another, I am compelled to admit to the priesthood all who can be found suitable for it.

In a letter to Watson drafted on the same day,[81] his high hopes for Augustine's are clear:

> Coleridge sends me from time to time encouraging and hopeful accounts of the progress of St Augustine's and very thankful was I my dear Mr Watson to find that the Archbishop had with his usual judgment and calm discrimination, placed your name on the list of his Committee. [...] The entire character of the Colonial Churches will be moulded according to what St Augustine's shall be during the next 20 years.

These two letters also indicate that the news of John Henry Newman's defection to Rome has reached Australia.[82] Although he does not comment much upon it, apparently following Coleridge's counsel, he is clearly aware that this event has done little for the St Augustine's scheme. Little did he realise the similar troubles that his own college would soon have to deal with on this score.

In June 1846, Broughton sent Coleridge a couple of sketches, one of which showed:

a turreted or castellated building. I am on the point of hiring the latter for about three years and a half, as the Site of a Seminary for Students in Divinity. At present we have eight under instruction. Formby you know disappointed me: but my most worthy friend Allwood adheres to me faithfully, and we between us carry on the concern. He lectures in general literature (Greek, Latin and english) and in the Greek Testament: I dissert in a weekly Lecture upon the 39 Articles: and we shall in due time undertake Edlenas/ [?] History between us. Our disciples are really all very promising and satisfactory.[83]

As he speaks of these developments, he catches himself, and reminds Coleridge that 'our Collegiate Institution is *meant* to be, if you will allow it, a branch of St Augustine's'.

This persistence with St. Augustine's shows a deep commitment to that institution, for the same letter reveals that the only subscriptions that he has been able to raise for the Canterbury college are his own and that of his old schoolmate, Governor Gipps.

> The malicious were prepared to raise, and foolish to adopt, a cry of the "Puseyite College at Canterbury". This I have reason to know would have been made the stalking-horse from behind which many were prepared to "shoot out their arrows, even bitter words". I was therefore unwilling to expose our *well-meaning* supporters to the pernicious sophistries and misrepresentations with which the opposite part were prepared to assail the proposal. The timidity and backwardness with which very good people here attach themselves to any cause which they hear evil-spoken of, even when in their consciences they believe it to be unjustly, is as lamentable as it is surprising. Therefore I thought it better to forebear pressing the matter (after holding one preliminary Meeting) and to keep our forces in reserve for a future effort; which may be made with more confidence of success when your College has commenced its operations; and the groundlessness of the insinuations which are uttered against it maybe shewn by an appeal to facts. There is, I am sure, a great reserve of good feeling in existence: but it is beaten down

and interminated by a bold noisy combination of schismatics, sceptics, semi-churchmen, and such like; while, I *should* say if it were not introducing too great a confusion of metaphors, the Roman Catholics blow the coals, and hope to see us all in a blaze. But in that hope they will be disappointed.

The following month has a good report of St James' happily ticking along, and the promise of a full report by way of Sir George Gipps, sailing on Saturday next.[84] Another comes in August,[85] with some estimated costs required to keep 'our Divinity College' running for the next two years. The shadow of the English institution still falls on Broughton, for he hopes that 'during that interval we shall ripen our plans; and by God's blessing may bring to maturity a school of the prophets which you may not think unworthy to be taken into association with St Augustine's'. Perhaps his own ambitions are also hinted at in his comment that 'I pray that the mantle [of the Bishop of Sydney] may fall upon some suitable shoulders, and that I may retire to obscurity and my books. This is what I often sigh for, but dare not contemplate while many things are to be done and I have strength to do them'.[86]

In October 1846,[87] he reports that the college:

stands erect I think there is reason for saying. I have hired an admirable house and grounds about a mile from Sydney at a rent of £150 a year: and we shall have from 12 to 20 students. My wish is to begin humbly, and to mount upward by degrees: drawing public attention to us in proportion as we can present any thing worthy of notice. I consider myself as Principal, and my excellent friend and colleague Allwood as Resident Tutor: and that will be the whole of our Staff at the commencement. Our greatest drawback and hindrance is the remoteness of the spot from my present residence (not less than three miles) which must prevent my taking that active and hourly part in the work which it would be my wish to take. At present I am trying to get rid of my house, in the hope of finding one nearer to the scene of action.

His letter of 12th October 1846 reports 'active operation', seeks for £200–300 pa from the friends in England, and announces that they will move to Lyndhurst by the end of the year.[88] Since Allwood is a potential candidate for an Australian bishoprick, Broughton also meditates upon a possible replacement for him, and upon Formby who almost came to the post:

> and yet more difficult still to be found, a man who can maintain the highest and most truly catholic principles without giving occasion to the timid or censorious to cry out (as they do even against me) that he is bringing in popery. At one time I had formed a notion that Mr Formby might be such another: but it is plain to see now that he had not the force of mind and superiority to trifles which would have made him suitable. What an escape too have I had, I could not help saying to myself, when in looking very lately over a list of those who had followed that fatal example of declension into Romanism, I found his name included in it. No one who has *that* tendency would be for our purpose. Yet it is odd to be thus talking, of who will suit and who will not, in this somewhat imperious style, when we are in fact beggars and therefore not entitled to choose. But really the truth is that unless we could have an effective man it would be better to have none, and to allow the institution to drop. But I do form my plans, and after what we have seen and known cannot help forming them, upon the hypothesis that there are others yet remaining like Allwood, who will engage in such a work for its own sake, and not shrink from a laborious life and then a narrow income; when the aim is to provide a succession of the ministry in so wide-spreading a branch as this is of the tree which sprang but yesterday from its grain of mustard-seed.

Before referring to another letter on its way, describing three potential sites (presumably for the college?), he once again turns to how the college is to be funded, and argues that it is absolutely essential that the funding should come from outside the colony.[89]

> With respect to the endowment of the College, or any provision whatever for its maintenance, I will candidly express my belief, even at the risk of being thought exorbitant, that it is not only *better*, but altogether *indispensable*, if we wish it to go upon sound church-principles, that we should obtain assistance

without, until we are so firmly set up as to be able go alone, and insist upon having our own way. I do not think the people of the Colony would give *much* towards the erection and maintenance unless every one who gave might have a voice in appointing the system according to which a College should be founded and regulated. In most cases people's presumption would be in the exact ratio with their ignorance of the subject: and I could not face this with any hope of doing good. [...] we can thus go on and establish our own rules, and then merely have to ask people to come and enjoy the benefit if they will.

In these remarks it is not difficult to hear an echo of the suspicions being raised about the College's churchmanship. These suspicions had clouded Broughton's educational institutions for several years at least. After a visitation of clergy in mid 1844, at which he delivered a charge on the hot issue of General Education, the speaker of the Legislative Council had asked how the colony can put its schools under the Church of England if the Bishop refuses to give assurance that their clergymen can be trusted. Broughton answered him in terms of the clergymen being endorsed by holding his licence, but, as he informs Watson, he was well aware that this concern arose from the desire 'to lay down another test, and to require a disavowal of what they call Puseyism'.[90] News of Newman's defection, and then that of further defections to Rome in England, such as that of Formby, could not have helped the situation at all.

His letter of the 15th October 1846, speaks of the need for a permanent abode for the college, and so for further funds.[91] The 'incipient college':

indeed at present forms the chief subject of my anxiety. I have engaged (as you know) a house near Sydney from year to year, and we move to it at Christmas. But the great object of exertion must be a *permanent* settlement. If one had the cap of Fortunatus, I believe nothing could be so desirable as the house and the premises which we have hired. But I do not think in the way of purchase any thing effectual could be done with a smaller sum than £8000: so it is out of the question. Secondly there is a house and pretty good quantity of land opposite to the former. It is not nearly so good in any point of view, excepting that I think £4000 would set us going there. Again there is a residence with seven Acres of land adjoining the place which we have taken. It is a poor place certainly: but might be made to answer. The cost I imagine would not exceed £1500. The place which I have taken is called Lyndhurst. The Bishop of Tasmania who has seen it can tell you about it. If we had means, the Bishop's residence might be fixed there; and there would still be space enough to build the College upon. But all this must cost money: much more than we have, or probably can have.

The Glebe property, "Lyndhurst", was originally part of a 400 acre grant to the Colony's first chaplain, Rev. Richard Johnson in 1789, then absorbed into the 'Church and Schools Grant', subdivided and sold in 1828. A Dr Bowman purchased part of the land, and by 1845 when he died, 'Lyndhurst was a splendid house which stood in twenty acres of ground lying between what is now Glebe [Point] Road, St John's Road, Pyrmont Bridge Road and Blackwattle Bay'.[92] In October 1846, Broughton informed Coleridge that the Glebe college could accommodate 12 to 20 students,[93] but when it opened in 1847,[94] there were only four divinity students under the care of Rev. Robert Allwood, as well as four or five students, who probably attended lectures at Sydney College.[95]

In March 1847,[96] Broughton's two chief concerns were 'the partition of the Diocese, and St James' College', reporting that the latter is going very well, now, since February 1st, at Lyndhurst. Allwood is working too hard, but Lyndhurst is too far away for Broughton to be involved as he would wish, with the students coming to him now only on Thursday mornings. He then adds,

> As to our final site (should we ever obtain means to build) nothing is yet determined. But wherever it may be, my design is that the Bishop should form a proximate and integral portion of the College here as in New Zealand. Otherwise there can never be that vigour and uniformity of action which ought to be maintained. [...] We do want resources most sadly. That is not to be denied and I cannot yet see how it will be possible upon this narrow and frail foundation to raise up a succession of the ministry such as is

required for the service of this immense region: immense it will be even when two thirds shall have been lopped off from my charge and handed over to the direction of others.

On May the 8th 1847, he reported that 'St James college has been finally opened and the students are now in residence', and he now names 'bishop-elect' Allwood as 'at present the principal of the college to which his whole energies are devoted'.[97] By October he reports that Allwood was not disappointed about not receiving the bishoprick, and was working away steadily at the college.[98] In November, Broughton once more returns to his need for clergy, and expresses concerns about the future of the college, given that in the last eighteen months they have overspent by some £250.[99] By January, the bishop is buoyed up again by the arrival of some funds, and the prospect of ordaining three students next Lent.[100] He also noted that Joshua Watson had asked him to express his judgement 'as to the comparative advantages of an English or a Colonial education for those who are to minister at *our* altars', which he would endeavour to do in due course. At the same time,[101] he sent his subscription to St Augustine's, sorry 'to hear of difficulties and differences in connexion with that noble establishment, impeding its starting on its course'. In view of these troubles, he advises that 'to conduct it you must find a man who can have, at the same time—his own way *and* the confidence of everybody. I hope that Bishop Coleridge will prove such'.

But in this same year, St James would also fall under a similar cloud of its own, and by the next year, it would be closed.[102]

Part of the reason for its failure was the loss of the secular students whose fees had helped to keep the college afloat. When Sydney College closed in 1848, the Sydney Diocesan Committee resolved to 'use their utmost endeavours to promote [St James'] permanent establishment'.[103] No doubt the university opening in 1850 exerted some further pressure on the college.[104] However, a major reason for its decline was its reputation for being connected with the Tractarian movement.[105] It was not only that Bishop Broughton and Allwood were known to be sympathetic to these teachings emanating from Oxford, but the students had also received lectures from Rev. Robert Knox Sconce.[106] Sconce arrived in March 1841 at Port Phillip, and Bishop Broughton had invited him to be ordained in Sydney, at the prompting of Edward Coleridge. He was ordained on the 19th December to serve at Penrith and South Creek, before being priested at the largest ordination thus far in Australia on 18th December 1842. He took up the incumbency of St Andrew's in 1844, and when St James' College opened, he was one of the extra clergy who taught there from 1845 to 1847. When enrolments fell away in 1848, this was partly, as it came out later, because Sconce had been teaching the Tridentine view of Justification and advocated Catholic doctrine. After a time of severe self-questioning, through which he claimed Broughton and William Walsh at Christ Church St Lawrence had been of no help,[107] he, with Makinson (who, when Sconce was at Penrith, had served next door at Mulgoa, but was now at St Peter's Cook's River), on 21st February 1848, became one of the two Sydney Anglican Priests who joined the flood of those in England who followed Newman in going over to Rome. In May, Broughton reports that he had also dismissed a deacon, trained at St. James and influenced by Sconce, who had confessed to having knelt before an altar in a Roman Catholic chapel.[108] Rather strangely, he also appears to have disciplined another student who, just prior to his priesting, had made allegations regarding Catholic Doctrine being taught at St James's College.[109]

In the midst of the troubles of 1848, Broughton had drafted a quick note in response to the news of the death of Archbishop Howley —as its ship of delivery was spreading her sails. Here he ponders 'the influence which the new appointment may have on the state of the Church at large, and on St Augustine's in particular'.[110] Broughton had little cause for concern. Howley died on 11th February 1848, to be replaced by Archbishop Sumner, who expressed his full approval of the college whilst still Primate-elect, and the English college was inaugurated with due ceremony on St Peter's Day (29th June). By January 1849, Broughton was sharing his joy at reading the details of this glorious occasion,[111] and pledging his continued support. As he reflected upon the occasion, Broughton's own view of the genius behind the college is revealed quite clearly, for he asked Coleridge how he felt 'at witnessing this completion of *your own* glorious design, and this effect of your exertions'.

This same letter thanks Coleridge for further funding sent for St James's College, which he has banked, and then discusses some of the details about Sconce's defection, before turning to news of his own situation.

> Our position is certainly improved: but still I do not conceal from you it is full of cares, full of fears, and yet (for myself I speak) it is full of hope. Recently I have seen a spirit springing up, not in the highest class certainly, but among men who *can* work and *will* work: and who are now working for the College in a way which is gratifying at the moment and still more delightful in the prospect of its future efficacy. For any thing which you can do to encourage this disposition I shall be truly grateful.

Presumably the college closed its doors soon after, but there is no indication of this from Broughton's letters.[112] After such detailed reports at its inception, St James disappears from Broughton's correspondence without explanation.

St Augustine's and Australian Clergy

By the time the doors of St James's were closing, those of St. Augustine's were opening. Because of his influence on Coleridge by way of letter, Broughton was gradually credited as being the inspiration behind the new Canterbury Missionary College. This bouquet would later be voiced by Mr. Gilbert at the twenty-fifth anniversary of the college, heartily seconded by Mr. Coleridge,[113] and thereafter repeated in the chronicles of St. Augustine's.[114] In his 1843 private circular, Coleridge had diffused the inspiration somewhat, saying that 'such an institution will, I believe, meet with the general concurrence and approval of the Colonial Bishops;

especially when it is known that the project itself emanates in great measure from the suggestions of the Bishops of Australia, New Zealand, and Tasmania [...]'.[115] Whether or not Broughton had an English college in mind when he wrote the 'germinal letter' (16/6/1842), it was certainly one of the possibilities he mentioned in July 1842, and thereafter he swung his support behind it as the scheme emerged —although, as we have noted, he tended to credit the College to Coleridge.

Because of the connection with Broughton, St. Augustine's showed a particular interest in Australia at the beginning. At the opening of the college on St Peter's day 1848, twelve months after four new colonial bishops had been consecrated,[116] a donation of £1000 was announced for the establishment of the first of two Australian scholarships—the other would be established in memory of Broughton in 1854.[117] When the first outgoing student, Rev. Charles Joseph Gillett, was farewelled, 'the destination designed for him was Sydney, chiefly out of duty and obligation to the Bishop of Sydney'.[118] In the evening, 'an impressive address' was delivered 'by Rev. W.H. Walsh of Sydney, one of the Bishop's dearest friends'. On departure, however, Gillett's ship ran into a storm, forcing it to return. Gillett then fell seriously ill and, upon recovery, went to Barbados instead.[119] It would be up to a native Australian to be the first graduate to grace Sydney's shores.

In early 1846, Bishop Broughton had received a letter from Rev. John Jennings Smith, incumbent at Paterson, near Dungog, inquiring about the proposed college at Canterbury and, given his financially straitened circumstances, about potential assistance in sending his son to be trained there for colonial service.[120] Broughton immediately alerted Coleridge to this situation,[121] and, in due course Percy Jennings Smith joined the first intake of St. Augustine's in 1849, being the seventh to matriculate to the college.[122] His studies completed, he sailed for Sydney in 1853, but by the time Bailey wrote his open letter in 1873, Smith was no longer in Sydney, but was serving in another foreign diocese.[123]

James Carter, who had entered in 1851, also sailed for Sydney with Smith in 1853, where he became the minister at Picton.[124] While at college he was the Mission Essay Prizeman for 1852 and 1853, writing on 'Compare the difficulties which attended the propagation of the gospel in early ages, with those which exist at present', and 'A Refutation of Mahommedanism considered as a corruption of Christianity'.[125] In Bailey's day he was listed as the Rev., but by the time Boggis wrote, he was the Rev. Dr. Carter. In 1907 Boggis listed him under some of the college's worthy graduates, who:

> Sent out in the earliest hours to work in the vineyard, are still bearing the burden and heat of the day, still true to their matriculation promises, and likely so to continue till the Lord of the vineyard Himself orders them to knock off work. It is fifty-three years since Dr. James Carter set out for New South Wales, and he is ministering there yet.[126]

Carter's brother-in-law was also a graduate of St. Augustine's. The grandson of Australia's famous, long-serving chaplain, Samuel Marsden, Parramatta-born Charles Marsden Betts entered the college in 1853 as the 'Hutchesson exhibitor', eventually sailing for Sydney in July 1856.[127] After being ordained in January of the next year in St Andrew's, the 'temporary cathedral', and a brief two months locum at Campbelltown, he arrived in Goulburn to minister to the outlying areas. He soon endeared himself to his parishioners, but, in a matter of months, on 28th July 1857, he was drowned in the flooded Wollondilly river whilst returning from ministry in some outlying diggings.[128] News reached St Augustine's in the autumn, and a sermon was preached in the chapel on the event, which was later published with a collection of Betts' own sermons gathered in his memory by his parishioners at Goulburn, and with a memoir from James Carter.[129] He was remembered in St. Augustine's 'Kalender of Deceased Students':

> 28th July 1857, Charles Marsden Betts: Grandson of the Rev. Samuel Marsden: from Paramatta, Sydney: through Bishop Broughton, of Sydney: admitted March 26, 1853: Sydney: Drowned in the Wollondilly River.[130]

His brother, James Cloudesley Betts also attended St. Augustine's some time later, and was the Mission Prizeman for 1871 for an essay on 'The best methods for diffusing a rigorous Missionary spirit amongst all classes and all ages in a Parish'.[131] He sailed for Goulburn Diocese in 1871,[132] where he later served as Archdeacon.[133] In 1907, Boggis praised him, saying that 'Australia [has reason to thank God] for [the long and faithful service] of Canon J.C. Betts'.[134]

By 1873, St Augustine's had sent 24 of its graduates to Australia, four having sailed to Sydney.[135] By the end of the century, when Australian Dioceses had received a total of 70, only one more had gone to Sydney.[136] Despite Broughton's hopes, quite evidently, Sydney was not one of the main beneficiaries of St Augustine's College.

The earliest three Sydney men, Percy Jennings Smith, James Carter, and Charles Marsden Betts, were Australians who had gone to St. Augustine's to train for service in their homeland. Although presumably Broughton could have enrolled Percy Smith at the college he opened in 1845, Carter and Betts had no local college to go to, for by the time of their enrolment, St James' had already closed its doors, and Moore was yet to open.

Towards the Opening of Moore's College

When Broughton writes on 8th May 1850,[137] he sounds lonely and depressed. On his own confession, 1848 had 'occasioned [him] intense anxiety and suffering',[138] and this was followed by his great year of domestic sorrow, in which he himself fell desperately ill, and, while he was ill, his dear wife Sarah passed away. He then lost a grandchild. His own reserves were probably rather low when he was forced to respond to the news that Bishop Coleridge, after such a brief time as Warden of St. Augustine's, had suddenly died.

> In *his* case it is more than his own home which suffers. That noble institution, which opened with such a reasonable prospect of sending forth into the harvest many labourers

trained under his judicious guidance, is suddenly bereaved; and being desolate shall sit upon the ground. It is more to be desired than expected that his place should be satisfactorily supplied.

Although it is too late for him to fill the vacancy,[139] as usual, Broughton is personally involved in this need. A long tour of his diocese, from 12th November to 23rd March, had satisfied him that 'if the country be left in its present state, that is with an increasing population and hundreds of miles often intervening without a vestige of the means of Church communion, the results must be the growth of barbarism and infidelity'. This had brought back to him the old concerns.

> The difficulties under which I labour are want of means; want of men; want of money. As to the former of these, namely want of men, I am well nigh reduced to despair; for in the country itself I see none prepared, none promising well, for the work of the ministry. And from without, the only dependence which I can place for a supply is upon the arrival of such clergymen as the Society may be able to send in charge of Emigrant vessels. There must also be great risk of some at least of these proving not serviceable. I hope they will not be induced to accept too large a proportion of *Irish* graduates.

Fresh from the failure of Lyndhurst, there is no hint here of any hopes for a local training institution. As the plans for the University of Sydney were coming to fruition, Broughton's mind turned to having a college attached, but this was foiled by those who argued that the university ought to be a thoroughly secular institution. Although Allwood was more amenable to the new institution, later serving on the Senate and even as Vice-Chancellor in 1869–82, Broughton would have nothing to do with this 'godless' institution, 'a most frightful and formidable instrument of evil', and refused the invitation to join its Senate. Bewailing the composition of the Senate, he particularly singles out the fact that 'the *lowest* of churchmen: *Edward Hamilton*, I regret to say, has accepted the office of Provost'.[140]

In subsequent letters, Broughton occupied himself with various other diocesan concerns, but there is no further mention of a local college. Then in 1853, whilst in England to press the issue of the establishment of Diocesan Synods, he died from an illness contracted on the voyage home. Although St. Augustine's College wished to have the privilege of interring his body, he was buried instead in the nave of Canterbury Cathedral on the 26th February.[141]

It was not until 30th November 1854 that his successor, Frederick Barker, was consecrated at Lambeth. He sailed for Sydney on 22nd February 1855, to arrive on 25th May and be enthroned in St Andrews' on the 31st.[142] As a symbol, perhaps, of the importance of the project to the new Archbishop, less than two weeks later, on the 13th June, Barker sat with the other trustees of Thomas Moore's Will, to discuss the establishment of a college at Liverpool.[143] Sydney's clergy would be Sydney trained. For by 1st March of the following year, Moore's Will would finally become Moore's College.

Notes

1. A shorter version of this essay was published in *Southern Cross*, February 2006.
2. Memorandum presented to the Trustees, 12th June 1885. *Trustees Minute Book* No. 2, pp.192–195, now printed in Loane, *Centenary History*, 73. On 21st July, he repeated the same statement to Synod: 'The position at Liverpool has so far as I can see the advantage neither of town nor of country. Never would it have been chosen for a Theological College had it not chanced that Mr. Moore's own house and land were situated there'; *Proceedings* of Synod of Diocese of Sydney, 1885, reprinted in Loane, *Centenary History*, 76.
3. Cable, 'The Cowpers', 34.
4. See his request for permission to resign as superintendent of public works and Goulburn's reluctant acquiescence; T. Moore to Goulburn, [19th] May 1823, and Goulburn to T. Moore 18 Oct 1823 (SDA 0853CH, Item 9, doc. 1 and 2).
5. *Trustees Record Book*, pp.3–4. See Loane, *Centenary History*, 8–9.
6. Including the fact that Moore Bank was under lease for 21 years, at a pittance, and the buildings in town required development to be suitable for a college.
7. Dickey, 'Secular Advance', 59.
8. Dickey, 'Secular Advance', 59. These three options continued into the twentieth century. It was only just before World War I that Moore College trained men predominated in Sydney.
9. The Diocese of New Zealand and Tasmania had come into existence in 1841 and 1842 respectively. In 1847 the Diocese of Australia ceased to exist and the Dioceses of Sydney (Broughton), Newcastle (Tyrrell), Melbourne (Perry), and Adelaide (Short)

were born. The Diocese of Brisbane was created in 1859, but North Queensland lay beyond its borders and was still under the jurisdiction of the Bishop of Sydney until the consecration of the first Bishop of North Queensland in December 1873. Loane, *Centenary History*, 14, 39.
10. Broughton to Coleridge, 19 Oct 1837. See also Boggis, *History*, 34.
11. Broughton to Coleridge, 19 Oct 1837, after discussing John Macarthur's attempts to secure a minister for Camden. See also Boggis, *History*, 35.
12. The letters of Broughton to Coleridge are held in the Moore College and Mitchell Libraries. Letters to and from other people are also amongst this collection. I have been greatly assisted in the preparation of this article by having a draft transcription kindly made available to me by Dr Bruce Kaye.
13. Broughton to Watson, 29 Nov 1838. For a profile of Watson, see Overton, 'Watson, Joshua'.
14. Thomas Moore, *Account Book 1828–1840* (SDA: 0885 CH, Item 6), entry for November 28th, 1838: 'Went to Sydney to alter my Will', and then 'Deeds to Sydney to be made out to the Deed of Gift to the Church'.
15. See Courtney, 'Warneford, Samuel Wilson'.
16. The Bishop no doubt meant that a direct challenge had not been tested. As we shall see below, the New South Wales courts had, in fact, already expressed their own opinion of the purview of these Statutes in the colony.
17. These Statutes were of concern when he turned his mind to acquiring land for the future endowment of the Church, Broughton to Coleridge 8 Sept 1837: 'It is proposed, you will remember, that the fee simple of all the property should be vested in the Bishop and his successors, who by their Letters Patent are appointed to be a perpetual corporation with power to hold lands to any extent. Of course this could not enable us (at least I presume so) to hold any such lands except in conformity with the law; and if the Statutes of Mortmain are in force here they must cut us off from any such power. My opinion upon such a subject is worth little or nothing; but I have taken pains to examine the matter as well as I could, and see reasons for thinking that the Statute of Charitable Uses does *not* prevail here; and that if others do prevail yet that the operation may be got over. At least I hope so'. For the information that follows in this paragraph, see Sloane, 'Mortmain'.
18. See Lewis, 'Practical Treatise'; cited in Sloane, 'Mortmain', 5. Pennsylvania alone of the states of the USA re-enacted the Statutes of Mortmain, in 1832, although only to prohibit superstitious use and grants to corporations without licence. England's *Mortmain and Charitable Uses Act 1888* would repeal the *Charitable Uses Act 1601*, although this still allowed for charities to be defined within the spirit of the preamble to Elizabeth's act; see Commonwealth of Australia, 'Charities Definition Inquiry', http://www.cdi.gov.au/report/cdi_chap2.htm, Ch. 2 (25/11/2005).
19. R. v Wentworth, Campbell and Dunn [1825] NSWSupC 26 (17 June 1825); see http://www.austlii.edu.au/au/other/NSWSupC/1825/26.htm (25/11/2005).
20. Walker v Scott (No. 1) [1825] NSWSupC 60 (21 December 1825); see http://www.austlii.edu.au/au/other/NSWSupC/1825/60.htm (25/11/2005).
21. John Kinchela, L.L.D. (Judge), like Moore, was linked with Liverpool. He died on 21/7/1845 and was buried in St Luke's cemetery, Liverpool. See Freame, *St. Luke's*, 17.
22. Broughton to Coleridge, 15 Feb 1841 no. 1. In a letter of 4 Dec 1841, he says it was the 9th, but there are two extant letters written on 15th.
23. Broughton to Coleridge, 15 Feb 1841 no. 2.

24. Broughton to Coleridge, 15 Feb 1841 no. 1.
25. Broughton to Coleridge, 4 Dec 1841.
26. Moore's sister Elizabeth was elderly and blind, cared for by her son Joseph Scott (Thomas's nephew); see William Moor to Thomas Moore, 24 Dec 1839 (SDA: 0851 CH, Item 6, doc. 35; and 0853 CH, Item 8, doc. 10).
27. Surviving letters from Thomas's brother William show that he had indeed made provision for his relatives during the last years of his life, to the tune of £100 p.a.; See Thomas Moore to William Moor, Address label, 31 May 1839 (SDA 0853 CH: Item 8, doc. 11); William Moor to Thomas Moore, 2 July 1839 and 24 Dec 1839 (SDA: 0853 CH, Item 8, docs. 9 and 10; 0851 CH, Item 6, doc. 35); William Moor to W.G. Broughton, 5 Nov 1842; and 7 July 1842 (SDA: 0851 CH, Item 7, docs. 28 and 65). After Moore died, the Trustees continued to provide money to his relatives; see Rev. G. Fielding to Trustees of Moore's Estate, 12 July 1847 (SDA: 0851, Item 10, doc. 45).
28. Broughton to Coleridge, 27 Dec 1841.
29. Broughton to Coleridge, 14 Feb 1842.
30. Broughton to Coleridge, 14 April 1842. Although this copy of the opinion came by way of E. Coleridge, the actual opinion was apparently received from the lawyers a little later, on 1 June 1842; see W.W. Follet and H.N. Coleridge to Trustees, Opinion of counsel on Will & Codicil received 1 June 1842 (SDA: 0851 CH, Item 7, doc. 3).
31. The Trustees continued to provide money to them; see William Moor to W.G. Broughton, 7 July 1842 and 5 Nov 1842 (SDA: 0851 CH, Item 7, docs. 28 and 65); Rev. George Fielding to Trustees of Moore's Estate, 12 July 1847 (SDA: 0851, Item 10, doc. 45).
32. Broughton to Coleridge, 16 June 1842. See also Bailey, *Twenty Five Years*, 14–17.
33. Broughton to Coleridge, 11 July 1842.
34. Benjamin Lucas Watson, priested 22/5/1842; Loane, *Centenary History*, 174.
35. See Bailey, *Twenty Five Years*, 65; Boggis, *History*, 168–170.
36. This statement is strangely prophetic of the later attempt, in 1952, to make St Augustine's 'the Central College of the Anglican Communion'; see Neill, *Anglicanism*, 412.
37. Broughton to Watson, 11 July 1842.
38. Broughton to Coleridge, 14 Jan 1843. The proposal to establish two King's schools feeding a college was floated in 1830 by a committee of the Church Corporation, which included all three of the men who would become the original Trustees of Moore's Estate. See [Broughton], *Plan for the Formation and Regulating of the King's Schools*. They were both established, but the Grammar School in the city did not survive.
39. Broughton to Coleridge, 1 April 1845.
40. Broughton to Coleridge, 9 April 1845.
41. Despite Bailey, the letter of the 11 July 1842 seems to be a better candidate for being so labelled.
42. Cable, 'The Cowpers', 32.
43. Cable, 'The Cowpers', 32. W.M. Cowper was the first Australian born admitted to Holy Orders, see Broughton to Coleridge, 14 Feb 1842.
44. See Cowper, *Autobiography and Reminiscences*.
45. Boggis, *History*, 31.
46. Boggis, *History*, 30–31.
47. Broughton to Coleridge 19 Oct 1837. See also Bailey, *Twenty-Five Years*, 12; Boggis, *History*, 30–31.
48. Broughton to Coleridge, 14 Jan 1843.
49. Broughton to Coleridge, 3 Feb 1843.

50. Broughton to Coleridge, 16 Feb 1843. See also Boggis, *History*, 36.
51. Bailey, *Twenty-Five Years*, 14, 17, calls it 'germinal', largely because it provoked the enthusiastic support of Edward Coleridge, and things simply snowballed from there.
52. Bailey, *Twenty-Five Years*, 20–21.
53. The Archbishop wrote on 5th March. Bailey, *Twenty-Five Years*, 20; Boggis, *History*, 40.
54. Bailey, *Twenty-Five Years*, 21.
55. He wrote on August 9th 1843; see Boggis, *History*, 43.
56. Broughton to Watson, 22 Dec 1843.
57. Broughton to Coleridge, 3 Jan 1844. See also Boggis, *History*, 37.
58. Broughton to Coleridge, 4 May 1844. See also Bailey, *Twenty-Five Years*, 30.
59. Broughton to Cowper and Allwood, 6th May 1844.
60. Broughton to Coleridge, 28 Dec 1844, following it up further on 4 Jan 1845. See also Bailey, *Twenty Five Years*, 33–36. For Broughton and Selwyn's delight at the news of Hope's purchase of the site, see Boggis, *History*, 61–63.
61. Broughton to Coleridge, 30 Jan 1846.
62. Bailey, *Twenty-Five Years*, 45.
63. Boggis, *History*, 56–57.
64. Boggis, *History*, 54. Beresford Hope's motives were 'the retrieving for the English Church of her ancient possessions' (i.e. St Augustine's monastery). His sympathies were definitely towards asserting the 'Catholic' character of Anglicanism, as became clear when he later published *Worship in the Church of England*.
65. For this paragraph, Boggis, *History*, 55–56.
66. Boggis, *History*, 56.
67. Boggis, *History*, 42–43.
68. Broughton to Coleridge, 7 Sept 1845.
69. Despite his own need for clergy, Broughton had been extremely reluctant to receive the Evangelical missionaries from the Colonial Church Society being urged upon him by the Bishop of London, due to the fact that the Society's missionaries were required to pledge that their own doctrine was not that of the Tractarians. See Broughton to Watson, Nov 1844 (letter only partially preserved), and Broughton to Coleridge, 5 Nov 1844.
70. Broughton to Coleridge, 14 Jan 1846.
71. Broughton to Coleridge, 30 Jan 1846. See also Bailey, *Twenty Five Years*, 44.
72. Broughton names Allwood as principal in Broughton to Coleridge, 3 Oct 1846, but in his letter of 8 May 1847, he himself takes that title and calls Allwood his tutor.
73. Cable & Annable, *St James' Church, Sydney. An Illustrated History*, 23. Cf. Cable & Annable, *St James' Church 1824–1999*, 7; Cable, 'Allwood, Robert', 11.
74. Broughton to Coleridge, 28 Dec 1844; Bailey, *Twenty Five Years*, 35.
75. This would be Frederick William Addams, see Loane, *Centenary History*, 174.
76. Broughton to Coleridge, 4 Jan 1845; Cf. Bailey, *Twenty Five Years*, 35–36.
77. Broughton to Coleridge, 1 July 1845.
78. Broughton to Coleridge, 30 Jan 1846.
79. The earliest students were Philip Agnew (ordained 24/6/1846) and Cheyne Macartney, ordained in Melbourne; Robert Chapman and Thomas Wilkinson (ordained 20/9/1846); George Fairfowl Macarthur, Charles Priddle, James Hassall and George Gregory (ordained 19/3/1848). See Loane, *Centenary History*, 12–13, 175.
80. Cf. Bailey, *Twenty Five Years*, 44.
81. Broughton to Watson 30 Jan 1846. See also *Memoir of Joshua Watson*, II, 133, as

CHAPTER 10 ~ *Training Colonial Clergy* [291]

recorded in Boggis, *History*, 81.
82. Newman was received on 9th October 1845, and in October 1846 he was ordained a priest and given a D.D. in Rome. He returned to England at Christmas, 1847. See Lilly, 'Newman, John Henry'.
83. Broughton to Coleridge, 12 June 1846. He mentions Agnew by name.
84. Broughton to Coleridge, 3 July 1846.
85. Broughton to Coleridge, 18 Aug 1846.
86. He also tells of his daughters writing a hymn for use in St Augustine's.
87. Broughton to Coleridge, 3 Oct 1846.
88. Broughton to Coleridge, 12 Oct 1846.
89. He mentions the £1000 already placed in trust by Dr Warneford (in 1838). This gift is also mentioned in his letter of 15 Oct 1846. It was eventually applied to Moore College, see Loane, *Centenary History*, 10–11, 21–22, 24–25, 201.
90. Broughton to Watson, 8 May 1844.
91. Broughton to Coleridge, 15 Oct 1846.
92. Loane, *Centenary History*, 200.
93. Broughton to Coleridge, 3 Oct 1846.
94. Loane, *Centenary History*, 176. Cable & Annable, *St James' Church, Sydney*, 23. Cable, 'Allwood', 11.
95. Loane, *Centenary History*, 201, has five, quoting the Sydney *Guardian* Vol. 1, No. 11, 2 April 1849, whereas Broughton to Coleridge, 6 Mar 1847 has four.
96. Broughton to Coleridge, 6 Mar 1847.
97. Broughton to Coleridge, 8 May 1847.
98. Broughton to Coleridge, 26 Oct 1847. Cable & Annable, *St James' Church, Sydney*, 23, informs us that Allwood missed out on being Bishop of Newcastle, but 'Broughton bungled the arrangements'. Perhaps this is hinted at when Broughton commented: 'the awkward part of the affair was as he very justly says, that in fact the offer was *never made* to him: the utmost that I could say to him being that I had reason that he *would* be fixed upon, and the newspapers shortly afterwards bringing word that he *had* been'.
99. Broughton to Coleridge, 15 Nov 1847. Broughton is also hopeful of more support from Dr Warneford and from an unnamed lady. On 5 Jan 1848 he reveals that the funds coming from Warneford are the accumulated interest upon his previous donation.
100. Broughton to Coleridge, 5 Jan 1848. The ordinands would be George Fairfowl Macarthur, Charles Frederick Durham Priddle, and James Samuel Hassall, who were deaconed in St Andrews' on 19 Mar 1848; see Loane, *Centenary History*, 175.
101. Broughton to Coleridge, 5 Jan 1848.
102. Loane, *Centenary History*, 176, gives its closing day as 1848, and Cable, 'Allwood', 11, gives the year 1849. See below for the evidence from his own letters that the college, at least in his own mind, was still in existence through to April 1849.
103. The Sydney *Guardian* Vol. 1, No. 11, 2nd April, 1849; Quoted in Loane, *Centenary History*, 201.
104. Cable & Annable, *St James' Church, Sydney*, 23.
105. '[Allwood] was an able and devoted principal, but charges of Tractarian influence made the college unpopular with some of the clergy and laity', Cable, 'Allwood', 11.
106. For the biographical details which follow, see Daly, 'Sconce, Robert Knox'.
107. Broughton disputed some of Sconce's claims in regard to himself; see Broughton to Cowper, 27 April 1848, printed in Cowper, *Autobiography and Reminiscences*, 51–52.

108. Broughton to Coleridge, 21 May 1849. This would be George Edward Gregory, see Loane, *Centenary History*, 175.
109. T.F. Cusack Russell, who was deaconed 19 Sept 1847 with Robert Lethbridge King, future principal of Moore College. After his allegations were dismissed by the Bishop's Consistorial Court, he was priested by Perry in Melbourne; for details, see Loane, *Centenary History*, 175, 201–202.
110. Broughton to Coleridge, 4 July 1848. The Royal Charter of the college was issued on 28 June 1848, the same day the deed of the site was conveyed. See Bailey, *Twenty Five Years*, 46–47.
111. Bailey, *Twenty Five Years*, Ch. 3; Broughton to Coleridge, 15 Jan 1849.
112. Broughton to Coleridge, 15 July 1848 mentions £140, which has not arrived. They are desperate for the money, but Broughton can't advance it himself, so is planning to ask the Bank to do so. He is not confident they will, however, because the College's funds need replenishing. On 15th January 1849, Broughton refers to this gift again, saying that he has now advanced the money to the College (and £10 to Mrs Jennings Smith, as requested), so presumably it is somehow still in existence at this stage. Since there were plans for the Bank to sue him later that year, in March (26/3/1849) and April (2/4/1849) he instructs Coleridge to send any moneys for the College by way of the Bishop of Newcastle. Again, this sounds like the College still exists in his mind, in some capacity. In May, however, his requests for funding deal with general diocesan needs, making no mention of the College. The mention of a College in 1851 (1st February and 9th May) would most likely refer to his plans to have a college attached to the future Sydney University.
113. Bailey, *Twenty-Five Years*, 197. Boggis. *A History*, 131, later informs us that Canon Gilbert, 'was a Canterbury boy, who was educated at the King's School with the future Bishop Broughton, and as the Vicar of Syston near Grantham was an ardent supporter for the missionary cause, and bequeathed the greater part of his possessions to St. Augustine's'.
114. Bailey, *Twenty-Five Years*, 7, where he adds the rider 'however this may have been', perhaps indicating that this had *not* been the prevailing view previously, although he does concede that Coleridge received his impulse from his correspondence with Broughton. He later seeks to prove, however, that 'Bishop Broughton is the real, prime, conscious founder of a Missionary College for the Church of England', by reference to this correspondence; p.10. See also Boggis, *History*, 80–81.
115. For Coleridge's circular, see Boggis, *History*, 43–50.
116. Perry (Melbourne), Tyrell (Newcastle), Short (Adelaide), and Grey (Capetown).
117. Bailey, *Twenty-Five Years*, 57. The first came from Rev. H.J. Hutchesson in honour of Bishop Broughton, his friend and former pupil. For the Broughton scholarship, see p.70.
118. Bailey, *Twenty-Five Years*, 67.
119. Bailey, *Twenty-Five Years*, 68.
120. Smith to Broughton, 29 Jan 1846.
121. Broughton to Coleridge, 31 Jan 1846. He followed this letter up with another on 3 Oct 1846, after Percy's father had had an accident leaving him in a stupor.
122. Boggis, *History*, 312.
123. Bailey, *Twenty-Five Years*, 233.
124. Boggis, *History*, 313; Bailey, *Twenty-Five Years*, 29.
125. Bailey, *Twenty-Five Years*, 78.
126. Boggis, *History*, 226.

127. Boggis, *History*, 313; Bailey, *Twenty-Five Years*, 234. Carter, 'Memorial'. For the family tree, see Yarwood, *Marsden-Survivor,* 292–3.
128. Carter, 'Memorial'.
129. Bailey, *Twenty-Five Years*, 72–73. Betts, *Eight Sermons*.
130. Bailey, *Twenty-Five Years*, 183. The Kalendar refers to *Occasional Paper* 25.
131. Bailey, *Twenty-Five Years*, 79.
132. Bailey, *Twenty-Five Years*, 237.
133. I suspect that J.C. Betts may be the anonymous writer cited by Bailey, *Twenty-Five Years*, 125, numbered (13), who tells that his mother 'often travelled with my grandfather amongst the heathen he visited; she often told me when I was a boy at school that her highest ambition was that I should follow the examples of my grandfather, and of my eldest brother who you know was sent to St. Augustine's'. The allusion certainly fits the details of the Marsden family see Yarwood, *Marsden-Survivor,* 258, but there are several other potential 'brothers' on Bailey's list that ought to be excluded before identification can be absolutely certain.
134. Boggis, *History*, 227.
135. William Kildahl entered in 1866, and sailed in 1869; Boggis, *History*, 316; Bailey, *Twenty-Five Years*, 233–238.
136. Boggis, *History*, 311–327. Herbert Francis Alexander Champion, who entered 1899, sailed for Sydney. His brother (see p.230) Stanley Adolphus Thomas Champion, who had entered in 1898, went to Bathurst; Boggis, *History*, 325.
137. Broughton to Coleridge 8 May 1850.
138. Broughton to Coleridge, 15 Jan 1849.
139. He later asks Coleridge to thank Mrs Keate for thinking of him for this vacancy, 'and you too for your expression of good will. But if I were *ever* equal to it, it would not do now. Canterbury would be to me a place of ghosts'; Broughton to Coleridge, 1 Feb 1851.
140. Broughton to Coleridge, 1 Feb 1851; and 9 May 1851.
141. Bailey, *Twenty Five Years*, 84.
142. Loane, *Centenary History*, 16.
143. Loane, *Centenary History*, 17.

[294] *Thomas Moore of Liverpool: One of our Oldest Colonists*

ABBREVIATIONS

ADEB	*The Australian Dictionary of Evangelical Biography* (B. Dickey, ed.; Sydney: Evangelical History Association, 1994).
ADB	*Australian Dictionary of Biography*
AIGS	Australian Institute of Genealogical Studies, Blackburn, Victoria.
CMS	Church Missionary Society
Col.Sec.	Colonial Secretary's papers.
DEB	*The Blackwell Dictionary of Evangelical Biography* (D.M. Lewis, ed.; Oxford: Blackwell, 1995).
DNB	*Dictionary of National Biography* (Oxford: Oxford University Press, 1949–1950 [1917]).
HRA	*Historical Records of Australia*
HRNSW	*Historical Records of New South Wales*
IJMH	*International Journal of Maritime History*
JRAHS	*Journal of the Royal Australian Historical Society*
MC	Moore College, 1 King St, Newtown.
OCD	*The Oxford Classical Dictionary* (S. Hornblower & A. Spawforth, eds.; Oxford, Oxford University Press, 2003).
ML	Mitchell Library, Macquarie St, Sydney
PRO	Public Records Office
RTS	Religious Tract Society
SDA	Sydney Diocesan Archives
SLNSW	State Library of New South Wales, Macquarie St, Sydney.
SPCK	Society for the Promotion of Christian Knowledge
SPG	Society for the Propagation of the Gospel
SRO	State Records Office
WAMS	Wesleyan Auxiliary Missionary Society

Thomas Moore of Liverpool: One of our Oldest Colonists

BIBLIOGRAPHY

1. Primary Sources

Books & Registers

Ashe, Thomas ~ *The Liberal Critic, or Memoirs of Henry Percy. Conveying a Correct Estimate of the Manners and Principles of the Present Times* (1812), 3 Vols.

[Broughton] ~ *Plan for the Formation and Regulating of the King's Schools Preparatory to the Institution of a College* (Sydney: R. Mansfield, January 1830).

Carter, J. 'Memorial', in C.M. Betts, *Eight Sermons by the Rev. Charles Marsden Betts, SAC, Curate of Goulburn NSW* (Canterbury: St Augustine's Press, 1859).

Charterhouse Register 1769–1872 (R.L. Arrowsmith, ed.; Phillimore & Co, 1974)

Collins, D. ~ *An Account of the English Colony in New South Wales, from its first settlement in January 1788 to August 1801* (London, 1804), 2nd edition.

Cowper, W.M. ~ *The Autobiography & Reminiscences of William Macquarie Cowper, Dean of Sydney* (Sydney: Angus & Robertson, 1902).

Crockfords Clerical Directory (London: Church House Publishing)

Flinders, Matthew ~ *Narrative of his Voyage in the Schooner Francis, 1798, Preceeded and Followed by Notes on Flinders, Bass, the Wreck of the Sydney Cove &c by Geoffrey Rawson* (G. Rawson, ed; Golden Cockerel Press, 1946).

Foster, J. ~ *Alumni Oxoniensis*, 1500–1714 (4 vol. [in 2]; Repr. of the ed. of 1891, 92); – 1715–1886 (4 vol. [in 2]; Repr. of the ed. of 1887, 88); (Nendeln: Kraus Reprint, 1968).

Ryan, R.J. (ed.) ~ *Land Grants 1788–1809. A Record of Registered Grants and Leases in New South Wales, Van Dieman's Land, and Norfolk Island* (Sydney: Australian Documentary Library, 1974).

Venn, J. & Venn, J.A. ~ *Alumni Cantabrigienses*. Pt.1: to 1751 (4 vol.; Cambridge: Cambridge University Press, 1922–27); Pt.2: 1752–1900 (6 vol.; Cambridge: Cambridge University Press, 1940–54).

Historical Records of Australia (F. Watson, ed.; Sydney: Library Committee of the Commonwealth Parliament, 1914–1925).

Historical Records of New South Wales (F.M. Bladen,ed.; Sydney: 1892–1901; reprinted: Mona Vale, NSW: Lansdown Slattery, 1978–1979).

Hunter, John ~ *Remarks on the Causes of the Colonial Expense* (London, 1802).

Lloyds ~ *Lloyds Register of British and Foreign Vessels* 1790, 1791, 1792.

Proceedings of Synod of Diocese of Sydney, 1885.

Census Documents, Australia: Musters

Baxter, C.J. *Musters & Lists. 1801–1802* (Sydney: ABGR in association with the Society of Australian Genealogists, 1988).

Census Documents, Britain

Microfiche copies, Australian Institute of Genealogical Studies, Blackburn, Victoria.

Correspondence & Conversations

Moor, David, to Peter Bolt, 9 August 2006, per email.

Robinson, Donald, personal conversation with Peter Bolt, 1st March 2006.

Genealogical Records

International Genealogical Records, see www.family.org

NSW Registry of BDM: 380 Vol. 3A and 240 Vol. 4.

NSW Registry of BDM: V18256640 2C/1825 and V18251145 8/1825.

Government Reports & Court Records

Bigge Report ~ *Report of the Commissioner of Inquiry into the state of the colony of New South Wales* (3 vols.; Adelaide: Libraries Board of South Australia, 1966).

Bigge Report, Appendix, Mitchell Library.

Charitable Uses Act 1601

Commonwealth of Australia, 'Charities Definition Inquiry', http://www.cdi.gov.au/report/cdi_chap2.htm, Ch. 2 (25/11/2005).

Mortmain and Charitable Uses Act 1888.

R. v Wentworth, Campbell and Dunn [1825] NSWSupC 26 (17 June 1825); see http://www.austlii.edu.au/au/other/NSWSupC/1825/26.htm (25/11/2005).

Walker v Scott (No. 1) [1825] NSWSupC 60 (21 December 1825); see http://www.austlii.edu.au/au/other/NSWSupC/1825/60.htm (25/11/2005).

Journals and Memoirs (published)

Matthew, Sarah Felton ~ O. Havard, 'Mrs Sarah Felton Mathew's Journal', *JRAHS* 29.2, 3, 4 (1943), 88–128, 162–195, 217–244.

Murry, Robert ~ Extract from Begg, *Dusky Bay*.

Paine, Daniel ~ *The Journal of Daniel Paine, 1794–1797: together with documents illustrating the beginning of government boat-building and timber-gathering in New South Wales, 1795–1805* (R.J.B. Knight & A. Frost, eds.; Sydney: Library of Australian History in association with the National Maritime Museum, Greenwich, England, 1983).

Watson, Joshua ~ *Memoir of Joshua Watson* (E. Churton, ed.; 2 vol.; Oxford & London: J.H. & J. Parker, 1861).

White, John ~ *Journal of a Voyage to New South Wales* (R. Rienits, ed.; Sydney: Angus & Robertson, 1962 [Original: 1790]).

Manuscripts, Catalogues & Archival Material

Arnett File: Portrait of Thomas Moore (Moore College)

Broughton Papers, Moore College and Mitchell Libraries

Catalogue for the Exhibition of Fine Arts, 1847, Mitchell Library.

Cathedral Church—Dean's Correspondence [Morton], Sydney Diocesan Archives.

Clark, Nathaniel, Journal, Trustees of the Estate of the Late Thomas Moore Esq., Sydney Diocesan Archives.

Colonial Secretaries Papers, Microfiche, Mitchell Library.

Hassall Correspondence, Mitchell Library.

King Papers, Mitchell Library.

Macarthur Papers, Mitchell Library.

Macquarie, Lachlan, Diary, Mitchell Library.

Macquarie, Lachlan, Memoranda, Mitchell Library.

Moore Papers, Moore College

Trustees of the Estate of the Late Thomas Moore Esq., Sydney Diocesan Archives.

Wardell Papers, Mitchell Library.

Waterhouse Papers, Moore and Mitchell Libraries.

Wentworth Papers, Mitchell Library.

Newspapers, Magazines, and Press Clippings

Bain, W.H. ~ 'St. Luke's, Liverpool. Our Oldest Existing Anglican Church', [Press Clipping with Freame, *St. Luke's* in Moore College library; probably from 1936]

Australian

Dalgety's Review

Guardian

Morning Herald [London]

Quarterly Review

Societas

Southern Cross

Sydney Gazette

Sydney (Morning) Herald

Truth

Yorkshire Daily Observer

Parish Registers

Lesbury (Nbl), St Mary's, Baptismal Register.

Lesbury (Nbl), St Mary's, Burial Register.

Liverpool (NSW), St Luke's, Burial Register.

York St [Sydney], St Philip's Register.

Portraiture

Cash, F. ~ 'Portrait of Thomas Moore', printed in Loane, *Centenary History*, facing p.16. Original originally at Moore College, since stolen.

Dayes, Edward, ~ 'View of Sydney Cove—1804', now printed on the covers of *Journal of Daniel Paine* and Russell, *Thomas Moore*.

Griffith(s), W. ~ 'Portrait of the Late Thomas Moore Esq.', now housed at Moore College, Sydney.

Realia

Commemorative plaque in the grounds of St Luke's, Liverpool.

Commemorative plaque of the opening of Moore College dining room by Archbishop Gough on the 13th May 1961.

Moore, Rachel, memorial, St Luke's, Liverpool, NSW.

Moore, Rachel, tombstone, Pioneer Park, Liverpool, NSW.

Moore, Thomas, tombstone, Pioneer Park, Liverpool, NSW.

White, Andrew, tombstone, Pioneer Park, Liverpool, NSW.

2. Secondary Sources

[ADB] ~ 'McLeay, Alexander (1767–1848)', *ADB* 2.177–180.

Albion, R.G. ~ *Forests and Sea Power: The Timber Problem of the Royal Navy 1652–1862* (Cambridge, Mass., 1926).

Atkinson, A. ~ *The Europeans in Australia. A History.* Vol. 1: *The Beginning* (3 vols.; Oxford: Oxford University Press, 1997).

[*Ausralian Encyclopedia*[2]], ~ 'Moore, Thomas (1762–1840)', *The Australian Encyclopedia* (Sydney: Angus and Robertson, [2]1958), VI.145.

[*Ausralian Encyclopedia*[2]], ~ 'Scott, Thomas Hobbes (1773–1860)', *Australian Encyclopedia* (Sydney: Angus & Robertson, [2]1958), VIII.41.

[*Ausralian Encyclopedia*[2]], ~ 'Waterhouse, Henry (– – 1812)', *Australian Encyclopaedia* (Sydney: Angus & Robertson, [2]1958), IX.213–214.

Backhouse, J. and C. Tylor, ~ *The Life and Labours of George Washington Walker of Hobart Town, Tasmania* (London: A.W. Bennett, 1862).

Bailey, H. ~ *Twenty Five Years at St Augustine's College. A Letter to Late Students* (Printed for the Warden of St Augustines, by S. Hyde; 1873).

Barrie, D.M. ~ *The Australian Bloodhorse* (Sydney: Angus & Robertson, 1956).

Begg, A.C. & N.C. ~ *Dusky Bay* (Christchurch: Whitcombe & Tombs, 1968 [1966]).

Bernard, J.R.L. (gen.ed.), ~ 'Moore, 12' and 'Moore Theological College', *The Penguin Macquarie Dictionary of People and Places. A Handy Guide to Who & Where* (Ringwood, Vic.; Penguin [Australia], 1987).

Betts, C.M. ~ *Eight Sermons by the Rev. Charles Marsden Betts, SAC, Curate of Goulburn NSW* (Canterbury: St Augustine's Press, 1859).

Blake, G. ~ *Lloyds Register of Shipping 1760–1960* (Crawley: Lloyds, 1960).

Boggis, R.J. ~ *A History of St. Augustine's College, Canterbury* (Canterbury: Cross & Jackman, 1907).

Bolt, P.G. ~ 'An Overdue Birth Announcement: In Quest of the Long-Lost Family of Thomas Moore', *Journal of the Anglican Historical Society, Sydney Diocese* 51.2 (December 2006), 35–45.

Border, R., ~ 'Scott, Thomas Hobbes (1773–1860)', *ADB* II.431–433.

Boyce, F.B. ~ *Thomas Moore. An Early Australian Worthy* (London: Rowell & Sons, 1914).

Boyce, F.B. ~ *Fourscore Years and Seven: the Memoirs of Archdeacon Boyce, for over Sixty Years a Clergyman of the Church of England in New South Wales* (Sydney: Angus & Robertson, 1934).

Bremer, F.J. & T. Webster (eds.), ~ *Puritans and Puritanism in Europe and America. A Comprehensive Encyclopedia* (Santa Barbara, Ca.: ABC-Clio, 2006).

Bremer, F.J. ~ 'Hooker, Richard (1554–1600)', in Bremer & Webster, *Puritans*, 1.130.

Brinton, C. ~ *English Political Thought in the Nineteenth Century* (London: Brenn, 1933, [2]1954).

Cunningham-Browne, J.V. ~ 'Scott, Thomas Hobbes (1773–1860)', *Australian Encyclopedia* (Sydney: Angus & Robertson, 1926), II. 430-31.

Cable, K.J. ~ 'Allwood, Robert (1803–1891)', *ADB* I.11.

Cable, K.J. ~ 'The Cowpers—Father and Son', in A.M. Blanch (ed.), *The*

Parish of St Philip Church Hill, Sydney. Three Bicentennial Lectures (Sydney: The Churchwardens of St Philip, 2002), 23–40.

Cable, K.J. & R. Annable, ~ *St James' Church 1824–1999* (Sydney: Churchwardens of St James' Church, 1999).

Cable, K.J. & R. Annable, ~ *St James' Church, Sydney. An Illustrated History* (Sydney: David Ell Press for Churchwardens of St James' Church, 2000).

Canby, C. ~ *The New Illustrated Library of Science and Invention. A History of Ships and Seafaring* (London: Leisure Arts Limited, n.d. [1963]).

Carter, J. ~ 'Memorial', in C.M. Betts, *Eight Sermons by the Rev. Charles Marsden Betts, SAC, Curate of Goulburn NSW* (Canterbury: St Augustine's Press, 1859).

Cash, F. ~ 'The John Francis Cash Memorial Chapel', in *A Centenary History of Moore Theological College* (Sydney: Angus & Robertson, 1955), 206–220.

Chisholm, A.H. ~ 'Editor's Introduction', to John White, *Journal of a Voyage to New South Wales* (Sydney: Angus & Robertson, 1962 [Original: 1790]), 9–16.

Claeys, G. (ed.), ~ *The Political Writings of the 1790s* (Pickering Masters, 8 vols; London: Pickering & Chatto, 1995). The list of pamphlets collected here can be examined at http://www.pickeringchatto.com/index.php/pc_site/major_works/the_political_writings_of_the_1790s. (17/4/07).

Clark, C.M.H. ~ *A History of Australia* I. *From the Earliest Days to the Age of Macquarie* (Melbourne: Melbourne University Press, 1962, repr. 1985).

Clarke, J. ~ 'Comments on Simon Ville, "Rise to Pre-Eminence: The Development and Growth of the Sunderland Shipbuilding Industry, 1800–1850"', *IJMH* 2.2 (1990), 183–194.

Courtney, W.P. ~ 'Warneford, Samuel Wilson (1763–1855)', *DNB* 20.848.

Craig, R. ~ 'A Note on Shipbuilding in the Port of Sunderland', *IJMH* 3.2 (1991), 109–119.

Crimmin, P.K. ~ '"A Great Object With Us to Procure This Timber ..." The Royal Navy's Search for Ship Timber in the Eastern Mediterranean and Southern Russia, 1803–1815', *IJMH* 4.2 (1992), 83–115.

Daly, R.A., ~ 'Sconce, Robert Knox (1818–1852)', *ADB* I.424–426.

Dickey, B. ~ 'Moore, Thomas', *ADEB*, 265–266.

Dickey, B., ~ 'Secular Advance and Diocesan Response 1861–1900', in B.N. Kaye (ed.), *Anglicanism in Australia: A History* (Melbourne: Melbourne University Press, 2002), 52–75.

Dykes, E.W. ~ 'Doddridge, Philip (1702–51)', in Vickers, *Dictionary*, 98.

Dyton, S. ~ 'Milton, John (1608–74)', in Bremer & Webster, *Puritans*, 1.174–176.

Ellis, M.H. ~ *Francis Greenway. His Life and Times* (Sydney: Angus & Robinson, 1949, rev. 1953).

Encyclopedia Britannica, ~ 'Pufendorf, Samuel, Freiherr von', *The New Encyclopedia Brittanica* (Chicago, ^{15}1994), 9.789.

Estensen, M. ~ *The Life of Matthew Flinders* (Sydney: Allen & Unwin, 2002).

Estensen, M. ~ *The Life of George Bass.*

Surgeon and Sailor of the Enlightenment (Sydney: Allen & Unwin, 2005).

Flagg, A.C. ~ *Notes on the History of Shipbuilding in South Shields 1746–1946* (South Shields: South Tyneside Borough Council Library Service, 1979).

Fletcher, B.H. ~ 'Christianity and Free Society in New South Wales 1788–1840', *JRAHS* 86.2 (2000), 93–113.

Fletcher, B.H. ~ 'Sydney Town: The First Twenty Years', in A.M. Blanch (ed.), *The Parish of St Philip Church Hill, Sydney. Three Bicentennial Lectures* (Sydney: Churchwardens of St Philip's, 2002), 7–22.

Forsaith, P.W. ~ 'Fletcher, Rev. John William (1729–85)', in Vickers, *Dictionary*, 124.

Freame, W. ~ *The Early Days of Liverpool* (Liverpool: Liverpool News, 1916).

Freame, W. ~ *St. Luke's Church of England, Liverpool* (Parramatta: Federal Press, 1930).

Frost, A. ~ *Convicts and Empire: A Naval Question* (Melbourne: Oxford University Press, 1980).

Green, I. ~ 'Appendix 1: Sample of Best-Sellers and Steady Sellers First Published in England c.1530–1729', *Print & Protestantism in Early Modern England* (Oxford: Oxford University Press, 2000), 591–672.

Gribben, A. ~ 'Introduction', in *Reading for Moral Progress: Nineteenth Century Institutions Promoting Social Change. Papers from the Conference on Faith and History, Messiah College, Grantham, Pennsylvania, October 7–8, 1994* (Occasional Papers, Graduate School of Library and Information Services, University of Illinois at Urbana-Champaign; 1997), 1–4.

Grocott, A.M. ~ *Convicts, Clergymen and Convicts* (Sydney: University of Sydney Press, 1980).

Grundy, D.M. ~ 'Whitefield, George (1714–1770)', in Vickers, *Dictionary*, 392.

Hamst, O. ~ " Notes and Queries," fourth series, vol. ii. p. 340, 1868, cited from http://www.isle-of-man.com/manxnotebook/manxsoc/ms vol24/p122.htm (16/4/07).

Hassall, J.S. ~ *In Old Australia, Records and Reminiscences from 1794* (North Sydney, N.S.W.: Library of Australian History, 1981 [1902]).

Havard, W.L. ~ 'Note on the Naming of Liverpool, N.S.W.', *JRAHS* 22.5 (1936), 370. See also notice of typographical error in 22.6, p.452.

Hope, A.J.B. ~ *Worship in the Church of England* (London: John Murray, 1874).

Horde, D.M. ~ 'The Library is a Valuable Hygenic Appliance', in *Reading for Moral Progress: Nineteenth Century Institutions Promoting Social Change. Papers from the Conference on Faith and History, Messiah College, Grantham, Pennsylvania, October 7–8, 1994* (Occasional Papers, Graduate School of Library and Information Services, University of Illinois at Urbana-Champaign; 1997), 19–42.

Hughes, R. ~ *The Fatal Shore. A History of the Transportation of Convicts to Australia, 1787–1868* (London: Collins Harvill, 1987).

Hunter, M., G. Mandelbrote, R. Ovenden, & N. Smith (eds.), ~ *A Radical's Books. The Library Catalogue of Samuel Jeake of Rye, 162390* (Cambridge: D.S. Brewer, 1999).

Ingleton, G.C. (comp.) ~ *True Patriots All, Or, News From Early Australia As*

Told In A Collection Of Broadsides (Sydney: Angus & Robertson, 1952).

Johnstone, S.M. ~ *The Book of St. Andrew's Cathedral Sydney* (Sydney: Edgar Bragg & Sons, 1937).

Kemp, P. ~ *The Oxford Companion to Ships and the Sea* (Oxford: Oxford University Press, 1988).

Ker, J. ~ 'The Wool Industry in New South Wales 1803–1830', Parts 1 & 2: *Bull. Of Business Archives Council* 1.8 (1961), 28–49, and *Business Archives & History* 2.1 (1962), 18–54.

Knight, R.J.B.& A. Frost, ~ 'Introduction', *The Journal of Daniel Paine, 1794–1797: together with documents illustrating the beginning of government boat-building and timber-gathering in New South Wales, 1795–1805* (Sydney: Library of Australian History in association with the National Maritime Museum, Greenwich, England, 1983), i–xxix.

Lewis, W.D. ~ *A Practical Treatise on the Law of Perpetuity, or, Remoteness in Limitations of Estates: As Applicable to the Various Modes of Settlement of Property, Real and Personal, and in Its Bearing on the Different Modifications of Ownership in Such Property* (Philadelphia, 1846).

Lilly, W.S. ~ 'Newman, John Henry (1801–1890)', *DNB* 14.340–351.

Loane, M. ~ *A Centenary History of Moore Theological College* (Sydney: Angus & Robertson, 1955).

Loane, M. ~ 'Moore, Thomas (1762–1840)', *ADB* (Melbourne: Melbourne University Press, 1967), II.254.

Loane, M.L. ~ *Hewn From the Rock. Origins & Traditions of the Church in Sydney* (The Moorhouse Lectures 1976; Sydney: AIO, 1976).

Lyons, M. ~ 'New Readers in the Nineteenth Century: Women, Children, Workers', in G. Cavallo & R. Chartier, *A History of Reading in the West* (L.G. Cochrane, transl.; Amherst: University of Massachusetts Press, ET 1999 [French: 1995, 1997]), 313–344.

Macarthur Onslow, S. (ed) ~ *Some Early Records of the Macarthurs of Camden* (Adelaide: Rugby, 1973).

Macintosh, N.K. ~ *Richard Johnson. Chaplain to the Colony of New South Wales. His Life and Times 1755–1827* (Sydney: Library of Australian History, 1978).

Marsden, J.B. ~ *Memoirs of the Life and Labours of the Rev. Samuel Marsden* (London: Religious Tract Society, n.d. [1857]). Reprinted as *Life and Work of Samuel Marsden* (J. Drummond, ed.; Christchurch: Whitcombe and Tombs, 1913).

McGee, J. S. ~ 'Sanderson, Robert (1587–1663)', in Bremer & Webster, *Puritans*, 1.227.

McKay, R.J. ~ 'Moore, William Henry (1788?–1854)', *ADB* II.255–257.

McLachlan, N.D. ~ 'Macquarie, Lachlan (1762–1824)', *ADB* II.187–195.

McLaughlin, J.K. ~ 'The Magistracy and the Supreme Court of New South Wales, 1824–1850. A Sesqui-Centenary Study', *JRAHS* 62.2 (1976), 91–113.

Monk, R.C. ~ 'Puritanism and Methodism', in C. Yrigoyen, jr. & S.E. Warrick (eds.), *Historical Dictionary of Methodism* (Lanham, Md.: Scarecrow, 1996), 173.

Monthly Review, ~ 2nd ser. 72 (Nov 1813): 327. www.british-fiction.cf.ac.uk/reviews/libe12-19.html (17/4/07).

Moore College Student Body, ~ *Societas '06* (Newtown, NSW: Moore College, 2006).

Morrison, W.F. ~ *The Aldine Centennial History of New South Wales, Illustrated* (2 vols.; Sydney: Aldine, 1888).

Neal, D. ~ *The Rule of Law in a Penal Colony. Law and Power in Early New South Wales* (Cambridge: Cambridge University Press, 1991).

Neill, S. ~ *Anglicanism* (Harmondsworth: Penguin, 1958, repr. 1960).

Newton, J.A. ~ 'Puritanism', in Vickers, *Dictionary*, 285.

Nicholson, I.H. ~ *Log of Logs. A Catalogue of Logs, Journals, Shipboard Diaries, Letters, and all Forms of Voyage Narratives, 1788 to 1988, for Australia and New Zealand, and Surrounding Oceans* (Roebuck Society Publication 41; Nambour, Qld: Ian Nicholson, n.d.), Vol. 1.

Nockles, P.B. ~ *The Oxford Movement in Context. Anglican High Churchmanship 1760–1857* (Cambridge: Cambridge University Press, 1994).

Nord, D.P. ~ *Faith in Reading. Religious Publishing and the Birth of Mass Media in America* (Oxford: Oxford University Press, 2004).

Overton, J.H. ~ 'Watson, Joshua (1771–1855)', *DNB* 20.928–930.

Power Institute of Fine Art, ~ 'Griffith (Griffiths), William', *Dictionary of Australian Artists. Working Paper II. Painters, Photographers & Engravers 1770–1870 A–H* (University of Sydney: Power Institute of Fine Art, 1984), 313–315.

Railsback, R.D. ~ 'Bowdler, John', *DEB*, 1.126.

Rees, S. ~ *The Floating Brothel* (Sydney: Hatchette, 2001, reprint 2006).

Rienits, R. ~ 'Biographical Introduction', to John White, *Journal of a Voyage to New South Wales* (Sydney: Angus & Robertson, 1962 [Original: 1790]), 17–34.

Robinson, D. ~ 'Thomas Moore and the Early Life of Sydney', *JRAHS* 56.1 (1970), 165–192. [Round brackets are page numbers cited from offprint.] Soon to be reprinted in *Donald Robinson: Select Works. 2: Biblical and Historical Studies* (P.G. Bolt & M.D. Thompson, eds.; Camperdown: Australian Church Record & Moore College, 2007 [forthcoming]).

Robinson, D. ~ 'Postscript', to 'Thomas Moore and the Early Life of Sydney'. Moore College Library. Soon to be reprinted in *Donald Robinson: Select Works. 2: Biblical and Historical Studies* (P.G. Bolt & M.D. Thompson, eds.; Camperdown: Australian Church Record & Moore College, 2007 [forthcoming]).

Robinson, D. ~ 'Thomas Moore of Moore Bank 1762–1840: The Father of Liverpool, Benefactor of Mankind', Ward Havard lecture for City of Liverpool and District Historical Society, 2/8/1975. Soon to be published in *Donald Robinson: Select Works. 2: Biblical and Historical Studies* (P.G. Bolt & M.D. Thompson, eds.; Camperdown: Australian Church Record & Moore College, 2007 [forthcoming]).

Robinson, K. ~ 'Anglican Libraries in Australia: Moore Theological Library (1840)', in P. Harvey & L. Pryor (eds.), *"So Great a Cloud of Witnesses". Libraries & Theologies. Festschrift in Honour of Lawrence D. McIntosh* (Melbourne: United Church Theological Hall & ANZ Theological Library Association, 1995), 70–73.

Russell, E. ~ *Thomas Moore and the King's Dockyard 1796–1816* (Somersby, NSW: Old Sydney Town, 1975).

Scott, J. ~ 'The Scottish Martyrs' Farms', *JRAHS* 46.3 (1960), 161–168

Shaw, G.P. ~ 'Judeo-Christianity and the Mid-Nineteenth Century Colonial Civil Order', in M. Hutchinson and E. Campion (eds.), *Re-Visioning Australia, New Essays in the Australian Christian Experience 1788–1900* (Sydney: Centre for the Study of Australian Christianity, 1994), 29–39.

Sheehan, E.M. ~ 'The Identity of Richard Rice, "The Left Handed Flogger"', *JRAHS* 70.2 (1984), 124–132.

Sloane, C.W. ~ 'Mortmain', *Catholic Encyclopedia*, http://www.newadvent.org/cathen/10579a.htm (25/11/2005).

Smith, B.M. (ed.) ~ *Quench Not the Spirit. Merino Heritage* (Melbourne: Hawthorn Press, 1972).

Smith, J.W. & T.S. Holden, ~ *Where Ships are Born. Sunderland 1346–1946. A History of Shipbuilding on the River Wear* (Sunderland: Thomas Reed & Co, 1946).

Spurr, J. ~ 'Baxter, Richard (1615–1691)', in Bremer & Webster, *Puritans* 1.19–21.

Stancombe, G.H. ~ 'Youl, John (1773–1827)', *ADB* II.632–633.

Stephen, L. ~ *History of English Thought in the Eighteenth Century* (London: Smith, Elder & Co, 1881), Vol. 2. .

Swanzy, H.B. ~ *Succession Lists of the Diocese of Dromore* (Belfast: Carswell, 1933), now published in *Clergy of Down and Dromore* (Belfast: Ulster Historical Foundation, 1996).

Thompson, A.J. ~ *Australia and the Bible. A Brief Outline of the Work of the British and Foreign Biblie Society in Australia 1807–1934* (London: British & Foreign Bible Society, 1935).

Vickers, J. A. (ed.) ~ *A Dictionary of Methodism in Britain and Ireland* (Peterborough, UK: Epworth, 2000).

Vickers, J. A. ~ 'Edmondson, Jonathan (1766–1842)', Vickers, *Dictionary*, 107.

Vickers, J.A. ~ 'Hervey, Rev. James (1714–58)', in Vickers, *Dictionary*, 156.

Ville, S. ~ 'Rise to Pre-Eminence: The Development and Growth of the Sunderland Shipbuilding Industry, 1800–1850', *IJMH* 1.1 (1989), 65–86.

Ville, S. ~ 'Sunderland Shipbuilding: Pre-Eminence Restated', *IJMH* 2.2 (1990), 195–211;

Ville, S. ~ 'Craig on Sunderland Shipbuilding: A Comment', *IJMH* 4.1 (1992), 155–158.

Wadia, R.A. ~ *The Bombay Dockyard and the Wadia MasterBuilders* (Bombay: R.A. Wadia, 21957 [1955]).

Walker, F. ~ 'Some Early Churches of new South Wales', *JRAHS* 3.9 (1916), 436–454.

Wallace, jr., D.D. ~ 'Alleine, Joseph (1634–1668)', in Bremer & Webster, *Puritans*, 1.3.

Wallace, jr., D.D. ~ 'Flavel (Flavell), John (1627–1691)', in Bremer & Webster, *Puritans*, 1.98.

Webster, T. ~ 'Hall, Joseph (1574–1656)', in Bremer & Webster, *Puritans*, 1.117.

White, C.A. ~ *The Challenge of the Years: a History of the Presbyterian Church of Australia in the State of New South Wales* (Sydney: Angus and Robertson, 1951).

Wittmann, R. ~ 'Was there a Reading Revolution at the End of the Eighteenth Century?', in G. Cavallo & R. Chartier, *A History of Reading in the West* (L.G. Cochrane, transl.; Amherst: University of Massachusetts Press, ET 1999 [French: 1995, 1997]), 284–312.

Wood, A.S. ~ 'Burnett, George', *DEB*, 1.171.

Wyatt, R.T. ~ 'A Wine Merchant in Gaiters', *JRAHS* 35 (1949–1950), 145–199, 209–254, 257–286.

Yarwood, A. T. ~ *Samuel Marsden* (Melbourne, 1968).

Yarwood, A.T. ~ *Samuel Marsden. The Great Survivor* (Carlton, Vic.: Melbourne University Press, 1977, 1996).

3. Websites

Airgale, 'The Descendants of Thomas Duffus':
http://www.airgale.com.au/duffus/pafn02 [and 03].htm (18/1/06).

All Experts, 'Jean Baptiste Bourguignon d'Anville':
http://experts.about.com/e/j/je/jean_baptiste_bourguignon_d'anville.htm (26/12/2006).

Amazon.com, 'Ship Builders Repository': http://www.amazon.com/Shipbuilders-Repository-1788-Limited-Facsmile/dp/B000KIVBOQ/sr=1-7/qid=1166857703/ref=sr_1_7/105-5427445-1759658?ie=UTF8&s=books.

Australian Commonwealth Government, Charities Definition Inquiry:
http://www.cdi.gov.au/report/cdi_chap2.htm, (25/11/2005).

Bowdoin College, Jesse Appleton Collection:
http://library.bowdoin.edu/arch/archives/jag.shtml (28/7/06).

British Fiction 1800-1829: http://www.british-fiction.cf.ac.uk (16/4/07).

Bruzelius, Lars, 'Transcription of Shipbuilders Repository':
http://www.bruzelius.info/nautica/Etymology/English/Repository(1788)_p443.html (23/12/06).

Catholic Encyclopedia, 'Mortmain':
http://www.newadvent.org/cathen/10579a.htm (25/11/2005).

CRC Studio, Revolution & Romanticism, 'Conrad the Corsair':
http://www.crcstudio.arts.ualberta.ca/streetprint/Pages/viewtext.php?s=browse&by=title&route=browseby.php&tid=210 (3/2/2007).

Eastern Woodland Indian, 'Voyages':
http://www.easternwoodlandindian.com/index_files/page0022.html (26/12/2006).

Fortuin, H.B., 'John Arden Radio Plays':
http://web.ukonline.co.uk/suttonelms/jarden.html (20/4/07).

June Dark, 'Nathaniel Lucas & Olivia Gascoigne',
http://www.jdark.linkt.com.au/childrenhtml.html (5/8/2005),

Longbottom, A., 'Prison Report 1839':
http://www.institutions.org.uk/prisons/info/prison_report_1839.htm (23/12/2006).

Longbottom, A., 'Prison Report 1842':
http://www.institutions.org.uk/prisons/info/prison_report_1842.htm (26/12/2006).

Maggs Rare Books: http://www.maggs.com//AU3800.asp (23/12/06).

Manx Society, http://www.isle-of-man.com/manxnotebook/manxsoc/msvol24/p122.htm (16/4/07).

Methodist Archives Biographical Index,
http://rylibweb.man.ac.uk/data1/dg/methodist/bio/biol.html (11/4/07);

Michigan State University, 'Marcet, Jane Haldimand. Conversations on Natural Philosophy': http://www.lib.msu.edu/digital/Exhibit1/Books/MARCET.htm (14/4/07),

Monthly Review, 2nd ser. 72 (Nov 1813): 327. www.british-fiction.cf.ac.uk/reviews/libe12-19.html (17/4/07).

Moore College Library Catalogue: http://www.library.moore.edu.au/

Old Bailey Online, 'Rachel Turner':
http://www.oldbaileyonline.org/html_units/1780s/t17871212-13.html.

Open Library, 'Marcet. Conversations on Natural Philosophy':
http://www.openlibrary.org/details/conversationsonn00marciala (14/4/07).

Pickering & Chatto Publishers, 'The Political Writings of the 1790s':
http://www.pickeringchatto.com/index.php/pc_site/major_works/the_political_writings_of_the_1790s (17/4/07).

Pickering & Chatto Publishers, 'William Cobbett: Selected Writings':
http://www.pickeringchatto.com/index.php/pc_site/major_works/william_cobbett_selected_writings

Project Canterbury, 'Izaak Walton': http://anglicanhistory.org/walton/index.html

Questia: http://www.questia.com.

Rumsy, David, Map Collection, 'Atlas Generale d'Anville':
http://www.davidrumsey.com/maps462.html (26/12/2006).

SLNSW, Papers of Sir Joseph Banks:
http://www.sl.nsw.gov.au/banks/series_23/23_43.htm.

Society for the Diffusion of Useful Knowledge, *The Penny Cyclopædia of the Society for the Diffusion of Useful Knowledge*
http://books.google.com/books?id=HGt_tlAq1R8C&pg=PA169&lpg=PA169&dq=%22christopher+sturm%22&source=web&ots=QyIcdQRlt9&sig=gOR0bIEvUN8tp_kiIjhBmw3JRNQ (12/4/07).

Superior Courts of New South Wales (pre 1900) Case Notes:
http://www.austlii.edu.au/au/other/NSWSupC/1825/26.htm (25/11/2005).

This is the Northeast:
http://www.thisisthenortheast.co.uk/the_north_east/history/shipbuilding

University of Chicago Library, *Voltaire électronique*
http://efts.lib.uchicago.edu/efts/VOLTAIRE (28/12/06).

Vail, J.W., Illustrations of the Works Lord Byron:
http://people.bu.edu/jwvail/byron_illustrations.html (3/2/2007).

Thomas Moore of Liverpool: One of our Oldest Colonists

Index of Names

Abell, Robert	28, 59
Addams, Frederick William	290
Addison, Joseph	174
Agnew, Philip	290, 291
Airds, NSW	14
Alleine, Joseph	169–170, 197, 198, 199, 200, 203
Alleine, Richard	170
Allestree, Richard	148–149, 166, 197, 200
Allwood, Robert	268, 270, 273, 275, 276, 277, 279, 280, 286, 290, 291
American Tract Society	210
Amiens, France	63
Andrewes, Lancelot	125–126, 132, 153, 197, 198, 271
Andromache	256, 257
Anglican Church	See Church of England
Annesley, Samuel	170
Antigua	13, 42
Antill, Henry Colden	25, 246
Appleton, Jesse	144–145, 197, 198, 200
Argyle, NSW	20
Arndell, Thomas	58
Arnett, Elisabeth	236
Ashe, Thomas	158–159, 202, 208
Atkins, Judge-Adv. Richard	58, 228
Atlas	215
Aurora	169
Australian Immigration Association	22
Bagot, Richard	265, 266
Bailey, Henry	265, 284
Bampton, William	12
Banks, Sir Joseph	48, 49, 92
Banks Town, NSW	14, 15
Barker, Frederick	29, 249, 264, 287
Barker, Matthew	171
Barrington, George	58
Barry, Alfred	249
Barwell	55

Bass, George	45, 66, 68, 98, 192
Bass, Elizabeth (nee Waterhouse)	45, 98, 192
Bass(es) Straits	89
Baxter, Richard	146, 156, 170, 190, 197, 198, 199, 203
Bay of Islands, New Zealand	103
Bedell, Gregory	168–169, 199
Benelong	66
Benevolent Society	111, 220
Bent, Jeffrey Hart	57
Berens, Edward	128–129, 197, 198
Bethel Union	166, 203
Betts, Charles Marsden	284, 285
Betts, John Cloudesley	285, 293
Bevan, David	55
Bewson, George	242, 245, 247
Bible Society	18, 19, 111, 201, 202, 220
	See also British and Foreign Bible Society
Bigge, Comm. J.T.	9, 28, 39, 56, 93, 103, 218, 229
Bingley, William	132, 197
Bishop of London	264, 267
Bishop-Auckland	9, 10, 32, 33, 37, 41, 257
Bishop's College, Calcutta	265
Blackman, John	115, 116, 235
Blair, Hugh	122–123, 197, 198
Bligh, Gov. William	21, 109
Board of Admiralty	79
Bobart, Henry Hodgkinson	240
Botany Bay, NSW	94
Bourke, Gov. Richard	22, 218
Bousmard, H.J.B. de	182, 186
Bowdler, Thomas	147, 197, 198, 200, 201, 202
Bowen, John	80
Bowles, John	155–156, 197, 201, 210
Bowman, Dr James	279
Bowring, Bernard	168, 193, 202
Boyce, F.B.	1, 18, 235
Brampton	231
Brandes, M.E.	184
Braithwait, Lieut.	49
Bray, Thomas (& associates)	119, 164, 167, 202, 208
Brickmaker's Creek, NSW	27
Brisbane, Gov. Sir Thomas	213, 230
Britannia (Melville)	24
Britannia (Raven)	3, 6, 11, 13, 24, 25, 30, 38, 39, 45, 48, 56, 58, 72, 73, 74, 108, 179, 211, 233, 234
British and Foreign Bible Society	154, 157
Brocklehurst, John	216
Brooks, Richard	28

Broughton, Sarah ("Sally")	285
Broughton, William	28
Broughton, William Grant	3, 4, 8, 9, 10, 17, 19, 20, 22, 29, 30, 31, 32, 33, 36, 37, 106, 113, 115, 118, 196, 226, 227, 235, 237, 241, 242, 243, 246, 247, 250, 251, 252, 253, 254, 255, 256, 257, 260, 261, 264, 265, 269, 273, 276, 277, 279, 280, 281, 282, 284, 285, 287, 290, 291, 292
Brownrigg, Marcus Blake	1, 5
Broxbornebury	57
Bryan Boroo	28
Buchan, William	125, 194
Buffalo	101, 102
Bulanaming, NSW	14, 20, 21, 28, 40, 58, 59, 75, 99
Bull, George	164
Bunker, Ebor	75
Bunyan, John	157, 201
Burnet, Gilbert	129, 197
Burns	25
Burder, George	138, 157, 166, 168, 197, 198, 200
Burridge, James	230
Burton, George	165–166, 197, 200, 203
Burton, Judge William W.	31, 40, 223, 226, 239, 240, 252, 254, 256
Buturlin, Dmitry Petrovich	186
Byron, Lord George Gordon	236, 239
Cabramatta Creek, NSW	27
Calcutta, India	143
Calcutta	53, 59, 88, 89, 90, 91, 93, 102
Cambridge, England	5
Camden, NSW	288
Campbell, Robert snr.	28
Campbell, Robert (son of snr.)	115, 235
Campbelltown, NSW	16, 17
Canada	70, 93
Cape Horn	11
Cape of Good Hope	11, 48, 55, 59, 70, 73, 169, 246
Capetown	49
Carion-Nisas, Marie Henri Francois de	180
Carlyle, W.B.	231
Carter, James	283, 284, 285
Cartwright, Robert	16, 17, 18, 26, 27, 219, 231, 240, 246
Cash, Frank	242
Cash, John	242
Castlereigh, NSW	14
Cervantes Saavedra, Miguel de	139–140, 201
Champion, Herbert Francis Alexander	293

Champion, Stanley Adolphus Thomas	293
Chapman, Robert	290
Charles, Archduke of Austria	181
Charterhouse	31, 116, 121, 128, 142, 193, 196
China	90
Chipping Norton, NSW	25
Christ Church Newcastle	15
Church Corporation	289
Church Missionary Society	18, 27, 112, 150, 154, 221, 230, 246
Church of England	8, 29, 31, 32, 44, 111
Churchill, Awnsham & John	160
Churchill, John	183
Churchill, Sir Winston	183
Clarke, Joseph	42
Clarke, Nathaniel	35–37, 41–42
Clarke, Sarah, 'Sally' (nee Moor)	36, 38, 41
Clarke, William	41
Clementson, Isaac	55
Cobbett, William	135, 194, 195
Coldwell, Jonathan	101
Coleridge, Edward	9, 251, 255, 256, 257, 258, 262, 266, 267, 269, 271, 274, 275, 279, 281, 282, 283, 289, 290, 292
Coleridge, Samuel Taylor	163
Coleridge, William Hart	261, 266, 280, 285
Collins (Sunderland)	25
Collins, David	74, 89, 210, 229
Colnett, Capt. James	59, 83, 84, 85, 86, 88, 101, 102
Colonial Church Society	290
Colquhoun, Patrick	133–134, 194–195, 202
Cook, Capt. James	11, 72, 98, 161
Cook's River, NSW	14, 20
Cotton, Dr George E.L.	265
Cowley, Abraham	174
Cowper, William	114, 264
Cowper, William Macquarie	1, 5, 110, 249, 264, 268, 269, 289
Cromwell, Oliver	71, 146
Dampier, William	161
Darlinghurst, NSW	260
Davey, Col.	45
Davy, Charles	156, 197, 198
Davys, George	175
Dayes, Edward	97, 100
De Brosses, Charles	161
Deletanville, Thomas	187
Deptford Naval Yard	66, 68, 166
Derwent River, Tas.	80, 89

INDEX OF NAMES [313]

Dido	79
Dickson, L.W.	231
Divine, Nicholas	58, 67
Doddridge, Phillip	137, 164–165, 197, 198, 200, 203
Dorrington, Theophilus	162, 193, 197, 200
Douglass, Henry Gratton	228
D'Anville, Jean Baptiste Bourguignon	190
D'Oyly, George	120, 197, 199, 200
Dromedary	93, 94
Duaterra	55
Duffus, John	2, 5, 20, 240, 246–247, 255
Duffus, Mrs & children	246
Duffus, Elizabeth	See Taylor, Elizabeth
Duffus, Susan	240
Duguid, Leslie	231
Dundas, Henry	133
Durham, England	9, 32, 34, 37
Dusky Bay, New Zealand	11, 12, 39, 72, 73, 74, 234
Dutems, J.F.H.	183
East India Company	11, 24, 42, 62, 97
Eastern Farms, NSW	58
Ebenezer, NSW	25
Eden	246
Edmondson, Jonathan	137–138, 149, 197, 198, 200, 203
Elizabeth	215
Elizabeth Henrietta	77, 97, 100
Endeavour (Bampton)	12, 73
Enfield, William	157–158, 197, 203
Euler, Leonhard	127, 193
Evangelical Magazine	138, 157, 179, 198, 200, 222
Experiment	99
Falconer, William	169, 193
Falmouth, England	11
Featley, Daniel	190
Fenelon, Francois Salignac de la Mothe	187, 192
Fielding, Allen	10
Fielding, Charles	10
Fielding, Henry	10
Fielding, George	9, 10, 32, 33, 41, 257
Fitzgerald, Maurice	228
Fitzgerald, Richard	28, 58
Flavel, John	149, 197, 198
Fletcher, John	138–139, 157, 197, 198, 201
Flinders, Matthew	55, 66, 68
Forbes, Francis	254
Formby, Mr.	263, 264, 271, 272, 275, 277, 278
Fort William, Bengal	24

Foster, James	137, 178, 197, 198, 203, 208
Foxe, John	201
Francis, Mr	257
Francis	74
Frank, Elizabeth	127–128, 193
Gale, John	178
Galloway, J.J.	2, 5, 6
Galvin, Paddy	228
Gascoigne, Olivia	See Lucas, Olivia
George III	47
George's River	14, 20, 27, 28, 45, 54, 80, 109, 194, 212, 249
Gilbert, Mr.	282
Gillett, Charles Joseph	283
Gillot, C.-L.	181
Gipps, Gov. Sir George	268, 275, 276
Gerrald, Joseph	97
Glatton	59, 79, 80, 81, 82, 83, 84, 85, 86, 87, 88, 91, 93, 99, 100, 101, 102
Glenholme, Capt.	28
Good, John Mason	150. 194, 198, 200, 208
Goodchilds	25
Goodwin, John	190
Gordon, Col.	48
Gordon, Mrs	48, 49
Gorgon	72, 99
Goulburn, F.	25, 287
Goulburn, NSW	284, 285
Grammar School, Sydney	263, 289
Grant, Sir William	254
Gregory, George Edward	290, 291
Greenway, Francis	16, 26, 111, 238
Greenwich	101, 102
Grenville	151
Grenville College, Parramatta	242, 247
Grey, Robert	292
Griffiths, William	106, 110, 233–247
Grimes, Charles	57, 58
Grose, Maj. Francis	52, 58
Grylls, J.C.	246
Guildford	215
Hale, Matthew	146–147, 195, 197, 201
Hall, Joseph	131, 197, 198, 199, 200
Hall, Robert	171
Hamilton, Edward	286
Hammond, Henry	146–147, 197, 201
Harris, John	55
Hassall, Elizabeth	240
Hassall, James Samuel	18, 221, 290, 291

INDEX OF NAMES [315]

Hassall, Rowland	18, 55, 58, 221, 240
Hassall, Samuel	18, 221
Hammond, T.C.	5
Havelock, Thomas	25
Hawkesbury, Lord	70
Haydon Bridge, Nbl	9, 41, 257
Hayes, Patrick	240
Heber, Reginald	143
Henry, Matthew	171
Herbert, George	152–154, 197, 201
Hervey, James	173, 197, 198, 200
Hill, Michael	236
Hobart, Lord	79, 81, 82
Hobby, Lieut.	58
Hodges, William	111
Holland, Sir Henry	143, 197
Holsworthy, NSW	14
Holt, Joseph	228, 229
Holy Island	See Lindesfarne
Hooker, Richard	152–154, 197, 201, 222, 273
Hope, Beresford	265, 268, 272, 273, 290
Horne, George	150, 151–152, 197, 200
Horne, Thomas Hartwell	163, 197, 203
Hoskings, Mr	226
House of Commons	213
Howley, William	264, 267, 268, 269, 274, 281
Humfrey, John	189
Hunt, William	66
Hunter, Gov. John	6, 52, 58, 62, 66, 67, 68, 69, 72, 75, 76, 79, 96, 109
Huntingdon, Countess of	165
Hutchesson	284, 292
Hutchinson, John	150
Hutton, W.	150
India	65, 70, 77, 97, 99
Integrity	89, 97
Ireland	33, 71
Jackson, Mary Ann	216
James, John Thomas	142–143, 197
James, Kerrison	115, 204, 235
Jamison, Sir John	218
Jeake, Samuel	119, 132, 156, 205
Jeffries, John	28, 59
Jensen, Phillip D.	234
Jervis, John (Lord St Vincent)	63, 64, 65, 71, 93
Jobbins, Boak	237
Johnson, Jane (nee Moor)	10
Johnson, Richard	30, 39, 55, 105, 107, 108, 113, 114, 119,

	128, 149, 164, 168, 175, 201, 219, 279
Johnston, George	28, 90
Johnson, Samuel	122, 136, 140, 197, 199
Jomini, Antoine Henri de	181, 183
Jones, William	150, 197
Jonson, John [William]	228
Keble, John	167
Kelly, Patrick	134–135, 194
Kemmis, Thomas	1, 5
Kent, William	28, 48, 49, 50, 51, 57, 58, 101
Kerr, Robert	160
Kildahl, William	293
Kilfod, Stephen	216
Kinchela, Dr John	255, 288
King's College, London	120
King's Dockyard	7, 14, 33, 45, 50, 54, 61, 62, 65, 66, 76, 81, 89, 92, 93, 95, 96, 102, 109, 114, 179, 211, 219, 249
King's Island	101
King's School, Canterbury	292
King's School, Parramatta	263, 289
King, Harriet (nee Lethbridge)	109
King, Gov. Phillip Gidley	12, 28, 44, 48, 49, 50, 54, 58, 73, 74, 79, 80, 81, 82, 83, 84, 85, 86, 87, 88, 89, 91, 92, 99, 101, 109, 254
King, Adm. Phillip Parker	109
King, Robert Lethbridge	109, 111, 292
Label, Alexandre-Jean-Maximin	182
Labaume, Eugène	186
Lady Juliana	28, 30, 39, 107, 113
Lady Nelson	101
Lawrence, John	123–124, 194, 222
Laycock, Thomas	57
Layton, John	5, 6, 115, 204
Leigh, Samuel	19
Leith, William	11, 39
Lempriere, John	120–121, 193, 197
Lesbury, Nbl	34, 35, 37, 38, 39, 42, 121, 163, 196, 219
Lethbridge, Robert	256
Levizac, abbé de (Jean-Pont-Victor Lacoutz)	184
Lindesfarne	37–38, 219
Liverpool	1, 2, 3, 4, 8, 14, 15, 17, 18, 20, 21, 22, 23, 25, 26, 27, 28, 29, 33, 35, 39, 41, 43, 45, 94, 95, 103, 109, 110, 119, 162, 194, 196, 204, 212, 214, 216, 217, 218, 219, 221, 222, 227, 230, 237, 241, 242, 249, 287, 288
Liverpool, Earl	15

Index of Names [317]

Lloyd, David	68
Locke, John	148
London Missionary Society	18, 96, 157
Longden, Henry	124, 201
Lorack, Anne	205
Lord, Simeon	21, 28
Louis XIV	188
Louis XV	188, 192
Louis Philippe, Compte de Ségur	186
Loyal Sydney Association	90, 145
Lubecki, Prince	246
Lucas, Nathaniel	16, 26, 111
Lucas, Olivia (nee Gascoigne)	26
Luxford, James	230
'Lyndhurst'	276, 277, 278, 279
	See also St James' College
Lyttelton, George	151, 203
Macarthur, Elizabeth	56
Macarthur, George Fairfowl	290, 291
Macarthur, Hannibal	55, 228, 229
Macarthur, John	28, 44, 46, 47, 48, 49, 50, 51, 56, 57, 59, 288
Macartney, Cheyne	290
McKenny, Thomas	58
Mackenzie, Mary Ann	See White, Mary Ann
McKinstry, Mr	231
McLeay, Alexander	115, 235
Macquarie, Gov. Lachlan	14, 15, 16, 21, 25, 26, 28, 35, 36, 40, 42, 109, 111, 113, 114, 212, 217, 218, 229, 238, 246, 249
Macquarie, Elizabeth	15–16, 26, 109, 111, 217
Macquarie, Lachlan jr.	16, 109, 111, 217–218
Madgett	183
Makinson, Thomas	281
Mann, Isaac	128, 197, 199, 200
Mant, Richard	120, 143, 152, 197, 199, 200
Marcet, Jane Haldimand	129
Margarot, Maurice	97
Mariner	215
Marlborough, Mary	99
Marquis Cornwallis	51
Marriot, Charles	265
Marsden, Samuel	17, 19, 44, 46, 47, 54, 55, 56, 57, 58, 59, 96, 103, 112, 119, 150, 208, 213, 214, 215, 219, 228, 229, 240, 246, 284
Marshall, Stephen	190
Mart, Byam	93, 94
'Mary Vale'	17
Massillon, Jean-Baptiste	188, 192

Mathew, Felton	16, 246
Mathew, Sarah	16, 113, 246
Mayniel,	182
Meehan, J.	25
Melville	65, 93
Methodist Magazine	136, 179, 197, 198, 200
Middleton, Lord	64, 96
Military Monitor	135
Miller, John	228
Milman, Henry Hart	143, 197
Milner, Joseph	157
Milton, John	121–122, 132, 197, 198
Minto, NSW	15, 25
Mitchell, Stanley	1, 5
Moffitt, William	136, 206, 207, 210
Molle, Col. & Mrs	26
Moor, David	35, 37
Moor, Elizabeth	See Scott, Elizabeth
Moor, George	24
Moor, George jr.	24
Moor, Henry	36, 38, 42
Moor, Isabella	10
Moor, James	39, 121, 163, 196
Moor, Jane	See Johnson, Jane
Moor, John	24
Moor, Joseph (sr.)	36, 38
Moor, Joseph (jr.)	38, 42
Moor, Mary (sr.)	38, 42
Moor, Mary (jr.)	36, 38, 42
Moor, Thomas (Whitfield)	24
Moor, William	8, 9, 32, 36, 38, 113, 221, 254, 289
Moor, William (jr.)	2, 8, 9, 32, 254, 257
Moor, dau. of William	114
Moore Bank (Moorebank)	14, 15, 20, 21, 23, 26, 45, 110, 119, 212, 219, 249, 252, 260, 263, 287
Moore College	1, 4–5, 7, 23, 32, 33, 34, 38, 43, 51, 52, 54, 105, 106, 109, 110, 112, 118, 196, 205, 211, 226, 227, 233, 234, 235, 243, 244, 249, 250, 251, 253, 263, 264, 285–287
Moore, Joshua John, Mrs	27
Moore, Lake	25
Moore, Rachel (nee Turner)	8, 14, 15, 16, 17, 18, 19, 20, 21, 23, 24, 26, 27, 28, 29, 31, 32, 39, 40, 59, 95, 98, 107, 108, 111, 113, 149, 164, 179, 195, 203, 212, 217, 219, 220, 221, 222, 223–226, 230, 231, 237, 238, 245, 250, 252, 254
Moore, Rachel (da. J.J. Moore)	209
Moore, Thomas (Liverpool)	See separate index

Index of Names [319]

Moore, Ensign/ Capt. William	50–51, 57, 58
Moore, William Henry	50, 57
Moravian Brethren	167
Morley	231
Most Worshipful Company of Shipwrights	35
Muir, Thomas	67, 97
Mulgoa, NSW	281
Munroe, Mr	6
Murry, Robert	74, 99
Napoleon	61, 64, 65, 93, 96, 163, 183, 185, 186, 210
Navy Board	64, 75, 82, 83, 84, 91, 93, 100, 102, 103
Nelson, Horatio	93
Nelson, Robert	164, 193, 197, 200, 202
Nepean, Sir Evan	84, 101
Nepean River, NSW	98
New South Wales Corps	11, 44, 50, 51, 72
New Zealand	18, 19, 55, 70, 93, 150, 221, 233, 250, 258, 272, 279
'Newlands', Parramatta	55
Newman, John Henry	143, 167, 268, 274, 278, 281, 291
Nichols, Isaac	55
Nicholson	25
Nixon, Francis Russell	251, 279, 283
Nobel, Capt. George	246
Noel, M.	184
Noizet-de-Saint-Paul, Gaspard	186
Norfolk Island	12, 16, 26, 51, 57, 62, 73, 74, 98, 102
North Ockendon, Essex	10
Ocean	215
Oddfellows, Order of	179, 202
Old Bailey	39, 245
Ord family	10
Ord, J.A.B.	24
Ord, William	24
Ord, Mrs Blacket-	24
Otter	67, 68
Owen, John	157, 171
Oxford Movement	See Tractarianism
Ozanam, Jacques	130, 193, 194
Paine, Daniel	6, 24, 39, 40, 66–69, 95, 192, 210
Paley, William	133, 197, 198, 203, 210, 222
Palmer, John	28, 58
Palmer, Thomas Fyshe	97, 210
Parramatta	28, 51, 57, 213, 214, 215, 229, 240, 241, 284
Pasley, Charles William	163, 192
Paterson, Col.	48, 49, 57, 58, 99, 101
Paterson, NSW	283

Paton family	240
Pearce, Zachary	133, 197, 198
Peat, Thomas	127, 193
Pelham, Lord	84
Penrith, NSW	281
Penton, Stephen	174–175, 202
Perry, Charles	287, 292
Petersham, NSW	14, 20, 21
Philippines	68
Phillip, Gov. Arthur	44, 54, 66, 72, 98
Phillips, Ambrose	176
Pickersgill	98
Picton, NSW	284
Pile	25
Pitt, William	70, 93, 151
Pitt Town, NSW	14
Place, M. de la	184
Plater, Count Lucien de Broel	240
Plater, Ferdinand	240
Plutarch	121, 139, 193, 195, 197, 201
Port Dalrymple	26, 101
Port Jackson	11, 49, 61, 62, 63, 70, 75, 78, 85, 101, 223, 251
Port Jackson Lending Library	119, 208
Port Phillip, Vic	89, 246, 267, 281
Porteus, Beilby	147, 154, 192, 197, 198, 200, 202, 203
Porpoise	101
Portland	See *Elizabeth Henrietta*
Powers, Capt.	103, 223, 231
Powlett, Henry William	155
Price, M.	231
Priddle, Charles Frederick Durham	110, 290, 291
Prony, Gaspard-Clair-Francois-Marie de	181
Providence	12, 73
Protestant Association	22, 112
Pufendorf, Samuel Freiherr von	148, 166, 195
Puibusque, L.V.de	186
Pusey, Edward Bouverie	268
Puseyism	See Tractarianism
Ramsay, James	166, 198
Raven, Capt. William	6, 11, 12, 13, 24, 30, 56, 74
Reay	25
Reddall, Thomas	246
Redfern, William	21, 25, 28
Redman, James	99
Reid, Robinson	66, 69, 76, 96
Reliance	6, 48, 66, 68, 77, 78, 100
Religious Tract Society	119, 148, 156, 157, 166, 201, 202, 205, 206

INDEX OF NAMES [321]

Renneville, Constantin de	160
Renou, Sarah	175
Restant, P.	184
Rice, Richard	228
Richmond, NSW	14
Ridley, Nicholas	271
Riley, Alexander	44, 46
Rippon, John	172, 197, 200
Risdon Cove, Tas.	51, 58
Robbins, Thomas	130–131, 200, 203
Robertson, William	171–172
Robinson, Donald	234, 235
Robson, Mr	24
Romaine, William	157, 173
Ross, Maj. Robert	98
Rouse Hill	90
Rouse, Elizabeth	240
Rouse, Richard	240
Rousseau, Jean Jacques	139, 148, 189, 192
Rowley, Capt. Thomas	50, 51, 52, 57
Royal Engineers	31, 94, 116, 145, 163–164, 180, 182, 191, 192, 222
Rudd, Henry	25
Ruse, James	44, 58, 72
Russell, T.F. Cusack	292
Sadleir, Capt. Richard	206, 240
Sadleir, Mrs. Ann (nee Cartwright)	240
St Andrew's (Thompson's farm)	25
St Andrew's Cathedral	15, 233, 234, 243, 247, 252
St Andrew's, Sydney	281, 284, 287, 291
St Augustine's College, Canterbury	261, 264–287
St Barbe, John	11, 25
St Hilda's South Shields	42
St James' College	270–282, 286, 291, 292
St James' Sydney	15, 245, 270, 273
St John's Parramatta	15, 26, 219, 240, 245
St Lawrence, Christ Church	281
St Luke's Liverpool	2, 15–16, 17, 18, 20, 24, 29, 31, 40, 105–114, 119, 203, 216, 219, 225, 238, 240, 245, 250, 252, 288
St Mary's Lesbury Nbl	34, 38
St Marys, NSW (suburb)	109
St Matthew's Windsor	15, 26, 245
St Paul's Cathedral, London	143
St Peter's Campbelltown	15, 284
St Peter's Cook's River	281
St Philip's, Sydney	219
St Thomas' Port Macquarie	15

St Thomas's College	253
	See Moore College
St Vincent	See Jervis, John
Salter's Hall, Exeter	137, 178
Sanderson, Robert	152–154, 197, 198, 201
Santa Annabella	233
Schäffer, Phillip	45, 49, 52, 58, 72, 99
Sconce, Robert Knox	281, 291
"Scottish Martyrs"	67, 97, 98, 192, 210
Scott, Elizabeth (nee Moor)	8, 9, 32, 36, 38, 42, 257, 289
Scott, Joseph	289
Scott, Thomas Hobbes	9–10, 24, 29, 31, 32, 37, 39, 41, 250, 254, 257
Scott, William	101
Seller, John	176
Selwyn, George Augustus	250, 258, 259, 261, 265, 283, 290
Sheerness, England	77
Short, Augustus	287, 292
Sibly, Ebenezer	141, 194
Sibly, Manoah	141, 194, 198
Sikes, George	149
Sinclair, Sir I.	49
Skinner, Capt.	93
Skirving, William	97, 210
Smyth	58
Society for the Diffusion of Useful Knowledge	210
Society for the Promotion of Christian Knowledge	120, 150, 156, 164, 167
Society for the Propagation of the Gospel	120, 164, 167, 247, 258, 261, 267
Solomon, Lewis	229
Sotyk, Count Roman	186
South Church, Co. Durham	37, 108, 114
South Creek, NSW	281
South Seas	65, 70, 74, 93
South Shields, Co. Durham	24, 38, 42
Southern Cross	17
Southern Fisheries	11, 25
Southland Museum, Invercargill NZ	234
Smith, James	26, 111
Smith, John Jennings	283, 292
Smith, Mrs Jennings	292
Smith, Percy Jennings	268, 283, 285
Staël-Holstein, Germaine de	184
Stebbing, Henry	144, 178, 197, 198, 203
Steel, David	134, 159, 193
Steele, Richard	172, 174, 201, 202
Stewart, John	151, 194

Stone, William	26
Straiter, James	229
Straits (of Magellan or Malacca)	13, 42
Strong, William	171
Stroud, NSW	249, 264
Sturm, Christopher	126, 130, 199, 200
Sumner, Archbp John Bird	281
Sunderland	13, 25, 38, 97
Supply	6, 48, 66, 72, 83, 96
Surry	94, 103, 215, 223, 231
Sutton Forest, NSW	20
Suttor, George	239
Swammerdam, Jan	149
Sydney, NSW	7, 21, 30, 38, 78, 80, 90, 102, 103, 112
Sydney College	279, 280
Sydney Diocesan Committee	268, 269, 280
Sydney Diocesan Library	118
Sydney	91, 92, 93
Tahiti	18
Taleby, Thomas	58
Taylor, Cecil	246
Taylor, Elizabeth (nee Duffus)	246
Taylor, Esther	231
Taylor, Jeremy	132, 139
Taylor, Richard	18, 219, 246
Tegg, James	119
Temperance Society	220
Thompson, Andrew	21, 28
Tiffin	25
Tilsitt	185
Timber Trust	64, 74, 93
Tindal, Matthew	178
Tom Thumb	68
Toogood, John	150, 194
Toone, William	136, 195
Tombs, John	189–190
Towgood, M.	170
Townson, Dr Robert	25
Tractarianism	268, 269, 270, 275, 278, 280, 290, 291
Trafalgar	63, 93, 94, 96
Trustees of Moore's Estate	6, 32, 36, 39, 115, 117, 235, 250, 258, 287, 289
Turner, Rachel	See Moore, Rachel
Tyrrell	287, 292
University of Sydney	270, 280, 286, 292
Valentine, Henry	166, 198
Van Diemen's Land	93, 94, 102
Vale, Benjamin	57
Venus	101, 102

Vernon, Simon-Francois Gay de	180
Vinegar Hill	See Rouse Hill
Vineyard, Parramatta	44, 49, 99
Voltaire, Francois Marie Arouet de	188, 192
Waldo, Peter	128
Walker, George Washington	17, 25, 113, 216, 220
Walker, J.	2, 6
Walker, Mrs	6
Walker, William	240
Walsh, William H.	281, 283
Walton, Izaak	152–154
Warneford, Dr	253, 291
Warng, W.	13
Waterhouse, Capt. Henry	45, 46, 48, 51, 52, 53, 55, 57, 66, 77, 78, 79, 90, 98
Waterhouse, William	46, 55
Waterhouse, Elizabeth	See Bass, Elizabeth
Washington, George	67
Waterloo	31, 63, 94, 95, 116–117, 163, 191, 222
Watson, Benjamin Lucas	261, 289
Watson, Joshua	9, 252, 253, 254, 255, 262, 267, 274, 278, 280
Watts, Isaac	136–137, 157, 168, 170, 197, 198, 200, 222
Weeks, Thomas	See Wickey, Thomas
Wells, Edward	130, 195, 197, 199, 200
Wentworth, William Charles	217, 228, 254
Wesley, Charles	127, 200
Wesley, John	123, 127, 139, 141, 152, 165, 172, 197, 198, 199, 200, 219, 222
Wesley, Samuel	199
Wesley, Susannah	199
Wesleyan Auxiliary Missionary Society	19, 27, 112, 200, 221, 230
Wesleyan Methodist Missionary Society	138
Whateley, Richard	175
Whitfield, Nbl	9, 10, 32, 33, 34, 41, 257
'Whitfield Hall'	10
White, Andrew Douglas(s)	4, 8, 23, 29, 31, 39, 40, 45, 55, 94, 95, 98, 103, 107, 116, 117, 121, 128, 130, 135, 145, 162, 163, 164, 168, 180, 180–190, 191–193, 195, 196, 200, 203, 205, 222, 223, 231, 250, 252
White, Surgeon John	29, 98, 107, 192, 195, 205, 222
White, John	170, 197
White, Mary Ann (nee Mackenzie)	31, 116, 193, 205
Whitefield, George	123, 141–142, 144, 149, 152, 157, 165, 197, 198, 200, 201, 210, 222
Whitmore, Lucy E.G.	155
Whittle, Thomas	85

Whytehead, Thomas	272
Wickey, Thomas	79, 86, 101
Wilberforce, NSW	14
Wilberforce, William	165
Wilkinson, Frederick	246
Wilkinson, Thomas Hattam	205, 290
Williams, Arthur Lukyn	1, 2, 3, 4, 41, 106, 111, 112, 113, 226
Williamson, James	50, 57
Wilson, Thomas	167–168, 193, 197, 200, 202
Windsor, NSW	14, 28
Wollondilly River, NSW	284
Woodriff, Daniel	89, 102
York, Archbishop of	267
Youl, John	15, 18, 26, 111, 219
Youl, Mrs Jane	15, 111
Young, D.	13
Zinzendorf, Count	167

[326] *Thomas Moore of Liverpool: One of our Oldest Colonists*

Thomas Moore Index

Arrival in Australia	3, 30, 38, 72, 108, 233
Australian Immigration Association	22
Banking, Finance & Business	110, 134, 203–204, 239
Benefactor of Church of England	4, 8, 31, 32, 44, 243, 253
Benefactor of Moore College	1, 4, 8, 23, 32–33, 39, 51, 105, 196, 231, 227, 243–244, 249–293
Benefactor of St Andrew's Cathedral	243, 253
Benevolent Society	111, 220
Bethel Union	166
Bible Society	18, 19, 111, 220
Books	115–231, 222, 238–239
Charity	vii, 3, 110, 124, 134, 204, 239
Church Missionary Society	18, 112, 221
Death	vii, 3, 7–8, 20, 29, 115
Education	121, 162, 191, 196–197, 203–204
Education, interest in	23, 134, 175, 197, 203–204, 263
Emancipist sympathy	21
Family	5, 8–10, 29–42, 94–95, 105, 107–108, 116–117, 128, 130, , 135, 145–146, 159, 162–164, 180–190, 191–193, 203, 217, 220–227, 237–238, 250, 254–255, 257
Farming	21, 39–58, 110, 124, 149, 194, 203–204, 239
Hospitality	17–18, 107–108, 217
Humane Treatment of animals	123–124, 194
Intellectual history	115–231
Land & Property	20, 75–76, 110, 249
Law reform	134, 148, 216–218
Liverpool House	2, 162, 249
Liverpool Period	13–14, 33, 35, 45, 94, 109–110, 194, 211–231, 241
Liverpool School	2, 110, 219
Loyal Sydney Association	90, 145
Magistrate	15, 21, 95, 110, 134, 193, 194–195, 203–204, 211–231, 239
Master Boat Builder	3, 7, 30, 33, 45, 61, 65, 66, 76, 89, 90–91, 95, 108–109, 134, 176, 178–179, 180, 192,

	193, 203–204, 219, 231, 249
Ministry	166–167, 179, 200, 203–204
Missionary interest	18, 19, 112, 200, 204, 221
Moore Bank	109–110, 212, 219, 249, 252
Moral Reform	195–202
Origin	7, 12–13, 29–38, 108, 159, 219
Piety	2, 3, 4, 22–23, 106, 110, 115–231, 197–200, 219–227
Political Reform	195, 204, 216–218
Portrait	106–107, 110, 233–247
Protestant Association	22, 112
Representative Government	21, 217
Reputation	3, 12, 73–75, 216
Rum Rebellion	21, 109
Ship's Carpenter on *Britannia*	3, 11, 38, 61, 72–74, 78, 108, 134, 166, 169, 176, 178–179, 180, 193–194, 216, 231, 233
St Luke's Liverpool	16, 20, 105–114, 219, 238, 249
Temperance Society	220
Timber S/Purveyor	53, 61–102
Trial by Jury	21, 217
Wesleyan Auxillary Methodist Society	112, 221
Will	2, 4, 8–9, 20, 23, 29, 115, 249–287

www.ingramcontent.com/pod-product-compliance
Lightning Source LLC
Chambersburg PA
CBHW051934290426
44110CB00015B/1979